reproduced on the cover:
Kenneth Noland. *Transist.* 1965.
Acrylic on canvas, 5′ square.
Courtesy André Emmerich Gallery, New York.

cover design: Marlene Rothkin Vine

DESIGN THROUGH DISCOVERY

DESIGN THROUGH DISCOVERY

third edition

Marjorie Elliott Bevlin

HOLT, RINEHART AND WINSTON
New York Chicago San Francisco Atlanta Dallas
Montreal Toronto London Sydney

Figs. 30–35, 295 from *The Penland School of Crafts Book of Pottery,* edited by John Coyne, photographs by Evon Streetman. The Bobbs-Merrill Company, Inc., Indianapolis/New York, 1975.
Figs. 51, 140, 144 from *Forms and Patterns in Nature,* by Wolf Strache. Copyright © 1973 by Random House, Inc. Copyright © 1956 by Pantheon Books. Reprinted by permission of the publishers.
Fig. 138 © Deborah Remington.
Fig. 151 from *The New Churches of Europe,* by G. E. Kidder Smith. Holt, Rinehart and Winston, Inc., New York, 1964.
Figs. 169, 331 from *How to Wrap Five More Eggs,* by Hideyuki Oka. John Weatherhill, Inc., Tokyo, 1965.
Fig. 209 © 1971 by Paul Strand.
Fig. 213 from *Alice in Wonderland* and *Through the Looking Glass,* by Lewis Carroll. Copyright 1946, by Grosset & Dunlap, Inc., New York.
Fig. 226 from *The Art and Architecture of the Ancient Orient,* by Henri Frankfort. Penguin Books, Ltd., Harmondsworth, 1970.
Figs. 239, 514 courtesy of Rizzoli Film S.p.A.
Fig. 242 from *This is the American Earth.* The Sierra Club, San Francisco.
Fig. 455 from *Urban Spaces,* by David Kenneth Specter, by permission of Little, Brown and Co. in association with New York Graphic Society.
Fig. 456 from *Rabbit & Pork,* by John Lawrence. Hamish Hamilton Ltd., London, 1975.
Fig. 458 reproduced by permission of *Esquire* Magazine © 1976 by Esquire Inc.
Fig. 517 from *The King and I* © 1946 Twentieth Century-Fox Film Corporation. All rights reserved. Courtesy of Twentieth Century-Fox.
Fig. 521 from the MGM release *Million Dollar Mermaid* © 1952 Loew's Incorporated.
Fig. 532 from the MGM release *Gone With the Wind* © 1939 Selznick International Pictures, Inc. Copyright renewed 1967 by Metro-Goldwyn-Mayer Inc.
Fig. 573 from *Arcology: The City in the Image of Man,* by Paolo Soleri. M.I.T. Press, Cambridge, 1969.
Pl. 4 from *Photography: A Handbook of History, Materials, and Processes,* by Charles Swedlund. Holt, Rinehart and Winston, Inc., New York, 1974.
Pl. 47 from the motion picture *Barry Lyndon,* courtesy of Warner Bros. Inc., copyright © 1975.

Editor Rita Gilbert
Picture Editor Joan Curtis
Production Assistants Barbara Curialle, Polly Myhrum, Hope Davis Rost
Production Supervisor Sandra Baker
Designer Marlene Rothkin Vine

Library of Congress Cataloging in Publication Data

Bevlin, Marjorie Elliott.
Design through discovery.

Bibliography: p. 395.
1. Design. I. Title.
NK1510.B53 1977 745.4 76-54980
ISBN: 0-03-089701-7

Composition and camera work by York Graphic Services, Inc., Pennsylvania
Color separations and printing by Lehigh Press Lithographers, New Jersey
Printing and binding by Capital City Press, Vermont
7 8 9 10 138 9 8 7 6 5 4 3 2 1

Preface

There is probably no more effective way to discover how rapidly the world is changing than to write a textbook. One expects this to be true in the fields of science and technology, but it is no less so in design. Nearly every change in the world today influences the designer, and this edition of *Design Through Discovery* has been touched by many of them. An author needs a certain audacity to present a new book, knowing that—in a time of continuous and dramatic evolution—parts of that book may be outdated even before it reaches the bookstore.

With all the currents sweeping through the design world, however, certain ideas remain constant. First, design is an all-pervasive activity that governs every area of human endeavor, from the visual arts through industry, communications, and transportation. Second, the human designer can find endless inspiration in the ingenious and beautiful designs created by nature. These two premises together form the basis for *Design Through Discovery*.

Not everyone aspires to be a professional designer, but everyone is affected by design. Thus, *Design Through Discovery* is directed at those who wish to *look* as well as those who wish to *do*. It functions as a basic introduction to the elements and principles of visual expression, both for the design student and for the individual who wishes to develop an understanding of the world's art, past and present.

The 1970s have witnessed such tremendous growth in the fields of art and design that this third edition of *Design Through Discovery* has required a drastic revision. To keep pace with these developments, I have replaced nearly all the illustrations in the book, of which there are now more than 600—50 in full color. Moreover, I have tried to select examples that will be interesting as well as informative, that will evoke a direct response in the reader. The entire text has been rewritten, with 15 completely new chapters, and there are major structural changes in the book's format.

Part I of *Design Through Discovery* has been reordered to analyze in detail the elements and principles of design, both two- and three-dimensional. A full chapter each is devoted to line, space, shape, color, and texture, with numerous visual examples from all areas of design. In this Part, also, will be found a new chapter on the fascinating topic of symbolism—from ancient signs to corporate logos—and the ways in which this powerful tool can function for the designer.

Part II of the text introduces the materials in which designers work—wood, metal, clay, glass, fiber, and plastics. Each of these is considered in terms of the special design challenges and potentialities it offers for various kinds of work. Part III explores different media of visual expression, from painting and sculpture through photography, prints, graphic design, industrial design, and apparel. Another new chapter, on the performing arts, recognizes the expansion of design into fields both very old and very new: drama, dance, film, and television.

The final Part of *Design Through Discovery* focuses upon areas of design that, perhaps, touch each individual most closely—the structures we inhabit, the cities and towns in which we live, and the environment that sustains us. Following these summary chapters, the reader will find a Glossary of design terms, as well as a Bibliography with suggestions for those who would pursue certain topics in greater depth.

In a period of turbulence that cuts across political, economic, religious, and aesthetic concerns, many people will find it satisfying to discover design principles that exist universally in nature and in human expression. Once understood, these principles can have a stabilizing effect on one's personal philosophy as well as on one's work. I hope that the themes and concepts woven through *Design Through Discovery* will help to foster a recognition of the order in design.

Acknowledgments

In producing this revision of *Design Through Discovery,* I have been fortunate in having the help of literally hundreds of people. A questionnaire survey organized by my publisher yielded more than 800 responses from teachers all over the United States and Canada. The consensus of their opinions—and many of their individual suggestions—have been incorporated in the new text.

More specifically, a number of professional designers and teachers have been exceedingly generous with their assistance. David A. Lauer of the College of Alameda served as advisor on the chapters in Part I, and his comments and criticisms were indispensible in developing the ideas they contain. Harvey K. Littleton and Glenn C. Nelson, recognized as foremost authorities in their respective fields of glass and clay, offered much valuable advice on those two chapters. Deli Sacilotto of Siena Studios read the chapter dealing with prints, enabling me to feel confident that it is accurate and up to date. The expertise in plastics of Richard B. Platt at Polyproducts Corporation guided me through the mysteries of this highly complex subject. Gary Switser of IBM Design Center contributed many ideas to the chapter on industrial design.

I am indebted to Nathan Knobler of the University of Connecticut for his forthright appraisal of the chapters devoted to painting and sculpture. James Hoekema, a rare Renaissance man who combines the aesthetic with the practical, helped me to cast these two chapters in the light of contemporary writing in the visual arts.

At the helm throughout the development of the book was Rita Gilbert, my editor at Holt, Rinehart and Winston, who devoted herself wholeheartedly to fulfilling her own high goals for the project, often under nearly insuperable handicaps. To her must go full credit for the form into which it ultimately evolved. Joan Curtis, the picture editor, displayed impeccable taste in recommending illustrations and remarkable ingenuity in obtaining them. The stunning new design and layout is the creation of Marlene Rothkin Vine, whose mastery of the elements and principles of visual design offers the best possible demonstration of the book's message. Polly Myhrum, Hope Davis Rost, and Barbara Curialle kept track of endless production details, and Francesca Friedrich-Herrmann read the entire manuscript, screening out convolutions of prose and making a number of inspired suggestions about the illustrations. To all of them go my sincere thanks.

Finally, I am grateful as always to my family, whose interest and support have been invaluable. My acknowledgments would not be complete without expressing my special debt to my husband, Ervin W. Bevlin, for his moral sustenance and help in innumerable ways. His sudden and untimely death as this edition entered its final phases only served to emphasize dramatically how much he had contributed to my work and to my life.

Cragbourne
Orcas Island, Washington
December 1976

M.E.B.

Contents

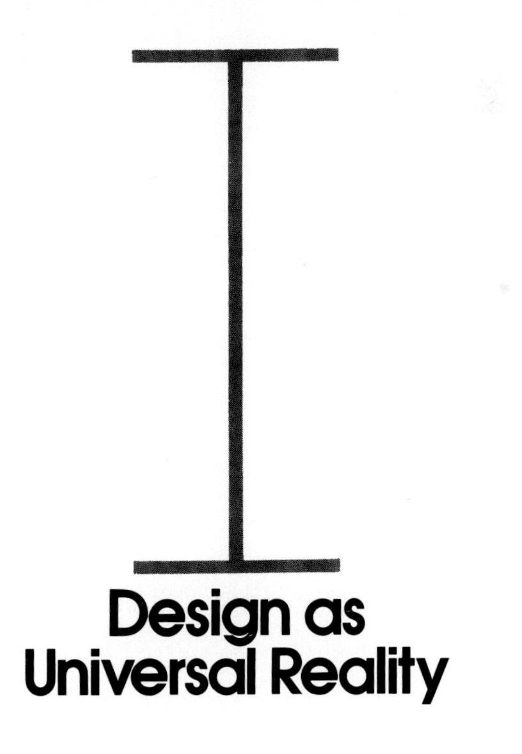

Design as Universal Reality

1 The Essence of Design

Design is the organization of parts into a coherent whole. Although it is considered to be a human expression, design is in reality the underlying process by which the universe was formed through orderly procedures of selection and evolution. The resulting phenomena often reveal a perfection far beyond the capabilities of human designers, yet they have the potential to offer limitless inspiration (Fig. 1).

The incredibly complex design of our universe continues to baffle scientists. No choreographer could plot a network of movements as intricate as the revolution of moons around planets, planets around their stars, stars whirling in their galaxies, and galaxies interrelated in a system whose limits we have only begun to explore. On our own Earth—a small planet belonging to a small star, Sun—we can identify a complicated design of water and land, rivers and mountains and plains and deserts. The landscape that through the centuries has been erected over this topography seems to be the creation solely of human designers—a superficial pattern laid upon the surface of the land. Yet these human constructions, farms and cities and nations, were influenced by the natural design that existed before them. Areas of fertility yield patches of growth (Fig. 2), rivers and natural harbors make the

1. Paul Caponigro. *Sunflower.* 1965. Photograph.

obvious sites for construction of cities, mountain ranges and again rivers mark the boundaries between nations, while deserts, tall mountains, and dense jungles defy the possibility of any human imprint. In a sense, our constructed environment is the very character of the earth coming to its surface from deep within.

We find other natural designs, of astonishing complexity, in the food chains of animals and fish, the interdependence of insects and plants, and the mechanisms of various organisms. Most sophisticated of all is the design of the human body, with its neurological, muscular, circulatory, digestive, eliminatory, and reproductive functions all evolved to a high degree.

The desire for order seems to be a basic human characteristic. In every culture, every mythology, every religion, the world began when order was created out of chaos. The Book of Genesis, foundation stone

2. Aerial photograph of terraced farms in central Peru.

3. *The Creation of the World,* vault mosaic. 13th century. St. Mark's Cathedral, Venice.

of the Judao-Christian tradition, reads like a classic design scheme (Fig. 3). Greek mythology is founded upon a process in which the entire complicated genealogy of the gods can be traced back to the ancestors who sprang from chaos and then sorted the universe into categories, giving Zeus dominion over the land, Poseidon over the seas, and Hades over the Underworld. Further subdivisions allocated the Dawn, the Harvest, the Hunt, Love, and so forth. Both the ancient Chinese and the ancient Egyptians believed in a nebulous state that existed before the earth came into being. In all these versions the world as we know it began only when confusion or nothingness gave way to form and order—in other words, to design.

The great religions of the world have carried designs further into the systems of ethics by which people can live in harmony with one another and the universe. The Hebrew Torah, the writings of Confucius and Lao-Tse, the Hindu Vedas, the New Testament, and the Moslem Koran are all bodies of instruction seeking to create order in both individual and collective human lives.

The quest for order did not stop with the arrangement of cosmic priorities. It continued in the establishment of nations, the formation of medieval guilds, and the design of planned communities. Today the process goes on with the proponents of Esperanto (the international

4. Beran and Shelmire. Interior of the World Trade Center, Dallas Market Center. Completed 1974.

language), the European Common Market, the Arab League, and the Women's Movement.

System designs take concrete form in such areas as the design of a New Town (Fig. 570), a city mall, or a large apartment complex. The new World Trade Center in Dallas (Fig. 4) exemplifies functional design to achieve certain identified goals.

The World Trade Center is the last in a six-building complex comprising the Dallas Market Center, a 125-acre beehive of trade shops. In planning the World Trade Center, the builders wished to erect a structure that would be usable year-round, even in Dallas' hot climate; would provide for easy passage within the building and to the others in the complex; would categorize certain types of shops; and finally would give the feeling of a town square.

Architects Beran & Shelmire solved all these problems with a soaring, open-core structure of seven floors (eventually to be twenty). Since the entire facility is enclosed, climate can be regulated to a comfortable springlike atmosphere. All the shops open from balconies located mostly around the central courtyard. The various floors are connected by high-speed escalators and glass-enclosed elevators, while carpeted halls lead to the other buildings. Each level has been assigned to an individual type of shop, with gifts on the second floor, fabrics on the third, and so forth. Best of all, the core of the building succeeds beautifully at creating the effect of a pleasant city plaza. The floor is cobbled, trees and plants abound, a central pool-fountain provides a gathering point for people, and the whole is lighted by an immense natural skylight. In all respects, the World Trade Center has been pronounced a resounding success—a brilliant fulfillment of purpose.

Walt Disney World, near Orlando, Florida, has been cited as one prominent new example of design (Fig. 5). In constructing this center for family entertainment, the planners took nearly everything into

left: 5. Cinderella Castle, in the Magic Kingdom. Walt Disney World, near Orlando, Fla.

above: 6. Aerial view of San Gimignano, Italy, a medieval town.

consideration. Walkways are paved in a soft material to cushion the feet for a long day of exploration. Food service units are strategically located and supplied from underground tunnels. An underground air-propelled system carries away wastes. Nothing is left to chance in this total design for pleasure.

All the designs we have mentioned so far could be described as *functional.* They deal primarily with physical, emotional, or moral interrelationships. In this text, however, we will be concerned primarily with *visual* designs, which are basically aesthetic in nature. The two are interrelated, but it is important to make the distinction. Many functional designs are also visually satisfying. A town that has grown up naturally around the needs of its inhabitants may present an attractive design when seen from the air (Fig. 6). At the same time, many visual designs are functional as well. The design of a book, a pot, a skyscraper, or a house must adapt its visual elements to the function it will be required to perform. Functional designs can emerge either from nature or from the minds of people, but visual designs, strictly speaking, are considered to be the deliberate creative acts of men and women.

Many visual designs are inspired by natural ones. In fact, a great portion of the world's art has been based on forms discovered in

right: 7. June Schwarcz. Electroformed enamel bowl. 1970. Diameter 11″. Courtesy the artist.

below: 8. *Haliotis fulgens,* a shell found on the beaches of California.

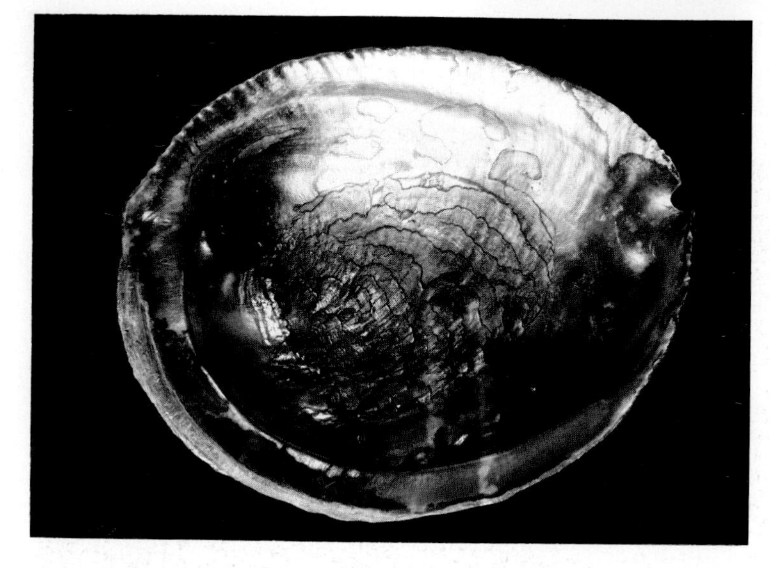

nature. The contemporary enamel bowl shown in Figure 7 closely resembles the design of a haliotis shell (Fig. 8), with its iridescent interior and rough outside. This is not to say that June Schwarcz, when she set out to design the bowl, consciously sought to imitate the shell. More likely the artist had once seen a shell like this, perhaps long ago, and the impression of its striking design stayed with her, buried as part of her total experience of perceptions. When she began to make the bowl, then, the design came naturally to her mind and hands. Many design inspirations arise in just this manner, as the artist draws upon a lifetime of visual impressions.

The desire to bring order to nature itself, to design the landscape visually, is as old as humankind. During prehistoric times many cultures constructed huge earthworks whose purpose is not fully understood. Throughout the Eastern Woodlands section of North America, as well as in Mexico and Central America, there survive vast ceremonial mounds, some in the shape of serpents, and measuring as much as a fifth of a mile in length. In Europe there are huge rectangular entrenchments—more than 3 acres in size and surrounded by walls—that date from the La Tène period, the five centuries before the birth of Christ (Fig. 9). These entrenchments were used in Celtic worship rituals, the walls probably serving to isolate the sacred ground from the profane. Lacking any high vantage point, the builders of these earthworks could not possibly have appreciated their creations in the way that we can through aerial photography. It seems difficult to understand what would impel designers to make something they could not really see.

Nearly two thousand years later the Bulgarian-born artist Christo, aided by modern technology, constructs gigantic landscape projects of parallel daring and scope. One of his first monumental environments was the *Wrapped Coastline* done in 1970, in which a mile of the craggy Australian coast was literally wrapped and tied in a million square feet of polyethylene sheeting. In the following two years Christo executed the plan for his *Valley Curtain* (Fig. 10) in Rifle Gap, Colorado. Here a 4-ton bright orange curtain was strung between two mountains 1250 feet apart. Unlike the prehistoric mounds and entrenchments, however, Christo's works are necessarily temporary, since the people of

right: 9. Aerial view of rectangular entrenchment at Buchenberg, Starnberg, Bavaria. Earth, 115 x 130 yards. Celtic, Late La Tène period, 5th–1st century B.C.

below: 10. Christo. *Valley Curtain.* 1970–72. 2,000,000 square feet of nylon polyamide, 110,000 pounds of steel cables; height 185–365′, span 1250′. Grand Hogback, Rifle, Colo. (Project Director: Jan van der Marck).

left: 11. Piet Mondrian's studio in New York, 1940s.

below: 12. Piet Mondrian. *Composition with Red, Yellow, and Blue.* 1939–42. Oil on canvas, $28\frac{5}{8} \times 27\frac{1}{4}$". Tate Gallery, London.

Colorado would not be willing to have their gorges permanently curtained, nor the Australians their coastline forever wrapped in plastic. Actually, many critics have called his works *assaults* on the landscape, and this reaction agrees with the artist's intent. By causing us to feel shock and disquiet in usually neutral surroundings, Christo hopes to stimulate the imagination. By designing a new order for the landscape, he *disorders* our complacent ideas about art and nature.

Visual Design

In order to concentrate our attention on purely visual design, we must narrow the definition given at the beginning of this chapter. In visual terms, design is the *organization* of *materials* and *forms* in such a way as to fulfill a specific *purpose.* There are four ideas in this definition: organization or order, materials, form, and purpose. Although in practice they interconnect in the creation of an effective design, we will discuss each one separately.

A Plan for Order

Throughout the height of his career the Dutch artist Piet Mondrian created paintings that consist of precise squares and rectangles in black, white, and primary colors (red, yellow, and blue). It would be difficult to find more ordered works of art than these. Mondrian's sense of organization carried him to extremes of method, yet we can learn much about the way an artist organizes a composition from studying his working habits.

Figure 11 shows Mondrian's studio in New York, where he moved toward the end of his life. On the walls are fixed rectangles of black, white, and colors, in different sizes. According to his biographers, it was the artist's custom to arrange and rearrange these rectangles on the wall constantly until he had arrived at a pattern that satisfied him. Similar relationships can be found in his precise, geometric paintings (Fig. 12).

Many times artists use exactly this procedure to plot out a design, working perhaps with scraps of paper or pieces of fabric, moving them around, making minute shifts, until the composition falls into place. Preliminary drawings for a painting or sculpture do the same job, as do architects' sketches and scale models. All of these are plans for order—the first step in creative design. Parallels can be found in all the arts. Writers make outlines or plot out the adventures of their characters, musicians decide upon an overall structure for their compositions. Nearly always design begins with a basic organization.

Expression of Materials

Much of the impact of a design will depend upon the way the artist uses particular materials. Oil paints can be thinned with turpentine and laid on in transparent glazes; or they can be applied with a palette knife in a thick, plastic buildup known as *impasto.* Wood can be finished until it is almost as smooth as glass or left rough, in the manner of driftwood.

The two sculptures shown in Figures 13 and 14 are the work of a single artist, Auguste Rodin. The strikingly different treatment of forms, surface, and modeling can be attributed at least in part to

below left: 13. Auguste Rodin. *The Danaïd.* 1885. Marble, $13\frac{3}{4} \times 28\frac{1}{2} \times 22\frac{1}{2}''$. Rodin Museum, Paris.

below: 14. Auguste Rodin. *Monument to Balzac.* 1897. Bronze, height 9′3″. Museum of Modern Art, New York.

Rodin's feelings about two different materials—marble and bronze. In the marble *Danaïd* (Fig. 13) we see a smoothly polished, luminous interpretation of the nude. Every bone, every muscle is beautifully expressed, and the figure's flesh almost seems as though it would be warm to the touch. Rodin clearly was responding to the pure perfection of the marble in designing this piece. The bronze *Balzac* (Fig. 14) is quite another matter. Here the artist wished to create an impression of overwhelming monumentality, of sheer power in the personality of the French writer. Physical characteristics yield to the dynamic flow of form in Balzac's cloak, culminating in a head whose features are highly stylized. The bronze is less important for its ability to describe than for its strength and force.

15. Michelangelo. *David.* 1501–04. Marble, height 18′. Academy, Florence.

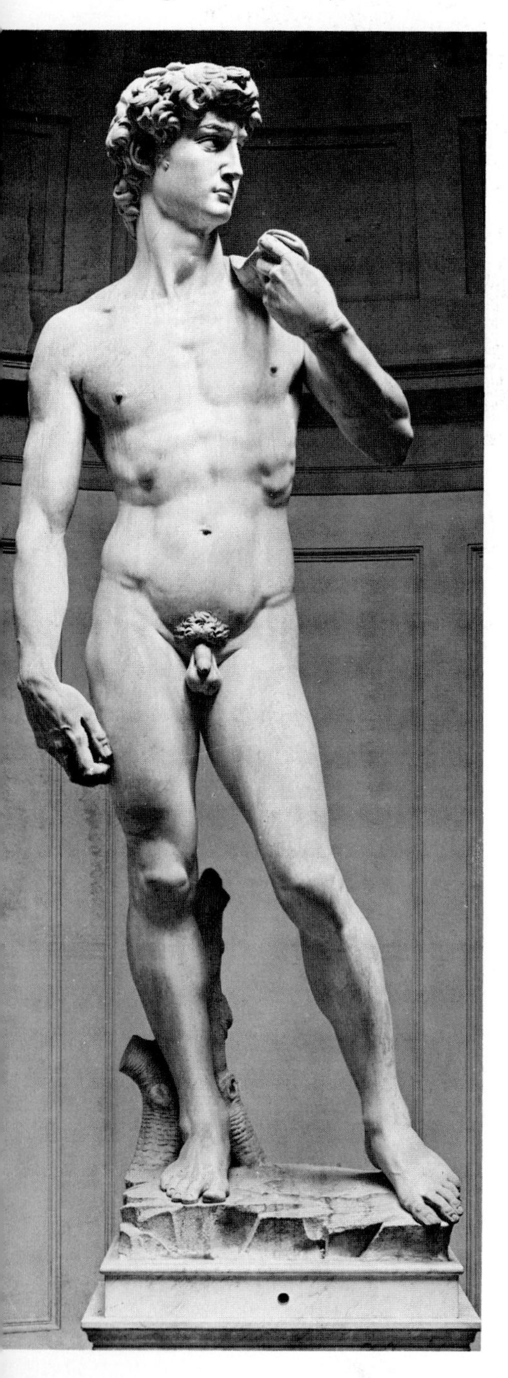

Some sculptors work almost exclusively in a single material: Michelangelo in marble (Fig. 15), David Smith in steel (Fig. 269). For them, the challenge is to discover the forms they envision within the chosen material. An artist who concentrates on one medium will see design in those terms, seeking always to exploit that medium to the fullest. When asked how he had carved the magnificent *David* (Fig. 15), Michelangelo replied that he had simply chipped away the stone until only David was left. The artist thought first of the material, of the living stone. Each block of marble was unique, with a form inside waiting to be released.

In contrast to Michelangelo, most designers visualize first in terms of form. They have ideas and then must choose a medium in which to express them. The sculptor, for example, in creating a portrait bust has the option of working in bronze, stone, plaster, clay, acrylic, wood, or even fiber. The selection of a material that will best realize the form becomes a major decision in the design process.

Form

To a certain extent, the term *form* is synonymous with shape or mass (see Chap. 5). It refers to the general outlines of something, as in the form of a ship or the human body. But designers use form in more complex ways, so that it takes on greater meaning. We can speak of something as having solid or liquid or vaporous *form,* by which we mean its substance. In the abstract sense, form conveys the idea behind shape. If, for instance, something were designed "in the form of a space ship," it might not be precisely like a space ship or attempt to look like one, but instead convey the speed and thrust and metallic gleam of a space ship (Fig. 16). All-inclusively form can mean a given medium or style. We speak of artists working in a certain "form."

Form may develop from a number of sources. It can spring entirely from the artist's imagination (Fig. 26) or be controlled to some extent by tradition. Christian tradition requires that a church be adorned with a cross, but it does not specify the particular form that cross will take, its size, or its placement.

Many forms are inspired by things present in nature, and actually the great majority of works in the history of visual art reveal a dependence on natural sources—paintings of landscapes, people, or still lifes, portrait sculptures, and so on. However, it must be remembered that inspiration is only the *beginning* of artistic form. No two designers would portray a tree in exactly the same manner or from the same point of view. The form of a tree and the form of a work based on a tree are not the same thing.

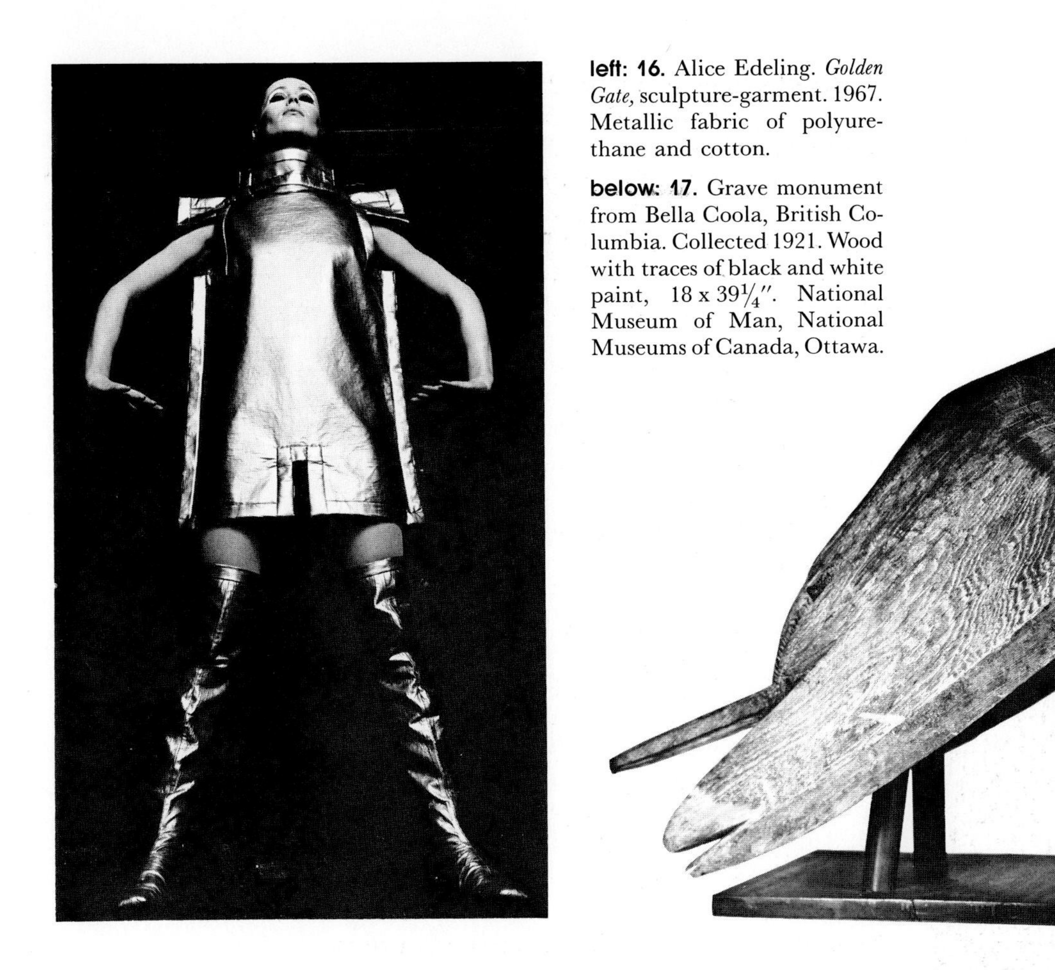

left: 16. Alice Edeling. *Golden Gate,* sculpture-garment. 1967. Metallic fabric of polyurethane and cotton.

below: 17. Grave monument from Bella Coola, British Columbia. Collected 1921. Wood with traces of black and white paint, 18 x 39¼″. National Museum of Man, National Museums of Canada, Ottawa.

Many times form will be partially guided by the material chosen for the design. Michelangelo participated directly in the quarrying of his marble blocks, and frequently he would plan his sculptures to conform to a particular veining pattern in the block. A wood sculptor may come upon a special piece of wood that has beautiful graining and work it to bring out the quality of the material (Fig. 17).

Outside the so-called "fine arts," form may be directly related to a function the designed object must perform. A chair must have some horizontal portion for sitting, a cup must be hollow to hold liquids, a ring must fit the finger. Again, as with material, these considerations are only the beginning of design form, yet they do bring us to the fourth concern in our definition of visual design.

Fulfillment of Purpose

Every design has some purpose, some role to play, or else there would be no point in designing it. In utilitarian objects—furnishings, utensils, textiles—this purpose is clear. But designs of a purely visual nature—paintings, sculptures, drawings, prints, photographs—also have a definite purpose, in fact *two* purposes. The first is expression on the part of the artist; the second, creation of a response in the viewer. Together these add up to communication. We should note that the viewer's response may be any number of things: delight, admiration, shock, rapture, intrigue, disquiet, or even revulsion. If the artist succeeds in communicating what was intended, the design must be considered effective.

Designers have been fulfilling specific goals since human design began. The totem poles carved by the Indians of the Pacific Northwest (Fig. 18) have as their purpose keeping the tribal record. Stylized characters of exciting variety are carved into the huge pole of Northwest cedar, adding visual drama and meaning to the depiction of the clan's history. Designs are not applied for purely decorative effect; the majestic tree remains visible in the sculpture and paint, but in it are embodied the social and religious philosophy of a people, as well as the personal and familial legend of a proud individual. Even to those who understand nothing of the interpretation of totem poles, however, the dramatic designs and colors remain striking. Effective design can operate on more than one level, depending upon the viewer's degree of understanding.

The Role of the Designer

The designer brings two important ingredients to any creative work: the *inspiration* that gives birth to a particular design, and the *originality* that sets it apart from other designs. If five painters were to walk down the same city street at the same time, they might well be inspired by five different design impulses. One might become fascinated by the faces of passersby, another by the pattern of light on the buildings, a third by the particular form of a street lamp, a fourth by the movement of vehicles, a fifth by the collection of trash in the gutter. One could go on with this indefinitely. The point is that each designer carries a host of impressions, memories, interests, and ideas that cause inspiration to be channeled in certain ways.

Once inspired, the designer will approach the project with his or her originality. We can see this effect in a life-drawing class, in which every student is drawing from the same model in the same pose under

above: 18. Totem pole, Stanley Park, Vancouver, B.C.

right: 19. Paul Gauguin. *Mahana No Atua* (*The Day of the God*). 1894. Oil on canvas, $27\frac{7}{8} \times 35\frac{5}{8}$". Art Institute of Chicago (Helen Birch Bartlett Memorial Collection).

the same lighting conditions. If there are twenty students, there will be twenty different designs.

Together, then, inspiration and originality ensure that there is infinite potential for creative design.

Inspiration

The creative designer observes the universe with sensitivity, absorbing impressions from all around. These impressions drop into the subconscious mind like cells that divide and combine to form new entities that could never be constructed by conscious effort. Often when one least expects it, one becomes aware of new relationships and, seeing them in terms of a unique vision, works to give them a form that will make them apparent to others. This, in essence, is the phenomenon known as inspiration.

Since inspiration is nourished by impressions, it becomes imperative that the artist absorb through the senses as much of the world as possible. One designer may find motivation in travel to other lands, another in films of space flight, yet another in the sight of a familiar weed. Some artists draw their ideas directly from their own memories and experiences. Generally speaking, the more one is exposed to sights, sounds, smells, and textures; the more one learns of the arts of theater, dance, poetry, and music; and the extent to which one attempts to understand the workings of science and technology—the better will be the likelihood of one's arriving at designs that will awaken response in a variety of people. Science can make the designer aware of the physical universe, a knowledge of history will reveal the heritage from centuries past, and philosophy will increase understanding.

The New Mexico-based artist Georgia O'Keeffe has executed a series of paintings based on flowers (Pl. 1, p. 53). Her particular approach, however, causes her to move in very close on the subject, so that the flowers open up and expand to create a whole universe. Seeing these natural forms through O'Keeffe's eyes we become aware of them almost as creatures, with personalities—perhaps slightly menacing ones—all their own. Here the artist's inspiration was a natural form, but she brings to the subject her unique viewpoint.

Travel acts as a source of inspiration for many artists, and one of the best known travelers in the history of art was the French painter Paul Gauguin. Gauguin was a prosperous businessman who, during his late twenties, took up painting as a kind of hobby. In 1883, at the age of 35, he concluded that his art was more important than anything else, so he abandoned his business, left his family, and began to paint full time. During the course of several short journeys he gradually developed a unique compositional style based on flattened forms and shapes, shallow space, and bold, bright colors (Fig. 95). In 1891 Gauguin traveled to Tahiti in the South Pacific, where he remained for most of the rest of his life. There at last he found themes consistent with his new style, in the lush tropical foliage and birds, the exotic native people, and the strange, primitive symbolism of the islands (Fig. 19). No environment in France or in all of Europe could have provided such an impulse for his creative genius.

Another type of journey that may bring inspiration for design is the journey into the mind, especially back into memory. Betye Saar creates "assemblage boxes" from objects that have particular meaning for her, that evoke an image of the past. The one illustrated in Figure

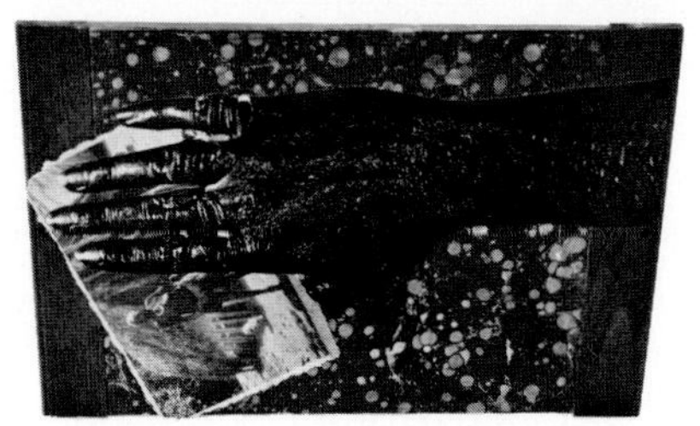

20. Betye Saar. *The Time Inbetween.* 1974. Assemblage box, mixed media; 16 x $11\frac{1}{2}$ x 2″ (closed). Courtesy the artist.

20, called *The Time Inbetween,* includes old photos, a hand, a fabric fan, velvets, a rose, a beaded bag, a leather glove, old jewelry—the whole contained in an antique wooden writing box. This collection has a special *personal* meaning for the designer, but the visual relationships among objects also create an emotional environment for the viewer.

Ever since primitive times artists have based their designs on ideas borrowed from other designers. A sculptor might adapt a pose found in classical Greek statuary, a painter develop some compositional device from an earlier work. Marcel Duchamp drew a moustache and beard on a reproduction of Leonardo's *Mona Lisa,* turned the early master's painting into a visual pun, and exhibited it as a unique work of art. Sometimes the borrowing from another source is very subtle; at other times we are meant to see immediately the work that inspired design and respond to the way it has been changed (Figs. 368, 369).

During the 1970s the Selig Furniture Corporation commissioned photographer David Vine to create a series of advertisements based on well-known paintings. Each of the works chosen contains a piece of furniture, and Vine's project was to recreate the scene using a modern piece manufactured by the Selig company. One of the earliest and most successful of these ads derives from John Singer Sargent's magnificent portrait of *Madame X* (Fig. 21). To recreate the scene (Pl. 2, p. 53), Vine chose a model who resembled closely the original "Madame X"—not an easy job when 19th-century faces and bodies are out of style! He dressed her in the same fashion as Madame X, posed her against a similar backdrop, and then substituted the strikingly contemporary Selig chair for the original table. Every detail was made as authentic as possible, so that the contrast of the new "prop" would be all the more telling. This example of direct reference to an earlier design is not at all uncommon. It is not plagiarism, but rather homage to the creations of another artist.

Originality

Originality of design results from individuality in the designer. As no two people are exactly alike, no two designs should be precisely the same. Each artist expresses a unique world, a personal experience reaching far back beyond birth into generations of genes and tenden-

21. John Singer Sargent. *Madame X.* 1884. Oil on canvas, 6′10⅛″ x 3′11¼″. Metropolitan Museum of Art, New York (Arthur H. Hearn Fund, 1916). (See also Pl. 2, p. 53.)

cies, mores and customs, racial and national traits and familial trends in thinking.

Today many people fear that such individuality will begin to break down, that cultures will become so standardized that there will no longer be the potential for uniqueness. Instant communication and the ease of transportation have joined to bring widely separated cultures together. In the world of the 70s, it is just as easy to get a hamburger in Tokyo as it is to eat sukiyaki in New York.

Former generations of children were first exposed to a common environment when they started school. The first five highly impressionable years could be filled with a wealth of personal exploration, uninhibited fantasy, and rich associations derived from family experiences and imaginative reactions to stories. The advent of television, however, has bombarded the child with a conformity of influences almost as soon as that child learns to focus. Thus, by the age of five, kindergarten classmates have a store of reference material in common

below: 22. John Marin. *Woolworth Building, New York, No. 3.* 1913. Etching, $12\frac{7}{8}$ x $10\frac{1}{2}''$. Brooklyn Museum (Dick S. Ramsay Fund).

right: 23. Joseph Stella. *Skyscrapers.* 1922. Mixed media on canvas, $8'3\frac{3}{4}''$ x $4'6''$. Newark Museum, N.J.

with children all over the nation, if not the world. Since characters, settings, and other data are presented on television with all details visually complete, the imaginative efforts of the child are not called upon to create but must be exercised in adaptations and expansions of things already seen.

In spite of this narrowing band of experience, there remains the potential for great originality in design. One of the most significant ways in which artists project their individuality is in the quality of their imagery.

Imagery

Imagery is a very simple idea that is difficult to explain. In the most basic terms, it is the art of making images, as in drawing or painting. Images can be direct representations of people, places, and things, but they can also be symbols that *evoke* a particular thing (see Chap. 11). One can think of an image as a *picture* representing something, whether it looks just like that thing or not. Perhaps the concept of imagery will become clearer when we contrast two types: *perceptual* and *conceptual.*

24. Philip L. Molten. *Mast of HMS "Bounty."* 1962. Photograph.

Perceptual Imagery

Perception relates to *real things* that actually exist or that actually did exist and survive in the memory. However, since no two artists perceive things in exactly the same way, the images they create will always be different. This relates back to our discussion of inspiration, and the example of five painters walking down the street.

We can get an idea of how perceptual imagery operates from two remarkably different interpretations of the New York City skyline. John Marin, an early-20th-century American watercolorist, was especially sensitive to atmospheric effects. In his etching of the *Woolworth Building* (Fig. 22) this sensitivity is translated into a less-obvious relationship, the attitude of a skyscraper being tossed about by the wind. The theme of human works bending before the forces of nature is not unique, yet the interplay of moving air with unyielding steel, glass, and concrete may suggest a new concept to Americans nurtured in the solidity of city architecture. Millions of people have seen the Woolworth Building from the exact spot where Marin stood, and many on just such a windy day. However, it was Marin's special *perception* of the scene that led to this particular *imagery.*

A more conventional attitude toward skyscrapers, though not necessarily a conventional image, appears in Joseph Stella's painting (Fig. 23). Here the image is one of strict geometry, soaring verticality, buildings reaching up to the skies. Stella's skyscrapers would never bend before the wind. They are instead closely spaced spires, almost like the spires on a cathedral, perhaps signaling the new religion of technology. Again, the artist builds his imagery from his own perceptions of a subject.

Philip L. Molten's photograph of a ship's mast illustrates a certain kind of perceptual imagery in his choice of an unusual vantage point (Fig. 24). So does Joan Semmel's painting *Patty and I* (Fig. 25), in

25. Joan Semmel. *Patty and I.* 1975. Oil on canvas, 5′8″ square. Courtesy the artist.

which the artist took a dramatic overhead position and cut off her field of perception drastically to convey a warm, close relationship between two women. Georgia O'Keeffe's flower paintings (Pl. 1) demonstrate yet another form of perceptual imagery—the monumentalization of something small and delicate.

Conceptual Imagery

A conceptual image is a kind of symbol, a shape or form that represents something in the artist's mind rather than what is actually seen. Conceptual imagery derives from emotion, fantasy, or invention.

One thinks of the eye as being like a camera, because the camera is designed upon the theory of the eye, but the human eye does not actually record complete and separate pictures. Instead, it registers a continually changing kaleidoscope of images, colors, shapes, sizes, textures, and lines, many of which are superimposed on others or rearranged from the order in which they actually appeared. To these impressions we must add memory, fantasy, dreams, nightmares, and personal visions. All of these together make up the raw material for conceptual imagery.

The fantastic creations of Hieronymus Bosch resemble nothing on this earth. His *Tree Man in a Landscape* (Fig. 26), for instance, shows a form based on a tree but which has assumed humanoid characteristics. The Tree Man is inexplicably standing in two little boats in the water, and a group of people are having dinner inside his body. On his head rests a jug, from which emerges a ladder being climbed by a tiny man. It is a characteristic of Bosch's work that his inventions manage to

left: 26. Hieronymus Bosch. *Tree Man in a Landscape.* c. 1500. Pen and brown ink, $10\frac{15}{16}$ x $8\frac{3}{8}$". Albertina, Vienna.

above: 27. Joan Miró. *Self-Portrait.* 1937–38. Pencil, crayon, and oil on canvas, 4'$9\frac{1}{2}$" x 3'$2\frac{1}{4}$". Collection James Thrall Soby, New Canaan, Conn.

seem at once whimsical and disquieting. All, however, are interwoven in a composition that unifies his conceptual imagery.

The conceptual imagery of Joan Miró is based on decorative progressions of real forms. His *Self-Portrait* shown in Figure 27 begins with the human form, but the artist then plays with each feature and contour until they become separate, though unified decorative elements. The result is still recognizable as a man, but like no man who ever lived. This self-portrait may express in a certain way how the artist feels about himself, but it may on a different level show his delight in experimenting with forms. Much of conceptual imagery depends on giving the imagination free rein.

The essence of design lies in its universal application. Design is not a project or an isolated attempt at aesthetic creation. Rather, design permeates every aspect of life and art. Many of the same considerations apply to the design of a master painting or sculpture as to the patterning of a blue denim jacket (Fig. 155), the visual effects of a rock concert (Pl. 10, p. 90), or the arrangement of a shelf of books. To some extent, everyone is a designer.

2 The Design Process

The most original designs are conceived intuitively, in a kind of "hunch" that the artist feels but could not present in words. To the experienced designer the process of development is largely natural and spontaneous. However, the beginner, approaching the formal study of design for the first time, may feel overwhelmed by the possibilities and have no idea where to begin. The infinite number of potential variations in any design can be at the same time liberating and terrifying. For the novice, then, it may prove reassuring that the act of designing can be analyzed as a logical process in which no sudden burst of inspiration need be expected.

Steps in the Design Process

Even the most seemingly straightforward design can present a wide range of possibilities. If the object to be designed is a teapot, for instance, one might think there are few decisions to be made. Over the centuries the teapot shape has assumed a fairly standard form, determined by the requirements for brewing and serving tea. It is a hollow container, usually rounded, with a lid, a spout for pouring, a handle,

below: 28. Anne Currier. *Teapot with Two Cups.* 1975. Slip-cast earthenware with slab-built handles and spout, luster glaze; height 9″. Courtesy the artist.

right: 29. Wilhelm Wagenfeld. *Teapot.* 1932. Heat-resistant glass, height $4\frac{3}{8}$″. Museum of Modern Art, New York (gift of Philip Johnson and Fraser's Inc., New York).

below right: 30. Marianne Brandt. *Teapot.* 1924. Nickel silver and ebony. Museum of Modern Art, New York (Phyllis B. Lambert Fund).

and often a strainer for the tea leaves. But we must bear in mind that the objective of design is to create something *better* than has existed before—a more beautiful appearance, a more functional shape.

One of the first decisions in designing a teapot would concern the material. Most teapots are ceramic, which is traditional and holds the heat well (Fig. 28). But some are glass, allowing one to watch the brewing process (Fig. 29). There is no reason why a teapot could not also be metal, like many fine past examples (Fig. 30). The spout should pour without dripping or spilling, but a straight or curved one will do this equally well. Frequently the handle reaches across the top of the pot, but if the overall form is carefully balanced, it can be placed on the side (Fig. 29). Teapots generally have flat bottoms, but since they are rarely used directly on the stove, this becomes a matter more of tradition than of function. A built-in stand to insulate the table from heat might be a sensible innovation (Fig. 30). When all these questions of performance have been resolved, there remains the potential for decoration, in which the choices are even wider.

In order to reduce the infinity of options in design to manageable proportions, we will discuss the design process as a series of decisions, taken one at a time. Each time a decision is made, the choices narrow, until there remains only one best solution. If the designer settles on a teapot, then cups, goblets, bowls, and the rest can be forgotten. If it is to be ceramic, that rules out all the other materials. The selection of a glaze eliminates other possible decorative techniques. This process of decision and elimination continues until the design is finished. For convenience, we have broken down the continuum into seven steps.

31. Hexagonal slabs are cut to size with templates.

32. The sides are joined to the base of the hexagon.

31–35. Stages in construction of *Hexagon Scroll Jar,* by Tyrone and Julie Larson. The jar is of stoneware with a glaze and gold luster, its finished height 13″. From *The Penland School of Crafts: Book of Pottery,* edited by John Coyne.

Definition of the project comes first. What will the designer design? Sometimes the answer will be governed by a classroom assignment, a commission, or just an idea that comes to mind. In functional objects, some of the best designs have sprung from a perceived need. A person who gets milk in the lap from a dripping pitcher may think, "Why can't somebody design a pitcher that doesn't leak?" Establishment of a goal represents the first decision that is to be solved by later decisions. Let us assume the project is to design a ceramic object.

Analysis of the possibilities means considering the various ways in which the project can be approached. This might include an analysis of available materials, sketches of possible shapes, and attention to different colors and textures. It may consider alternative uses for the finished product and means of expanding the design beyond the original concept. We will suppose that the ceramic piece will be a decorative jar and that it will be hexagonal in shape.

Definition of the specific problem involves more concrete decisions. How large will the jar be? Will it be tall and thin or short and squat? Should it seem heavy and monumental or light and delicate? Will its overall quality be coarse and earthy or more "formal"? Should the material therefore be porcelain, stoneware, or earthenware? Could it possibly function as a container, or must it be purely decorative? When these questions have been answered, the designer can begin to form a specific idea of the object to be created (Fig. 31).

Examination of the alternatives further limits the design options. The designer will now consider methods of fabrication (Fig. 32), possibilities for decoration, relationship of form to surface, colors (inherent in the material or applied), embellishments, and so forth. In the case of the jar, the decision to make it hexagonal ruled out throwing on the wheel and steered the designer to the slab method of construction (see Chap. 14). But there are still many alternatives. Should the jar have a lid? handles? a foot? an applied design? a glaze? If there is to be a lid (Fig. 33), how should it relate to the pot and how be made?

Selection of characteristics relates directly to the artist's vision. In this choice the designer draws upon a personal reservoir of impressions and experiences and tastes. The ceramic jar in question could be decorated with equal effectiveness in a bold, Japanese-style slash of colored glaze or an intricate filigree of applied clay forms (Fig. 34).

The act of production begins after the first five steps have laid the groundwork. Even at this point, however, the design process is not

33. A knob is thrown on the jar lid.

34. Decorative coils are formed and applied to the surface.

mechanical. While the larger decisions have been made, there remains much potential for intuition and inspiration. Each step in the development of a work may suggest modifications or elaborations not previously obvious. The designer should be flexible, so as to take advantage of unexpected implications in the material or the evolving form. In this way the design process becomes a continuous unfolding.

Clarification is the final stage. The designer stands apart from the completed work in order to appraise it (Fig. 35). Here the artist should try to become a critic, approaching the work as though for the first time. Rarely does the finished work measure up to one's original expectations. This is an important part of the design process, however, for the person who is completely satisfied might stop working altogether or go on to repeat the same design over and over. The artist who can be objective enough to analyze the strengths and weaknesses of a particular piece feels an impetus toward future work. Successful design not only carries the seeds for its own improvement but also generates completely new ideas.

35. The completed jar.

left: 36. Schipporeit-Heinrich, Inc. Lake Point Tower, Chicago. 1968. Reinforced poured concrete and bronzed aluminum with glass.

right: 37. Antoni Gaudí. La Sagrada Familia, Barcelona. Begun 1903; work terminated 1926 and resumed 1952; still under construction.

Structural and Decorative Design

Design books customarily distinguish two aspects of design, structural and decorative. However, the interrelationship between the two is so basic that it may be impossible to separate them. Every design has both. While a perfectly plain, glass-sheathed building, for example, may seem to have no ornamentation, the glass itself, shimmering with light, provides the decorative design.

Generally speaking, the most successful designs are those in which the structural and decorative functions are closely wedded. It is true that a designer may be involved first in the structure of a work and later turn to surface development, but the latter should evolve naturally from the former. If a particular piece, perhaps a ceramic pot, is completely finished with regard to structure and then the designer casts about blindly for a way to decorate it, the result probably will not be a happy one. Structural design should determine the decorative design in all its aspects: the shape and size, the techniques used, and the nature of the design, which should be related to the materials and basic structure of the piece. Architecture provides some of the clearest examples of harmonious structure and decoration.

At the turn of the century, when steel first became practical for skyscrapers, architects would frequently sheath their buildings in conventional patterns of stone or concrete, as though these were the only "proper" materials for a structure. Many also added classical friezes (decorative stone bands running around the building under the roofline). In this transitional period, architects were willing to accept a new *structural* material, but refused to abandon *decorative* techniques that belonged to a previous era. As the skyscraper evolved, the older decorative forms fell away, so that by the mid-20th century we had buildings like the Lake Point Tower in Chicago (Fig. 36). A 65-story apartment building, the Lake Point Tower exemplifies totally integrated structure and ornament. Its clover-leaf shape, which is its structure, acts at the same time as a kind of decoration, as does the aluminum-and-glass sheathing that reflects light throughout the day. There is no superficial ornament whatsoever.

Structure and decoration are just as closely interwoven in the work of Spanish architect Antoni Gaudí, but here the style is quite different (Fig. 37). Gaudí's architecture is totally organic, as though it had *grown* on its site instead of being constructed. The forms seem to have been molded freely by hand, with decorative elements emerging directly from the structure and then flowing back in again. It would be impossible to imagine a Gaudí building without the surface embellishments, because structure and ornament are created simultaneously. In visual appearance one could scarcely find a greater contrast than that between the Lake Point Tower and Gaudí's Church of the Holy Family, yet the two share a fundamental unity of concept.

Structural Design: Composition

In two-dimensional works such as paintings, structure is often referred to as *composition.* This means the underlying framework. Composition is relatively easy to analyze in geometric works like those of Mondrian (Fig. 12) or the 20th-century color-field painters (Pl. 31, p. 247). It may be more subtle in complex figural works or landscapes.

Jacques Louis David's *Oath of the Horatii* (Fig. 38) is often given as an example of compositional design, because its format is so clear. The three arched niches in the background provide the setting for three triangles in which the figures are arranged—the soldiers at left, Horatius in the center, and the lamenting women at right. Few paintings show so rigid and intellectual a compositional scheme, but

38. Jacques Louis David. *Oath of the Horatii.* 1784. Oil on canvas, 10′10″ x 14′. Louvre, Paris.

all have some underlying format, or else the result would seem haphazard. Unquestionably, David planned this structure with great care. Most painters arrive at a satisfying composition through intuition, trial and error. Different arrangements are tested, until the compositional elements settle into an order that has unity and balance. The remaining chapters in this Part I, which deal with the elements and principles of design, will expand upon the question of compositional order.

Decorative Design

The question of decorative design becomes particularly interesting with functional objects, which require no embellishment to perform the jobs they are supposed to do. An automobile, for example, once it has provided for an engine compartment, drive shaft, gasoline tank, and wheels, needs little more than a place to hold the passengers. Yet in the scant century during which motorized vehicles have been available, what a wealth of designs have been created!

The first automobiles tried to imitate the horse-drawn carriages that had preceded them (Fig. 39). They had rudder steering, large, thin wheels (sometimes only three), and generally looked as though they were missing something—the horse—at the front, as indeed they were. Later vehicles attempted, through their ornament, to establish an image of great luxury, with attachments of chrome and brass (Fig. 40). Special "custom" features, stuck on for effect and having little to do with the performance of the car, gave the owner a sense of riding like royalty.

During the late 1940s and early 1950s the "sports car" came into prominence (Fig. 41). Here decorative design was intended to give the driver a rakish appearance. The car would almost certainly be a convertible, have wire wheels and big lights, and perhaps have its spare tire mounted jauntily on the back. Other types of decorative design suggest speed and power (Fig. 42). The racing sports car, low-slung and streamlined, has a minimum of applied design, yet its body shape (independent of function) is planned to give the impression of unharnessed energy.

We can see from these examples that decorative design is not arbitrary. It aims at a particular effect—and that effect may be simplicity, grandeur, sleekness, conformity, eccentricity, or a thousand other qualities. We could just as easily apply these traits to the decorative design of other objects: chairs, bracelets, pianos, clothing, or television sets. Decorative design makes a statement about the personalities of both the maker and the user.

Integrity of Design

Stemming from the Latin *integritas,* the word integrity has as one of its meanings the quality or state of being whole. Integrity of design is primarily a matter of unity in the artist's conception and of honesty in bringing that conception into being. There are three specific areas in which we can consider design integrity: materials, form, and function.

Integrity of Materials

Before any structural design can be attempted, the designer should be aware of what materials are available and should be familiar with

left: 39. Mercedes-Benz, 1886.

below left: 40. Daimler Touring Car, 1907. Courtesy Long Island Automotive Museum, Southampton.

right: 41. MG TC, 1947. Courtesy British Leyland Motors, Inc.

below: 42. Maserati Merak, 1976.

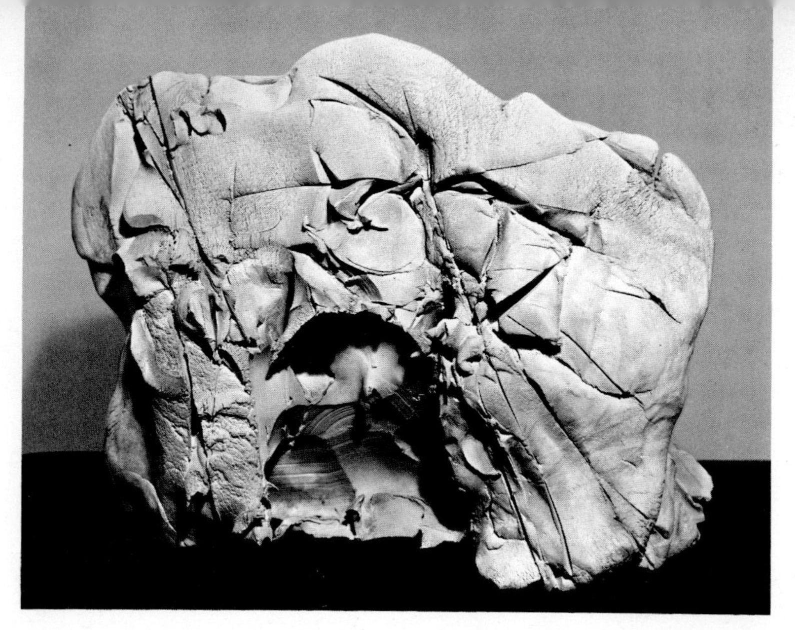

43. Reuben Nakian. *Rock Drawing* (study for *The Rape of Lucrece*). 1957. Terra cotta, 10 x 14¼ x 6″. Museum of Modern Art, New York (Philip L. Goodwin Fund).

their advantages and limitations. The chapters in Part II of this book have been offered to provide some basic information about raw materials, because the choice of a material is one of the first decisions a designer must make. The architect must know which materials are strong in compression (when pressed under weight) and which have more strength in tension (when stretched). The sculptor should understand which materials are capable of assuming certain forms, which will endure the longest, and how they will behave when exposed to weather. Painters will be better able to achieve the effects they are seeking if they are familiar with the various painting media available.

Some of the most exciting designs are those that truly express the substances of which they are composed. Reuben Nakian's sculpture in Figure 43, actually a study for a later work, quite obviously is made of clay. By its form, its texture, the deep impressions, and the dug-out portions it proclaims itself to be of the earth. Anyone who has worked with damp clay and felt its fascinating plasticity will experience the tactile richness of this work merely by looking at it. One has the feeling that even in the finished piece a touch of the fingers would leave an imprint. This is a particularly articulate expresssion of the material.

Industrial design today relies heavily on the materials that are especially of our own age—metal, plastic, and glass. In keeping with the qualities of these smooth, sleek materials, design tends to be clean and hard-edged, with a minimum of superficial ornament (Fig. 44). Forms are likely to express the function of the object, with the material implying efficiency, a "no-nonsense" approach.

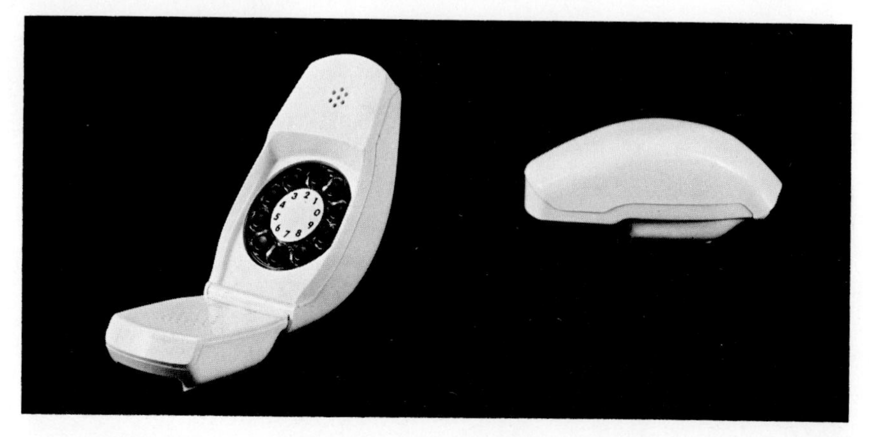

44. Marco Zanuso and Richard Sapper. *Folding Telephone.* 1968. Plastic housing, height 2¾″. Manufactured by Societa Italiana Telecomunicazioni, Italy. Museum of Modern Art, New York (gift of the manufacturer).

above: 45. Marilyn Levine. *Knapsack.* 1970. Slab-constructed stoneware with leather laces, 15 x 19 x 13″. Courtesy the artist.

right: 46. Marcel Breuer. *Armchair.* 1925. Chrome-plated steel tube and canvas. Museum of Modern Art, New York (gift of Herbert Bayer).

The advent of plastics brought a wave of simulation in which manufacturers imitated familiar surfaces with vinyl or melamine, advertising the advantages of increased durability and ease of upkeep. Americans walk on vinyl floors patterned to imitate the ceramic tile of Europe and set their hot kettles on counters topped with melamine grained to look like wood. Designers who imitate traditional appearances not only violate the concept of integrity in design but miss the opportunity to create new designs appropriate to plastic. The intrinsic qualities of the original materials are totally lost in imitation—the earthy quality of tile, the warmth and aroma of wood.

We must make an important distinction between imitations that try to deceive, such as those described above, and *deliberate* imitations created by artists for shock value, amusement, or whimsy. Marilyn Levine's *Knapsack* (Fig. 45), meticulously crafted in clay to mimic leather, stands as a visual pun. It is as though the artist is purposely contradicting the traditional role of ceramics for functional objects.

Integrity of Form

During much of the 20th century the idea of integrity in form has been summed up in the phrase "form follows function." Emerging from the writings of the 19th-century American sculptor Horatio Greenough, the concept has come to be associated with the Bauhaus, a school of design founded in Weimar, Germany, in 1919. Among the major aims of the Bauhaus program was the development of designs suitable for machine production. Its faculty and staff concentrated on architecture, textiles, furniture, and household items, paring them down to the essential form so that they would become a direct statement of the function they were intended to fill (Fig. 46). Each design was to be directly expressive of its material and of the machine process that

above: 47. John James Audubon. *Short-Billed Marsh Wren (Cisthothorus platensis)*, from *The Birds of America*. 1832. Watercolor, 21½ x 14½″. New York Historical Society.

below: 48. Gad-dam stilt tree house, Luzon Island, Philippines.

made it. A chair such as the one in Figure 46 must have seemed remarkable to the 1920s consumer accustomed to heavily carved oak and mahogany furnishings. Yet the fact that it still looks "modern" today testifies to its timeless purity of design.

Design in nature adheres rigidly to the principle of form following function. The bird's nest shown in Figure 47 is made from the materials in its immediate surroundings. Its form, too, harmonizes with the marsh grasses around it, which serves the function of camouflaging the birds' home from predators.

In character with the nest, but much more elaborate, the tree houses in the Philippines (Fig. 48) have been designed carefully to cope with a hostile climate. Deep in the jungle, in an area plagued by high humidity, floods, insects, and dangerous animals, the tree house avoids all by its position 40 feet above the ground. This elevation also permits cooling breezes to flow under the house. A steeply pitched roof shuns the torrential rains that are common to this area, while minimum walls give the greatest possible ventilation. Truly, function is satisfied in the form of this ingenious design.

Integrity of Function

The modern steel and glass office building can provide an example of functional design at its best—or its worst. In theory the office skyscraper makes ideal use of space. Cities that cannot grow outward grow *up,* stacking similar functions on top of one another. High-speed elevators carry people to their jobs quickly, while services—restaurants and shops, for instance—can be centralized. In practice, however, many newer buildings violate integrity of function in their designs. Windows that cannot be opened make year-round ventilation and temperature control essential, thus creating tremendous energy needs. Many offices have no windows at all, so that artificial lighting must be used at all times. Moreover, the lighting may be controlled by a master switch that operates for a whole floor or group of floors. If one person wants to work late, the lights for an entire complex of offices must be left burning. Some buildings constructed within this decade use, per building, the same amount of energy as a small city, and generate the same amount of waste.

Many of the irritations of modern life stem from objects lacking integrity of function. Furniture with drawers that do not run smoothly, automobiles that require a contortionist's skill to manipulate the seat belt, umbrellas that reverse under the slightest breeze—all of these are commonplace.

Integrity of design must play a role especially when the function of an object evolves. When electric irons were first introduced, their design remained close to the old heavy flat irons that had to be heated on top of the stove. It was not until many years later that manufacturers realized weight was no longer part of the function of the iron. We could cite many examples of this problem in objects that were refined after their original introduction.

Not surprisingly, then, some of the best—most functional—designs can be found in products that are uniquely of our own century, especially things related to sports, transportation, and communication. If a designer undertakes to create something that has never existed before, more thought undoubtedly will be given to integrity of function, since there are no preconceived ideas about how it should look. We see this in radios, stereo components, television sets, ski equipment, airplanes, and motorbikes (Fig. 49).

The process of design has many fundamental characteristics that apply whether one is designing a painting, a sculpture, a pot, or a set of modular furnishings. Certain underlying elements and principles guide the designer in every field. In the chapters that follow we will examine each of these separately, first the *elements of design*—space, line, shape, mass, color, texture, and pattern; then the *principles of design*—unity, variety, balance, emphasis, rhythm, proportion, and scale. We shall also consider the question of symbolism, which plays an important role in many designs. None of these qualities should be thought of as rules to be followed slavishly, but simply as guidelines to encourage the production of successful designs. Above all, the process of design is a *creative* act, and creativeness sometimes defies all logical rules.

49. Honda CB-500T, 1976.

Line

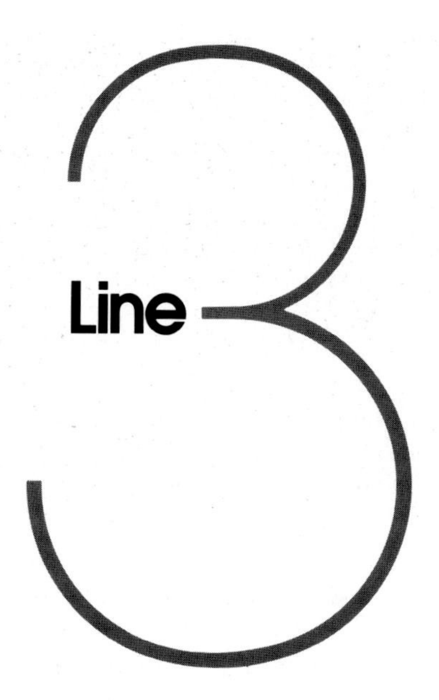

Line is perhaps the most fundamental element of design. Since civilization began people have been fascinated by lines. There may indeed be some basic human urge to draw a line, to "leave one's mark." Few people can resist the urge to draw with a stick in wet sand, to doodle in pen on a blank piece of paper, to scratch with a piece of charcoal. Children draw lines on the sidewalk and invent games around them. Primitive peoples left lines on the walls of their caves. A simple line can provide endless interest all by itself.

The mention of line suggests lines on a sheet of paper or on a canvas. But there are many other kinds of lines—some created by human hands, some occurring naturally, even some that are merely abstractions and do not "really" exist at all. The illustrations in this chapter are meant to expand the awareness of line in all its aspects.

It is difficult to discuss line without reference to *shape* and *space,* because a close interrelationship unites these three elements. The presence of one nearly always implies that both of the others are involved. For example, a line necessarily carves out areas of space on either side of it (Fig. 50). At the same time, any line except a perfectly straight one creates a shape, and it could be argued that even the

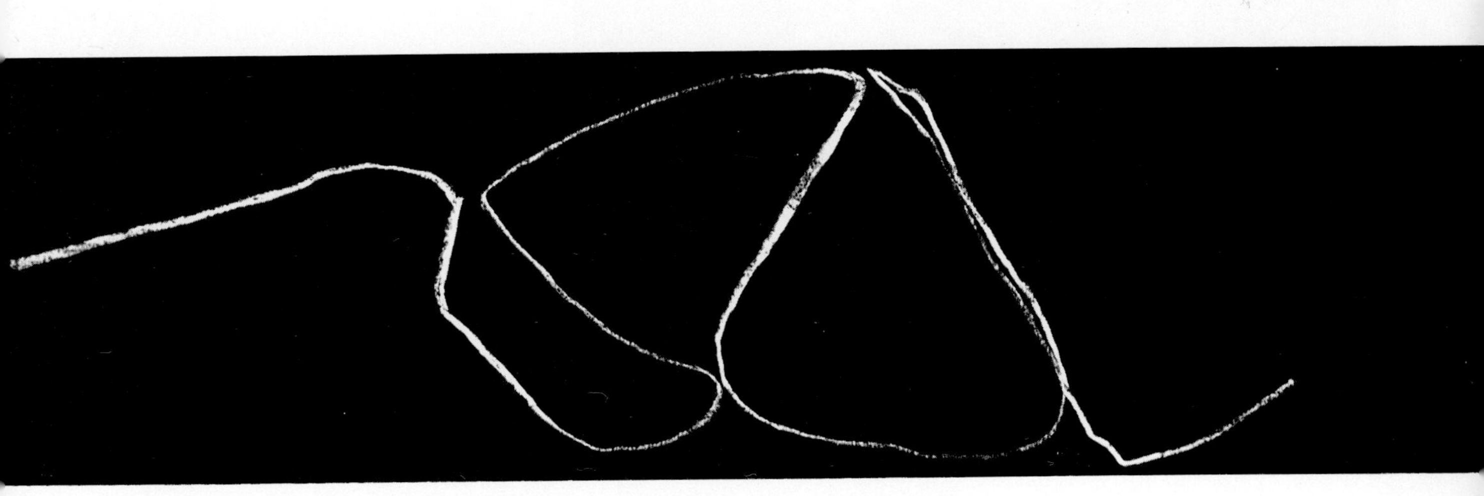

straight line marks geometric shapes on both sides. We cannot have shape without the lines that indicate its edges or without the space from which the lines carve a shape. The lines that operate as edges are particularly important, because we recognize most things by their shapes. Whenever we draw a line, such as the curved line in Figure 50, we automatically create a shape within the line and mold the space outside the line. Finally, although space is everywhere, we cannot *perceive* it until it has been limited, or *demarcated,* by lines and shapes. We can talk about the space within a building because the four walls and roof of the building have organized this space in a particular way.

In this chapter we shall isolate line for individual analysis, so that the reader can begin to see the special ways in which this element functions in any design. The following chapter treats space, and the next one shape, as well as its three-dimensional counterpart, *mass.*

Line in Nature

Lines fill every part of our world, from the endless reach of the horizon to the delicate veins in a leaf (Fig. 51), from the soaring vertical lines of

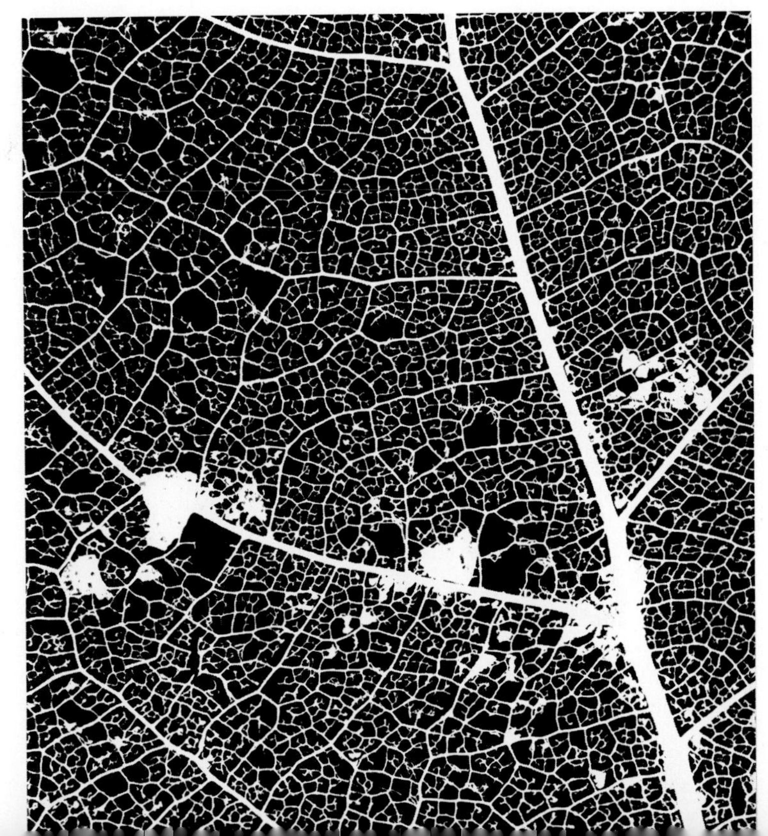

top: 50. Jan Groth. *Sign.* 1967. Tapestry weave, black wool with white line composition; 4′7″ x 16′5″. Museum of Art, Carnegie Institute, Pittsburgh (Patrons Art Fund).

right: 51. Wolf Strache. *Leaf Skeleton of Black Poplar.* 1956. Photograph.

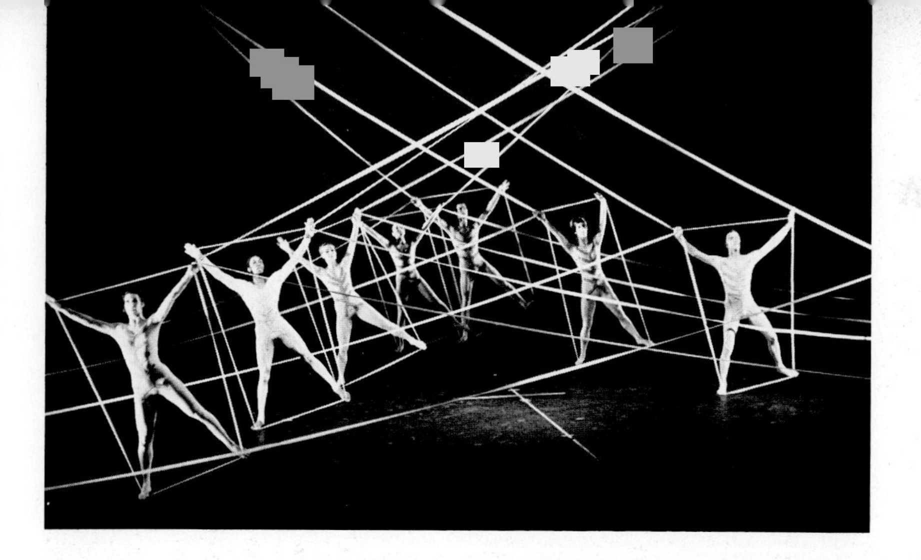

skyscrapers to the lines in a drawing or painting. The natural world abounds with lines of every description.

One of the most basic natural lines is that of the human body. We are accustomed to seeing each other as fleshed-out, three-dimensional forms. Unless someone presents us with a silhouette, we may overlook the outline of the human figure. In a stark photograph of the Alwin Nikolais dance company (Fig. 52) our attention is directed to the line of the body in graceful motion, here made all the more evident by the lines connecting the dancers. Except when the body is in repose, this line changes constantly. Anyone who works with people in programmed motion—a choreographer or director or even a drill master—will intuitively consider the visual impact of bodily lines and their interplay.

When we speak of lines in terms of the human body, we connect the everyday use of the word line with the concept of "designed" lines. People often refer to the *majestic* lines of a ship, the *flowing* lines of a gown, the *undulating* line of hills, and so forth. This is a way of expressing the overall feeling something conveys, its essential quality. If, for example, we talk about the "sleek" lines of an aircraft, we are not

top: 52. The Nikolais Dance Theatre performing *Tensile Involvement,* 1969.

right: 53. Charles Moore. *Death Valley.* 1970. Photograph.

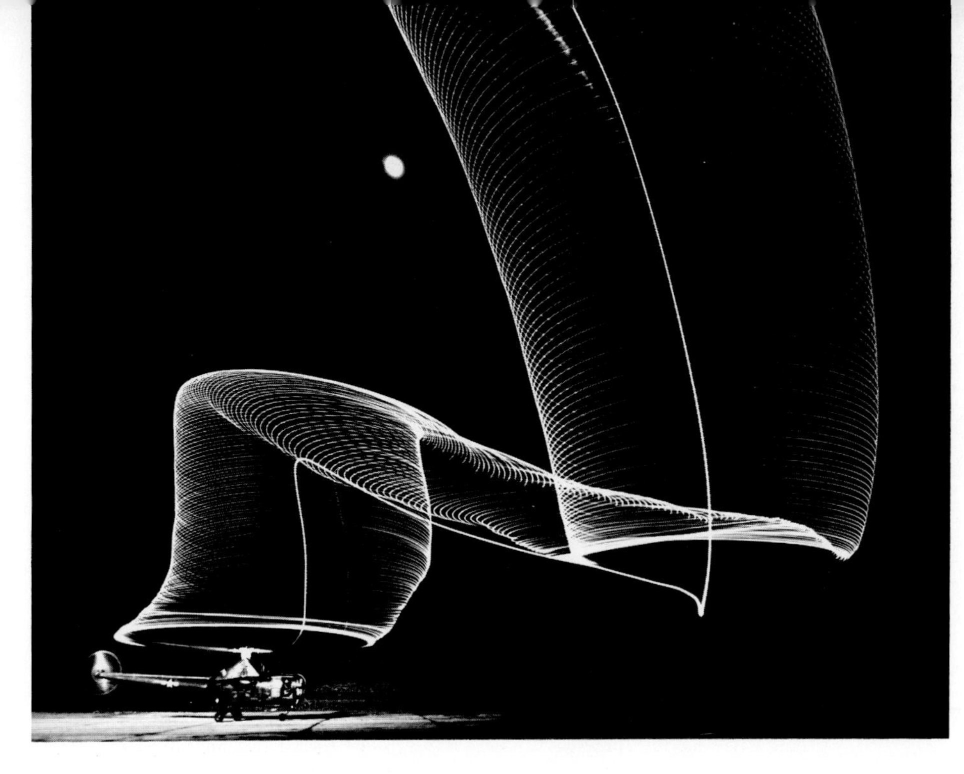

54. Andreas Feininger. *Navy Rescue Helicopter.* 1949. Photograph.

only describing its basic form but hinting at its potential speed, its power, its reflection of space-age technology. Line is such a vital element in design that it can determine the very character of the thing designed.

Besides the human form, an infinite variety of lines can be found in nature. Trees reaching upward create lines, as do the ripples in a pond, a range of mountains against the sky, a pattern of pebbles on a beach, a cactus on the desert, a column of ants marching from their nest. Some are static, some ever-changing. We tend to think of straight lines as being the products of the mathematician's or draftsman's straight edge, yet perfectly straight lines—lines that seem to have been drawn by a giant ruler—often occur naturally (Fig. 53).

The designer can find much inspiration by studying natural lines. For instance, the composition in Figure 53, if diagramed in line, would show the one sharp, dominant vertical, with softer wavy lines radiating out to the right. The curving lines of dunes terminate the long vertical, and a strong horizontal background line is formed by mountains in the distance. Of course, other elements, especially texture and value contrasts, play an important role in this composition, but it is instructive to separate one element for analysis. If you study the world around you, you will find a wealth of natural configurations in line.

Abstract Lines

At the beginning of this chapter we mentioned abstract lines that do not really exist, that is, lines we cannot actually see or trace. In about the 3rd century B.C. Euclid developed the science of geometry from imaginary lines connecting several points, such as the three points in an imaginary triangle. By these means he was able to calculate distances with great accuracy, even to the distances between planets.

The modern camera has given us the capacity to make concrete the abstract lines formed by motion and energy. We have all seen time-exposure photographs of a busy highway at night, in which the moving headlamps of the cars create long ribbons of light. A similar but more intriguing pattern of lines appears in Figure 54, a time-lapse photo of a helicopter landing. Here the "lines" are formed by the rapidly turning rotors as the craft swoops down in its descent. These lines are real enough in a sense, but we could not see them without artificial aids.

The fascinating lines resulting from modern technology are exemplified in Figure 55. This drawing of a "snail" came from no human hand. It is the product of a computer programmed to trace a repetitive pattern. What we see is a visual translation of coded instructions. The impulse comes from a person, the design from a machine.

Line as Symbol

A line becomes a symbol when a specific meaning is attached to it. When two or more people agree about the meaning, the symbol can serve as a method of communication. The lines of letters and numbers have particular symbolic meanings. Joined together in ways that are generally understood, lines represent words (and therefore ideas), mathematical quantities, or musical notes (Fig. 56). Without them, knowledge could not efficiently be stored or transmitted.

left: 55. Kerry Strand. *The Snail.* 1968. Computer graphic. Courtesy California Computer Products, Inc., Anaheim, Calif.

below: 56. Facsimile of autograph manuscript for Ludwig van Beethoven's *Missa Solemnis,* page 25, published by Hans Schneider (Tutzing). Performing Arts Research Center, The New York Public Library at Lincoln Center (Astor, Lenox and Tilden Foundations).

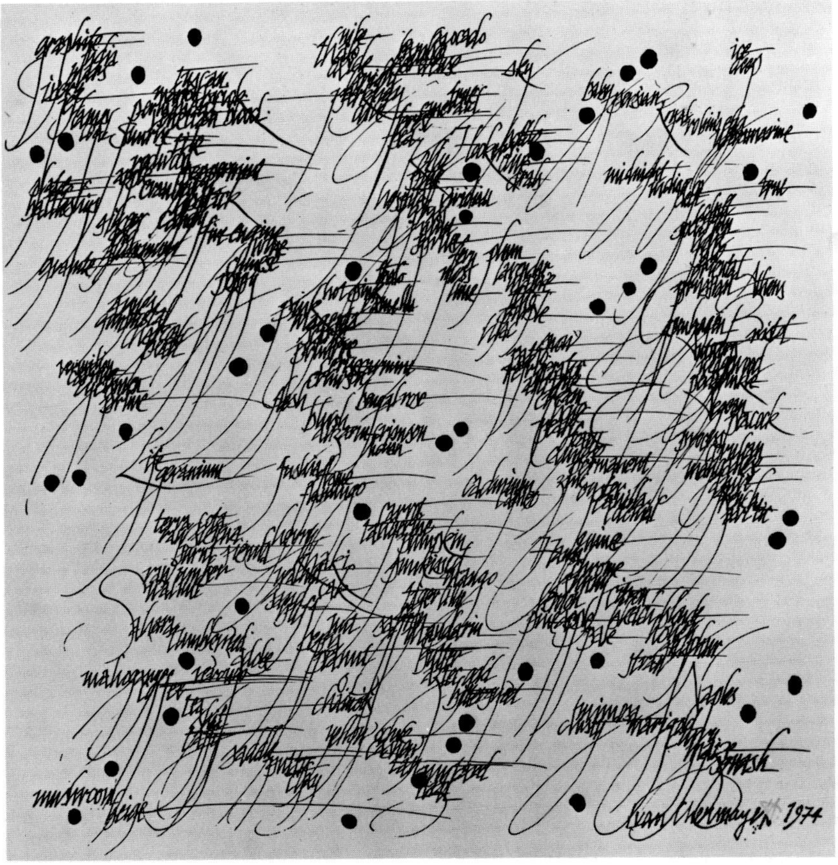

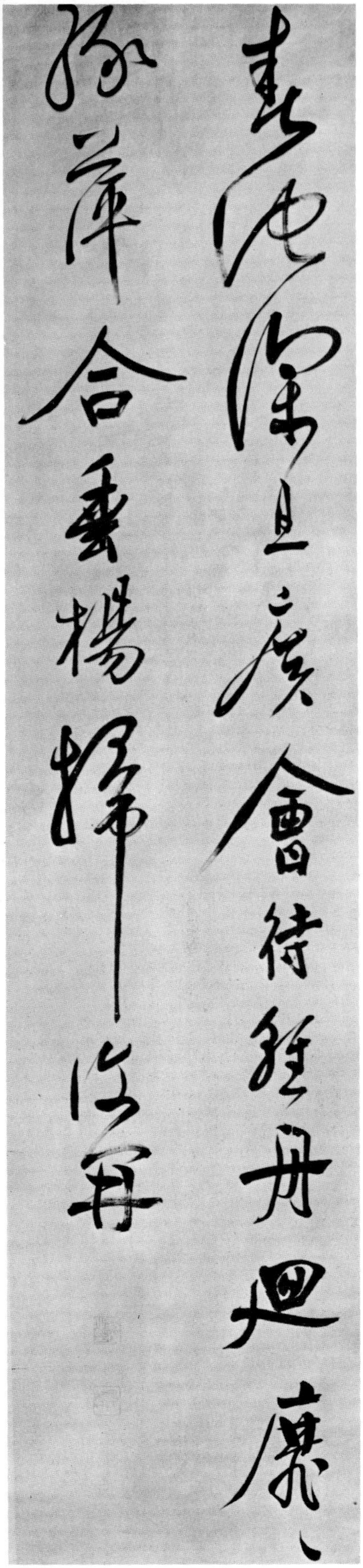

above: 57. Ivan Chermayeff. *All the Color Names.* 1974. India ink and prismacolor; image 22″ square, poster 35¾ x 23¾″.

right: 58. Hai Jui (Chinese, 1514–87). Hanging scroll, India ink on paper; 6′10⅞″ x 1′8″. Collection John M. Crawford, Jr., New York.

Nearly all civilizations have practiced a form of *calligraphy* (from the Greek "beautiful writing") whether in decorative forms of letters in the Western alphabet (Fig. 57), the Semitic scripts of the Middle East, or the highly stylized brushstrokes of Oriental characters (Fig. 58). The Chinese or Japanese calligrapher is considered a master artist, who may spend years—even decades—perfecting the technique. Each element of the craft is ritualized, including the way the brush is held, the relationship of the hand to the paper, the preparation of the ink, and especially the movement of the brush's tip onto the paper and away from it.

The letters in the Roman alphabet that we use can be considered arbitrary symbols; they are assigned to particular sounds in spoken language but have no visual meaning of their own. This is not true, however, of many forms of Oriental writing, which are *ideographic.* This means that the characters are abstracted images of what they represent. For example, the character that stands for "house" originated by actually resembling a house.

above: 59. Rachel Vine, age 4. Felt-tip pen drawing.

right: 60. Paul Klee. *A Child's Game.* 1939. Oil-tempera on papier mâché, $16\frac{7}{8}$ x $12\frac{5}{8}''$. Collection Felix Klee, Bern.

Children commonly use line symbols in their drawing (Fig. 59). A stick figure means a person, a vertical line with downward diagonals attached indicates a tree, and so forth. These naïve symbols are understood immediately. The Swiss artist Paul Klee adapted a technique based on such symbols for his works, many of which are done in simple, unshaded line (Fig. 60). Klee's drawings, and even his paintings, often include stick figures for people and animals, outline trees and foliage, crosses, flags, circles to represent the sun or moon, and other basic line symbols. In the hands of a sensitive artist these symbols become a highly sophisticated means of visual communication.

Line as Contour and Modeling

A contour line is a line that traces the outline or overall shape of something. It has no modeling or shading and tells nothing about the surface of the thing it pictures. Such a line can be used to draw flat, two-dimensional shapes (Fig. 61). A skilled artist can also make the

61. "Mickey Mouse" neon. Courtesy Let There Be Neon, New York.

contour line describe the volume of three-dimensional forms. In the drawing in Figure 62 Gaston Lachaise limited himself to the most economical means—a few swooping curves, a few smaller ones—in representing the voluptuous seated nude. The line varies hardly at all in thickness or darkness, and there is no shading whatever. Yet the artist's draftsmanship and amazing composition join to make us understand fully the rounded contours of the figure. This work is truly astonishing in its bold invention, a unified and daringly balanced outline drawing.

On the other hand, the artist who wishes to convey more specifically the details of surface, of feature, of different planes may use a modeled line. Such a line can be shaded, perhaps with the side of a pencil; or there may be closely spaced parallel lines (*hatchings*) or intersecting parallel lines (*cross-hatchings*). Overlapping lines give a soft contour and may suggest details. A page of sketched heads attributed to Leonardo da Vinci (Fig. 63) uses a complex system of lines and hatchings for facial modeling that is almost unbelievably plastic.

below: 62. Gaston Lachaise. *Seated Woman, Leg Raised.* c. 1933–35. Pencil drawing on paper, 24$\frac{1}{8}$ x 19″. Museum of Modern Art, New York (gift of Edward M. M. Warburg).

right: 63. Leonardo da Vinci(?). Page of portrait drawings. 1490–92. Pen and ink over red chalk on paper, 8$\frac{1}{2}$ x 6″. Royal Collection, Windsor (reproduced by gracious permission of Her Majesty Queen Elizabeth II).

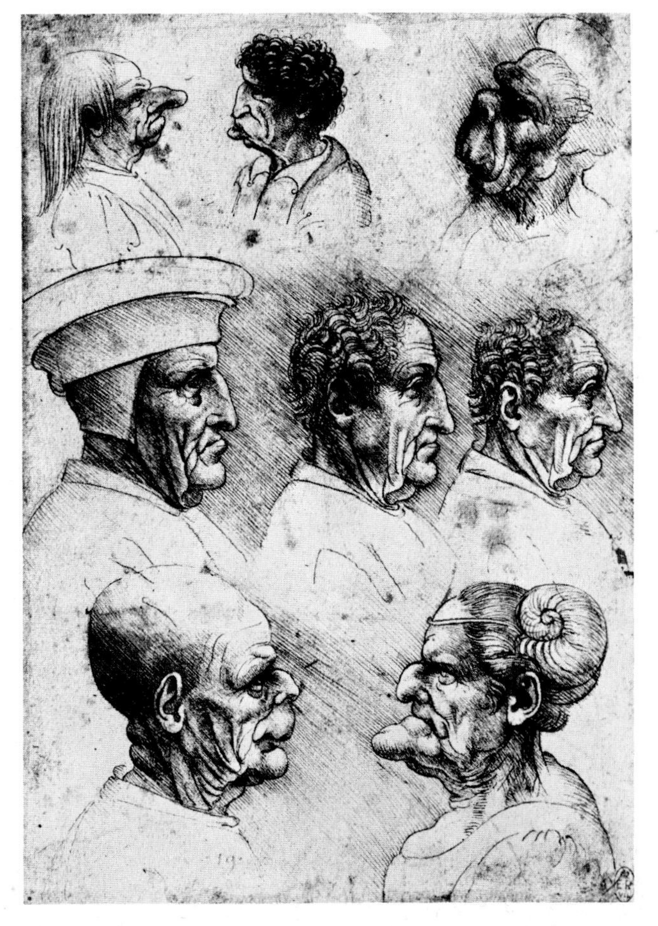

Leonardo began with a contour line to reveal the basic shape of each head, but then elaborated his details with modeling. The deeply wrinkled flesh of the man at lower left, the jutting, bulbous chin of the woman at right—all are achieved through line alone.

Line as Form

Sometimes line does not merely convey form but actually *is* form. We see this most readily in three-dimensional works—sculpture or constructions, for instance. Alberto Giacometti's *Chariot* (Fig. 64) is really nothing more than an assembly of lines, in this case drawn in bronze. Yet these delicate lines amply reveal the simplified figure of the charioteer on his wheeled vehicle.

Line is the major element in Robert Smithson's *Spiral Jetty* (Fig. 65), an artificial structure, 1500 feet long, that curves outward into Utah's Great Salt Lake. The *Spiral Jetty* is typical of modern "earthworks" that some artists have investigated as a means of establishing form in the landscape itself. A diagram or sketch of this work would simply be a long spiral line—not particularly interesting in itself. Yet translated into earth and rock, laid out on a gigantic scale, this single line becomes a powerful form.

Line as Pattern or Texture

When lines are drawn close together or when similar lines are repeated in a composition, they may create a visual pattern or texture. We can see this in the Leonardo heads (Fig. 63), and especially in the helicopter photo and the Chermayeff calligraphy (Figs. 54, 57). If we close our eyes for a moment to the actual letters and words in the calligraphy, the swirling lines and curves form an elegant pattern on the page.

left: 64. Alberto Giacometti. *Chariot.* 1950. Bronze, 4'9" x 2'2" x 2'4⅛". Museum of Modern Art, New York (purchase).

below: 65. Robert Smithson. *Spiral Jetty.* 1970. Black rock, salt crystals, earth, and red water (algae); coil 1500' long, 15' wide. Great Salt Lake, Utah.

In many different media lines are used as decorative design, because they provide an energetic visual texture. In a set of glasses designed by Michael Boehm for Rosenthal (Fig. 66), a pattern of thin lines swirls upward in a diagonal movement from the base of each glass to the rim. The delicate linear design helps to emphasize the swell of the forms. The lines formed by a potter's fingers in throwing a ceramic form provide the same kind of decorative design, as do the lines of the woodcarver's chisel. We could find many examples of this linear design in other media.

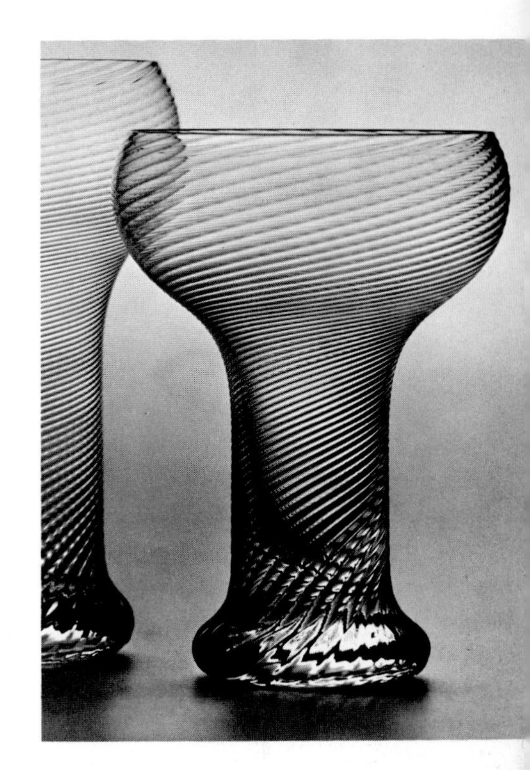

Line as Direction and Emphasis

In any design, line can perform the important function of leading the eye and creating emphasis. A pen drawing of *The Feast of Herod*, by Peter Paul Rubens (Fig. 67), illustrates this point clearly. If we were to diagram this drawing, we would see that a large portion of the lines, both contour and shading, are slanted in such a way that they direct our vision to Herod's head, which is the focal point of the work. Even as our eyes stray to other parts of the drawing, the diagonal lines pull us back repeatedly to Herod.

Figures 68 and 69 show opposite aspects of another way that line can lead the eye. In a painting by Al Held (Fig. 68), lines and forms

above: 66. Crystal glassware in the "Twist" pattern, designed by Michael Boehm for Rosenthal Studio-Linie.

below: 67. Peter Paul Rubens. *The Feast of Herod.* c. 1638. Pen and bistre with charcoal and red chalk on paper, $10\frac{3}{4} \times 18\frac{5}{8}$". Cleveland Museum of Art (Delia E. and L. E. Holden Funds).

68. Al Held. *Noah's Focus I.* 1970. Acrylic on canvas, 11′6″ x 2′1″. Courtesy André Emmerich Gallery, New York.

are carried right to the edge of the canvas and there chopped off abruptly. The viewer's eye is pulled continually *out* of the painting and back in again. The impression is of an infinitely expanding universe. By contrast, the lines in Amédée Ozenfant's *Fugue* (Fig. 69) all curve *inward* and are contained by a basically rectangular format. Their swelling and tapering widths encourage us to follow them around in their rhythmic paths throughout the drawing. There is nothing static about this work; the lines keep our eyes moving continually. For example, if we begin at center bottom, the line that serves as the left side of a rounded vase shape curves upward to become the side of the pitcher, then veers off into the pitcher's handle, which in turn is the side of another vase shape.

The Quality of Line

Our discussion of the Held and Ozenfant works has raised a significant point about line—the fact that it can have many different qualities. Lines can be thick or thin, can swell and taper or have uniform thickness, can be smooth or jagged. The Held painting consists entirely of bold, black, geometric lines, each of which is uniform in thickness from beginning to end. The emphatic, overlapping shapes they create have a powerful, almost overwhelming effect on the viewer. We do not experience individual lines, but rather the dramatic forms they suggest—forms that seem to be thrusting themselves out at us.

The Ozenfant drawing evokes quite a different response. Here the fine lines swell and taper to delineate the edges of forms, as in the curve of the pitcher at center. Without the accents of these swelling lines to suggest contour and shadow, the drawing would be an overall flat pattern.

Not only do lines have inherent qualities, but they can also imply qualities that cause an emotional response in the viewer. One of the simplest ways they do this is by their *direction.* Generalizations about this aspect can be dangerous, for one could always find exceptions. However, we can say that horizontal lines *tend* to suggest repose, stability, calm, as in the horizon line or the sturdy crossbeams of a building. In Caspar David Friedrich's *The Evening Star* (Fig. 70) nearly all the compositional elements are horizontal or predominantly so—the cloud lines, the distant horizon, even the row of figures. The very slight downward curve of the hillside prevents this format from becoming monotonous and adds to the feeling of tranquility and peace.

Vertical lines may represent a defiance of gravity. Sometimes strong verticals have an aspiring or uplifting quality, while at other times they establish a kind of balance set against a true horizontal. Diagonal lines tend to be dynamic and energetic (Fig. 71). They throw us off balance, demanding our attention. The designer may introduce a few diagonals into a composition to animate it, but as the diagonals

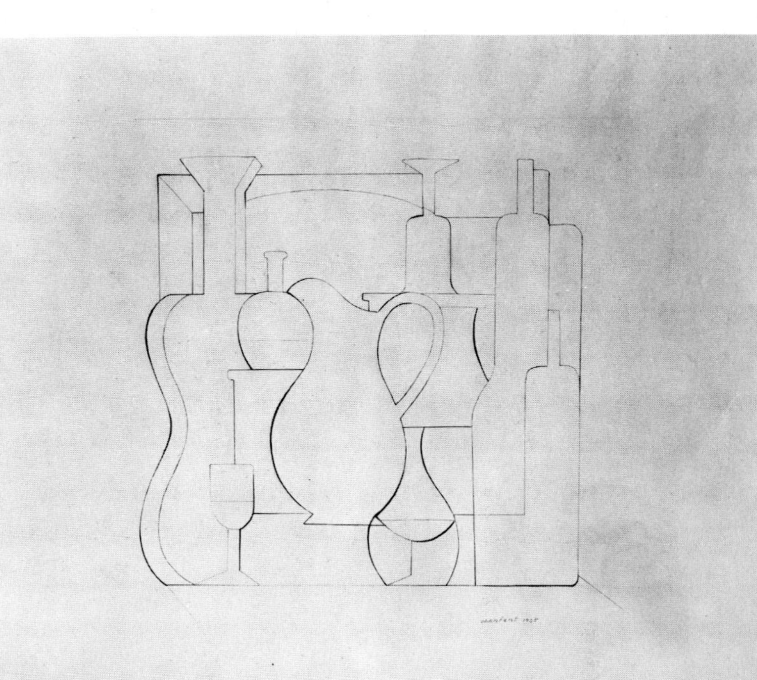

right: 69. Amédée Ozenfant. *Fugue.* 1925. Pencil, 18 x 22″. Museum of Modern Art, New York (gift of the artist).

below: 70. Caspar David Friedrich. *The Evening Star* (*Der Abendstern*). c. 1830–35. Oil on canvas, $12\frac{1}{2} \times 17\frac{1}{2}$″. Freies Deutsches Hochstift, Goethemuseum, Frankfurt.

left: 71. Kenneth Snelson. *Free Ride Home.* 1974. Aluminum and stainless steel, 30 x 60 x 60′. Collection Storm King Art Center, Mountainville, N.Y.; shown here in temporary installation at Waterside Plaza, New York.

right: 72. Honoré Daumier. *Fright* (*L'Epouvante*). Charcoal over pencil on paper, 8¼ x 9⅜″. Art Institute of Chicago (gift of Robert Allerton).

below: 73. Ronaldo de Juan. *Gate # 6.* 1976. Charcoal, 6′3″ x 3′10″. Courtesy Lerner Heller Gallery, New York.

increase, particularly if they are set in opposition to one another, the effect becomes ever more active.

Vigorous, ragged, curving lines may imply terror or turbulent emotions in general, as in a drawing by Honoré Daumier (Fig. 72). For this work the artist has used line in a compelling manner to create a tremulous form that seems visibly to be shrinking back in fear. A similar quality can be found in the characteristic frenzied line of Vincent van Gogh (Fig. 371), which tells us much about the artist's emotional state even before we know his life story. Yet another effect, a menacing one, is communicated by the lines in Ronaldo de Juan's *Gate #6* (Fig. 73). The heavy charcoal lines at the center of the composition seem to loom threateningly, while the curving lines at bottom are suggestive of whiplash strokes. As we can see, it is possible for line alone, without any recognizable shape or content, to convey a mood.

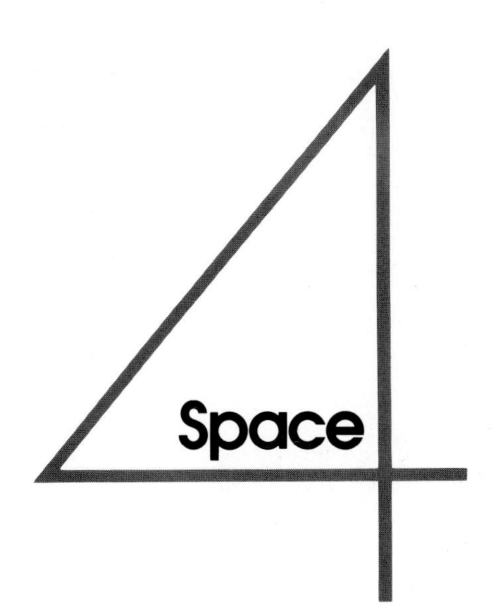

The layman tends to think of space as a void, a nothingness. Designers know better, for in creating form they must always manipulate space. The cut-paper design shown in Figure 74 illustrates this idea, for the design depends as much on the spaces as on the figures in the paper.

In any discussion of space as a design element, we must distinguish two kinds. *Actual* space is that which in fact exists in a composition. It may be the two-dimensional space within the borders of a canvas, the three-dimensional spaces inside and around a sculpture or within a building. *Pictorial* space is the illusionary space that we see in a two-dimensional work, such as a painting or drawing. We might analyze it in terms of the number of planes, or flat surfaces in depth that we *apparently* see. Pictorial space can vary from a perfectly flat, patterned surface to the illusion of deep space, as in a landscape that seems to recede to infinity.

Actual Space

Two-Dimensional Design

An artist who is about to make the first mark on a blank canvas or piece of paper has several important decisions to make. These include not only the shape of the mark, its size, perhaps its color, but also *where*

74. C. Schwizgebel. Cut-paper silhouette, from Switzerland. c. 1950. Schweizerisches Museum für Volkskunde, Basel.

the mark will be on the canvas or paper. It may be centered, off to one side, set high or low in the white field. Assuming for the moment a rectangular piece of paper with a *nonobjective* shape on it—a shape that does not resemble any natural form—we can see that the artist has established a *spatial relationship* between the shape and the page (Fig. 75). The shape relates to the space on all sides of it and to the rectangular field itself. This idea may seem very basic, but anyone who has ever tried to locate a shape on a blank piece of paper knows that it is not easy to find the "best" solution.

If the artist then introduces another nonobjective shape to the composition, the spatial relationships become more complicated (Fig. 76). Not only does each shape relate to the space of the paper, but the two shapes are related to each other in space. An example from graphic design may help to clarify this concept.

Let us suppose that the designer of this book, faced with a page 8¼ by 11 inches, wants to position the title of the book on that page. The words "Design Through Discovery," set into type, constitute a black shape. The designer has almost endless options in placing that shape, some of which are shown in Figure 77. In the end, the placement that seems most satisfying, most effective, will be the one that creates the best spatial relationship between the shape of the words and the space

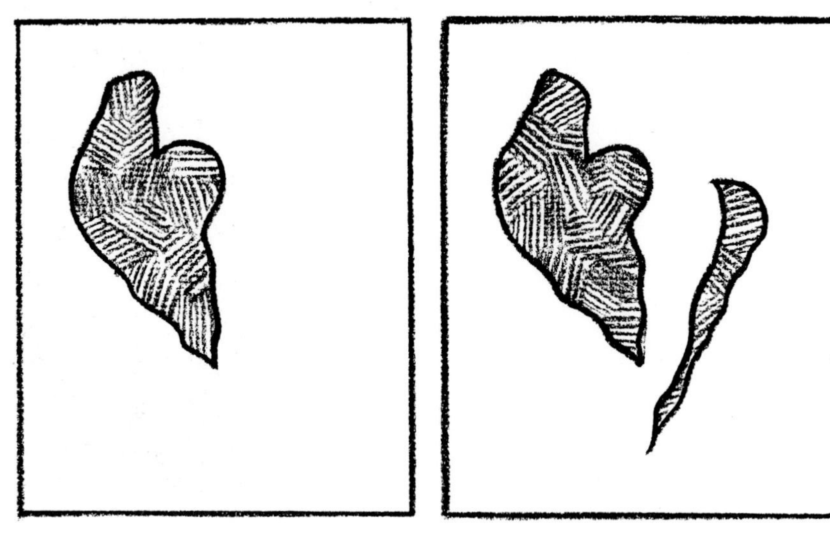

right: 75. One nonobjective shape positioned in a space.

far right: 76. Two nonobjective shapes positioned relative to one another in a space.

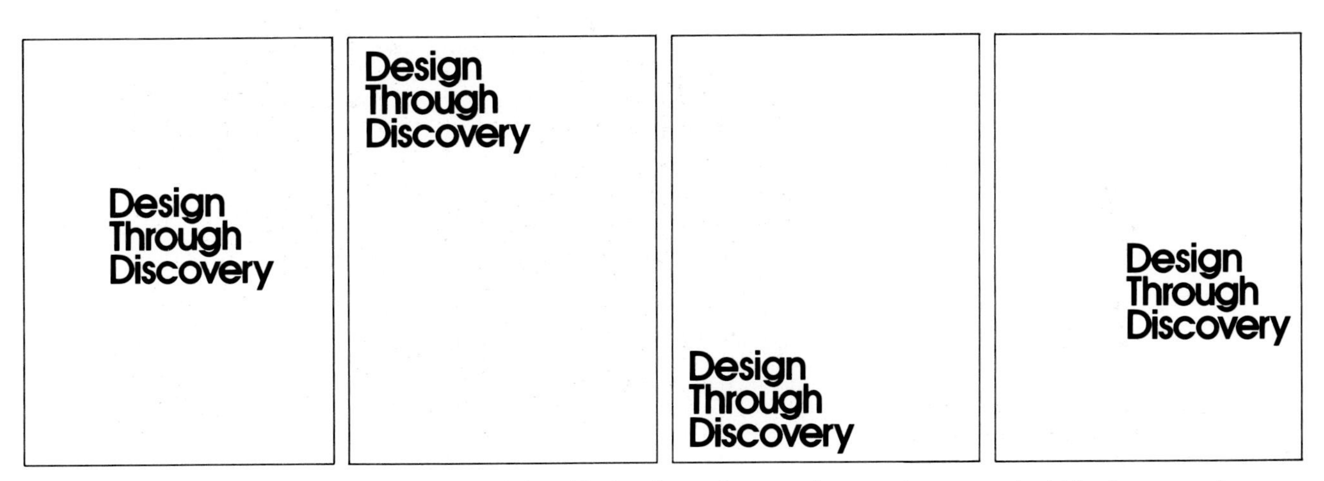

77. In graphic design, blocks of type become shapes to be arranged within the space of a page.

of the page. When another shape, perhaps a photograph, must be included (Fig. 78), the relationships multiply. The page can be made to *seem* more vertical or more horizontal through placement of elements, even though all four examples are the same size.

We can translate these fundamental exercises in space into a more complex visual expression. In the drawing by Leonardo da Vinci

78. Type and illustrations must be related to one another in the space of a page. Their placement can affect the sense of verticality or horizontality.

79. Leonardo da Vinci. *Copse of Birches.* c. 1508. Red chalk drawing on paper, $7\frac{1}{2}$ x 6″. Royal Collection, Windsor (reproduced by gracious permission of Her Majesty the Queen).

reproduced as Figure 79 the cluster of birches was deliberately set high on the page to create a unique spatial experience. A less sensitive or less confident artist might have located the drawing in the center of the paper or expanded it to fill the available space. But Leonardo was a supreme designer. The composition becomes much more interesting because of its unexpected spatial relationships.

Late in his life the painter Henri Matisse was too feeble to hold a brush or stand before an easel. Instead, he took to making cutouts of colored paper, then arranging and pasting them on a paper background (Fig. 80). The beginning designer often follows an exercise like this. By taking several cutout shapes and moving them around until their compositional relationships are most effective, one can develop a sense of the way space operates.

Three-Dimensional Design

Sculpture has always had as much to do with space as with material substance. When we look at the work in Figure 81, we see not only an assembly of forms but also a complex of different-shaped spaces. Of course, we are more aware of the positive forms than of the negative ones (or spaces), but we also cannot help taking note, perhaps unconsciously, of the latter. If we were to put a sheet of tracing paper over this photograph and fill in the spaces only, the result would look something like Figure 82—another interesting composition. Moreover,

above: 80. Henri Matisse. *The Parakeet and the Mermaid.* 1952–53. Paper cutout with gouache, 11′3⁄4″ x 25′4½″. Stedelijk Museum, Amsterdam.

left: 81. David Smith. *Voltri Bolton VII.* 1962. Steel, height 7′2″. Collection Howard and Jean Lipman, Wilton, Conn.

below: 82. Diagram of the spaces in David Smith's *Voltri Bolton VII.*

83. Jean Dubuffet. *Four Trees*. 1972. Prefabricated steel framework covered with fiberglass and plastic resin, painted with polyurethane; height 40′. Chase Manhattan Plaza, New York.

because we are looking at a photograph, our position is fixed. If we were actually standing next to this sculpture, we would be free to move around it, and every time our viewpoint changed even slightly, the forms—*and the spaces*—would alter in shape. Clearly the sculptor must keep in mind not only the forms being created but the spaces as well, and from every potential vantage point.

Architectural sculptures, such as are found in our parks and plazas today, throw this concept of space into a grand scale (Fig. 83). The spectator can walk not only around the work but *under* and *through* it, perhaps even climb *on* it. Looking at the Dubuffet work illustrated, we can imagine what it would be like to stand directly under it and look straight up. Certainly our perception of its space would be very different from the long view offered by this photograph. Moreover, the sculpture also activates the space all around it and maintains a spatial relationship with the building in front of which it stands.

When we talk of space in terms of a large work like the Dubuffet, and especially in relation to architecture, we cannot avoid introducing the concept of *time*. It takes time to walk around and through a monumental sculpture, time to pass through a building and gradually experience its spaces. Public buildings illustrate this most clearly. Upon entering a large cathedral, for instance, we cannot possibly grasp its complex open spaces all at once. The architects of Romanesque and Gothic churches were especially conscious of this fact. They planned their structures, therefore, so that the act of walking through would create a series of space-time "events." The vestibule of a cathedral would be a relatively enclosed space. Passing through it into the nave

above: Plate 1. Georgia O'Keeffe. *White Trumpet.* 1932. Oil on canvas, 30 x 40″. Fine Arts Gallery of San Diego, Calif. (gift of Mrs. Inez Grant Parker).

left: Plate 2. David Vine. Advertisement based on John Singer Sargent's *Madame X*, for Sweet & Co. Advertising, Inc.; client: Selig Manufacturing Company. (See also Fig. 21.)

Plate 3. Henri Matisse. *Harmony in Red (Red Room).* 1908–09. Oil on canvas, 5′11¼″ x 8′⅞″. Hermitage Museum, Leningrad.

84. Chartres Cathedral. c. 1194–1221. View through nave, looking toward the apse. Chartres, France.

(Fig. 84), the spectator would have a breathtaking experience of vast space leading directly to the altar. As one progressed through the church, one would gradually take in the spaces of chapels opening off to the sides, perhaps the soaring space of a dome, and finally the space around the altar. All of these perspectives would be different.

Often smaller-scale architecture has the same effect. The house shown in Figure 85 seems to have been sculpted, rather than merely built. Its complex of shapes, curves, spaces, hollows, and projections would offer a fascinating adventure to anyone walking through. In looking at this photograph we can see that, if the photographer had

85. G. E. Arenas. Hernandez House, Mexico City.

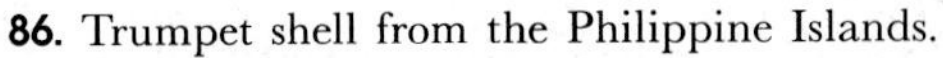

86. Trumpet shell from the Philippine Islands.

87. Architect Rodney Friedman's own house in Belvedere, Calif.

stood just a few feet to either side of the present vantage point, the spaces would have changed. This house was designed for a woman who collects shells as a hobby. Its great swooping curves and intersecting arcs seem to echo the configurations of a shell (Fig. 86), without directly imitating them.

Our notions about domestic architecture have altered considerably in the last hundred years. The most important change is in the way modern houses demarcate space. Until quite recently a proper house was a box enclosing a cube of space, with boxlike rooms breaking the total volume into smaller cubes of space. Thick walls and small windows made a rigid barrier between outside space and inside. The house pictured in Figure 87 shows how far we have come from that standard. Here rooms spill into one another, passageways give visual access to several areas, and there is only the slightest division between outdoor space and indoor space. One could almost say that this house is more a designed space than a structure.

Pictorial Space

Pictorial space begins, and sometimes ends, with the *picture plane*—a flat surface that is synonymous with the surface of the canvas or paper

88. *Harold Swearing Oath,* detail of *Bayeux Tapestry.* c. 1073–88. Wool embroidery on linen; height 20″, overall length 231′. Town Hall, Bayeux.

being drawn upon. Artists throughout history have tried to create the illusion of "real" or three-dimensional space on this surface. This means simply that in a given work some things appear to be behind other things. When we look at a landscape in the natural world, our eyes automatically make a judgment and inform our brains that certain things are farther away than other things. Pictorial space attempts to mimic this effect. In a landscape painting, for convenience, we often refer to the *foreground, middle ground,* and *background.* A few paintings actually do show this triple division of planes in space, but in a competent representation of space the various degrees of depth (or distance from the viewer) recede gradually to infinity, with no sharp divisions.

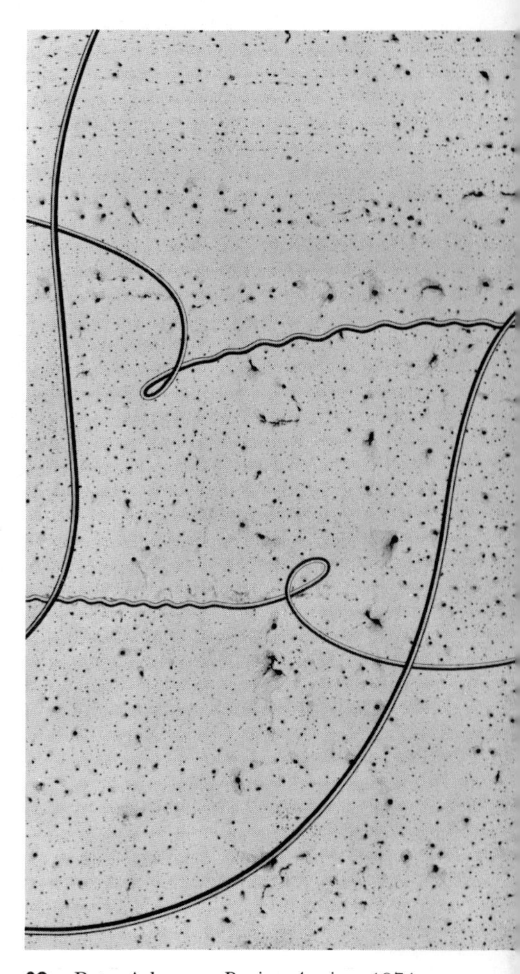

89. Pat Adams. *Begin Again.* 1974. Gouache, $22\frac{3}{4} \times 13\frac{1}{2}''$. Courtesy Zabriskie Gallery, New York.

Figure 88 shows a portion of the *Bayeux Tapestry,* an embroidered cloth banner depicting the Norman invasion of England and the events leading up to the Battle of Hastings in 1066. In all, the tapestry is 231 feet long. It shows many different episodes, which are arranged *sequentially,* so that the viewer reads them from left to right like a book. Very little attempt has been made here to create pictorial space. In fact, the space is almost totally flat. Ships in the water seem to be in the same plane as a man sitting on a throne or a knight storming a castle. Rather than being "realistic," the effect is decorative and charming. The *Bayeux Tapestry* also recalls our discussion of time in relation to actual space, since the whole banner cannot possibly be read from any vantage point. The viewer must walk along in front of it, gradually following the episodes.

One simple device prevents the *Bayeux Tapestry* from having absolutely flat pictorial space, and that is the technique of *overlapping.* Occasionally, as the narrative unfolds, we will come upon a group of figures whose bodies are partially overlapped. Here the designer has made a cautious effort to place one figure behind another, to create pictorial space. For the most part, though, the action remains on the surface.

Pictorial depth by means of overlapping can be accomplished with the simplest of means, as the line drawing in Figure 89 shows. Here the finer, more erratic lines are clearly behind the long curving ones. We get a sense of depth from just four simple lines.

Since the earliest cave paintings artists have understood that *size* could indicate distance. Things far away from the viewer seem to be smaller than those near at hand. We find a suggestion of this device in the *Bayeux Tapestry,* where the figures on the boat are smaller than the

others. However, the treatment of relative size is not convincing, because the boat still appears to be in the same plane as the adjacent figures and throne. No doubt the boat figures were made smaller primarily to fit them into the composition. The main concern of the tapestry is *narrative,* story-telling, rather than depiction of deep space.

In drawings made by children we often find another elementary device for creating space, and that is *placement.* Objects that are meant to be read as far away are placed higher in the composition than those supposedly nearby. Artists in many cultures have used this same system. In the Persian miniature reproduced as Figure 90 the figures at bottom should be understood as closest to us, the two higher ones as farther away, seated in the recessed area of the Turquoise Palace. From the Western point of view this representation has many flaws. For one thing, the figures, no matter how far away, are all the same *size,* which

right: 90. Mahmud Muzahib or Follower. *Bahram Gur in the Turquoise Palace on Wednesday,* page from the *Khamsa of Nizami.* 16th century. Illuminated manuscript. Metropolitan Museum of Art, New York (gift of Alexander Smith Cochran, 1913).

below: 91. Giotto. *Annunciation to Anna.* c. 1305–10. Fresco. Arena Chapel, Padua.

is not the way we perceive things in real life. Furthermore, the rug that is supposed to be flat on the ground seems to be parallel to the picture plane, with the figures not sitting on it but in front of it. We read the supposed "space" of the palace room as being absolutely flat. This version of pictorial space, however, was perfectly understandable to the audience for which it was created, and we cannot deny that the result is delightful.

Yet another method of indicating depth, called *aerial* or *atmospheric perspective,* is still to be found in some contemporary art. Stated most simply, aerial perspective is based on the fact that objects seen in the distance seem less clear, their colors more muted. This effect is caused by two factors: the softening quality of the air in between the viewer and the subject, and the inability of the human eye to distinguish clearly forms and colors at a distance. Aerial perspective tries to duplicate this reality by a progressive graying and blurring as the composition goes back into space.

The most painstaking and self-conscious search for "true" representation of space on a flat surface took place during the Renaissance. Artists of the 14th century had attempted to place their figures in a shallow space, frequently in little buildings, to create an architectural setting (Fig. 91). The progression into space ends right behind the figures, and the result often looks like a stage set.

By the 15th century artists had formulated the principles of *linear perspective* into an exact science. As practiced then it is extremely complicated, but the basic assumptions are simple. First, as had long been realized, objects in the distance appear to be smaller than those close to the viewer. Second, parallel lines or planes receding into the distance seem to meet at some point, which is known as the *vanishing point* (Fig. 92). We have all noticed this phenomenon in rows of telephone poles or in looking down an expanse of railroad track, for instance. The Renaissance painters sharpened their mastery of linear perspective by actually constructing lines and vanishing points in their pictures. In theory, once the lines were removed, we would have the same visual experience in looking at the painting as in viewing the actual scene (Fig. 93).

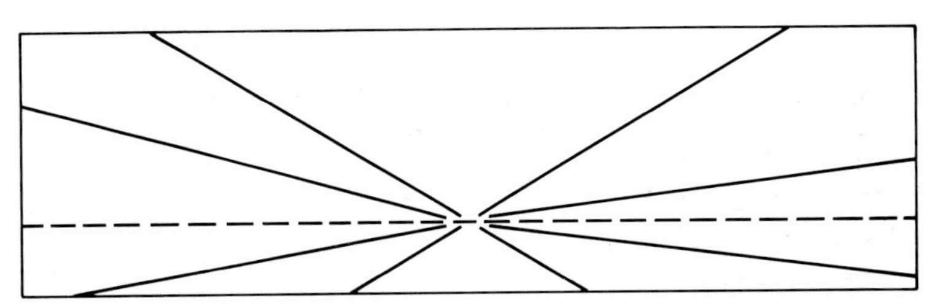

right: 92. Perspective drawing based on *View of an Ideal City* (Fig. 93).

below: 93. Piero della Francesca and Luciano Laurana. *View of an Ideal City.* c. 1460. Tempera on panel, 1′11⅝″ x 6′6¾″. Galleria Nazionale delle Marche, Palazzo Ducale, Urbino.

left: 94. Pablo Picasso. *Daniel-Henry Kahnweiler.* 1910. Oil on canvas, $39\frac{5}{8}$" x $28\frac{5}{8}$". Art Institute of Chicago (gift of Mrs. Gilbert W. Chapman).

below: 95. Paul Gauguin. *Vision After the Sermon (Jacob Wrestling with the Angel).* 1888. Oil on canvas, $28\frac{3}{4}$ x $36\frac{1}{4}$". National Gallery of Scotland, Edinburgh.

Naturalistic linear perspective reigned as the ideal in painting for some three hundred years. Then, in the late 19th century, a number of artists began to experiment with different kinds of pictorial space. In the works of Henri Matisse and Paul Gauguin (Pl. 3, p. 54; Fig. 95), for example, we find a flattened space, with all the "action" brought close to the picture plane. The forms depicted, even human forms, often seem as flat as cutouts, and the colors are flat and decorative. The Matisse painting is a masterpiece of spacial ambiguities. We cannot really tell where the table (if it is a table) leaves off and the wall begins, nor are we sure how the table drops off at the bottom. Although the window at left seems to give a view to the outdoors, this landscape does not really strike us as being behind the house.

Another manifestation of shallow pictorial space from the same period was Cubism. The works of its leading practitioner, Pablo Picasso, demonstrate how Cubism breaks up the planes of a human or inanimate form and brings them close to the picture's surface (Fig. 94). Picasso created *facets* of form and space as a gemcutter creates facets in a diamond. Moreover, these facets slip and slide over one another like the chips in a kaleidoscope, making a dynamic pictorial space. Cubism eliminates the traditional figure-ground distinction. The background becomes just as important as the subject, when both are facets.

Today artists are less concerned with depicting the "real" world on canvas or paper; photography has largely taken over this role. The contemporary artist finds more challenge in the discovery of a new reality beyond the physical world and of different kinds of space.

Implied Space

Implied space is a relatively new concept in design. The Held painting in Figure 68 provides a good example. By cutting off his forms sharply at the edges of the picture, and by leaving some of them incomplete, Held is suggesting that this space, and the forms within it, actually continue indefinitely around all sides of the painting. He has isolated a particular segment of space for our consideration, but in fact the space spreads out in all directions. In other words the artist has *implied* a much larger space.

Until the late 19th century, few Western artists concerned themselves with implied space. A figure or a scene would be neatly composed within the four sides of the picture as though the events shown stopped just at the edges. One of the painters who upset this view was the post-Impressionist Frenchman Paul Gauguin. In *Jacob Wrestling with the Angel* (Fig. 95) Gauguin gives us an unusual crowd's-eye view of the vision, with the apparent focus of interest pushed far into the upper right corner of the canvas. The heads of several peasant women are directly in front of us, almost blocking our view; we feel as though we might step a bit to the side to get a better angle. A daring composition like this one implies vast space around the segment of the world Gauguin chose to paint.

Spatial Perception

The art of creating spatial illusions on a flat surface is actually a way of "fooling" the viewer. One is persuaded by the artist's skill to see something that is not there at all—that is, deep space. So-called *trompe-l'oeil* (fool-the-eye) compositions do this with exaggerated clev-

96. Pedro Friedburg. *La Vida Sexual de Isabel la Carolica.* 1971. Acrylic on canvas. Courtesy El Taller Gallery, Mexico City.

erness (Fig. 96). A space constructed with such meticulous attention to detail and perspective makes us feel we could walk right into it, when in fact it is perfectly flat. Our perceptions of space have been distorted.

Having made us see what is not there, the artist can take another step: making us unsure about what we see. Jasper Johns' *Cup 4 Picasso* (Fig. 97) does this. With one glance at this work we see a classically proportioned vase. We blink our eyes and there are two profiles in silhouette, facing each other nose to nose (both, of course, Pablo Picasso). If we look at this work long enough, the two images (or perceptions of the image) will keep reversing, so that we alternately see one and then the other. This effect is known as *figure-ground ambiguity.* In most works of visual art we can identify a distinct image, such as a human subject or still-life composition (the *figure*) set against a less-emphatic background (the *ground*). In the Johns print we have no way of telling which is which. The positive forms and negative forms (spaces) are completely interchangeable.

The master of illusion M. C. Escher goes one diabolical step further in unsettling our spatial perceptions. He makes us see what we could not possibly see (Fig. 98). In this delightful work walls become floors become walls again—but at a different angle. Every time we think we know where we are, we find ourselves going off at right angles. The little man at the center of the composition is walking up a flight of stairs to a floor, but the floor is actually a wall with a door in it. If we turn the image to make the wall upright, then another little man is walking incomprehensibly down a flight of stairs from the ceiling, defying all gravity. This process goes on indefinitely until we are forced to abandon all sense of spatial "correctness." Escher's wit simply clarifies the fact that what we see in a work of art is what the artist wishes us to see.

The optical or "Op" artists of the mid-20th century investigated spatial perceptions of a different sort. Through careful manipulation of

97. Jasper Johns. *Cup 4 Picasso.* 1972. Lithograph, 22 x 32″. Courtesy Leo Castelli Gallery, New York.

above: 98. M. C. Escher. *Relativity.* 1953. Lithograph, $10\frac{1}{2}$ x $11\frac{3}{4}$″. M. C. Escher Foundation, Haags Gemeentemuseum, The Hague.

right: 99. Victor Vasarely. *Sir-Ris.* 1952–62. Oil on canvas, 6′6″ x 3′3″. Courtesy Sidney Janis Gallery, New York.

lines or shapes, the Op artist creates the impression of bulges, undulations, or actual movement in space (Fig. 99). This type of visual illusion is purely sensory. It relates to the *optical* reaction of the human eye to light and color.

The concepts of space discussed here only begin to touch upon this enormous subject. And, as we have mentioned, space always interacts with other elements, with line and also with shape (if two-dimensional) or mass (if three-dimensional). The following chapter will analyze shape and mass, bringing the most basic elements together.

5 Shape and Mass

In common usage the word "shape" indicates the general outlines of something. We speak of the shape of a building, a pot, a room, a person, and so forth. The more precise language of design, however, often makes a distinction between two-dimensional *shape* and three-dimensional *mass*. The latter may also be called *volume*. (Many writers use *form* synonymously with mass, but as was pointed out in Chapter 1, form has many other meanings, so the more specific term mass will be used here.)

We can see the difference between shape and mass easily by reference to geometry, which distinguishes the plane geometric figures (shapes) of square, circle, and triangle from the solid geometric figures (masses) of cube, sphere, and pyramid. Just as solid geometry is a more complicated system of mathematics than plane geometry, the designer may find greater difficulty in working with three-dimensional masses than with flat shapes. This is because the spaces involved are more complex and the lines multiply, appearing in several planes. For convenience, we will separate shape and mass to give each an individual analysis.

100. Sengai (1750–1837). *Sign of the Universe.* Ink on paper. Idemitsu Museum, Tokyo.

Shape

Shapes can be divided into four broad categories: *geometric, natural, abstract,* and *nonobjective.* These are not rigid divisions but allow for some overlapping.

Geometric Shapes

The drawing in Figure 100 shows an artist's interpretation of three basic geometric shapes—square, triangle, and circle. Generally speaking, these perfect shapes suggest stability and order. As we shall see in our discussion of geometric masses, these figures can be quite dynamic, even startling, especially when they are set at unusual angles or placed in opposition to one another. More often, however, they express repose. This idea has worked its way into our language. A century ago the designation of a person as "square" meant that person was honest, straightforward, and open. Later it came to mean a rigid conformity to safe, out-of-date ideas. The phrase "coming full circle" marks a return to what was before—a kind of stability.

Geometric shapes dominate the constructed environment. They appear in buildings, bridges, furniture, and machines of all kinds. Basic *post-and-lintel construction,* which sets a horizontal crosspiece over two separated uprights to create a square shape, has been a fundamental part of architecture since prehistoric times (Fig. 101). The

101. Stonehenge. 1800–1400 B.C. Height of stones above ground $13\frac{1}{2}'$. Salisbury Plain, Wiltshire, England.

107. Aubrey Beardsley. *The Peacock Skirt,* from *Salome.* 1907. Drawing, 9⅛ x 6⅝". Fogg Art Museum, Harvard University, Cambridge, Mass. (Grenville L. Winthrop Bequest).

colored examples of the style. The English artist Aubrey Beardsley worked intricate decorative patterns of natural shapes into his drawings and book illustrations (Fig. 107).

Abstract Shapes

When a natural shape is distorted in such a way as to reduce it to its essence, we say that it has been *abstracted.* This means that, while the source of the shape is recognizable, the shape has been transformed into something different. Usually, this is done by simplification, by omitting all nonessential elements. A series of lithographs by Picasso, taken from an edition of eighteen, will illustrate this principle.

The fifth print (Fig. 108) shows a fairly "natural" representation of two female nudes. Except for some Cubist distortion of the eyes and nose on the figure at left, the drawing seems lifelike, with normal shapes and volumes. By the tenth state (Fig. 109) Picasso has begun to abstract many of the elements in the drawing. Both figures are flattened, particularly the one at left, and the face at left has been drastically simplified into a circle with angular features. The left background form, which in the earlier print was a conventional suggestion of architectural space, has now become a geometric screen.

By the seventeenth state (Fig. 110) the composition has been highly abstracted. Both figures are transformed into flat collections of shapes. The face at left is a primitive mask, while the one at right has all but disappeared. Breasts are circles or simple curves. Fingers and toes now resemble oversize flattened cylinders. If we had only this print to look

108–110. Pablo Picasso. *Les Deux Femmes Nues* (*Two Nude Women*). 1945–46. Lithographs, eighteen states, each c. $10\frac{1}{8} \times 13\frac{5}{16}''$. Cleveland Museum of Art (J. H. Wade Fund).

108. State V.

109. State X.

110. State XVII.

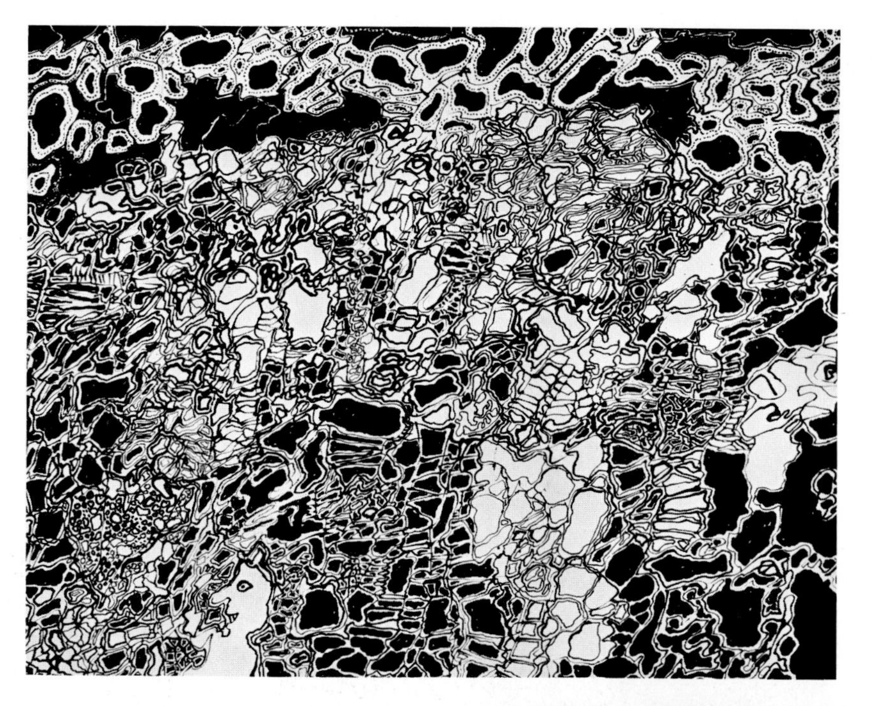

above: 111. Jean Dubuffet. *Radieux Météore,* from *Ferres Radieuses.* 1952. Drawing. Courtesy Pierre Matisse Gallery, New York.

right: 112. Joan Miró. *The Beautiful Bird Revealing the Unknown to a Pair of Lovers.* 1941. Gouache, 18 x 15″. Museum of Modern Art, New York (Lillie P. Bliss Bequest).

at, we would identify it as two female nudes, but we could not see how Picasso arrived at this particular interpretation. By comparing the three states we can follow his investigation of certain shapes, certain planes and outlines that fascinated him. The abstraction is not arbitrary but, in Cubist terms, a systematic development from the representational drawing.

113. Hans Hofmann. *Otium cum Dignitate.* 1964. Oil on canvas, 7 x 6′. Courtesy André Emmerich Gallery, New York.

Nonobjective Shapes

Shapes that do not relate to anything in the natural world are termed *nonobjective.* We cannot put specific names on them. The best we can do by way of identification would be to call them "blob" or "squiggle."

Dubuffet's drawing *Radieux Mêtéore* (Fig. 111) is composed almost entirely of nonobjective shapes. While we can identify a face here and there, most of the shapes have no specific reference. They are combined and interwoven into an overall decorative pattern of great intricacy. In this work the viewer responds to color, pattern, and texture, not to any individual shape.

Shape Relationships

A painting by Joan Miró (Fig. 112) combines the highly abstracted shapes of human heads and features with a network of geometric and nonobjective shapes. Unity in the composition is achieved by the general similarity among the various types of shapes. The dark circle that is in one place an eye becomes elsewhere just a circle or is distorted to make a blob. A rhythm of outline and filled-in shapes, of light and dark creates pattern. In other words, Miró has played with shape *relationships* in building his composition.

We might contrast this effect with the Hans Hofmann painting in Figure 113. Hofmann has used both dark, rectilinear shapes and broad, loosely brushed areas of color. The two elements are irregularly spaced on the canvas, and there is some overlapping, although the squared shapes never touch. It would be hard to imagine more contrasting shapes than these, yet somehow the painting "works" because of several devices, including a basic rhythm in the squared shapes and again in the loose strokes, as well as an overall balance of compositional "weight."

Another important relationship is that between shapes within a composition and the shape of the field—that is, the canvas or page or external outline. Many of the works of Josef Albers are a series of squares related to the square field (Fig. 114). Interest derives from the sensitive proportions of the squares, as well as from changes in color. In the Stella painting (Fig. 105) the internal shapes suggest but do not copy the geometric shape of the canvas. Certain shapes are set in opposition to others, and yet their basic similarity creates a harmonious effect. Among the other possibilities is a deliberate jarring contrast between internal shapes and field. Our discussion of the principles of design in Chapters 8 through 10 will consider other ways of combining shapes to achieve the desired effect.

Mass

The same categories that we identified in shape apply to mass as well.

Geometric Masses

The cube, sphere, and pyramid operate as the three-dimensional equivalents of square, circle, and triangle. To these we must add the cone (a triangle rotated on its axis) and the cylinder (a rectangle rotated on its bisector).

A cube may be the most visually stable of all forms. Most buildings are cubes, resting solidly upon the ground in a direct acknowledgment of gravity. However, it need not always be so. The sculptor Isamu

114. Josef Albers. *Homage to the Square: Silent Hall.* 1961. Oil on composition board, 40″ square. Museum of Modern Art, New York (Dr. and Mrs. Frank Stanton Fund).

115. Isamu Noguchi. *Cube.* 1969. Steel and aluminum, painted and welded, height 28′. Located in front of 140 Broadway, New York.

Noguchi sets us on our ears, so to speak, by tipping his cube up on one corner (Fig. 115). The lines of this work, which would otherwise have been placid verticals and horizontals, now become energetic diagonals thrusting upward. This cube makes an effective counterpoint to the conventional cube of the skyscraper behind it.

Just as a cube is normally a restful mass, the sphere is somehow a *satisfying* mass. Globes, rubber balls, and the earth itself—all are spheres. Most people, when they pick up a lump of clay or dough, automatically form it into a sphere. The glass sculpture in Figure 116, shimmering with light, is made in the form of an "earth satellite." Even while it rests on its pedestal, we can imagine this airy form beginning to lift upward and hover in the air, gently spinning as it goes. This idea expresses one of the most intriguing characteristics of the sphere. It seems ever mobile, always turning, never static. There are no sharp edges to bring motion to a halt, as there are in a cube. A sphere nearly always implies movement and time.

With the pyramid form, we again return solidly to earth. The pharaohs of Egypt built their burial pyramids to last for all time, and indeed they have withstood more than four thousand years of climate, wars, pillage, and geological upheaval. Many early civilizations constructed pyramids, from the first known residents of the Middle East and Southeast Asia to the Indians of pre-Columbian America (Fig. 117). While the cube is the most visually solid mass, the pyramid is immensely stable from an engineering point of view. Stresses begin-

above: 116. Pavel Hlava (in cooperation with the workshop of Miroslav Lenc, Czechoslovakia). *Satellite.* 1972. Blown crystal hemispheres joined by welding, diameter 13¾″. Courtesy the artist.

left: 117. Soothsayer Pyramid. 3rd–8th century. Uxmal, Yucatán, Mexico.

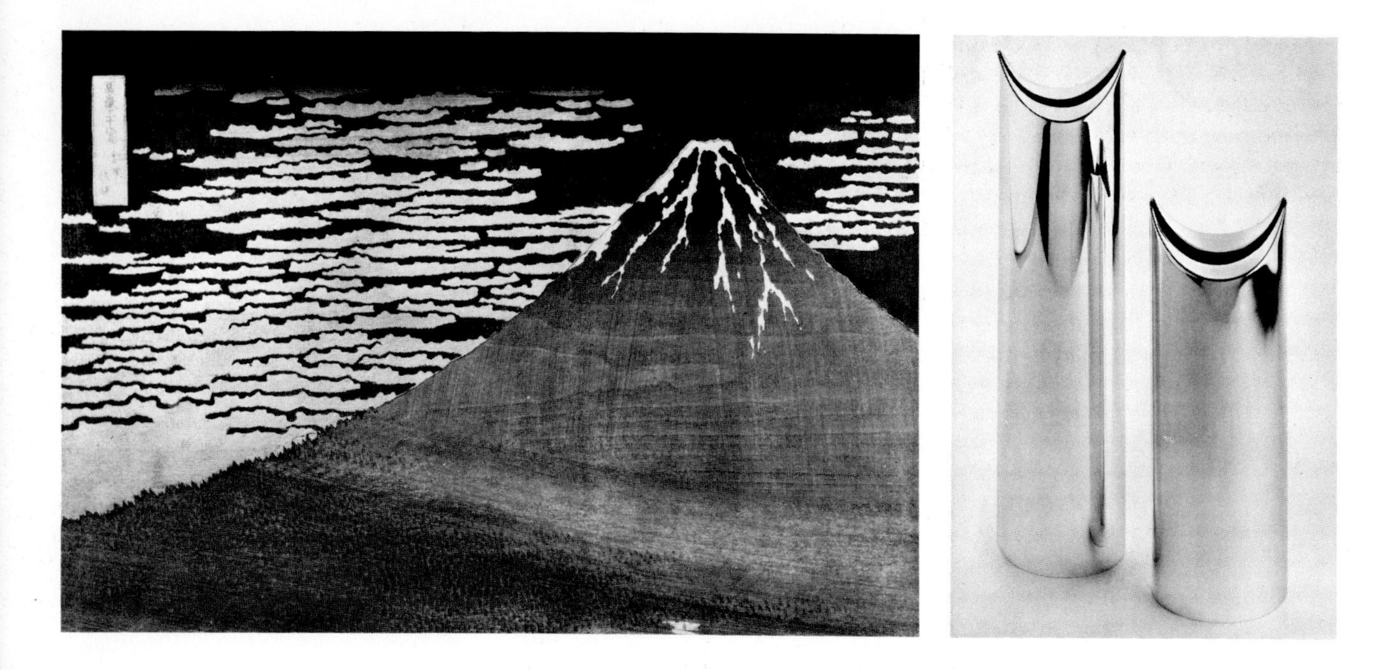

left: 118. Katsushika Hokusai. *Fire and Breeze,* from *Thirty-six Views of Mount Fuji.* Later recut of original dated 1823–29. Color woodcut. Riccar Museum, Tokyo.

right: 119. Silver-plated flower vases designed by Lino Sabattini for Argenteria Sabattini, Italy. Heights 14″ and 10½″.

below: 120. Fernand Léger. *The Card Players.* 1917. Oil on canvas, 4′2⅜″ x 6′4″. Kröller-Müller Museum, Otterlo, The Netherlands.

ning at the tip spread out in all directions to the broad base. It is no accident that these structures have outlasted all the other wonders of the ancient world.

The cone appears by nature to be a *thrusting* mass, as in the nose cone of a spaceship or the cone of a volcano (Fig. 118). While the form of a cone may be just as firmly rooted in earth, we somehow expect something to be coming *out* of it. A volcano, even a dormant one, remains mysterious. At any time it could erupt, spewing smoke and ash and lava over the countryside. Similarly, the Indian tepee, one of the most portable habitations ever invented, was planned with a hole in the center to permit the escape of smoke from the cooking fire.

Finally, the cylinder is a generally utilitarian mass. Cans, tubes, vases, cooking pots, cups, and many machine parts take the form of cylinders (Fig. 119). In purely practical terms the cylinder functions well because it can contain a great deal yet has no corners or crevices. We can even visualize the human body as a collection of rough cylinders, one for the trunk and one each for the limbs. The painter Fernand Léger developed this idea during the early 20th century (Fig. 120). At the beginning of the modern industrial age, many artists celebrated the coming of machine technology. Léger abstracted portions of the human anatomy—legs, arms, fingers, toes—into precision-formed cylinders, thus emphasizing the merger between human intellect and mechanical power.

Natural Masses

Like natural shapes, natural masses abound in the history of art. Any sculpture that represents the human form is a natural mass, and such works make up a great portion of sculptures. Today many artists rely on natural forms but use them in unexpected ways. The mushroom ring in Figure 121 gives an example of this. The form of the mushroom itself is reproduced faithfully, but one does not expect to find it on a ring. Contemporary designers can adapt an endless range of natural forms to their work.

Abstract Masses

The series of heads by Matisse shown in Figure 122 resembles the progressive abstraction in the Picasso prints. Here we can see that the *actual* rather than pictorial, planes of the face and head have been abstracted increasingly as the artist's insight progressed. The first bust, at far left, probably shows most precisely the "real" appearance of the subject. But the last interpretation, at right, may in fact express the

above: 121. Vada Beetler. "Mushroom" ring. 1975. Fabricated and reticulated, sterling silver with enamel. Courtesy the artist.

below: 122. Henri Matisse. *Heads of Jeannette.* 1910–13. Bronze, heights $10\frac{3}{8}''$ to $24\frac{1}{8}''$. Los Angeles County Museum of Art (gift of the Art Museum Council in memory of Penelope Rigby, 1968).

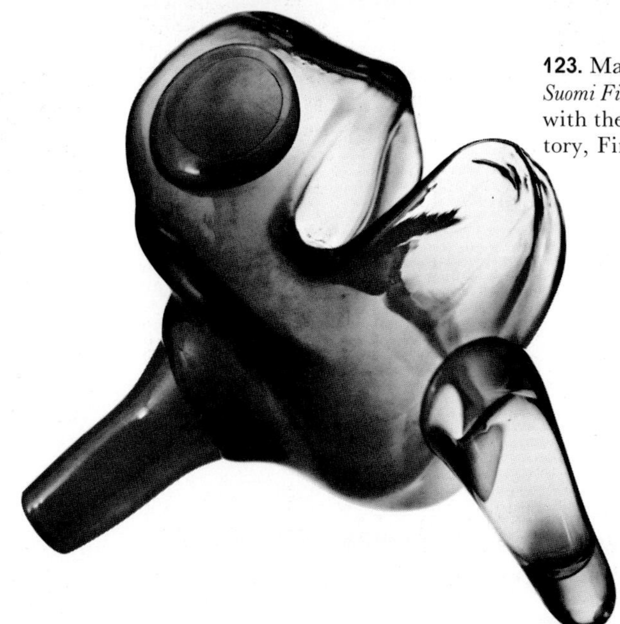

123. Marvin Lipofsky. Blown glass from the *Suomi Finland Series.* 1970. 12 x 14″. Executed with the assistance of Nuutajärvi Glass Factory, Finland.

character of the sitter more accurately. The last bust is not pretty but in many ways is the most interesting view. As the states progress, Matisse gradually selects particular features for intensification, while others diminish in importance. By the third state the hair has collected into three lumps, and by the fifth it has receded to the back of the head. The nose gradually becomes bigger, stronger, and more prominent, while the eyes deepen and take on a hooded quality. Perhaps Matisse sought to capture the essence of this woman, or of Woman personified. Perhaps he was fascinated by the new relationships of mass (features) on the mass of the head. At its best, abstraction can touch the basic quality of a form, while distorting its contours. By its definition an *abstract* concentrates on the *essence* of a thing.

Nonobjective Masses

Nonobjective masses do not refer to any specific recognizable form. When they *seem* organic, as though they might be part of some living thing, they are termed *biomorphic.* The glass form in Figure 123 could be some prehistoric sea creature or a resident of an undiscovered planet. It does not resemble anything known, and yet it seems alive. This is because of its fluid quality, its mouthlike opening, its big "eye." We have learned to recognize symbols, such as the circle for an eye. The power of nonobjective masses lies in their ability to evoke response in the viewer, perhaps a hundred different responses in a hundred viewers. Each person who looks at such a form brings to it special associations and experiences, which will help to give the form a personal interpretation. The artist who works in nonobjective mass invites the participation of the spectator.

Mass and Movement

The picture in Figure 124 shows a definite mass—a wave. Yet a second after this image was captured, no single molecule of water here in the wave would still be part of it, and the wave would have changed its outlines. We could point to numerous examples of this phenomenon—waterfalls, avalanches, clouds, tornadoes.

124. Rising wave.

The performing arts are also concerned with mass and movement. In the dance, for instance, each dancer's body can be considered a mass—one that changes its outlines with each movement (Fig. 125). As two or more dancers come together, they form another mass capable of transforming itself or breaking apart again. Each movement creates new mass and space relationships. These factors are equally present in a drama or a rock concert.

In visual expression many artists have experimented with works that move or seem to move. Otto Piene's *Citything* (Fig. 126), a structure of polyethylene tubes more than a third of a mile long, is billed as a "Sky Ballet." This huge helium-filled object can be partially controlled from the ground by strings. As wind currents shift it, its mass changes constantly, as do the relationships it establishes with masses in the cityscape—buildings and skyscrapers. Although the word "mass" often calls to mind something solid and heavy, we see that mass can in fact be fluid and endlessly changing.

above: 125. Maurice Béjart's Ballet of the 20th Century, performing *Stimmung,* 1972.

below: 126. Otto Piene. *Red Helium Sky Line,* from the event *Citything Sky Ballet.* 1970. Helium-inflated polyethylene tubing, c. 2000′ long. Shown flying over Pittsburgh, Pa.

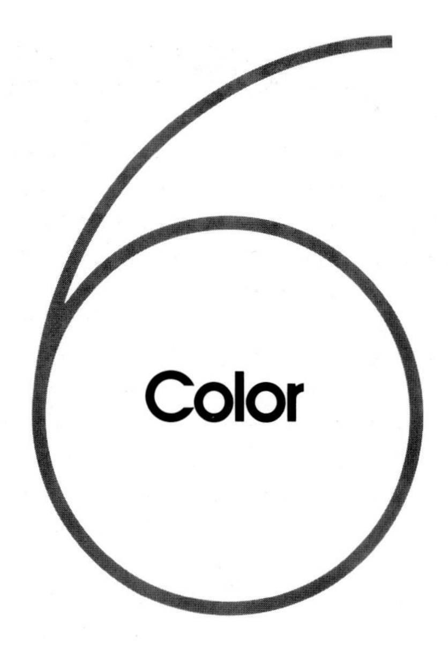

Color

Of all the design elements, color is perhaps the most appealing. It has been called the "music" of the visual arts. While color is not necessary for the creation of great art, it brings a mood and a depth of experience that cannot be achieved in any other way. Like the notes of the basic scale when expanded into a symphony, color has seemingly unlimited variation and enormous capacity to manipulate our emotions. It is therefore one of the most powerful tools of the designer.

One cannot discuss color exclusively as either a science or an art, for it is both, and the two aspects overlap. The designer must have some knowledge of each. Physicists explain the abstract theories and sources of color sensation, as well as the optical principles involved. Chemists formulate rules for mixing and applying colors. Psychologists provide information about emotional response to specific colors. The artist should seek to understand all these factors and then go further—developing personal variations and a distinctive symbolism by which color will fulfill an aesthetic purpose.

Color and Light

Without light there can be no color. Things that we identify as being "red," "green," or "orange" are not innately those colors. Rather we *perceive* them as being red, green, or orange because of the way light strikes them and the way our brains interpret the message transmitted by our eyes.

Although the perception of color has psychological overtones, it is fundamentally a neurophysiological process, which means that it makes use of both the nervous system and the physiological apparatus for seeing. The dynamics of color are not fully understood, but we do know that color is actually produced by light broken down into electromagnetic vibrations. What we call light represents only a very small portion of the electromagnetic field, that part which is visible (Fig. 127). Within that portion, variations in the wavelength of the vibrations cause the viewer to see different colors. The longest wavelength is perceived as red, the shortest as violet.

In about 1666 Isaac Newton demonstrated that color is a natural part of sunlight. Passing a beam of sunlight through a prism, he knew that the beam would bend—or *refract*—because the glass of the prism had a greater density than the air around it. His results depended upon the fact that when the beam of light emerged from the prism, the long waves were refracted less and the short waves more. The waves were of different colors, which arranged themselves in the order of colors in the rainbow: indigo, blue, green, yellow, orange, and red (Fig. 128). Newton continued his experiment by using a second prism to recombine the waves into sunlight. This established the fact that color is, basically, sunlight and further that *in light* all colors mixed together result in white.

When light strikes organic molecules, some of its energy is absorbed and some is reflected. A surface that we call "red" will absorb all the rays *except* those from the wavelength producing red, and so we perceive red. When light is totally absorbed by a surface, the result is black. Many factors influence the way in which light is absorbed or reflected, including the texture of a surface and, of course, the direc-

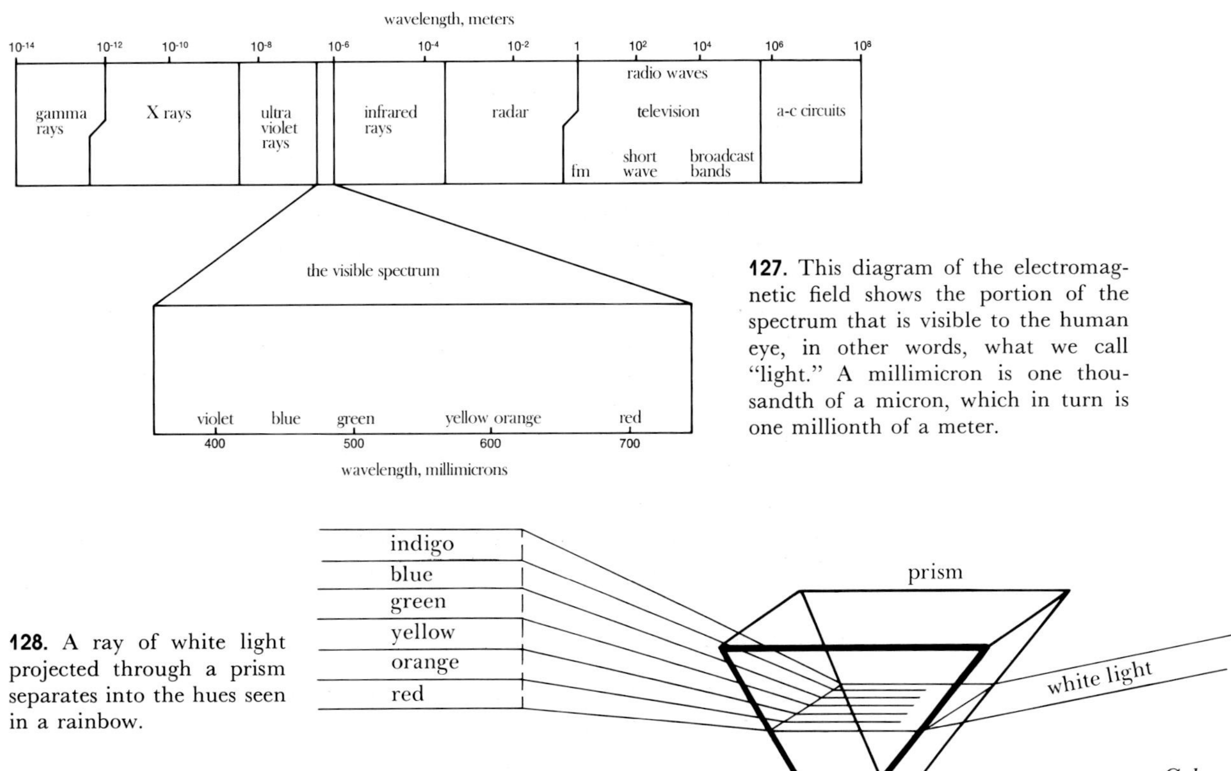

127. This diagram of the electromagnetic field shows the portion of the spectrum that is visible to the human eye, in other words, what we call "light." A millimicron is one thousandth of a micron, which in turn is one millionth of a meter.

128. A ray of white light projected through a prism separates into the hues seen in a rainbow.

tion of the light source. A tree in the sunlight will seem a different color on its shaded side than on the side in direct light, and its leaves can show tremendous color variation depending upon the way light strikes them. The Impressionist painters of the late 19th century exploited this fact to the highest degree.

Impressionism sought to divorce art from intellectual interpretations, to paint what we actually see rather than what we *think* we see. If we know a house to be red, we might be tempted to paint it all the same color red, when in fact the light striking it would produce many different reds and perhaps other colors as well. The Impressionists, then, tried to see forms in terms of shimmering light and color, breaking up visual images into tiny dabs of colored paint (Pl. 15, p. 125). Hard edges and lines were abandoned, because it was felt that these do not really exist in nature but are supplied by our reasoning process. The aim was to bypass the brain, to translate visual impression directly into sensory experience.

In dealing with light, any color can be produced by mixing various quantities of the rays producing red, blue, and green, or in other words, by adding them together. For this reason, these colors are known as *additive primary colors.*

One can demonstrate this principle by projecting white light through gelatin filters, either from three projectors onto a screen or from three spotlights onto a stage (Pl. 4, p. 87). A red filter will transmit the color red because the gelatinous film of the filter has absorbed the waves of all the other colors. Similarly, a green filter will cast a green light, a blue filter blue light. When red and green are focused on the same area, the light will be yellow. Cyan (turquoise) is produced when green and blue are overlapped, and magenta results from a combination of red and blue. Where all three projected colors overlap, we have white, or *all light,* from the three additive primaries.

The *subtractive primary colors* cyan, magenta, and yellow operate by subtracting from white light all the colors except the one produced (Pl. 4, p. 87). A cyan filter will produce cyan, and so forth. By overlapping two of these filters one obtains an additive primary—red, blue, or green. However, when all three subtractive primaries are overlapped, all color is subtracted from the white light, yielding black. (It must be noted that these mixtures apply *only* to light. Pigments mix differently and will be dealt with later in the chapter.)

Some of the most dramatic colors in nature are directly associated with light—the vivid red tones of a sunset, for example. A volcano, when it erupts, often creates extraordinarily brilliant colors reminiscent of a giant fireworks display (Pl. 5, p. 87). Extravagant artificial light shows have been popular for centuries; one example from the mid-18th century (Fig. 129) shows the brilliant effects that could be obtained long before the invention of electric lights. Today artists are using light itself as a medium in new forms of sculpture, painting, and construction (Fig. 130).

Although we assume that color is dependent upon light, there remain a number of unexplained phenomena. It is sometimes possible to see color by pressing the fingers against the closed eyelids or to experience a flash of color after sustaining a blow on the head. Some people see bright colors when feverish or when under the influence of certain drugs. Others dream in color. One more optical effect with colors is *afterimage,* which the reader can test easily. Cover the yellow and blue circles in Alexander Liberman's *Interchange* (Pl. 6, p. 88)

left: 129. J. Besoet. *Fireworks in an Outdoor Theater, The Hague.* 1749. Engraving. Gemeentemuseum, The Hague.

below: 130. Eric Zimmerman. *Kinetic Neon Light Sculpture.* 1975. Neon and mercury-filled tubes with two-way mirror, 20 x 47″. Commissioned by Mr. and Mrs. Robert Pauley, Los Angeles.

with a piece of opaque white paper or cardboard. Stare fixedly at the red circle for about thirty seconds, then quickly turn your eyes to the white paper. You should see an afterimage of the circle in *green,* the complementary color to red. No one is quite sure how these experiences work, but it is obvious that color is dependent upon the action of the retina in the human eye as well as upon the reaction of a surface to the effects of sunlight.

Color Theory

In his experiments with color in light, Newton found that six colors arranged themselves in the beam of light, each fusing into its neighbor. At one end of the spectrum was indigo, or blue-purple, and at the other was red verging also toward purple. Realizing the relationship between these two colors at opposite ends of the spectrum, Newton joined the ends into a circle. He found that in this way the two end colors produced a seventh color—purple or violet—and that with this color as a transition the hues of the spectrum now flowed together in a continuous band. This band or circle led to the development of the color circle, or *color wheel.*

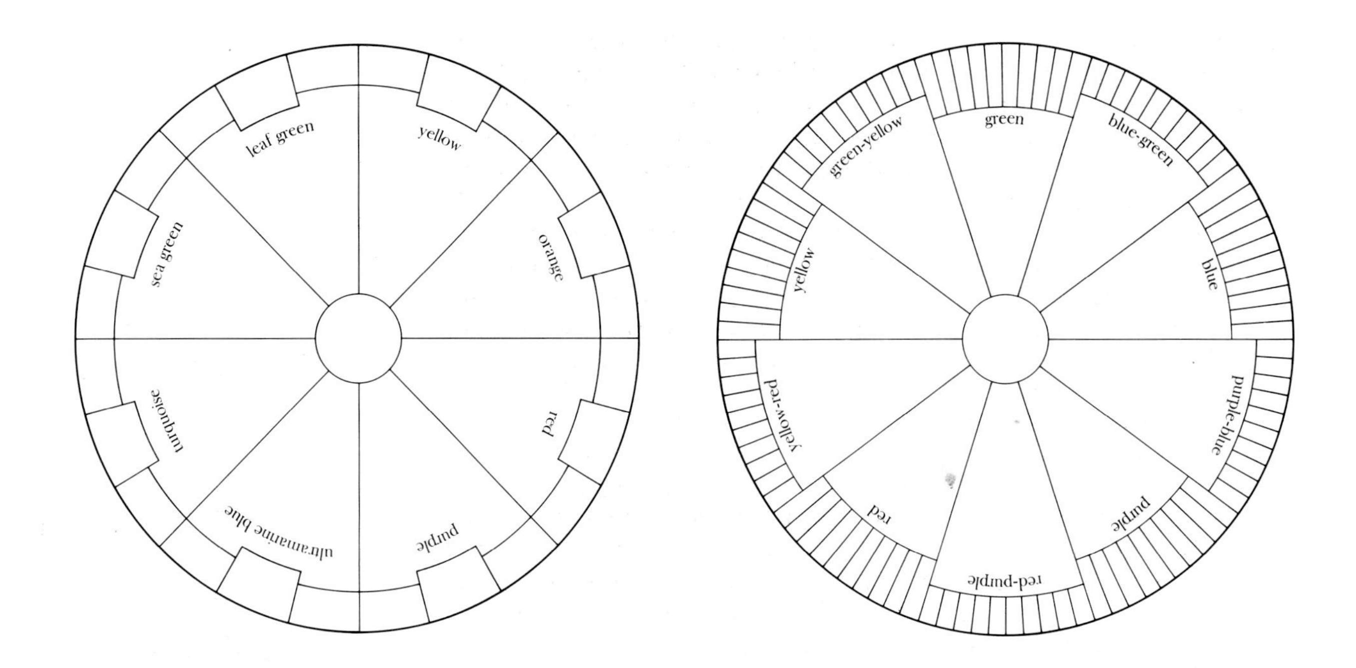

left: 131. The Ostwald color wheel considers red, yellow, green, and blue to be the primary colors.

right: 132. The Munsell color wheel is based on five key hues: red, yellow, blue, green, and purple.

For many years color theory was taught to students on the basis of studies begun in the 18th century and culminating in the work of Herbert E. Ives. Ives devised a color wheel based on red, yellow, and blue. These were called *primary colors* (Pl. 6, p. 88), because it was thought that they could not be mixed from other colors. By mixing any two of the primaries together, one obtains a *secondary color:* green from yellow and blue, orange from yellow and red, violet from red and blue. Going a step further will produce a third group of colors called *tertiaries:* yellow-orange, orange-red, red-violet, violet-blue, blue-green, and green-yellow. When all the colors from these three groups are placed in such a way that they seem to flow naturally, or *modulate,* into one another, there results the basic color wheel (Pl. 7, p. 88).

Any color wheel is to some extent arbitrary and is valid only insofar as it serves the purpose for which it was intended. Ives himself designed another wheel for use in mixing dyes and pigments, and this has for its primaries magenta, yellow, and cyan. Physicists who work with light base their color wheel on red, green, and blue-violet. Still other wheels concern themselves with human vision and the sequence in which we see colors. One design, created by the German physical chemist Wilhelm Ostwald, takes yellow, green, blue, and red as the basic colors (Fig. 131). Albert Munsell's wheel, part of an elaborate system of color structure, establishes five key hues—red, yellow, green, blue, and purple (Fig. 132).

In all color wheels it is assumed that the two colors directly opposite one another are as different in character as possible. These pairs are called *complementary.* When placed side by side, complementary colors tend to intensify one another, a factor called *simultaneous contrast.* However, a mixture of complementaries causes both to become grayed, or less brilliant. If mixed in equal proportions, complementary colors will produce a *neutral,* with characteristics of neither color.

The afterimage that we see following prolonged staring at a color will always be some version of that color's complementary. This phenomenon, known as *successive contrast,* is a means by which the human eye strives to compensate for the separation of complements, as if the two colors formed a whole that is incomplete when only one is seen. If a shape in neutral gray is placed on a yellow background, the gray takes on a violet cast. Conversely, a neutral placed on violet assumes a tinge of yellow. This is another phenomenon that holds true for all complementary colors: With each hue, gray tends to take on the color of its complement.

The term "complementary" arose from the work of still another pioneer in color theory, Michel Chevreul. Chevreul extended the idea of complements into *split complements,* which join a color with the two colors on either side of its complement. For example, on the color wheel in Plate 7, a split complement could be composed of yellow, red-violet, and blue-violet.

In discussing these relationships on the color wheel, we are really talking about *color harmonies,* or the use of two or more colors together in a design. *Monochromatic* harmonies are based on the use of one color, with light or dark variations. *Analogous* harmonies join colors that are adjacent on the color wheel, such as orange, yellow-orange, and yellow. A *triad* harmony would unite three colors equidistant on the wheel, such as yellow, blue, and red. There are many variations on this idea. Artists and designers have used such schemes, whether consciously or unconsciously, since civilization began. When we look at Pierre Bonnard's *Breakfast Room* (Pl. 8, p. 89), we have an overall impression of warm, harmonious colors. But in analyzing the painting we may realize it is composed entirely in tertiary colors, with no primaries or secondaries.

Color Properties

Most authorities identify three distinct properties of color, which are *hue, value,* and *intensity.* In layman's terms colors have subjective names—hunter green, teal blue, rose red, and so forth. These are imprecise, being understood differently by different people. An objective terminology of color properties gives the designer the ability to convey with great accuracy the quality of a particular color.

Hue

Hue is the name by which we identify a color. It refers to the pure state of the color, unmixed and unmodified. The hue red means pure red, with no black, white, or other colors added. Hue is the basis for the other color properties.

Value

Value refers to the relative lightness or darkness of a color. It can be understood best by a study of the *gray scale* (Fig. 133). The average person can distinguish perhaps thirty to forty steps or value gradations between white and black, while an individual with high visual acuity might be able to see as many as 150 gradations. However, for convenience, the gray scale customarily is broken down into about nine steps, as here. The colors on the gray scale have no hue and are therefore termed *achromatic.*

In drawings, which more often than not are achromatic, subtleties of mood and effect can be achieved by value alone. Two drawings, one by Picasso and the other by Jean-Auguste-Dominique Ingres, illustrate

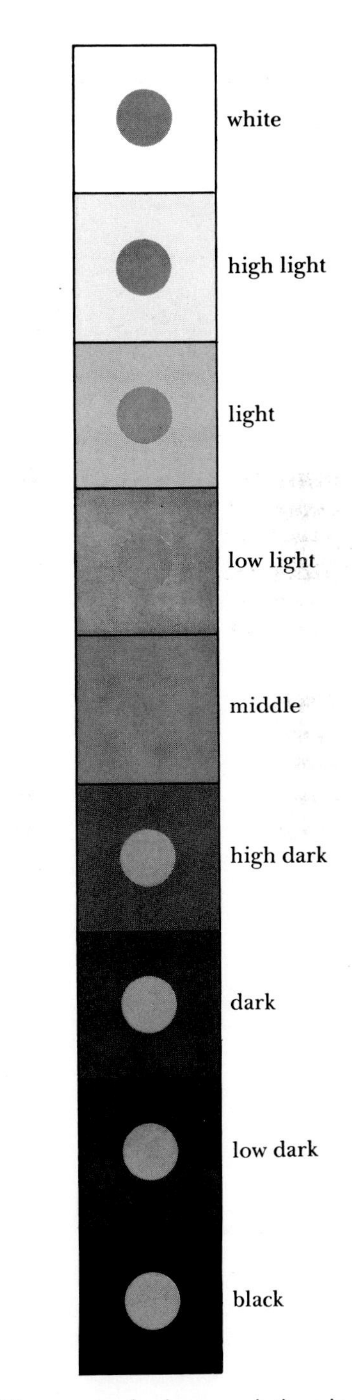

133. The gray scale shows variations in value from white to black. The circles in the centers are all middle value, although they seem different against lighter or darker backgrounds.

right: 134. Pablo Picasso. *Woman at Mirror.* 1934. Ink and colored chalk, $9\frac{3}{8} \times 13\frac{3}{4}''$. Los Angeles County Museum of Art (Mr. and Mrs. William Preston Harrison Collection).

below right: 135. Jean-Auguste-Dominique Ingres. *Family of Lucien Bonaparte.* 1815. Graphite on white woven paper, $16\frac{1}{4} \times 20\frac{3}{16}''$. Fogg Art Museum, Harvard University, Cambridge, Mass. (bequest of Grenville L. Winthrop).

this point. Very dark values dominate the Picasso drawing (Fig. 134), giving the work a brooding, melancholy, almost threatening quality. This feeling is augmented by the anguished expression on the face of the woman, as well as the masklike apparition at upper right. Heavy dark lines delineating the figure also add to the "dark" quality. By

136. A scene from the television program "Monty Python's Flying Circus."

contrast, the Ingres drawing (Fig. 135) consists entirely of light values. We get a feeling of delicacy, gaiety, and fragile charm from this work, a feeling that is intensified by the fine, decorative lines throughout.

It is possible to translate value gradations of gray into any hue. The reverse process—a conversion of colors into values of gray—takes place in black-and-white photography, television, and films (Fig. 136). Every hue can be said to have a *normal* or *natural value*—very light for yellow, very dark for violet (Pl. 9, p. 89). Color values that are lighter than normal value are called *tints,* those darker than normal value *shades.* Thus, pink is a tint of red, and maroon is a shade of red. In mixing paints, the addition of white will lighten value, black darken it.

Intensity

Intensity, also known as *chroma* or *saturation,* indicates the relative purity of a color (Pl. 9, p. 89). Colors that are not grayed, that are at their ultimate degree of vividness, are said to exhibit *high intensity,* while *low intensity* implies that the hue has been grayed, usually by mixing with its complementary color. It is also possible to lower the intensity of a color by adding white *and* black (gray), as compared to the practice of adding white *or* black to alter value. For any hue it would be possible to construct a spectrum in which the color becomes successively more grayed until it cannot be distinguished from a neutral. Certain colors known by everyday names are actually low-intensity versions of a particular hue. For example, the browns are most often low-intensity orange, with tan being a *high-value,* low-intensity orange, dark brown a *low-value,* low-intensity orange. Low-intensity colors often are referred to as *tones.*

Color and Pigment

Pigments are substances of various kinds that have been ground into a fine powder to color paints and dyes. Paints are classified not by their pigments but by their *binders*—the substances used to hold them together. Thus, the same pigment that is added to linseed oil to make oil paint can be bound in gum arabic for watercolor or in acrylic.

Originally, pigments came from the earth or from other natural sources. The so-called "earth tones" got their names during the Renaissance, when they were dug from the soil around the city of Siena or in the region of Umbria. These pigments retain today the names of raw sienna and raw umber in their natural state or, when baked to give a deeper hue, of burnt sienna and burnt umber. Other colors were taken from plants, sea creatures, or insects. Most pigments today are produced by chemical means, which increases their supply and also improves their durability and intensity.

The designer's approach to color will depend on the medium involved. The absorptive and reflective qualities of pigments can be affected by the binder, so it is necessary to become familiar with a medium by experimentation before definite results can be predicted. Mixing two colors of oil paint, for instance, may yield a different result from mixing the same two colors in acrylic.

Whenever pigments are mixed, a certain amount of light is lost. The amount of this loss depends upon both the reflective capacity of the individual pigments and their relationships to each other—the pigments most closely related losing the least reflective light. Since

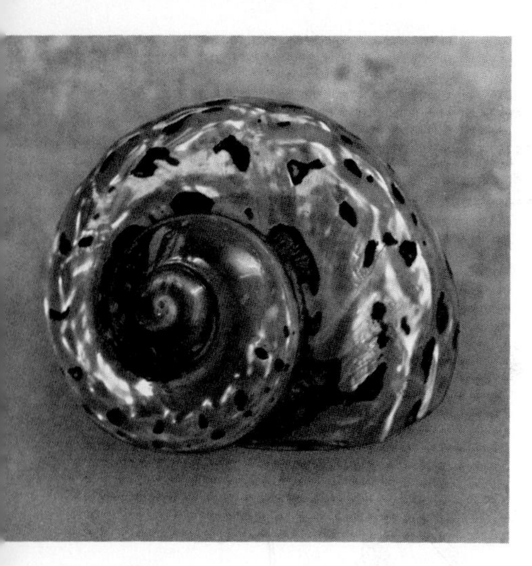

above: 137. Turk's cap shell (*Turbo sarmaticus*), from Capetown, South Africa.

below: 138. Deborah Remington. *Capra.* 1974. Oil on canvas, 6′4″ x 5′7″. © Deborah Remington.

complementary colors are the least chromatically similar of all possible combinations, a mixture of two complementaries causes their light to be totally absorbed, with the effect that the resulting pigment is neutral. Therefore, the most effective way to subdue a color is to add a little of its complement. Colors can be grayed by adding black, of course, but this has a tendency to darken the value.

In mixing gray itself, awareness of the complements makes possible a whole range of vibrant shades. Gray mixed from black and white will be neutral, but varying degrees of complementary colors can result in slight reflective qualities to produce warm grays, blue grays, reddish grays, and so on. Similar diversity is possible in the range of browns. A mixture of three primaries will generally result in brown, and for this reason some combinations of complements will produce a neutral that is closer to brown than gray. The best way to master these subtleties is to experiment with different mixtures in the specific medium chosen.

Expansion of Color

The uses of color can be expanded to achieve considerable diversity of effect in the areas of iridescence, luster, luminosity, and transparency. *Iridescence* is the rainbow effect evident in a raindrop or a seashell (Fig. 137), where the play of light on the surface color gives the appearance of including all the hues of the spectrum separately. Iridescence can be difficult to achieve with paint, but many sculptures and constructions, especially in plastic, are sparklingly iridescent.

Luminosity implies an actual or illusionary giving off of light. We can see this effect in a work by Deborah Remington (Fig. 138), in which subtle modulations of value from white to electric gray bring an aura of mystery to the painting. Remington manipulates oil paint in such a way that light seems to be coming from behind the canvas, casting a glow outward.

Plate 4. According to the additive principle in light (*left*), the three primary colors red, blue, and green together add up to white light. In the subtractive principle (*below left*), the primaries cyan, magenta, and yellow subtract from white light all the colors except the one seen.

Plate 5. Eruption of Mount Hekla in Iceland, 1970. The vaulted ridge, 4892 feet high and 3½ miles long, has erupted fourteen times since 1104.

left: Plate 6. Alexander Liberman. *Interchange.* 1951. Oil and enamel on Masonite, 4′2⅛″ x 2′6½″. Courtesy André Emmerich Gallery, New York.

below: Plate 7. The traditional color wheel begins with primary colors of red, yellow, and blue. From these three hues are formed the secondary colors orange, green, and violet. Tertiary colors result from combining a primary with a secondary.

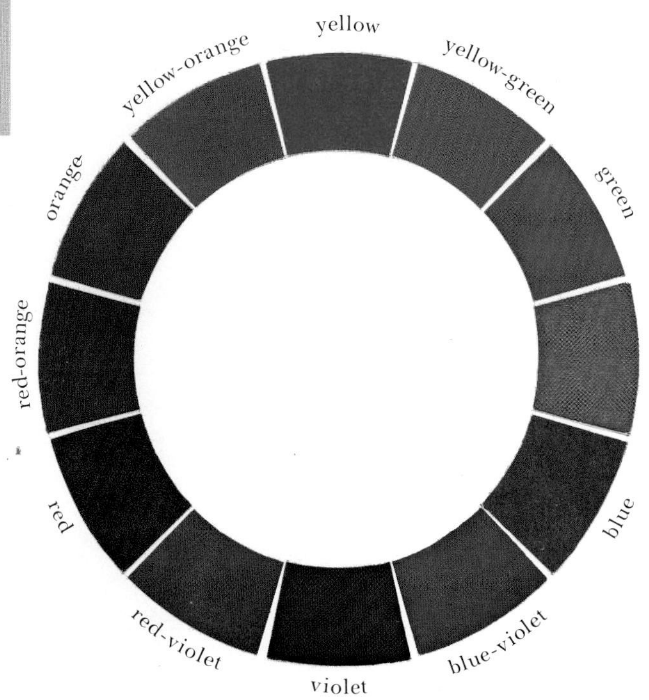

left: Plate 8. Pierre Bonnard. *The Breakfast Room.* c. 1930–31. Oil on canvas, 5′2⅞″ x 3′8⅞″. Museum of Modern Art, New York (given anonymously).

below: Plate 9. The value scale indicates shades of gray between pure white and absolute black. Hues in the color wheel, at their normal value, can also be arranged in such a value scale. The intensity or chroma scale shows the relative purity or grayness of a color.

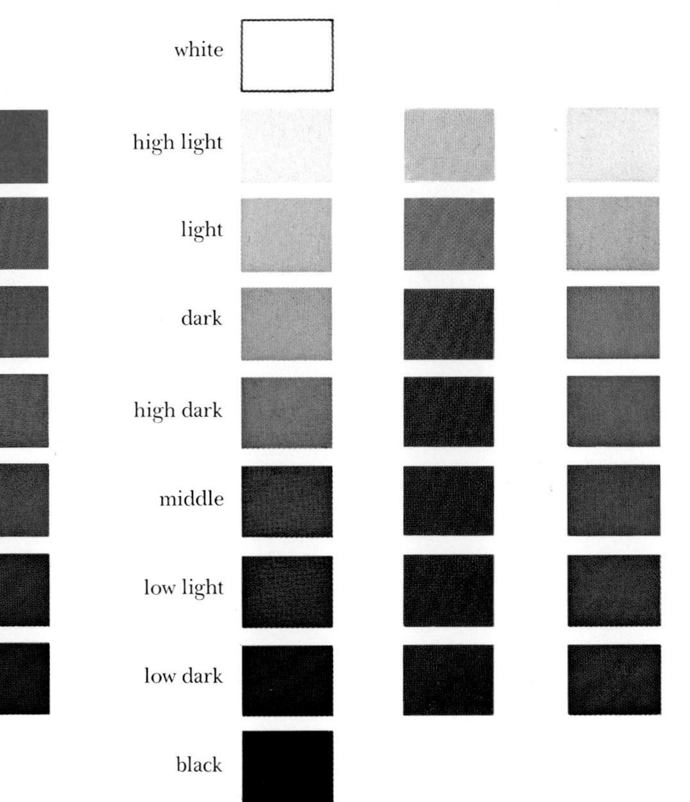

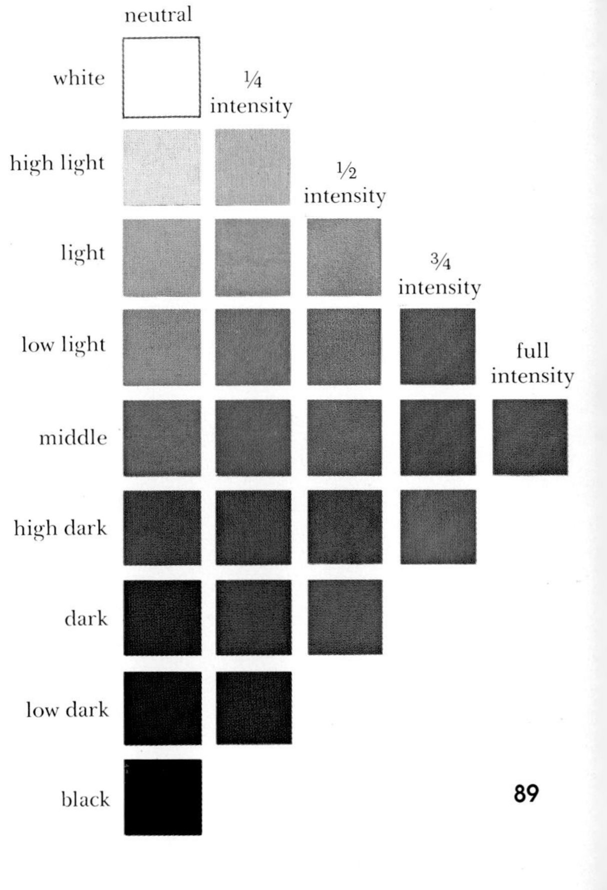

left: Plate 10. Procol Harum in concert.

below: Plate 11. Clayton Pond. *Self Portrait in the Bathtub*, from the series *Things in My Studio.* 1973. Serigraph, 23 x 29″. Courtesy Associated American Artists, New York.

Luster in a work of art is the quality of shine or brilliance, the glow of reflected light. Specially formulated luster glazes are common in ceramics (Fig. 307), and contemporary metal sculptures often display a high degree of luster. The painter can build luster effects through the use of glazes—colors thinned with paint solvent and applied in successive layers. Touches or areas of gold will also contribute luster to the painted surface (Pl. 14, p. 108).

Finally, *transparency,* of course, permits one to look through something. Looking through a transparent colored form to other forms or simply to tinted air provides a special experience. All of these potential ways of expanding the use of color show that its range is limitless.

Psychological Aspects of Color

The photograph in Plate 10 (opposite) illustrates one of the ways in which color affects us psychologically—its power to engage our senses. At a rock concert the dominant sensation is of course one of sound, but very often brilliant lights and colors are part of the overall sensory experience. The performers' intent may be to suspend intellect in their audiences (and themselves), so that a direct contact can be made with the emotions and the senses. High-keyed flashing colors operate with the sounds to produce an almost overwhelming effect.

Psychologists have long known that *specific* colors have the power to evoke emotional responses in the viewer. Among other qualities, colors seem to have a psychological temperature. Red, yellow, and orange are referred to as "warm" colors, perhaps because we instinctively associate them with sunlight and fire. Conversely, blue and green—related to forests, water, and the sky—are considered to be "cool" colors.

Human response to color has become of sufficient importance that people now make careers of color styling, designing color schemes for anything from subways to factories, and maintaining a counseling service for industrial concerns and small businesses. Color stylists base their services on a thorough knowledge of the relationship of color to human reaction.

In general, warm colors stimulate, and cool colors relax. A room with green-painted walls, for example, can actually make people feel cold, and office workers have been known to have chills when working in blue surroundings. With the room temperature held constant, the chills lessened when the walls were repainted in yellow or the chairs slipcovered in orange. Employers have also found that their workers produce at higher levels when they are stimulated by bright colors.

The famed Notre Dame football coach Knute Rockne had the locker rooms for his own team painted red and those for the visiting teams painted blue. When halftime came, the visitors instinctively relaxed in their soothing quarters, while the home team remained keyed up and ready for a winning second half. Similar psychology has been adopted in painting the stalls of racehorses, proving that color psychology is not limited to human reaction. Color can even be an important factor in traffic situations. Study has shown that most automobile drivers, when moving along the highway, feel a greater urge to pass a red, maroon, cream, or yellow car than a black, blue, or green one.

Although cats and dogs are color blind, insects react emphatically to color. Mosquitoes avoid orange but will approach red, black, and blue. Beekeepers wear white to avoid being stung, for they have found that if they wear dark colors they are besieged. The knowledge that flies dislike blue has helped the meat-packing industry.

Warm colors tend to make objects look closer than cool colors do. For instance, a red chair seems closer than a blue one placed at the same distance from the observer. Knowing this effect, the interior designer will use vivid colors to cut down the size of a room or to lower high ceilings, and will employ soft, cool colors to make a small room seem larger.

Beyond these general, shared responses to color, each individual may react in a special way to particular colors. Each of us brings to the perception of visual stimuli a collection of experiences, associations, and memories that may be triggered by a given color. This could be something like the color one's room was painted when one was a child, or the color of the sky on a special well-remembered day. In such an instance color may evoke a strong response, pleasant or unpleasant, even if the viewer does not understand the reason for the response.

Color in Contemporary Art

One of the most interesting developments in 20th-century art was Color Field painting, which emerged during the late 1940s. In a work such as Barnett Newman's *Dionysius* (Pl. 31, p. 247) color and form are indistinguishable. We are meant to experience the colors directly, to see them and understand them for what they are—pure color. There need be no psychological or emotional content in the color, and the artist has deliberately omitted any form references that could distract from the sensory response to color.

In the history of Western art most paintings until the late 19th century attempted to mimic "real" color—known to artists as *local color*—on the canvas. Great pains were taken to make the hues naturalistic, and colors were *modulated* into one another to create a lifelike quality. For example, in painting draperies, the artist might use areas of closely related colors to give the effect of light and shadow. But in the late 1800s artists began to move away from naturalistic color and toward *arbitrary color*—color for its own sake—and attempts were made to find new color relationships and purposes.

As was mentioned in Chapter 4, many artists experimented with flat, unmodulated colors. In the Matisse painting (Pl. 3, p. 54), for instance, the vivid, saturated pink dominates the entire canvas. There are no real highlights or shadows, just pure, flat color. This same aesthetic can be found in the work of many artists today, particularly in the graphic arts (Pl. 11, p. 90). In Clayton Pond's serigraph print the flat colors have been intensified to an extreme. A flattened pictorial space helps to create the impression of pure form and color, so that a foot, for example, can be studied as an abstract pink form, rather than a real human appendage.

The *Fauve* or "wild beast" painters got their name from the horrified response of a critic to their first exhibition in 1905. For these artists color was an almost arbitrary device, meant to be used for the sheer visual pleasure and excitement it could evoke. In a work such as André Derain's *The Turning Road, L'Estaque* (Pl. 12, p. 107) trees may be red or blue or yellow, and the earth may be almost any color at all. The exciting patterns of saturated hot colors take precedence over any visual reality. As we can see from these various examples, color may lead a life all its own in a work of art.

7 Texture and Pattern

Both texture and pattern are surface elements. *Texture* in particular refers to the surface quality of a thing, the way it might feel if we were to run our fingers over it—smooth, bumpy, rough, fuzzy, and so forth. However, designers identify two kinds of textures: *tactile* and *visual.* Actual changes in plane result in tactile textures that can be felt, whereas variations in light and dark produce visual textures. A chunk of porous lava rock has definite tactile texture; by passing the fingers over it, we could feel bumps and hollows. But a smooth granite pebble has visual texture as the result of flecks in the composition of the stone. A glaze on pottery may be perfectly smooth to the touch, yet be textured to the eye by fragments of chemical oxides suspended in the glaze (Fig. 298). When a texture is repetitive and/or decorative, we call it *pattern.*

Texture

Textures are so much a part of our environment that we generally take them for granted. Figure 139 shows two extremes of texture—the very smooth and the very rough—that decorate our own bodies and those of

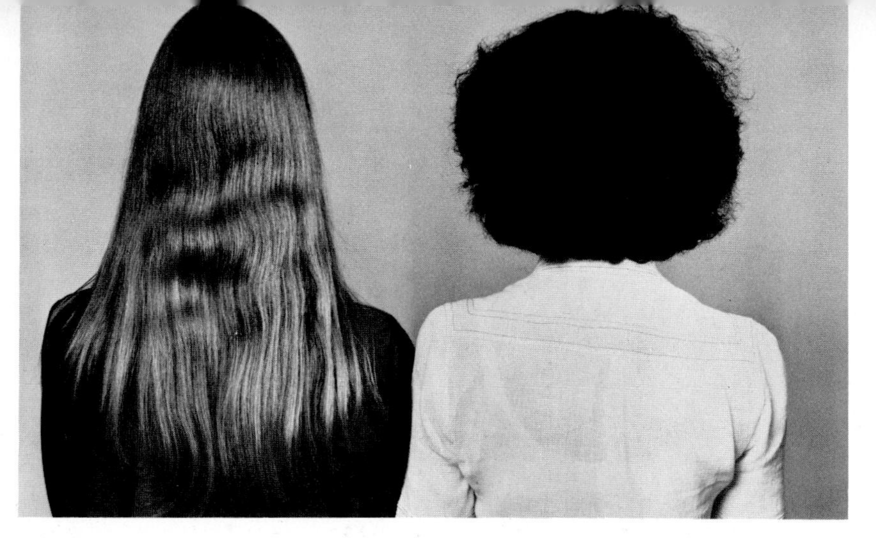

139. Two extremes of texture—the very smooth and the very rough.

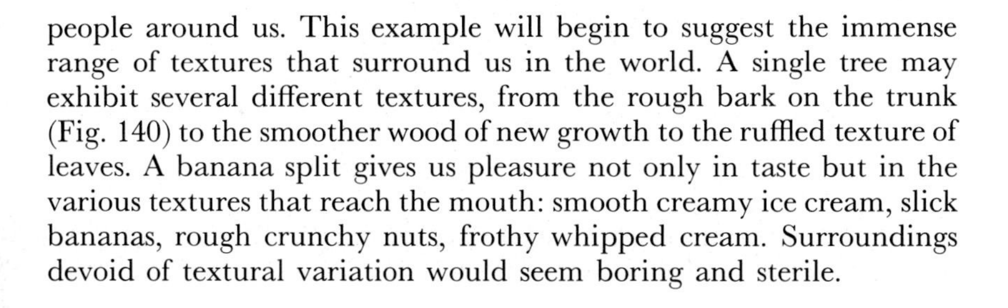

people around us. This example will begin to suggest the immense range of textures that surround us in the world. A single tree may exhibit several different textures, from the rough bark on the trunk (Fig. 140) to the smoother wood of new growth to the ruffled texture of leaves. A banana split gives us pleasure not only in taste but in the various textures that reach the mouth: smooth creamy ice cream, slick bananas, rough crunchy nuts, frothy whipped cream. Surroundings devoid of textural variation would seem boring and sterile.

above: 140. Wolf Strache. *Bark on the Trunk of a Plane.* 1956. Photograph.

right: 141. Cesar (Cesar Baldaccini). *The Yellow Buick.* 1961. Compressed automobile, 4′11½″ x 2′6¾″ x 2′⅞″. Museum of Modern Art, New York (gift of Mr. and Mrs. John Rewald).

Tactile Textures

Cesar's *Yellow Buick* (Fig. 141) illustrates an extreme tactile texture. This work, which is actually an automobile compressed into a cube, has very deep indentations all over the surface. Even if we could not touch it, we know from experience how it would feel to run the hands over this piece. Although these textures are real, they operate visually as well, for the eye translates one kind of perception into another. Just as taste is somewhat dependent upon smell, vision and touch interact in tactile textures.

The works of Japanese sculptor Nubuo Sekine provide beautiful examples of textural *contrast.* In *Phases of Nothingness* (Fig. 142), done in black granite, the artist has juxtaposed the absolutely smooth, pure surface of the cone against a rough base suggestive of rock. The two portions blend, and yet each acquires greater interest from contrast with the other.

One of the principal reasons that handcrafted objects are so treasured is the variety and warmth of their textures. No machine would be able to capture an intriguing pitted texture like that evident in Gertrud and Otto Natzler's bowl (Fig. 143), with its specially developed "crater" glaze reminiscent of the crater-struck surface of the Moon. Textures that remind us of natural ones establish a close relationship with the world around us.

Fabrics offer some of the richest textures in everyday life, from the smoothest satin to the deepest plush velvet. The Inca of pre-Columbian Peru wove entire garments from feathers (Pl. 13, p. 107), for an unusually lush texture. Feathers were carefully sorted for color to create not only broad areas of hue but also fine gradations within a color section. In this instance the Inca weavers certainly took their cue from nature; some of the most luxuriant textures are to be found in the plumage of birds (Fig. 144).

above left: 142. Nobuo Sekine. *Phases of Nothingness—Cone.* 1972. Black granite, height 11¾″. Courtesy Tokyo Gallery.

above: 143. Gertrud and Otto Natzler. Bowl with "crater" glaze. 1972. Courtesy Otto Natzler.

below: 144. Wolf Strache. *Back View of a Peacock.* 1956. Photograph.

left: 145. A "Minimal," all-white living room designed by Bil Ehrlich is nearly all smooth in textural surfaces.

below: 146. Designed by Kipp Stewart, the interior of this home at Big Sur in California shows rich and varied textures and materials.

We become particularly aware of textures in interior design, since variations in texture have much to do with physical and emotional comfort in the home. Generally speaking, smooth textures seem "cold," and when they predominate in a room the atmosphere itself may actually feel chilly. Very rough textures, on the other hand—associated with plush fabrics and rugs, uneven wall surfaces, and live plants—contribute a sense of warmth. The two rooms in Figures 145 and 146 show extremes of textural composition. The first has nearly all smooth textures with only the human occupants for relief; the second contains predominantly rough textures in walls, furniture, and fabrics. Most people prefer to live in surroundings that have some variation in texture, so that the eye and hand experience changing

above: 147. Vincent van Gogh. *Cypresses* (detail). 1889. Oil on canvas. Metropolitan Museum of Art, New York (Rogers Fund, 1949). (See also Fig. 371.)

right: 148. Georges Braque. *Musical Forms* (or *Guitar and Clarinet*). 1918. Pasted paper, corrugated cardboard, charcoal, and gouache on cardboard; $30\frac{3}{8} \times 37\frac{3}{8}''$. Philadelphia Museum of Art (Collection Louise and Walter Arensberg).

sensations. A room with smooth flooring and walls, for example, might have soft fabrics, carved (textured) furniture, and leafy plants.

For centuries artists have tried to simulate textures on the flat surface of canvas, but texture in painting can also be quite real. Certain artists, including Vincent van Gogh (Fig. 147), developed a technique of laying oil paint on canvas in a thick, pastelike *impasto.* This effect not only contributes to the illusion of reality on the flat surface, but it also lends an energetic physical texture to the work.

In this century a number of artists have experimented with pronounced textures in painting, to the extent that it becomes difficult to classify such works as painting or sculpture. The Cubists, particularly Georges Braque, pasted bits of newspaper and other "real" objects onto the canvas and then integrated them with the painted portions (Fig. 148). This type of composition is known as *collage.* Then, in the mid-20th century, artists such as Robert Rauschenberg (Fig. 393) incorporated actual three-dimensional objects into their paintings, so that the result becomes a challenge to the critic who is trying to establish categories. Tactile textures in painting make an important contribution to contemporary expression.

below: 149. A quilted linen coverlet from the first half of the 18th century interweaves circular and radiating forms to produce a rich textural surface. Victoria & Albert Museum, London.

right: 150. Cherwell cotton velvet printed from William Morris' design. c. 1885. Victoria & Albert Museum, London. This velvet presents a uniform surface to the hand, so the texture is largely visual.

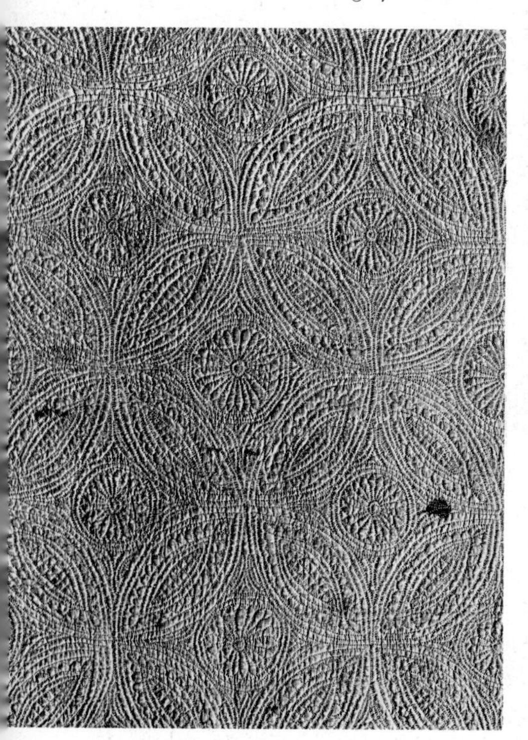

Visual Textures

The two fabrics shown in Figures 149 and 150 illustrate the difference between tactile and visual textures. The first (Fig. 149), a quilted coverlet from the 18th century, has a raised surface that we could perceive by touching it, even with our eyes closed. By contrast, the printed velvet designed by William Morris (Fig. 150) would present a uniform surface to the touch, but it offers much visual texture. This is because of changes in light and dark, separation of design areas from background, and so forth. The brain translates this visual perception into texture.

Contrasts of light and dark play a vital role in architecture, enlivening the interiors of buildings with ever-changing visual textures. Le Corbusier designed his chapel of Notre-Dame-du-Haut at Ronchamp with deliberate attention to the patterns of light that would be admitted by windows of varying size, placement, and angle (Fig. 151). Throughout the day, as the sun moves, light entering the chapel creates a fascinating visual texture both in the windows themselves and in the light cast on the floor and walls. Cathedrals with stained glass windows show this effect even more brilliantly, for here the light is translated into a vivid texture of color. Of course, even without the light streaming in, the cutout squares of windows in a wall give texture to the surface.

Visual textures can also appear in many other media. The Chinese scroll illustrated in Figure 152 has a very rich texture acquired from the dense concentration of black characters on white set against the clump of bamboo. A page of type in the Roman alphabet has texture as well. The pages of this book should demonstrate that idea. For example, a page on which only a few words appear (p. iii) has quite a different visual texture from a page solid with small type (p. 80).

Visual texture plays a vital role in all the pictorial arts. The chalk drawing by Pierre Paul Prud'hon, shown in Figure 153, presents such

right: 151. Le Corbusier. Notre-Dame-du-Haut, Ronchamp, France. Interior view of the south wall. 1950–55.

below left: 152. Li Shan (1711–after 1754). *Bamboo and Calligraphy.* Hanging scroll, ink on paper; 4′4″ x 2′5$\frac{1}{4}$″. Collection John M. Crawford, Jr., New York.

below right: 153. Pierre Paul Prud'hon. *La Source.* c. 1801. Black and white chalk on blue-gray paper, 21$\frac{3}{16}$ x 15$\frac{5}{16}$″. Sterling and Francine Clark Art Institute, Williamstown, Mass.

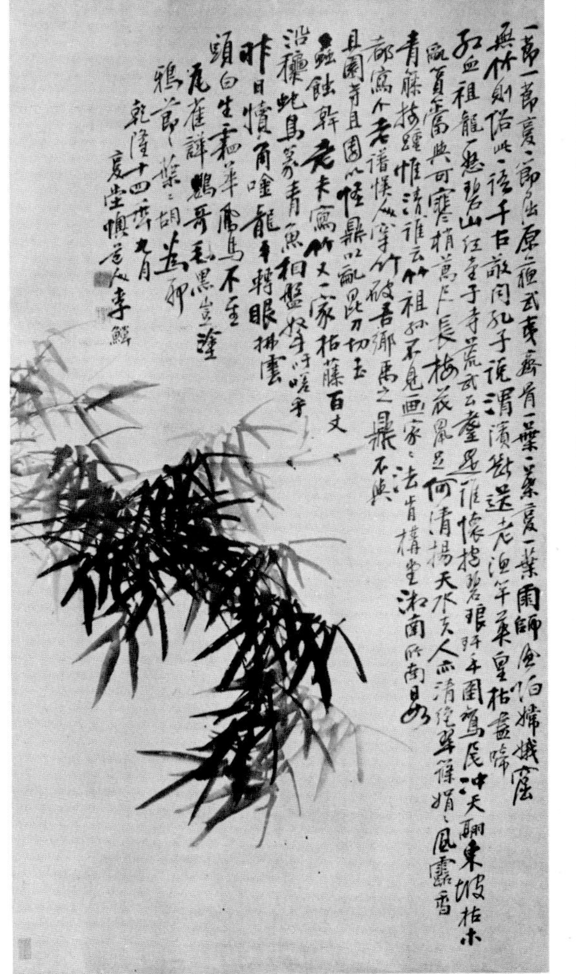

right: 154. Georges Seurat. *La Parade (The Come-On).* 1889. Oil on canvas, 39½ x 59¼". Metropolitan Museum of Art, New York (bequest of Stephen C. Clark, 1960).

below: 155. Denim jacket designed by Chris McDonald for "Levi's Denim Art Contest," 1974. Courtesy Levi Strauss & Co.

a rich, velvety texture that the sensory experience is almost tactile. In a painting by Georges Seurat (Fig. 154) the visual textures seem to pulsate with energy. This effect comes from Seurat's unique method of working, the application of tiny dots of paint to the canvas in a manner known as *pointillism.* This technique results in a visual texture that is nearly independent of the subject matter.

Every drawing, painting, sculpture, or other work of art can be characterized by its textural qualities, whether tactile or visual. A texture can be smooth, coarse, regular, uneven, harsh, or sensuous. The artist must be aware that this element has a strong bearing on a viewer's reaction to a piece.

Pattern

Pattern is difficult to separate from texture. We have said that pattern is repetitive, or in other words that the same motif is used over and over. Also, pattern usually is thought of as decorative, but "decorative" is a subjective word. People have different ideas about what is or is not visually attractive. Pattern may be an applied design laid onto the surface of something, but it can also emerge from structure.

Appliquéd designs on fabric (Fig. 155) can turn a plain, workaday material into a riot of design. When arranged in an imaginative interplay of shape and space (background), they become a pattern. On the other hand, a textile may create pattern just from the interweaving of its yarns.

A painting by Gustav Klimt (Pl. 14, p. 108) provides a good example of pattern in the visual arts. Works by this artist tend to be described as "decorative." His exotic, elongated figures swim in a sea of intricate pattern and color, often made all the richer with broad areas of gold. The forms are closely entwined in the elaborate, patterned backgrounds so that the two seem inseparable. Overall, the effect is lush and ornate.

Sometimes the introduction of pattern can give a completely fresh approach to a work of art. A metal cutout of an owl by Picasso gives a good example (Fig. 156). The pattern does not relate specifically to

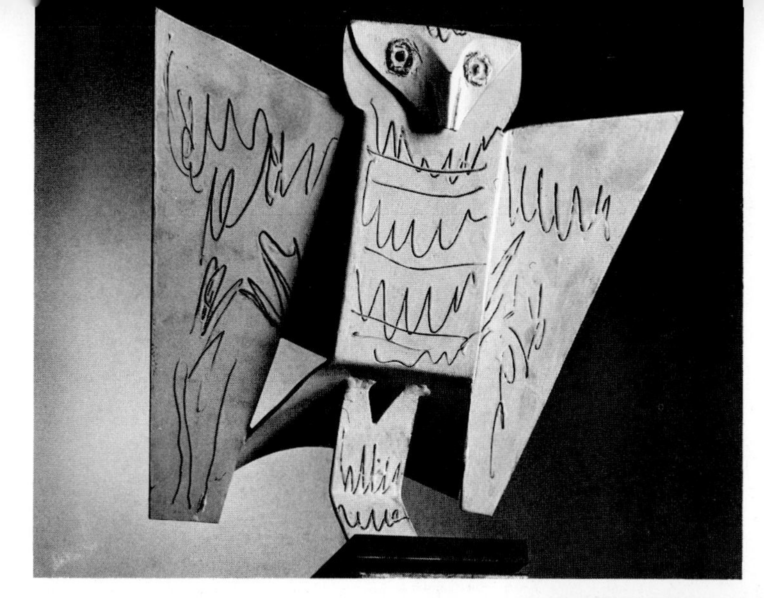

above: 156. Pablo Picasso. *Owl.* 1961. Metal cutout, folded and painted; height $9\frac{7}{8}''$.

right: 157. Paul Caponigro. *Negative Print.* 1963. Photograph. Courtesy the artist.

the owl shape, although there may be a suggestion of feathers. Instead, the pattern is applied for the sheer joy of its fanciful arrangement. The pattern is integrated with the form but not subject to it—the "icing on the cake," so to speak.

Pattern can serve an artist in many different ways. With Klimt, obviously, the pattern emerges from the artist's fascination with complex, interwoven designs. In an Op Art painting (Fig. 99), however, the pattern of dots or other repetitive forms acts to create the illusion of movement or vibration on the surface of the canvas. Both of these are strong, obvious patterns, which dominate the visual field of the work. But pattern can also operate in more subtle ways, perhaps to unify a composition, to establish balance among diverse elements, or to create a sense of rhythm and movement (Fig. 157). These concerns, as well as the principles of variety, emphasis, and balance, form the subject matter of the next two chapters.

8 Unity and Variety

A composition devoid of any unifying element will nearly always seem haphazard and chaotic. A composition that is totally unified, without the relief of variety, will nearly always be boring. These two overriding principles of design, *unity* and *variety,* are like two sides of the same coin. Unity represents the *control* of variety, whereas variety provides the visual *interest* within unity. In most cases, the ideal in a composition will be a balance between the two qualities—diverse elements held together by some unifying device (Fig. 158). The only possible exception to this would be when an artist deliberately sets out to create chaos or monotony in order to produce a certain effect.

In this chapter we shall discuss several ways in which a design can be unified and in which variety can be introduced. The illustrations will largely be interchangeable, for the most effective compositions demonstrate both principles.

Unity

Examples of underlying unity surround us in the natural world. All people, for instance, look somewhat different from one another, but we

above: 158. M. C. Escher. *Mosaic II.* 1957. Lithograph, 12½ x 15½″. Escher Foundation, Gementemuseum, The Hague.

right: 159. Great variety can be found in types of starfish.

have no difficulty identifying them as people. A collection of starfish (Fig. 159) might exhibit quite different characteristics of color, texture, even number of points, yet each is recognizable as a starfish. A unity of design—in this case points moving out from a central body—marks them all as starfish.

The beginning designer often faces the problem of establishing unity in a composition made up of many elements. There are several ways of doing this. *Repetition* of motif, shape, pattern, or size will create an underlying unity, as will *harmony* of color, texture, or material. An enclosing border can unify a composition of many elements.

Repetition of *motif* can be purely straightforward, as in an Andy Warhol silk screen print (Fig. 160). Here the artist literally duplicates the same image over and over, with variations of color and value.

160. Andy Warhol. *Mao 14, Mao 15, Mao 16, Mao 17, Mao 18.* 1973. Silk screen and acrylic on canvas, each 12 x 10″. Courtesy Leo Castelli Gallery, New York.

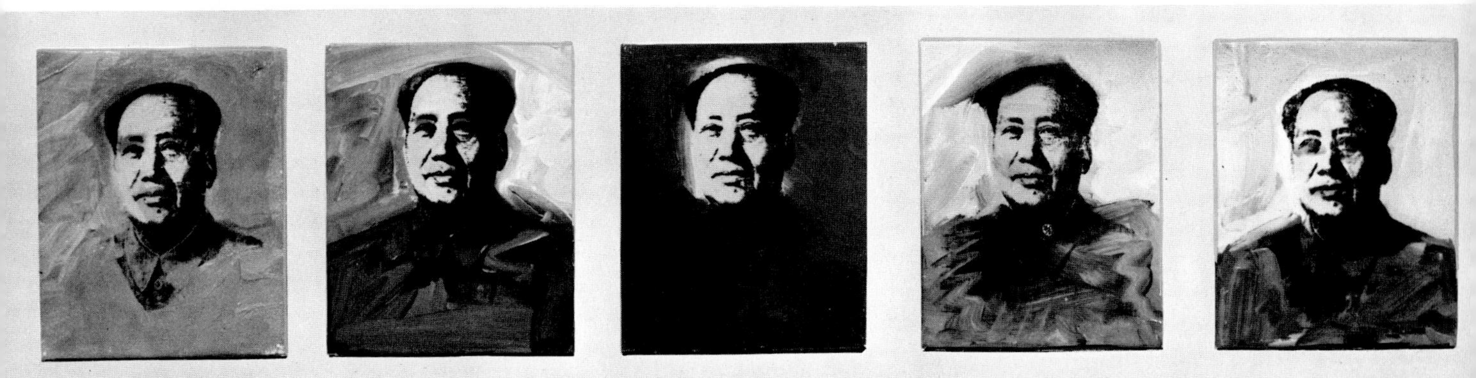

However, a more subtle repetition of motif will also pull a composition together. In Stuart Davis' *Report from Rockport* (Fig. 161) a highly complex assortment of shapes becomes unified because of a recurring motif or pattern running through the painting, a kind of jagged line that is not always the same but has the same general quality. Unity of motif also marks the lush canvases of Gustav Klimt (Pl. 14, p. 108), in which elaborate decorative patterns spill over from figure to ground, making them one flowing universe.

This is not to suggest that pattern is essential for unity in a composition. A work with only one figure set against a plain back-

above: 161. Stuart Davis. *Report from Rockport.* 1940. Oil on canvas, 24 x 30″. Collection Mr. and Mrs. Milton Lowenthal, New York.

right: 162. Georget Cournoyer. *Set of 3 Ceramic Bags.* 1973. Stoneware, tallest 12″. Courtesy the artist.

above: 163. Auguste Renoir. *Le Moulin de la Galette.* 1876. Oil on canvas, 4′3½″ x 5′9″. Louvre, Paris.

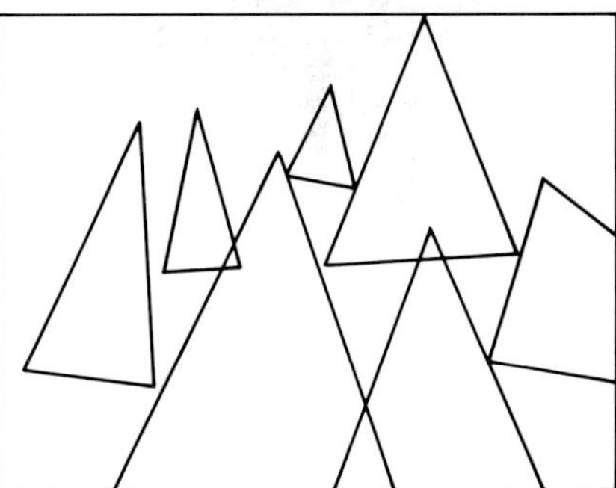

164. Diagram of *Le Moulin de la Galette.*

ground can be perfectly coherent. However, as the compositional elements multiply in number and complexity, the need for a unifying device becomes more apparent.

Repetition of *shape* is usually the underlying principle in a "set" of things. Georget Cournoyer's *Set of 3 Ceramic Bags* (Fig. 162) takes its form from the standard brown paper bag, which we know to be uniform. The craftsman has introduced variety by "bending" the bags into shapes that they could assume if they were made of paper.

Shape repetition also functions in painting, being most evident in a geometric work such as one by Mondrian or Albers (Figs. 12, 114). In a much less obvious way shape repetitions can help to unify a complex composition, for example, a painting that contains many figures. Renoir's *Moulin de la Galette* (Fig. 163) seems at first to be a completely random crowd scene, the kind of image we might get if we snapped an unposed photograph at a café. However, if we analyze the composition more carefully, and diagram its shapes, we realize that Renoir has deliberately composed his groups in a series of triangles (Fig. 164). By means of this subtle structure, a large, diffuse scene is organized into manageable configurations.

left: 165. Li Ch'eng (Ying-ch'iu). *Buddhist Temple Amid Clearing Mountain Peaks.* 10th century. Ink and color on silk, 44 x 22". Nelson Gallery-Atkins Museum, Kansas City (Nelson Fund).

below: 166. Brent Kington. *Air Machine #1.* 1966. Cast sterling silver, height 7". Courtesy the artist.

This device, if carried too far, can become stilted. One should not be able to look at a landscape or portrait or still life and immediately say, "Oh, look, three triangles." The construction must be subtle, or else its purpose will disappear in the face of meaningless geometry.

Harmony of *texture* is an important unifying device in many works of art, but especially in landscape painting. The great Chinese landscape painters were masters at blending diverse topographical elements. In a work by Li Ch'eng (Fig. 165) soft feathery textures unify the trees and hills in the foreground, the cluster of temple buildings, and the tall, craggy mountains in the background. The smoother sections of water lend contrast and prevent the work from being an overall decorative pattern.

Harmony of *material* is illustrated by the sculpture in Figure 166, a cast-silver piece by Brent Kington. In this work a charming collection of forms and curlicues is unified by the single material. It would be difficult to imagine this little "air machine" being composed of mixed media, for it is the silver that pulls the composition together.

above: Plate 12. André Derain. *The Turning Road, L'Estaque.* 1906. Oil on canvas, 4′3″ x 6′4⅞″. Museum of Fine Arts, Houston (John A. and Audrey Jones Beck Collection).

left: Plate 13. Inca feather tunic, from Peru. 1100–1400. Feathers knotted on cords, stitched to cotton ground; 5′11″ x 2′9″. Los Angeles County Museum of Art (gift of Mr. and Mrs. William T. Sesnon, Jr., 1974).

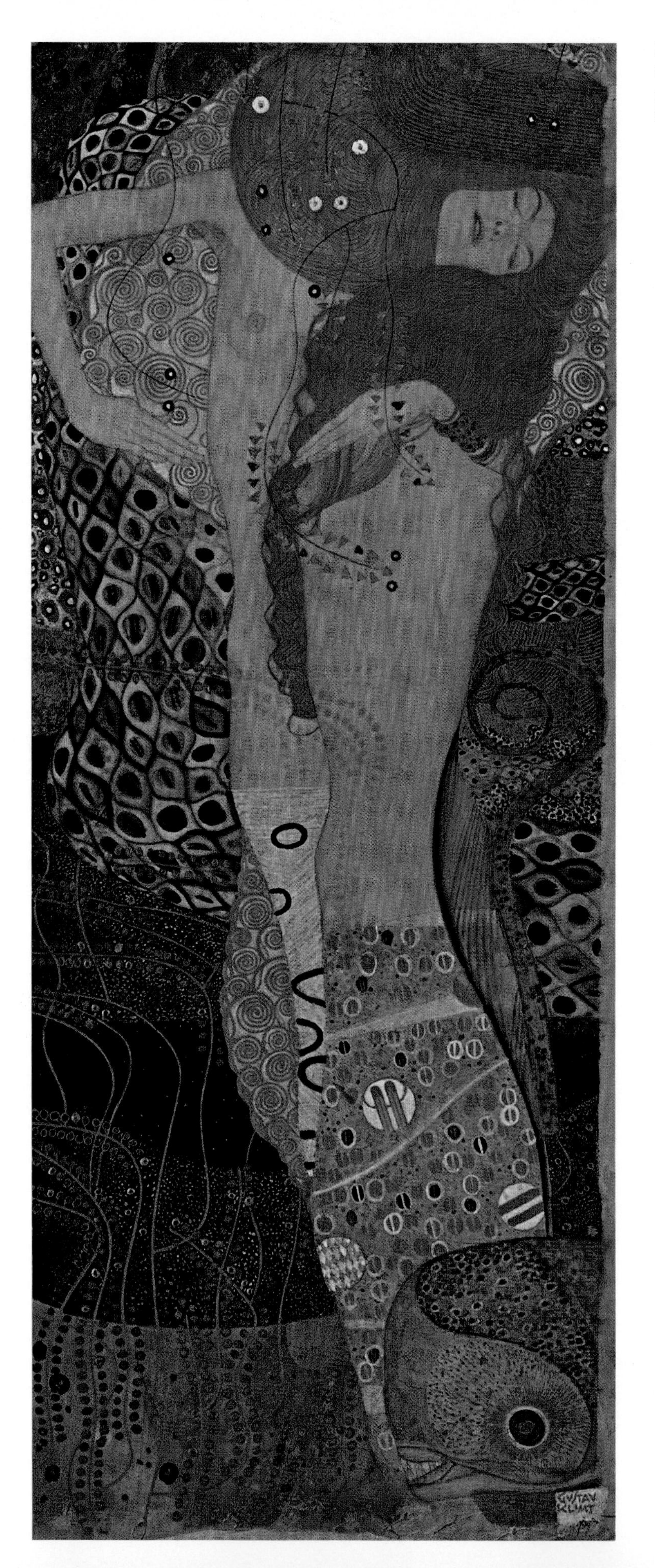

Plate 14. Gustav Klimt. *Water Serpents*. c. 1904–07. Mixed technique on parchment, 19½ x 7¾″. Österreichische Galerie, Vienna.

167. Louise Nevelson. *Sky Cathedral.* 1958. Painted wood construction, 11′3½″ x 10′¼″ x 1′6″. Museum of Modern Art, New York (gift of Mr. and Mrs. Ben Mildwoff).

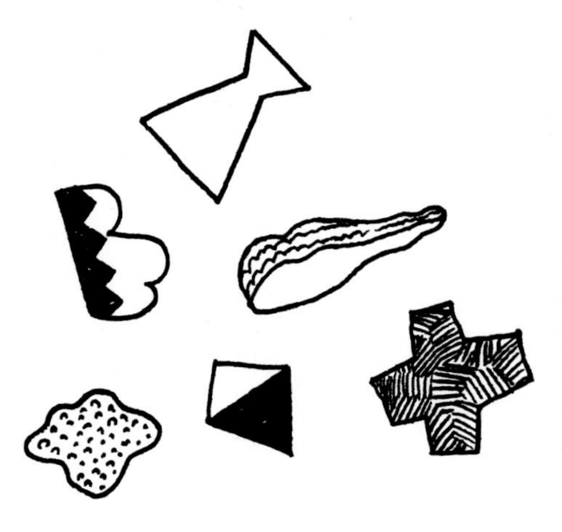

Harmony of *color* can mean the actual predominance of one color, as in Matisse' *Harmony in Red* (Pl. 3, p. 54). It may also result, however, from the quality of an artist's *palette,* the range of colors an artist uses for a particular painting or for all paintings. We speak of the Fauve palette as being very *high-keyed,* which means the colors are bright, saturated, and usually primary (Pl. 12, p. 107). As such, they are closely related in everything but hue, and the work achieves a color harmony. A low-keyed palette would be one in which the colors are dark and grayed.

The sculptor Louise Nevelson concentrated for many years on large assemblages of "found" objects—bits of wood, wheels, old newel posts, and miscellaneous oddments. To bring unity to these unrelated objects, Nevelson enclosed them in boxes and painted them all the same color (Fig. 167). Thus, two unifying devices operate in her works—the color and the enclosure.

A good exercise in learning to develop unity in two-dimensional compositions is to arrange several dissimilar shapes within a rectangular framework (Fig. 168). The forms shown in this example have been pulled together into a unified composition by means of *placement,* with all but one of the shapes *overlapping* in two balanced groups. The other shape serves to balance, by its distance from the groups, their visual weight. The placement of darker (and therefore heavier) shapes near the center gives a stability that adds to the unified effect.

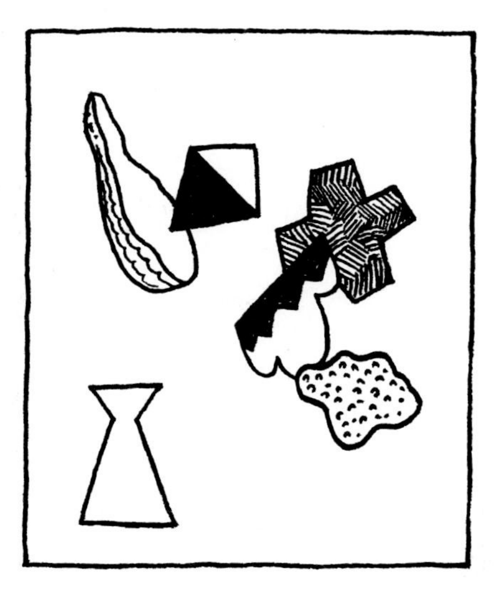

168. A variety of dissimilar forms can be unified in a composition by means of placement and disposition of weight.

169. *Kyo no Yosuga* (*Reminders of Kyoto*), a box of seasonal confections referred to as Yojohan (Four and a Half Mats). The interior sections of the box imitate the arrangement of a Japanese-style room whose size is always expressed in the number of standard mats (*tatami*) it contains. From *How to Wrap Up Five More Eggs,* by Hideyuki Oka.

Sometimes an enclosing border will be sufficient by itself to create unity. Japanese designers in particular have a finely tuned sense of unity and variety, which carries over into every realm of life. Even a Japanese meal will be arranged with a balance of colors and textures, held within the enclosing module of the plate. Figure 169 shows an example of traditional Japanese packaging, in this instance a box of commercial confections. While all the candies are different in size, color, and texture, the assortment has been beautifully composed inside the four sides and partitions of the box.

Unifying elements are an intrinsic part of some media. In mosaics, the grout that holds the tesserae together helps to unify the composition (Fig. 327), as does the lead between pieces in a stained-glass work. To some extent the enclosing borders of a canvas help to control a design and bring a kind of unity.

In sum, if the designer maintains unity in one or more of the elements discussed above, there is a strong likelihood that the composition will seem coherent and "together." One can then vary the other elements to achieve interest. An analogy could be made with the theme-and-variations form in music, in which a composer weaves a recognizable theme throughout a work but varies it in pitch, key, rhythm, or tempo. The visual designer can do much the same thing.

Variety

One of the most famous paintings in the history of art is Diego Velázquez' *Las Meninas* (Fig. 170), which shows the artist himself painting the Spanish royal princess with her friends and attendants. Nearly three centuries later, Velázquez' countryman Pablo Picasso did a series of variations on *Las Meninas,* one of which is shown in Figure 171. Most obviously, Picasso has altered the shapes in this work, even to the shape of the canvas itself, which now has a horizontal format. In working out his variation, he has selected for study the details most interesting to him. The dog and the two figures in the right foreground have become mere outlines, while the tall figure to the princess' left,

left: 170. Diego Velázquez. *The Maids of Honor (Las Meninas).* 1651. Oil on canvas, 10′5″ x 9′. Prado, Madrid.

below: 171. Pablo Picasso. *The Maids of Honor (Las Meninas).* 1957. Oil on canvas, $6'4\frac{3}{8}''$ x $8'6\frac{1}{4}''$.

who is prominent in Velázquez' painting, has been reduced to a mere animal, something like a horse. The Princess Margarita herself ceases to be the focus of the painting. Instead, Picasso has chosen to develop the figure of the painter, and especially of the girl next to him. The figure standing in the doorway at rear assumes new drama. Surprisingly, Picasso has elaborated on the two ceiling hooks, which are inconspicuous in the Velázquez original. The more we study these two works, the more we see how daringly Picasso has played with Velázquez' masterpiece. However, a person familiar with *Las Meninas* could not fail to recognize it as the source of Picasso's variations.

Besides the variety in shape that we have seen, there can be variety in all the other elements: motif, size, color, texture, or material. In this reference, variety is almost synonymous with *contrast*—white set against black, dark against light, smooth against rough, large against small.

Contrast is the stock-in-trade of the still-life painter. In effect, a still life is nothing more than a representation of objects assembled for their varied colors, shapes, and textures (Fig. 172): gleaming metal utensils, draped fabric tablecloth, the rough skins of peeled fruit, the intricate shapes of different shellfish. These objects may have little interest in and of themselves, but they become fascinating when set in contrast with one another.

The natural world is a dissertation on variety, and often the designer's success comes from capturing its many nuances. The beginning painter who sets out to transcribe onto canvas a particular section of the landscape soon discovers how complex are nature's colors. The painter may choose a particularly beautiful vista, a meadow or grove of trees, for instance. After an hour or so of work, frustration sets in. The sky has been painted blue, the trees, bushes, and grass are green, but the result looks like nothing so much as a mess of paint. This is because the painter has never learned to see properly. Grass is known to be green, so it is painted green. But nature provides the fields and forest with an incredible range of greens, from the

left: 172. Pieter Claesz. *Still Life.* 1643. Oil on panel, 35 x $39\frac{1}{2}''$. Minneapolis Institute of Arts.

opposite: 173. S. and J. C. Newson. William Carson Residence, Eureka, Calif. (now the Ingomar Club). 1884.

yellow-green of grass in sunlight to the deep blue-greens of fir trees in shade. Even a single blade of grass will not be the same color throughout its length, for the play of light and shadow causes minute changes as the blade twists in the breeze.

Rocks, soil, and dirt roads all have their own range of colors derived from mineral deposits, variations in moisture content, puddles, and the glint of changing lights. Some of the most dramatic variations can be found in water, because the high reflective ability and potential for movement cause the water to take on the colors of the sky and adjacent plant life, the sparkle of sunlight, the hint of underwater life. As was mentioned in Chapter 6, the Impressionist painters of the late 19th century set out deliberately to record that which is *actually* seen, rather that what one intellectually knows to be, in terms of light, color, and shape. Monet's *Water Lilies* (Pl. 15, p. 125) is a masterpiece of natural variations interpreted by the artist.

In sculpture, variety can be introduced in any of the elements of which it is composed—shape, size, color, texture, or form. Depending upon the artist's intent, the variety may be subtle or extreme.

Variety of form in architecture is a luxury to those conditioned by the post-World War II housing "development." Today, most houses except the very expensive, custom models are depressingly alike in basic shape, arrangement of rooms, and surface design. This was not always the case, however. The Victorian era—the late 19th century—specialized in domestic architecture that could perhaps be described as "creatively abandoned." Rooms might be square, round, octagonal, or totally irregular (Fig. 173). They might jut out from the

174. A house designed in excitingly varied geometrics is unified by the wood sheathing and the repetition of forms. Thomas M. Larson, architect.

core of the structure at almost any angle. The surface of the building would be adorned with pillars, scrollwork, shingles, carving, railings, and anything else that took the designer's fancy. Somehow, the whole happy mixture achieved a kind of architectural unity—perhaps a unity of extravagance.

Today some of the most varied and inventive designs in housing are created by amateur architects working on their own homes, with their own hands. Variety springs from the individual, from personal tastes, pleasures, interests. Free of the restrictive limits of standard materials and prohibitive builders' costs, generally too far in the woods to be censored by the zoning inspector, these designers can give their imaginations free play.

The house custom designed by an architect can also offer great variety—in the structure itself and as distinguished from other houses. The architect who planned the house in Figure 174 clearly was fascinated with variety of shapes and angles, especially of projections from the main body of the building. Both walls and roofline go off at peculiar angles, resulting in zany interior room shapes. These projections further create an energetic texture of light and shadow. A tiny "widow's walk" at the top completes the unique design experience. All told, there is an intriguing mix of elements in this design, but harmony is maintained by the single material (wood) and its uniform color.

Once unity and variety have been satisfied, the designer can go on to work under the guidance of other principles, as they seem appropriate. Balance, emphasis, and rhythm also play an important role in effective design, and these form the subject of the next chapter.

The three principles discussed in this chapter come almost intuitively to the work of sensitive designers, because they are intrinsic to the world around us and to life itself. A particular type of *balance* causes human beings to walk erect, in contrast to most other creatures on the earth. In all forms of life, balance is necessary to survival. For every intake of breath, one must exhale, and periods of activity must be balanced by times of rest. Emotionally ill people are described as being "unbalanced." Science and mathematics are founded on the principle of balance. In an algebraic equation, for example, the two sides must balance. Politicians seek a "balance of power," with Democrats balancing Republicans, the Western bloc balancing the Eastern bloc. We find visual balance all around us in the natural world. Broad areas of blue sky offset vistas of green field or of water (Fig. 175). It is, in fact, natural to seek balance.

A point of climax, a visual element that attracts our attention, anything that is highest, deepest, brightest, loudest—all these bring *emphasis,* and with it a relief from monotony. In nature, a violent storm provides emphasis, an interruption of the daily cycle of weather. A mesa jutting up from the flat landscape commands our attention because it is different, emphatic. Composers write moments of climax

left: 175. Philip L. Molten. *Angel Island No. 7.* 1969. Photograph.

below: 176. The New York City Ballet in a performance of *Movements for Piano & Orchestra.* Choreography by George Balanchine to music by Igor Stravinsky.

bottom: 177. The Moiseyev Dance Company in a performance of *Dance of the Buffoons.* Courtesy Hurok Concerts.

into their music, and a mystery novel reaches its climax when the villain is discovered. Emphasis, like variety discussed earlier, lends interest to life and art.

The universe we inhabit depends utterly on *rhythm.* Planets in our solar system have a rhythm of revolution around the sun, our moon around the earth. The seasons follow regular rhythms, and as a consequence there has developed a rhythm of planting and harvesting. Animals, birds, and fish in their migrations and breeding habits follow precise rhythms that astound less instinctive human beings. The annual arrival of the legendary swallows at Mission San Juan Capistrano can be timed almost to the minute. The daily rhythms of light and dark, sunrise and sunset are deeply ingrained in us. When travelers fly great distances in a short time, they suffer "jet lag," because they have upset the natural rhythm of the body. Every aspect of our biological being depends on rhythm—the heartbeat and throb of the pulse, the regularity of breathing, the pattern of waking and sleeping. We might even say that rhythmic movements of the body—as expressed in the dance—emerge from this internal rhythm (Fig. 176).

If these three principles of balance, emphasis, and rhythm play such an important role in all forms of life, it is inevitable that they will occur in visual designs. The remainder of this chapter, then, will show some of the ways in which they appear—or can be introduced—in the visual arts.

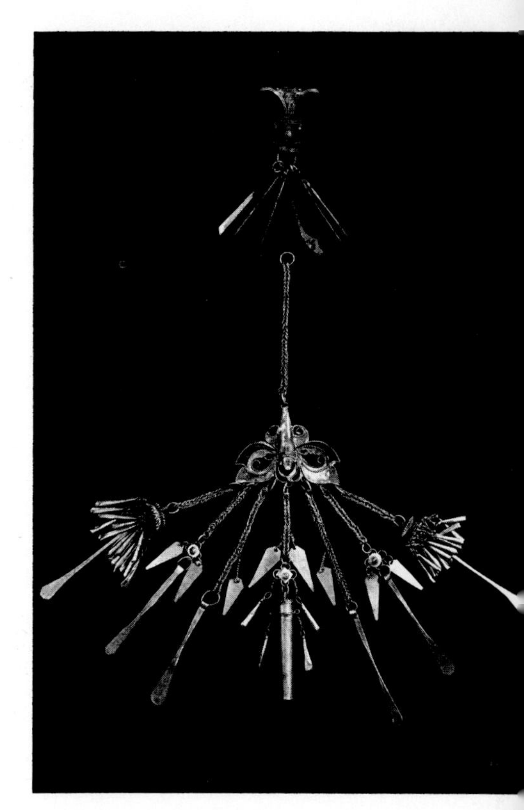

178. Toilet articles from India and Burma. American Museum of Natural History, New York.

Balance

The absence of balance will usually be noticeable, and its removal can be catastrophic. If we remove the lowest card in a house of cards or topple the first domino in a line, the structure collapses (Fig. 177). The lack of balance in a composition is equally unsettling, making us feel vaguely uneasy. Of course, this may be the designer's intent, in which case it is perfectly valid. More often, however, the artist wishes to achieve balance. We might divide visual balance into several categories, including balance of *shape, value, texture,* and *color.*

Balance of Shape

Traditionally, balance of shape is further subdivided into three types—symmetrical, asymmetrical, and radial.

Symmetrical balance means that we can draw an imaginary dividing line through the center of a composition, and the two resulting halves will form a mirror image of one another (Fig. 178). Another term for this is *bilateral* or "two-sided" symmetry. This is the visual balance of the human body and therefore of most things associated with it, such as furniture and clothing. Perhaps this is why symmetrical balance comes so naturally to the designer, and there can be no question that it is the easiest to achieve.

A composition that is balanced symmetrically tends to seem stable, dignified, and calm. It creates a sense of repose. Most architecture, and especially public architecture, is symmetrical. "Colonial" and Federal Period houses in the United States often had a door set directly in the middle of the façade, with windows evenly arranged on either side and a chimney at each end. (Children tend to draw houses like this, too.) A great many 20th-century color-field paintings are based on symmetrical balance (Pl. 16, p. 126).

179. Maurice Béjart's Ballet of the 20th Century in a performance of *Tombeau.*

In *asymmetrical* balance the two imaginary halves of a composition will have equal *visual weight,* but the forms will be disposed unevenly. Figure 179 shows how figures in different poses can be arranged irregularly in the space of a stage to create a balanced composition. To understand asymmetrical balance, we can use a mathematical analogy. In arithmetic, 2 plus 2 equals 4, but so does 1 plus 3. Furthermore, 1 plus 3 equals 2 plus 2.

Translated into visual terms, we can see this principle operating in a mobile by Alexander Calder (Fig. 180). The large single form at right balances the eight lighter forms on the left, both physically and visually. If one were to set this piece in motion, it would eventually come to rest in perfect balance. The visual balance, in this instance, is successful because the actual weights are equal.

The chest of drawers shown in Figure 181 illustrates both symmetrical and asymmetrical balance. When it is closed, its balance is

left: 180. Alexander Calder. *Pomegranate.* 1949. Sheet aluminum and steel; height 6′, diameter 5′8″. Whitney Museum of American Art, New York.

right: 181. John Makepeace. Storage unit. 1972. Pillar of birch plywood and acrylic drawers cantilevered on a stainless-steel column, height 4′10½″. Courtesy the artist.

symmetrical, but the open position reveals an exciting asymmetry. If symmetry tends to suggest repose, asymmetry is characteristically active and dynamic. Interior designers use asymmetry to create a more energetic effect in a room, perhaps by balancing two chairs against a sofa or two small paintings against a large one. Two chairs may have the same visual weight as one sofa, but this will depend to some extent on their materials and color. We will discuss the latter factors more fully under the other types of balance.

Radial balance results when a number of elements point outward from a central core, like the spokes in a wheel. It is possibly most common in architecture, where the dome and other forms based on the circle have always been important (Fig. 182). Of course, radial balance is really an extension of symmetrical balance, but it is more complicated than bilateral symmetry.

Balance of Value

A balance of value simply means a balance between lights and darks. We see this in the hanging by Herman Scholten (Fig. 183), in which the tone graduates from dark through medium to white. Generally speaking, dark values have more visual weight than light ones. The designer can balance a small dark area against a larger light one and achieve equilibrium. This is not always the case, however. In Mark Rothko's *White and Greens in Blue* (Pl. 16, p. 126) the relatively small white rectangle has more visual weight than any element in the painting—more than enough to balance the two brooding dark rectangles above it. Here contrast is responsible for giving the light value such importance, since the remainder of the canvas is in dark values.

Architects work with values in balance when they design the projections and openings in a building. Any projection from the

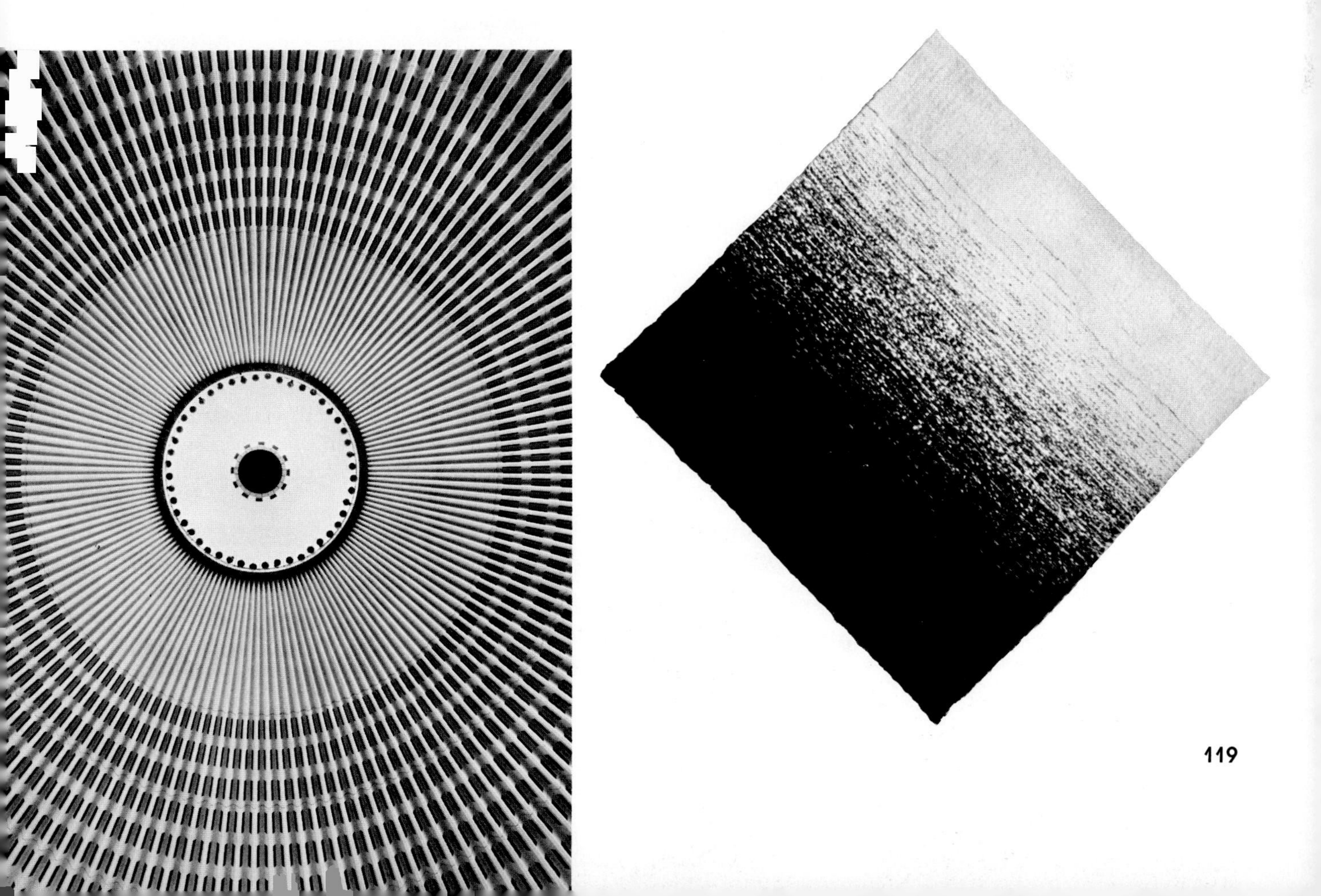

left: 182. Pier Luigi Nervi and Annibale Vitellozzi. Cupola and dome, Palazzo dello Sport, Rome. 1957.

right: 183. Herman Scholten. *Square Red-White.* 1974. Wool and sisal tapestry, 6′ square. Collection Benno Premsela, Amsterdam.

right: 184. Architect James Flynn's own residence on the Gulf of California.

below: 185. Arnaldo Pomodoro. *Traveler's Column.* 1965–66. Bronze, height 11′10″. Collection Nelson A. Rockefeller, New York.

exterior will create dark values of shadows, which can be balanced against light values where sunlight hits the smooth façade (Fig. 184). Similarly, light entering a building's interior through the windows will result in a pattern of light and dark values. The effect can be surprisingly rich when these values are sensitively balanced (Fig. 151).

Balance of Texture

As a rule—but again with exceptions—rough textures have more visual weight than smooth ones. Arnaldo Pomodoro's *Traveler's Column* (Fig. 185) is a pillar of smooth bronze interrupted by cutout sections of very coarse texture. The surface of the sculpture appears to be balanced, even though the rough areas occupy a relatively small portion.

Landscape architects are always working in textural balance. A large expanse of smooth lawn can be offset by just a few feathery shrubs, a single tree, or a flower bed (Fig. 560). As with value, the principle of contrast can operate to reverse these roles. A small area of smooth texture could actually balance a greater area of rough ones if the contrast is strong enough to direct our attention always to the smooth portion.

Balance of Color

Warm, advancing colors—red, yellow, and orange—tend to have more visual weight than the cooler blues, greens, and purples. A painter who is trying to balance a composition of many colors may find that a very small amount of red will be equal to a large field of blue and green. To some extent, perhaps, we are conditioned to this response because of nature's example. The overwhelming portion of our landscape is composed of cool colors—the blue of sky and water, the green of grass and trees. Bright, warm colors appear primarily as accents, as in birds and flowers. We expect red, for instance, to be either isolated (in a clump of flowers) or transitory (in the flush of sunset or the brief glory of fall colors). This may be why we attach greater visual weight to bright hues.

A composition of predominantly warm colors can, of course, be in perfect balance (Pl. 12, p. 107), as can one of all cool colors. However, when the designer mixes strongly contrasting hues in a single work, their visual weights must be taken into account if there is to be balance. A color—or for that matter, a shape or texture or value—that has much visual weight almost automatically becomes a focal point, a point of emphasis.

Emphasis

One of the most frustrating problems of the beginning designer is to create emphasis in a composition. A number of elements will have been assembled, with due consideration for unity, variety, and balance. Still, something is wrong. The different parts of the composition seem disjointed, even haphazard. A viewer's eye moves restlessly through the composition without ever coming to light on any particular place. No part of the work seems more important than any other. In short, there is no emphasis.

Certain types of designs have no special emphasis. They are repetitive and decorative by nature. Textiles offer a good example of this. However, many works of visual art benefit from having a *focal point* or points, some element that attracts the eye and perhaps that acts as a climax for other sections of the composition. In Jacques Louis David's *Death of Socrates* (Fig. 186) the focal point is patently obvious. Following the theme of the painting, emphasis is directed to the figure of Socrates himself. The compositional devices employed by David to create this emphasis are also obvious, but they are worth enumerating because they function less distinctly in many works of art.

First, the figure of Socrates is isolated, whereas all the others are grouped. Second, David has calculated his light source so that the brightest light falls on the philosopher. Three of his disciples (presumably the closest) are in slightly less bright illumination, the remainder in degrees of shadow. Third, the body of Socrates is rigidly vertical, whereas all nine of the men surrounding him lean toward him. (Compare Rubens' *Feast of Herod,* Fig. 67.) Fourth, the upraised finger is the highest point in the foreground, creating a focal point within a focal point. An upraised finger or hand—always an attention-getting device—usually focuses attention all by itself. Fifth, David has positioned Socrates almost at the center of the canvas. Sixth and

186. Jacques Louis David. *The Death of Socrates.* 1787. Oil on canvas, 4′3″ x 6′5¼″. Metropolitan Museum of Art, New York (Wolfe Fund, 1931).

187. Francisco Goya. *Executions of the Third of May, 1808.* 1814–15. Oil on canvas, 8′9″ x 13′4″. Prado, Madrid.

finally, a color reproduction of this painting would show that Socrates alone is dressed in white, whereas his followers are all garbed in cool tones of red, blue, and orange.

To sum up, then, the six focal devices in this painting are: *isolation, light, direction, height, position,* and *color.* In order to make a general statement about emphasis, we would add *size* (not evident in this work), because large size usually attracts the most attention. Strong *contrast* also creates a focal point. As suggested in Chapter 2, David's style was a thoroughly classic, intellectual one. His aim was utmost clarity. Few designers today would attempt a "textbook" composition

188. Henri Rousseau. *The Dream.* 1910. Oil on canvas, 6′10″ x 9′10½″. Museum of Modern Art, New York (gift of Nelson A. Rockefeller).

like this one, yet all the principles involved can be applied to other types of works.

All of the same emphatic devices operate in Goya's *Executions of the Third of May, 1808* (Fig. 187). The figure of the man about to be shot is isolated from his fellows and struck by the brightest light in the composition. He raises his arms in a crucifixion pose, which is an automatic center of attention. The soldier's rifles, with fixed bayonets, point directly to him, and the angle of their bodies further directs the viewer's eye toward the victim. Here the focal point—the condemned man—is off center, but his strong form is balanced by the heavy group of figures at right.

Any element that contrasts with the rest of a composition will automatically become the major focal point. A nude among clothed figures rivets attention, as would a clothed figure among nudes, a 20th-century costume among togas, a human among animals (Fig. 188).

Many compositions depend on several focal points to provide emphasis. In Tom Wesselmann's *Smoker #8* (Fig. 189) a series of focal points appear in all the dark (actually blood red) areas—lips, fingernails, glowing cigarette end. The major focus is unquestionably the lips, not only because of their color but because they jut out to the side of the shaped canvas. This extension into space acts as a pointing device, a way of leading the eye into the composition and across it to the cigarette. The eye has a tendency to swing from the lips to the cigarette end, back and forth in a sweeping curve. The work therefore shows a sense of rhythm in its emphasis.

190. The rhythm of a drumbeat can be interpreted visually as a series of dots. Dots of different sizes indicate complex rhythms and points of emphasis.

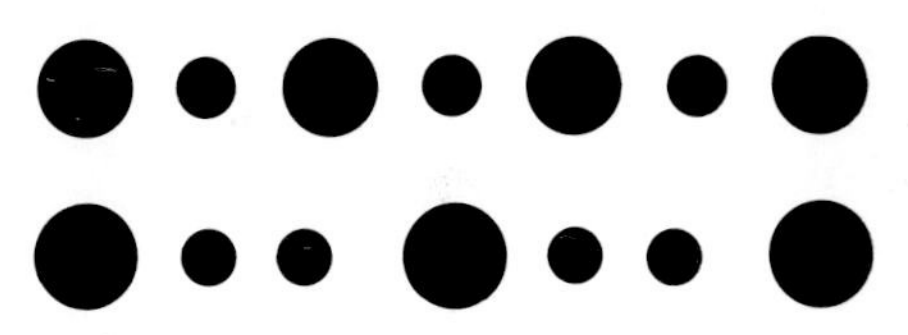

Rhythm

Rhythm is a regular pulsation, like the beating of the heart or a drum beat. Figure 190 shows a visual translation of three different patterns, the first consisting of all regular pulsations, the other two having evenly spaced points of emphasis. One could easily tap out these patterns with a drumstick or pencil, giving more intensity to the stronger beats—the larger dots.

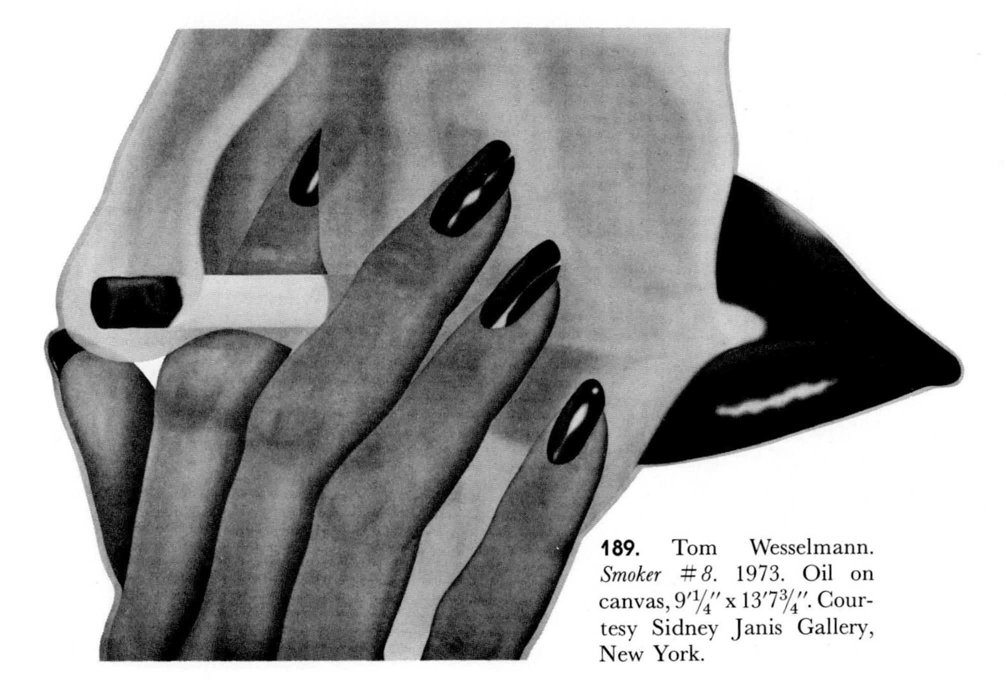

189. Tom Wesselmann. *Smoker #8*. 1973. Oil on canvas, 9′1/4″ x 13′7 3/4″. Courtesy Sidney Janis Gallery, New York.

191. José Clemente Orozco. *Zapatistas.* 1931. Oil on canvas, 3′9″ x 4′7″. Museum of Modern Art, New York.

Some contemporary artists work to the accompaniment of music in the hope that the rhythmic sounds will be transmuted into the visible forms of their work. Others express a natural sense of rhythm without conscious effort, much as rhythm is expressed naturally by a dancer. In creating a visual design the artist may develop a *physical* rhythm (Fig. 381) in the application of brush strokes, the impact of hammer on chisel, and so forth. On the other hand, the rhythms may be purely *visual* and deliberately introduced into the composition to provide an impression of flow and unity.

In José Clemente Orozco's *Zapatistas* (Fig. 191) the diagonal figures in the lower half of the composition establish a very strong visual rhythm, echoed by the horse's head and portions of the landscape. The predominant movement is from lower right to upper left, but a strong counterrhythm leads back to the right side. This is maintained by the action of the swords and hats. The imagery seems particularly evocative, since the visual rhythms suggest the marching beat of the soldiers. One could almost count out the rhythm in this painting just as one does the drumbeat pattern in Figure 190.

Swirling, curved rhythms mark William Blake's *Michael Binding Satan* (Fig. 192). Here the strongest rhythm is found in Michael's arched body, and this is directly opposed by the great coil of the serpent for an extremely dynamic composition. Smaller curves carry through the basic rhythm—the pattern of scales on Satan, the curling hair of Michael, the defined musculature. So intense are these rhythms that the figures seem almost to leap off the paper and continue their frenzied contest.

Both of the works just discussed show readily identifiable rhythms. In many compositions, however, this pulsation may be more subtle.

Plate 15. Claude Monet. *Water-Lilies,* detail. c. 1916. Oil on canvas, 6′6¾″ square. Kunsthaus, Zurich. © 1976, copyright by Cosmopress, Geneva.

Plate 16. Mark Rothko. *White and Greens in Blue.* 1957.
Oil on canvas, 8′6″ x 6′10″. Private collection.

Arshile Gorky's *The Liver is the Cock's Comb* (Fig. 193) has a definite rhythmic coherence in its shapes, values, and direction of forms. For example, there is a regular pattern of strong, dark verticals moving across the canvas. This rhythm does not leap to the eye as it does in the Orozco painting. Instead, we become aware of it as we study the composition, allowing our eyes to search back and forth.

Balance, emphasis, and rhythm are closely related principles. Each contributes to the other two. Both emphasis and rhythm foster an underlying balance, and focal points within a rhythm enliven the rhythm, just as the accented drum beats do. These principles which are basic to existence cannot help but find expression in human creations.

left: 192. William Blake. *Michael Binding Satan.* c. 1805. Watercolor, $14\frac{1}{4} \times 12\frac{13}{16}$″. Fogg Art Museum, Cambridge, Mass.

below: 193. Arshile Gorky. *The Liver Is the Cock's Comb.* 1944. Oil on canvas, 6′ x 8′2″. Albright-Knox Art Gallery, Buffalo, N.Y.

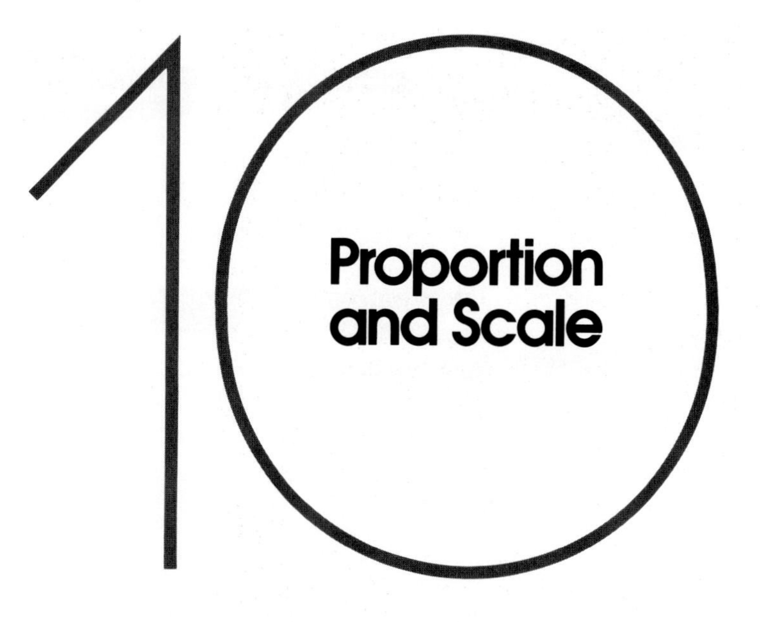

10 Proportion and Scale

Proportion and scale are closely associated principles of design. Both deal with the relative size of things. *Proportion,* however, usually refers to size relationships within a composition, whereas *scale* indicates size in comparison to some constant, such as the size of the human body or the size that something "ought to be." One illustration may help to clarify this difference.

The leather chair in Figure 194 is *in proportion* to the room it occupies. Since the room itself is large, two-story, and virtually open to the outdoors, a small or delicate chair might be dwarfed in such a space. The oversize piece seems in fitting proportion to the generous surroundings. However, considered as a receptacle for the human body the chair is very *large scale* indeed, even as contrasted to the other furniture in the room. And seen as a baseball glove, this piece has absolutely enormous scale!

Of course, since size is a factor in both proportion and scale, the two can often overlap. Something that is too large to be in satisfying proportion to its surroundings might also be large scale, or the reverse. We will separate proportion and scale for individual study, with the knowledge that they may be interwoven in any design.

left: 194. An enormous baseball-glove chair was selected by interior designer Ann Hartman for a home in the suburbs of Washington D.C., designed by the architectural firm of Hartman-Cox.

below: 195. René Magritte. *La Folie des Grandeurs.* 1961. Private Collection.

Proportion

Proportion usually involves some ideal, something the designer should strive for. Things that are "out of proportion" always jar to some degree, whether we are speaking of a tiny painting hung on a broad expanse of wall, a huge pattern on a dress for a diminutive woman, or an overreaction to an imagined verbal insult. This is not to say that disproportion in a design is necessarily "bad." Sometimes an artist will deliberately vary the proportions in a composition to call attention to something or create impact (Fig. 195).

196. Ictinus and Callicrates. The Parthenon, Athens. 447–438 B.C.

The most elaborate proportional system ever devised was the ancient Greeks' *golden section,* which controlled relative sizes in architecture, sculpture, and nearly every other endeavor. The proportions of a classical Greek temple, for example, were rigidly prescribed in a formula that can be stated mathematically as $a:b = b:(a + b)$. Thus, if a is the width of a temple and b the length, the relationship between the two sides becomes apparent. Similar rules governed the height of the temple, the distance between columns, and so forth. When we look at a Greek temple today, even without being aware of the formula, we sense that its proportions are somehow supremely "right," totally satisfying (Fig. 196). The same mean rectangle that determined the floor plan of the temple has been found to circumscribe Greek vases and sculpture as well.

For today's designer, a framework like the golden section would seem unnaturally rigid. Satisfactory proportions are more likely to be

197. In graphic design, many different proportions of shape to space may be effective.

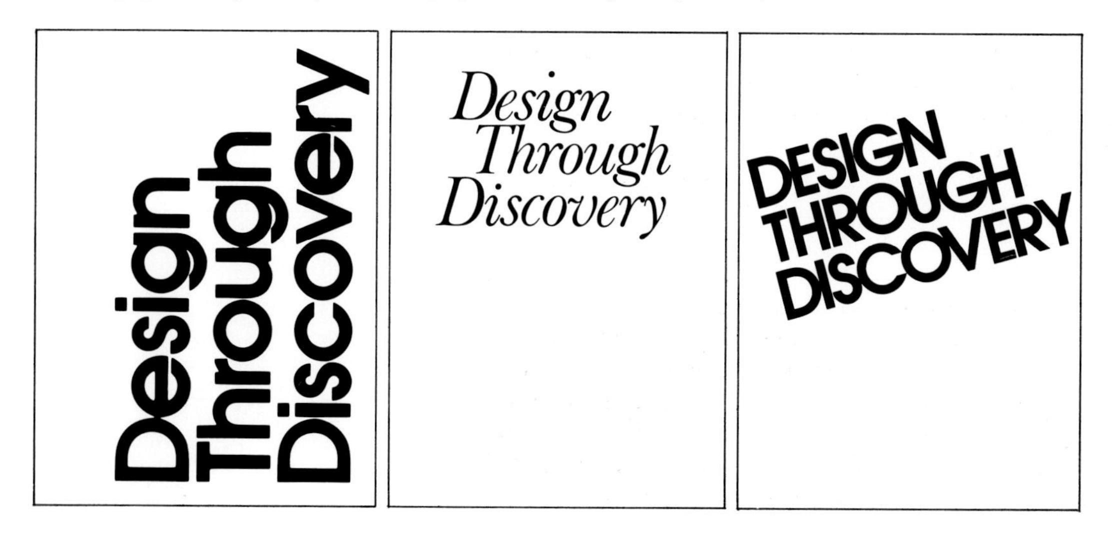

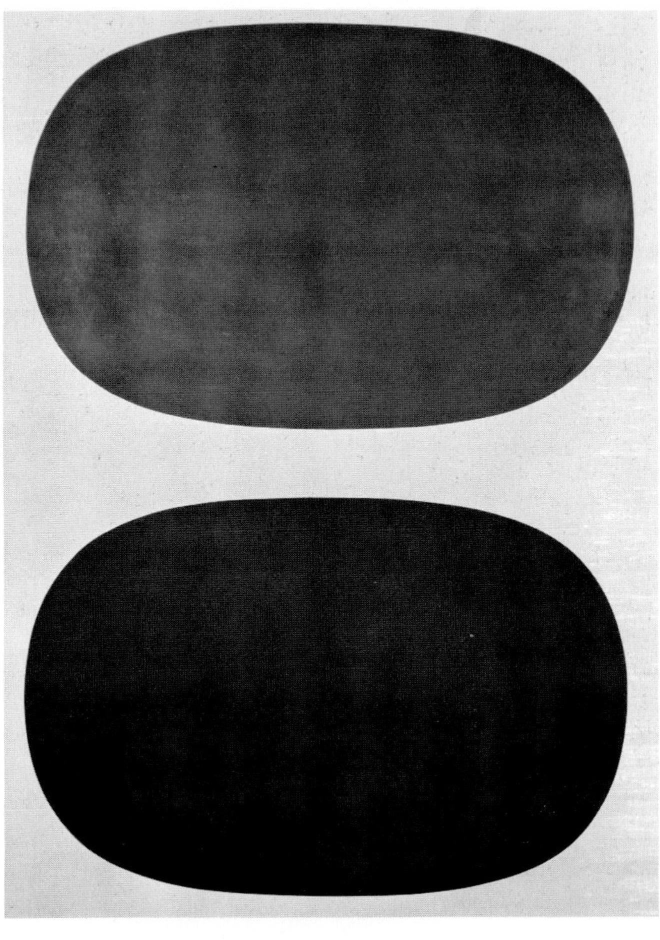

left: 198. Jasper Johns. *Target with Four Faces.* 1955. Encaustic on newspaper, on canvas, 26″ square; plaster faces in wood frame, 3¾″ x 26″. Museum of Modern Art, New York (gift of Mr. and Mrs. Robert C. Scull).

above: 199. Ellsworth Kelly. *Red, White, and Blue.* 1961. Oil on canvas, 7′4″ x 5′6″. Whitney Museum of American Art, New York.

worked out by trial and error, by "feel." Furthermore, no contemporary artist would feel obliged to be limited to one "correct" set of proportions, for many different proportional relationships might work, depending upon the intended effect. To return to our earlier example of the words "Design Through Discovery" printed on a book page, we see from Figure 197 that several variations in the proportion of type (shape) to page could be effective.

The success of a painting by Mondrian or by Albers depends largely upon the elegant proportional relationships between the internal rectangles and the rectangle of the canvas (Figs. 12, 114). Many times as well, proportion will be a matter of repetition. In Jasper Johns' *Target* (Fig. 198) one large circular motif dominates the field, establishing a satisfactory proportional relationship to the square. Ellsworth Kelly's *Red, White, and Blue* (Fig. 199) arranges two rounded forms in the rectangular format of the canvas, again in effective

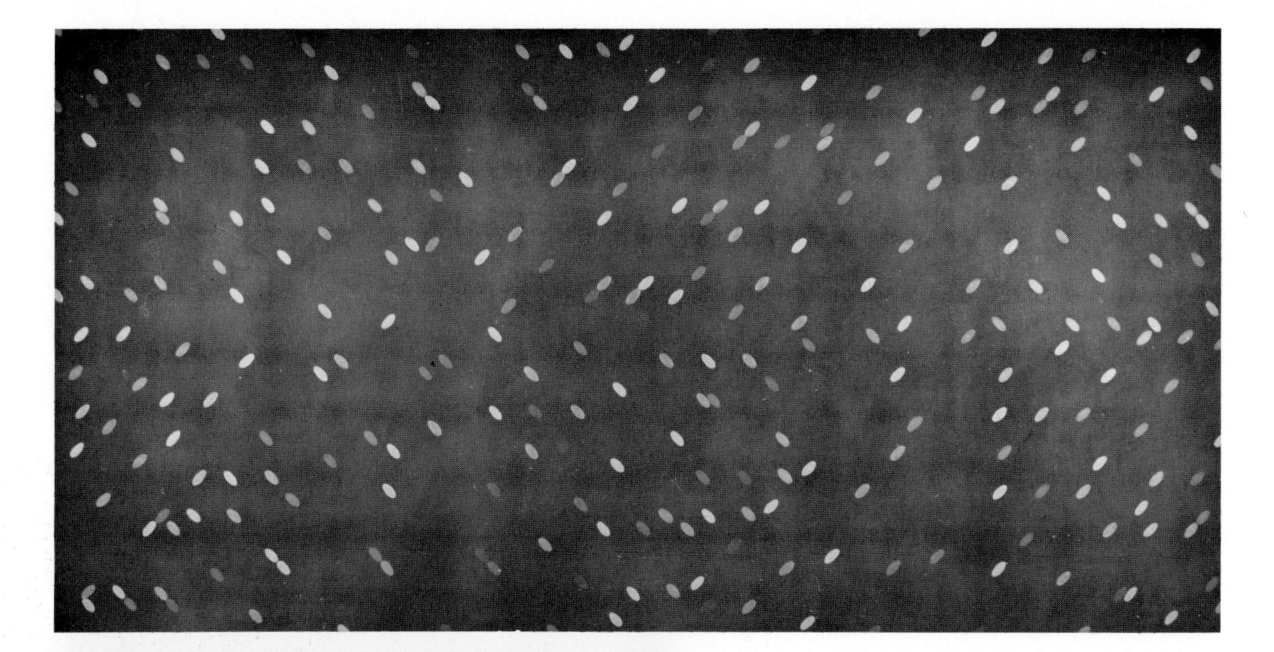

above: 200. Larry Poons. *Away Out on the Mountain.* 1965. Acrylic on canvas, 6 x 12′. Allen Art Museum, Oberlin, Ohio.

left: 201. Small-scale furniture seems appropriate for a tiny room in a house designed by Raymond Zambrano.

proportion. But the rounded shapes in Larry Poons' painting (Fig. 200) have been reduced to mere dots. Obviously, if only one or a few dots had appeared on the canvas, the result would have been ludicrous. The proportion is satisfied by repetition of shapes.

We have already seen how large, even oversize furniture works in proportion to a large room (Fig. 194). It is interesting to compare the dynamics that operate in a very small room, like the one in Figure 201.

Here the room is little more than a modified porch, and its tiny size could be an interior designer's nightmare. But a clever arrangement of very small elements—in other words, a keen proportional sense—have made it seem cozy and welcoming. A compact sofa, fragile chair and table, some delicate plants—all work together with the room's dimensions. There is even a generous amount of space left over, so that the elements do not seem crowded. It might be instructive to consider other proportional arrangements for this room. For example, if it did not need to be used as a sitting room, one huge plant—and nothing else whatever—could have completed the design.

Proportion functions through all aspects of design. A pendant composed of several semiprecious stones illustrates this principle in jewelry design (Fig. 202). Here the designer clearly wanted to focus attention on the one large, central stone. But the other stones are not mere fillers. Instead, their proportions are sensitively related to the principal stone and to the square format in which all are contained. The main round stone develops naturally into smaller, oval stones, which make a transition to the frame.

Figure 203 shows an instance in which proportion was deliberately adjusted for the sake of content. In this mosaic all the figures are in proportion to one another except the figures of Christ and two angels, which are disproportionately large. The great size is an indication of their importance. The image of Christ here seems, quite literally, "larger than life," as the artist no doubt thought appropriate. This illustration only serves to show that proportion is correct when it fulfills the aesthetic needs of the designer.

above: 202. Joseph Hoffmann, with Wiener Werkstätte, Vienna. *Jugendstil Pendant.* Silver and semiprecious stones, height $1\frac{11}{16}$". German National Museum, Nuremberg.

left: 203. *Last Judgment,* mosaic. 12th century. West wall, Cathedral at Torcella, Venice.

left: 204. Stone images, 17th century or earlier. Height c. 30′. Located outside crater of Rano Raraku, Easter Island.

below left: 205. Claes Oldenburg. *Clothespin.* 1976. Cor-Ten steel, height 45′. Centre Square, Philadelphia.

below right: 206. Clement Meadmore. *Upstart.* 1967. Welded Cor-Ten steel, height 20′6″. (Fabricated at Lippincott, Inc., New Haven, Conn.) Collection Mrs. Harry Lynde Bradley, Milwaukee, Wis.

Scale

The heads shown in Figure 204 are among thousands of similar carvings found on Easter Island in the South Pacific. These statues were first discovered in 1722 and were described in detail by Captain Cook when he visited the island in 1774. Centuries of drifting silt have buried many of them up to their necks, but they are actually full

207. Pyramid of Cheops. c. 2570 B.C. Height c. 450′ (formerly 480′). Giza, Egypt. Photographed from the pyramid of Chephren.

figures—some over 30 feet high. Who carved the megaliths and when and why—all these questions remain unanswered. Perhaps most fascinating is the problem of how a tribe with only primitive stone tools managed to erect such heavy structures. One romantic theory suggests a tribe of giants who planned the images in their own likeness, or in other words, in what to them was natural scale. A more likely explanation, however, assumes that these are ancestor images, elevated to superhuman scale by death. At the time of Captain Cook's voyage, most of the figures were standing upright, but later the inhabitants of the island toppled all those that were not buried. Again, the reasons for this are not clear. In any event, the sheer size of the Easter Island carvings, together with their stark abstraction of feature, makes them remarkable.

Scale, then, as was mentioned at the beginning of the chapter, is conceived in terms of some standard. The Easter Island figures are in very large scale because, although they are based on the human body, they are many times larger. We find a similar principle operating in Claes Oldenburg's *Clothespin* (Fig. 205). The unexpected material—Cor-Ten steel—would not alone be sufficient to rivet our attention on this piece. However, its outlandish scale requires the viewer to see this form in a completely new light, to come to terms with it on a new basis. By taking familiar forms and making them unfamiliar, Oldenburg forces us to look with an unjaded eye. He accomplishes this mainly through scale.

We might consider Clement Meadmore's *Upstart* to be aptly named, because its monumental scale challenges both the trees around it and the people who come to perch on it (Fig. 206). By its huge size, solid mass, and upward thrust this work seems to be saying, "Here I am! You cannot ignore me. Take me for what I am."

In architecture scale determines to a large extent how we feel about a building and how we feel when inside it. The great Christian cathedrals all are built on gigantic scale, so that they overpower us, giving a sense of awe and majesty. Similarly, the pyramids of the Egyptians (Fig. 207) were meant to overwhelm, to show the greatness of the pharaohs buried within them and stand as monuments for all time. Even the individual stones of the pyramids are of such scale that they make humans look like flies crawling on the outside. While the pyramids remain constant in scale—they are huge in terms of the human body or of architecture in general—their proportion may be a matter of viewpoint. The photograph in Figure 207, showing the great pyramid of Cheops, was taken from the adjacent pyramid of Chephren. Both pyramids are roughly the same height—about 450 feet. Because of the unusual photographic angle, as well as the telescoping properties of the camera, the mighty Cheops pyramid looks like a child's toy. We imagine that the man standing in the foreground could simply reach out and pat the pyramid on its top.

The temples and other public buildings designed by the ancient Greeks, such as the Parthenon (Fig. 196), seem to be very large scale and majestic. However, the visitor standing inside one of these structures does not feel overwhelmed. The Parthenon is built on a human scale, but a *grand* human scale. It thus symbolizes the aspirations of the human spirit to greatness, an elevation of mortals to immortality.

In contrast to the Greek temples, the architecture planned by the Nazi regime in Germany during the late 1930s had an enormous, overpowering scale (Fig. 208). Hitler assigned his architect, Albert Speer, the task of creating amphitheaters and other monumental public structures that would be suitable for the "master race" and the master empire that he envisioned. The hundreds of thousands of people who could be assembled in these colossal enclosures were to feel, simultaneously, *insignificance* as individuals and *greatness* as a group. The architecture thus participated in Hitler's program of uniting the people in mass fervor for conquest.

Paul Strand's photograph *Wall Street, New York* (Fig. 209) exploits the power of monumental architecture to intimidate people. Here the figures walking along seem insignificant beside the heavy concrete building that symbolizes financial power. Metaphorically, Strand's "little people" seem at the mercy of the politico-industrial establishment that rules their lives. We can see that, if the photograph had been composed differently, focusing on a small group of people perhaps, this effect would have been lost. By pulling his camera back, the photographer has given us the insight of scale.

Thus far we have talked about scale in terms of very large size, but many people are fascinated with miniaturization. At one time, there was a craze for engraving documents on the head of a pin—the Lord's Prayer or *Gettysburg Address,* for example. To read the words one needed a strong magnifying glass.

While not so drastic, the interest in doll houses and doll furniture shares this pleasure in the miniature. Few people can resist the charm of an object that is perfect in every way yet tiny in scale. Ceramist

208. Albert Speer. Model for a proposed reconstruction of Berlin. c. 1940. The domed hall of the secular cathedral was to have been seven times larger than the dome of St. Peter's in Rome. To the left of the cathedral in this photograph is the Führerpalast, meant to be seventy times the size of Bismarck's Chancellery.

209. Paul Strand. *Wall Street, New York.* 1915. Photograph.

David Furman has created a series of miniature environments in clay based on his own home and studio, always featuring his dog Molly (Fig. 210). The peaceful image of a dog curled up on a rug gives a warm atmosphere to the whole composition. Part of our delight in minuscule objects lies in the leisurely investigation of details. A very large work comes at us all at once, forcing us to take it in at a gulp. But a tiny object encourages us to pore over it, to examine it carefully.

It should be clear from these examples that we are made aware of scale primarily when it is distorted. The zany creations of Red Grooms, collectively known as *Ruckus Manhattan,* bring monuments of the New York landscape down to size and then decorate them with outlandish details. The Woolworth Building (Fig. 211; compare Fig. 22) emerges as a fantastic wedding cake, which just happens to

210. David Furman. *In the Den with Molly,* detail. 1974–75. Earthenware, 10 x 13 x 7″. Courtesy the artist.

have a dragon curling around it. The Brooklyn Bridge (Fig. 212; compare Fig. 263) seems to have been melted all out of shape. Grooms' inventions poke gentle fun at their full-scale originals while at the same time delighting the viewer in their whimsy.

Normal scale rarely attracts our attention. The person who is thrust into a too-small environment feels clumsy and overblown (Fig. 213), while large-scale surroundings can make the same person feel puny. Similarly, our interest is directed to objects that are unexpectedly out of scale, either large or small. The control of scale, therefore, enables the designer to create immediate impact.

above left: 211. Red Grooms. *Woolworth Building,* from *Ruckus Manhattan.* 1975–76. Mixed media, height 15′. Courtesy Marlborough Gallery, New York.

above right: 212. Red Grooms. *The Brooklyn Bridge,* from *Ruckus Manhattan.* 1975–76. Steel, 15′ x 33′ x 14′6″. Courtesy Marlborough Gallery, New York.

right: 213. John Tenniel. *Alice After Taking the Magic Potion,* illustration from *Alice in Wonderland* by Lewis Carroll, written in 1865. (New York: Grosset and Dunlap, Inc., 1946)

11 Symbolism

A symbol, in design terms, is anything that stands for something else. Usually, a symbol is a simplified image that, because of certain associations in the viewer's mind, represents a more complex idea or system. For example, the cross represents Christianity, the Star of David Judaism, the eagle with olive branch and arrows the United States of America.

As noted in Chapter 3, the lines that form letters, words, or musical notes are symbols. In fact, any drawing or painting could be considered a symbol. The drawing of a horse is not a horse but the representation of one. It stands for a horse, which makes it a symbol. In this chapter, however, we shall concern ourselves with deliberate visual images that convey certain ideas; the images may or may not be directly related to the form of what they represent.

Symbolism is a powerful tool for the designer. It permits the communication of enormously complicated, often abstract ideas with just a few lines or shapes. A design that makes use of symbols—whether they are universal, general, or very personal—becomes much the richer in its implications. Symbols provide a convenient "shorthand" in the artist's repertoire.

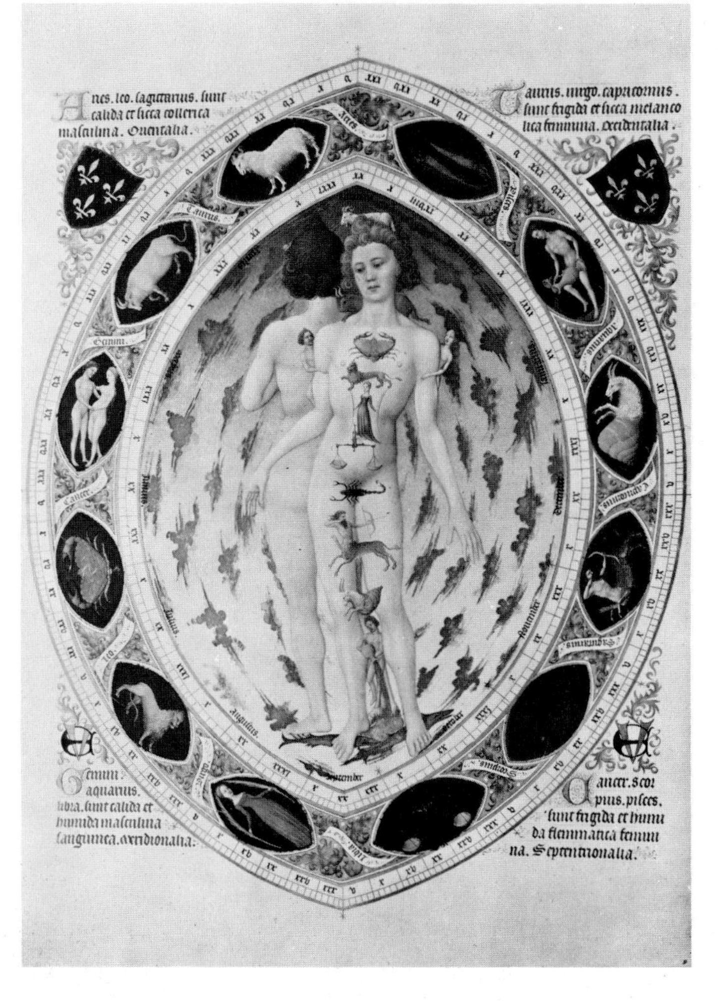

214. *Zodiac Man* designed for the Duc de Berry. 1413–16. Manuscript illumination, $10\frac{3}{16} \times 7\frac{3}{8}''$. Condé Museum, Chantilly.

A few symbols can be considered virtually universal. Nearly everyone, the world over, would identify a crescent as the moon. Other symbols are general to the culture in which one lives, such as the Stars and Stripes. Still others must be studied to be understood. In this group would fall the entire network of Freudian dream symbolism. Finally, the artist can invent personal symbols that become significant in one particular work or in the context of a life's work. Examples of all these forms will be found in this chapter.

The topic of symbolism is almost overwhelming in its scope. Each of the subheadings below could be the subject of an entire book. However, since it is impossible for us to cover the subject fully here, perhaps a few examples will show the importance of visual symbols to the designer.

Cosmic Symbols

No doubt the best known of cosmic symbols are the signs of the Zodiac (Fig. 214). The Zodiac is an imaginary belt in the heavens, 16 degrees wide, that includes the paths of the moon and all the principal planets, with the sun's path as the center line. It was originally plotted by the Chaldeans in the 2nd century B.C. with twelve divisions, each of which was given a symbol named for a constellation within the zodiacal belt. Through the centuries these signs have represented forces believed to govern not only the movement of bodies in the heavens but, through complex systems and movements, the behavior of human beings on earth. The visual images of these signs—the crab, the bull, the twins, and so forth—have taken on strong associations with regard to the temperaments of people born under the respective signs. Found in both Oriental and Western contexts, the Zodiac appears in numberless works of art that cut across cultural lines of all periods.

In Europe of the Middle Ages and early Renaissance, human behavior was thought to be dependent on a balance or imbalance of the four temperaments or humours: gall, phlegm, choler, and blood. It was believed that each of these substances existed in every human body, but if one came to dominate, the individual would have a distorted personality and lapse into sin. An engraving by the 16th-century German master Albrecht Dürer includes symbols of all four humours.

In Dürer's *Fall of Man* (Fig. 215), which shows Adam and Eve's temptation in the Garden of Eden, nearly everything in the composition symbolized something to the learned viewers of the time. The elk stands for an excess of gall, which leads to melancholy, despair, and greed. The ox is extreme phlegm, causing gluttony and laziness. Excessive choler is found in the person of the cat, who therefore represents cruelty, pride, and anger. Finally, the rabbit, emblem of blood, indicates sensuality and sins of the flesh. Dürer here is telling us that all of these sins emerged from Adam and Eve's fall from grace.

215. Albrecht Dürer. *Fall of Man.* 1504. Engraving, $9\frac{7}{8} \times 7\frac{5}{8}''$. Metropolitan Museum of Art, New York (Fletcher Fund, 1919).

216. Yin-yang symbol.

We could go on to describe the symbolism in this work with much greater detail. Nothing is introduced without reason. It is important for the designer to realize that we can appreciate this work without understanding its symbolic content. At face value, *The Fall of Man* remains a superb work of composition and draftsmanship. The lush, beautifully drawn bodies of Adam and Eve could provide study for generations of artists. Yet how much richer is our experience when we see all the hidden meanings in the work, how much more fully we can appreciate it. Symbols have the power to intensify a design by providing philosophical content.

In the Chinese cosmic system all qualities are divided into *yang,* the masculine (light, heat, dryness) and *yin,* the feminine (dark, cold, wetness). An ideal can be achieved only when yin and yang balance to complement each other (Fig. 216). Symbols of the yang and yin principles occur throughout Chinese design and indeed Chinese life. Even without knowing the philosophy behind this image, however, we sense a great deal by looking at it. We see that the two halves are the reverse of each other, that they are equal, and that the two together create balance and harmony. This symbol, then, operates for the viewer on different levels, depending upon the degree of knowledge.

Magical Symbols

Magical symbols deal with the most vital aspects of life—food, shelter, procreation, and the preservation of life itself. Primitive peoples drew pictures or fashioned masks in the image of animals they hunted to ensure success in the kill (Fig. 217). They made symbols of the mighty gods who controlled climate in the hope they could thus contain the elements. For example, rain is a tremendously powerful force. If one could personify it in a symbol (the Rain God) and hold that symbol in a tight enclosure, one could hope to control rain.

Tribal masks are among the strongest magical symbols in primitive art. Often their makers will endow them with great ferocity to frighten the enemies of the wearer. This element of warlike strength becomes even more symbolic when the masks are worn in the dance, either to anticipate or to commemorate victory in battle. Other masks, such as the Bamileke example in Figure 218, indicate the status of the wearer.

left: 217. *Bison,* prehistoric cave painting. c. 15,000–10,000 B.C. Pigment on natural rock. "Salon Noir," Niaux Cave, Ariège, France.

right: 218. Ceremonial mask made by the Bagam Chiefdom of the Bamileke tribe, Cameroon Grasslands, Africa. Wood, height 28″. Metropolitan Museum of Art, New York (Louis V. Bell Fund, 1971).

Plate 17. Cuna Indian *mola.* c. 1950–70. Appliqué fabric. Courtesy Michèle Herling, Quadrangle Galleries, Dallas.

Plate 18. Edvard Munch. *The Dance of Life.* 1900. Oil on canvas, 4′1 7/16″ x 6′2 15/16″. National Gallery, Oslo.

right: Plate 19. James Ensor. *Self-Portrait with Masks.* 1899. Oil on canvas, 46½ x 32½″. Collection Mme. C. Jussiant, Antwerp.

below: Plate 20. Tommy Simpson. *Blossoming.* 1968. Coffee table in butternut wood, 24 x 42 x 33″. Courtesy the artist.

In this instance the snakes on the crown are a royal symbol, which is fitting because this mask would have been used in the dance for installation of a new chief. More generally in Africa, the snake acted as a fertility symbol, since it was considered to be guardian of the waters. (It is interesting to compare this symbolism to Christian art, in which the snake always represents evil.)

Fertility was an overriding concern for primitive peoples. In order to survive they required both abundance in the crops and great numbers of children. Phallic images abound in primitive art, and the great size of these images suggests not so much sexual prowess as power in procreation. The ancestor poles in Figure 219, with their delicate openwork tracery, seem at first to be just ornate designs carved for their inherent beauty. Actually, the carved openwork symbolizes semen and hence the generative powers of sperm. Taken at face value, these figures are striking and beautiful, but again, familiarity with their symbolism enhances our appreciation of the work.

Many times symbols evolve and become disassociated from their original applications. This is true of the *mola,* an art form practiced by the Cuna Indians of the San Blas Islands off the coast of Panama (Pl. 17, p. 143). Designs used in the mola are an outgrowth of body painting originally done by this group. Until about a hundred years ago, these Indians used direct body painting as a means of making the tribesmen invisible to evil spirits. It is not clear when or why the transition was made, but eventually the designs were transferred to cloth, which is worn as a sort of blouse. The present mola panel consists of several layers of cloth of different colors stitched together, with designs created by cutting shapes from the upper layers to expose the colors underneath—usually red, orange, and black. On the top layer several more thicknesses of cloth are applied (or appliquéd) with a variety of stitches to lend further richness to the surface. The designs derive from flowers, trees, fruit, animals, and the native religion. With an intuitive sense of balance and unity, the designer will choose a central theme and cover all the surrounding area with intricate, harmonious detail.

above: 219. Ancestor poles, from the Asmat tribe, New Guinea. Wood, paint, and fiber; height c. 11′.

Symbols can evolve not only in their outward application but in their basic meaning. The Christmas tree is the descendant of a custom thought to have originated among the Romans of pre-Christian times. The tree in this context was a fertility symbol, both a phallic form and an emblem of plenty, with fruits and nuts decorating it. Germanic people later adapted it as a symbol of the feast surrounding the birth of Christ, associating it with the gifts brought by the Magi.

Religious Symbols

Beyond doubt two of the strongest religious symbolic systems are those of Christianity and Judaism. The cross, the Star of David, and the menorah are simple, perfect designs that lend themselves to abstraction or elaboration (Fig. 220). Moreover, both carry an enormous weight of association—traditions, theology, scripture, and history.

220. Tombstone menorah. A.D. 2nd–3rd century. Marble, engraved and inscribed, with traces of paint. Found in catacomb of Vigna Randanini, Rome. Jewish Museum, New York (gift of Henry and Lucy Moses Fund, Inc.).

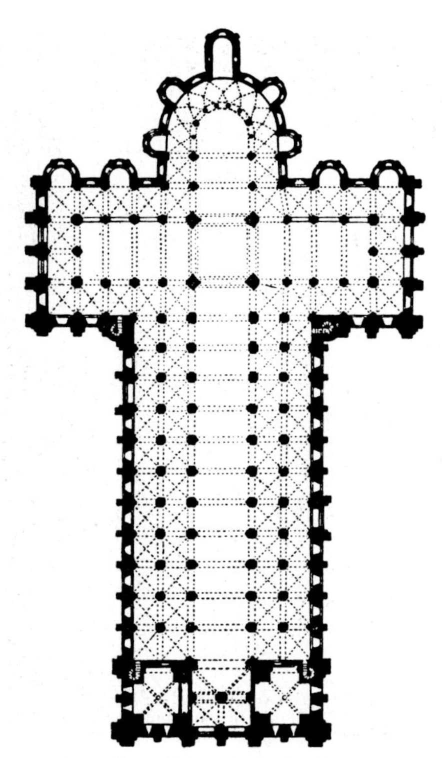

221. Plan, Church of St. Sernin, Toulouse. c. 1120.

222. Variations on the cross motif.

The cross permeates all areas of Christian practice. Most grand churches and cathedrals are built on a cross plan, so that the structure itself becomes a huge architectural symbol. We can see this clearly in the ground plan of the Church of St. Sernin in Toulouse (Fig. 221). The long nave or main section, terminating in the rounded apse, is cut by a transverse section, literally the "crossing." In later churches the architecture grew more elaborate, with chapels branching out from the nave, so that the cross form is not so easy to see. However, a great many churches are built on this plan today.

Besides architectural structure, of course, crosses appear in hundreds of different forms—as jewelry, in illuminated manuscripts, in paintings and sculpture. Figure 222 illustrates a few of the thousands of decorative cross designs that have recurred in art throughout the Christian era.

It may be enlightening to contrast some of the symbolism involved in two great religions, to see how they overlap or differ. A particularly interesting comparison can be made between an 11th-century image of the Amida Buddha and a Giotto painting of Christ in the Last Judgment (Figs. 223, 224). There are many different manifestations or versions of the Buddha. This one, the Amida Buddha, is the kindliest and most approachable. Here he is portrayed in the *Raigo* or descent from heaven, when the Buddha comes forward to welcome a worthy dead soul into his Western paradise. A similar event takes place in the Last Judgment, which occurs after the end of the world. Christ sits in judgment and triumph, separating the faithful who will be taken into heaven from those damned to hell for eternity.

Both Buddha and Christ are isolated from their compositional backgrounds by a rounded halo, and each further has a halo directly around his head. The Buddha sits in the traditional yoga meditation pose, which is one of his symbolic attributes. Buddha's hands usually are depicted in one of several ritual *mudras,* or gestures. The one shown in this painting, with thumb and forefinger touching, signifies the Wheel of Learning. Christ's hands, by contrast, are held in positions symbolic of the Last Judgment. His right hand is outstretched to welcome the faithful souls into heaven (the faithful always being on the right); the left hand, palm backward, seems to be casting away the damned.

The Buddha is surrounded by 25 Bodhisattvas, which are a kind of sub-Buddha—not quite deity, not quite angel. Behind and around the Bodhisattvas are angels playing musical instruments, indications of the lush pleasures to be found in the Western Paradise. Christ, as is usual in Last Judgment scenes, is flanked by his twelve Apostles. Legions of angels, some playing trumpets, gather about him and help to conduct the saints into Paradise.

One important difference exists between these two visions. In the Giotto *Last Judgment* we see in the lower right corner an image of hell, with Satan ready to torment the damned souls. But no suggestion of punishment mars the perfect tranquility and bliss of Amida's Western Paradise.

The symbolic details we have listed in these two paintings, the story behind the work of art, is called its *iconography.* In the same way, the four humours portrayed in the Dürer work (Fig. 215) make up part of its iconography. In order to understand fully any work of religious art, it is necessary to be familiar with its underlying iconography—in particular, the religious symbolism involved.

top: 223. *Amida Raigo Triptych.* Japanese, late 11th century (Heian Period). Color on silk, height 6′11″. Koyasan Museum, Wakayama.

right: 224. Giotto. *Last Judgment.* 1305–06. Fresco. Arena Chapel, Padua.

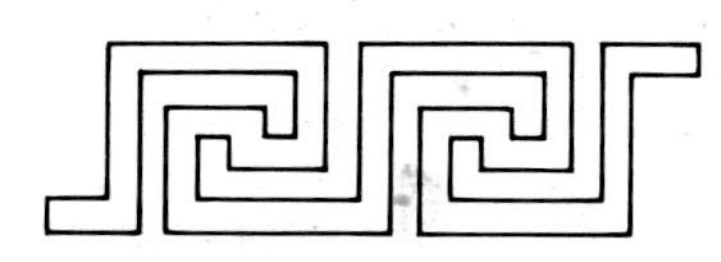

225. Traditional motifs: spiral, maze, key, acanthus leaf.

Traditional Patterns

There are a great many traditional patterns that have occurred over and over in the history of art since ancient times. Some only barely qualify as symbols, since they either have no particular meaning or have meanings subject to change. For example, the swastika is a very old sign that has appeared in Egypt, China, Persia, Crete, and throughout prehistoric Europe. It remained for the Nazis in the late 1930s and early 1940s to attach a special ugly meaning to the sign. Most of these patterns, however, no doubt found such widespread popularity because of their decorative, repetitive possibilities. Figure 225 illustrates a few of the most common—the spiral, the maze, the key, and the acanthus leaf. One image that appears in many parts of the world consists of paired animals, often winged griffins or lions, around a pillar or tree of life (Fig. 226). The balance and symmetry of this type of composition can lend itself to many interpretations.

Pure geometric forms also function as traditional patterns. In Christian symbolism the triangle represents the Trinity, with the three points standing for the Father, Son, and Holy Spirit. A circle generally symbolizes a wholeness, a totality. King Arthur and his knights met at a round table, and the Round Table of Camelot has come to mean a vision of perfect ideals, a unity of goodness (Fig. 227).

The great value of traditional patterns for the designer is that one can invent one's own symbolism to fit them. Paired animals around a tree can represent any kind of duality. A maze could be endless search, a spiral continuing ascent or descent. Images formed within a circle nearly always suggest some coherent whole. Depending upon the context, one can easily attach personal significance to these motifs.

Status Symbols

The term "status symbol" has gotten a bad name in recent years, implying as it often does the struggle to impress others with material possessions. Yet very real status symbols have existed from ancient times. These symbols do precisely what they say—they indicate the exact status or station in life of the owner. Wedding rings are status symbols, for they mark the wearer's role as "married person." All military insignia are status symbols, and so are special religious items, such as bishops' mitres. But far and away the most complicated system of status imagery can be found in the field of *heraldry*.

Heraldry began with the old custom of certain peoples adopting a particular symbol to identify their soldiers or citizens. The ancient Romans took as their emblem the eagle, the Goths used the bear, the French adopted the lion and later the fleur-de-lis (white iris or sword lily). By the 12th century, when both feudal wars and the Crusades were in progress, it became necessary for a knight to be recognized from a distance. Thus, each family would carry a personal emblem on the shield, which when decorated was known as an *escutcheon*. Later, the family arms came to be embroidered on a kind of coat worn over the armor, thus giving rise to the term *coat of arms* (Fig. 228).

In time, heraldry became so complex that it might almost be called a science. A knight who married an heiress could incorporate her family arms into his own. When he died, only his eldest son would be entitled to use the arms in their original form; other children would have to adapt them, perhaps by changing some of the *charges* or figures.

left: 226. Paired figures flanking a central tree. (*above*) Decoration on an ivory box, from Nimrud, c. 9th century B.C. (*below*) Reliefs from Carchemish, 8th century B.C.

below left: 227. *Round Table of King Arthur.* 15th century. Manuscript. Bibliothèque Nationale, Paris.

below: 228. Cornelis Engelbrechtsz. Detail of *Constantine,* from *Constantine and St. Helena.* c. 1510–20. Entire panel, $34\frac{1}{2} \times 22\frac{1}{4}''$. Alte Pinakothek, Munich. Constantine is pictured wearing a tunic decorated with his arms.

Not only families, but also kingdoms, towns, abbeys, and even corporations were (and are) entitled to display a coat of arms.

The importance of heraldry for the designer lies not so much in the significance of each motif but in the creation of a system of symbols to build upon. Quite apart from their status value, coats of arms are beautiful and fascinating as pure design images.

Patriotic and Political Symbols

The symbols that represent a particular nation or political orientation are among the most easily recognized. For those who enjoy symbols and their meanings, the study of national flags—many of which have developed and changed over the centuries—can prove endlessly fascinating. In the United States we have an especially rich array of symbols, from the Statue of Liberty to the eagle with olive branch and arrows. It begs the obvious to remember that our flag is composed of thirteen stripes to signify the original colonies and fifty stars in honor of the present fifty states. However, this focuses on the central fact about such emblems: they succeed because they are at the same time striking visual images and symbolic messages.

Each of our major political parties is identified by a symbol (the elephant and the donkey). Moreover, certain groups will adopt a symbol to exemplify their ideals. The symbol of the Women's Movement, which combines the biological symbol for woman with an image of strength and unity, clarifies the goals of a particular group (Fig. 229).

One of the most striking ways to suggest a change in viewpoint is to change one's symbol. Until a few years ago the flag of Canada had an English Union Jack in the Corner, symbolic of close ties with the Commonwealth. But when the Canadians wished to establish a very strong Canadian identity, they changed their symbol—their flag—to the distinctly Canadian maple leaf (Fig. 230). By this gesture they asserted: "We are Canadians, and not an offshoot of anyone else." Such is the power of political symbols.

left: 229. Button with symbol of the Women's Movement.

below: 230. The national flag of Canada.

left: 231. "Jenny Lind" figurehead from the ship *Nightingale* of Portsmouth, New Hampshire. Built 1851. Carved and gilt wood. Index of American Design, National Gallery of Art, Washington, D.C.

right: 232. *Man with Grapes,* barroom figure or tavern sign found in Wells, Maine. 19th century. Painted wood, bone, and wire; height 15″. Guennol Collection, New York.

Commercial Symbols

In many parts of the world the sign of three balls is recognized as a pawnbroker's shop. Before the era of modern dentistry, the huge tooth hanging outside a window marked the office of a feared "tooth extractor." These are both examples of commercial symbols; they advertise the service or product to be sold.

Not strictly commercial but related symbols were the magnificent figureheads that adorned sailing ships in their heyday. Most figureheads were women (Fig. 231). They were carved of wood and had spendid flowing hair and billowing skirts to suggest the speed of the ship in plying the waves. It is said that the captain of the ship was symbolically "married" to the figurehead. This would explain why, if his ship foundered, he was expected to "go down with the ship," with his symbolic "wife."

The little statue shown in Figure 232, a man holding aloft a bunch of grapes, was carved in the 19th century probably as a tavern sign. In both its forthright symbolism and its stylized detail the figure is absolutely charming. Today, corporations pay thousands of dollars to have advertising agencies or public relations firms develop symbols, called *logos,* especially for them. This is a real design challenge, since the company logo must be read and immediately understood by the

233. Logo for International Harvester, designed by DeMartin and Marona Cranston Downes. 1973.

consumer when very small (perhaps on letterhead) or huge (on the side of a factory). The logo for International Harvester Company (Fig. 233) consists of the stylized initials "IH," which manage to evoke the image of a farmer on a tractor. A logo designed for the American cotton industry shows a stylized cotton boll "growing" from the two central T's in the word "cotton" (Fig. 234).

Of course, it is not strictly necessary that great amounts of money be spent to create a logo. This fact was proved by an incident in which

234. Logo for Cotton, Inc., designed by Walter Landor.

the NBC television network in New York initiated a major design project, with a large staff and many sophisticated aids, to develop a new logo (Fig. 235). After the resulting image was presented with fanfare, the network discovered that a designer working for a small television station in Nebraska (KNBC) had come up with virtually the identical logo for his station.

As times change, so do company logos. Many companies that have been in business for a long time have found it necessary over the years to redesign their logos to make them seem "modern" (Fig. 236).

235. Logo for the National Broadcasting Company, Inc. 1976.

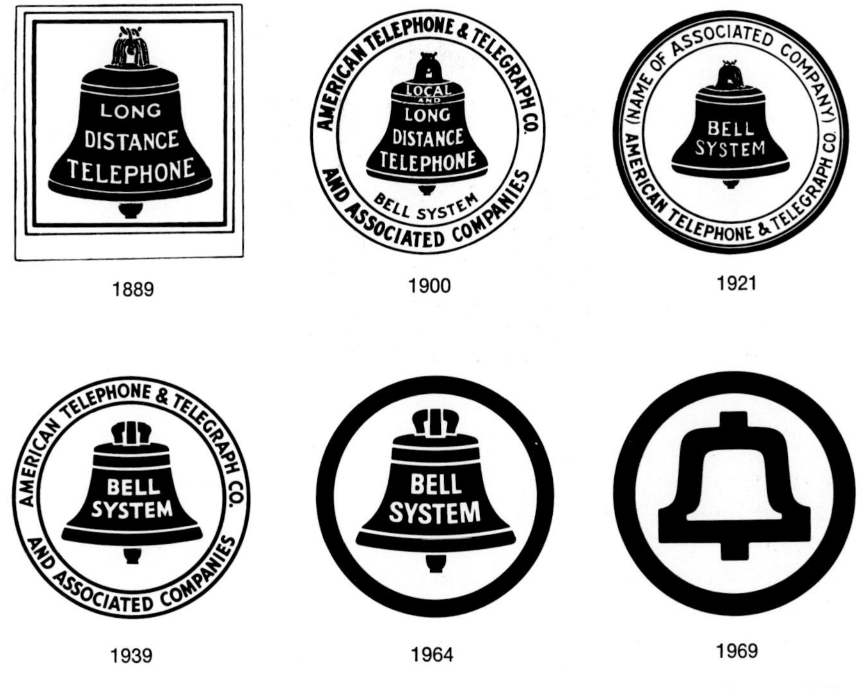

236. Logo for the Bell System, as it has appeared since 1889.

With increasing international travel, symbols have become a vital means of communication. Travelers on the roadway in Europe cannot possibly memorize all the various words for "stop," "danger," "slow," and so forth. Striking visual symbols take their place. To be successful these symbols must be: compelling enough to attract attention; clear enough to be read at sixty miles per hour; and understandable to people of many cultures. Figure 237 shows a selection of signs from the United States, on a travelers' road sign in Vermont. Computers are busy plotting the exact size of image, optimum colors, and spot identification of these symbols. In time, we may have a truly international system of signs—a civilized return to primitive sign language.

237. Highway symbols indicating (*left to right*): lodging, food, fuel, recreation, goods and other services.

238. Marc Chagall. *I and the Village.* 1911. Oil on canvas, 6′3⅝″ x 4′11⅝″. Museum of Modern Art, New York (Mrs. Simon Guggenheim Fund).

Psychological Symbols

When Sigmund Freud wrote *The Interpretation of Dreams* in 1900, he opened a Pandora's box of psychological symbolism that has become the staple of painters, photographers, and filmmakers ever since. Many, but by no means all of these symbols are sexual in content.

Marc Chagall's *I and the Village* (Fig. 238) represents a remembered dream vision of childhood in Russia. The images are tumbled and superimposed, with little attention to scale, just as they might be in a dream. Chagall remembers all these images—the cow, the milkmaid, the farmer with his scythe—but does not try to fit them into any logical order. They appear as a patchwork of impressions, in much the same way that dreams present us with impressions.

A number of filmmakers, including Ingmar Bergman and Federico Fellini, have made extensive use of symbols in their work. A scene from Fellini's *La Dolce Vita* (Fig. 239) illustrates this idea. We know only that the characters in this scene are exploring a run-down castle. But two strong symbols enhance the action. First, the man at right is garbed in a black robe and wears an eyepatch—surely a symbol of potential menace. Second, the candles offer the only light, symbolizing hope? brightness? reason? Fellini in one image has therefore created a duality: evil versus light. Symbols like this can be enormously powerful in building an impression, for they reach to the core of our sensibilities.

239. Scene from Federico Fellini's *La Dolce Vita.* 1960.

Personal Symbolism

Much of the symbolism in contemporary painting and sculpture could be described as "personal." That is to say, the artist creates a symbol that meets his or her particular needs. The symbolism to be found in the works of Edvard Munch seems at the same time obvious and subtle. Munch expressed passions in terms of *color,* as though the energies of human emotion translated themselves into vivid hue. The *Dance of Life* (Pl. 18, p. 143) shows three evolving stages in the life of woman. The earliest stage is represented by the young girl at center, dancing with the man. She is innocent, untried, and naïve—yet dressed in red in expectation of love's promise. At left stands a woman symbolizing ripe maturity. This figure, clad in white, seems confident and assured, in the full glory of her womanhood. We discover the morbid quality of Munch's symbolism in the woman at right, who, dressed in black, stands for love gone by and ultimate loneliness. All the background couples suggest sexual desire, which is the preoccupation of all three stages of Woman—future, present, and past. The leaden, purplish sky seems to be heavy with sexuality. Here the symbolism of colors supports the balanced composition and stance of the figures to convey Munch's idea.

The symbols drawn by Francisco Goya are more openly threatening. In *The Sleep of Reason Produces Monsters* (Fig. 240) the artist shows himself asleep, surrounded by fearsome, menacing creatures of every description. This etching forms part of the series, *Los Caprichos,* meaning caprices or follies. At the time he created it, Goya was tormented by deafness and possibly unsure about his mental stability. By giving animal form to the nameless horrors that assailed him, he may have hoped to ward them off. We cannot attach specific names to these creatures, as we might in a work by Dürer. Here the cat does not represent a particular quality. Instead, the group of monsters together

240. Francisco Goya. *The Sleep of Reason Produces Monsters,* from *Los Caprichos.* 1796–98. Etching, $8\frac{1}{2} \times 6''$. Metropolitan Museum of Art, New York (gift of M. Knoedler & Co., 1918).

symbolizes fear, evil, chaos, insanity. These are personal symbols constructed by the artist for his own use.

One of the most intensely personal symbolic systems in the history of art was that developed by the Belgian painter James Ensor, who worked at the turn of this century. Ensor spent his youth in the town of Ostend where his family were shopkeepers specializing in toys, souvenirs, and curiosities. During carnival time they made masks. In later life Ensor took the mask as his metaphor for his tortured vision of society. In *Self-Portrait with Masks* (Pl. 19, p. 144) we see the artist wearing a jaunty scarlet hat, surrounded by masked figures whose vacant or threatening expressions belie the gay colors of their dress. Although right in the center of the crowd, Ensor is totally alien from it. The masks operate as a mirror for what he felt to be the ugly, vacant spirits of the bourgeoisie. It is as though the artist is saying all people wear masks to cover their genuine selves. He has merely drawn the masks to reflect the true qualities underneath.

The many and varied examples of symbolism in this chapter should help to demonstrate that this tool can reveal layers of meaning far beyond the actual content of a work. Whether the designer uses age-old symbols or invents personal ones, the device can add immeasurably to the depth in a work of art. Symbols make intimate connections between viewer and artist on many levels, from the overt to the subconscious.

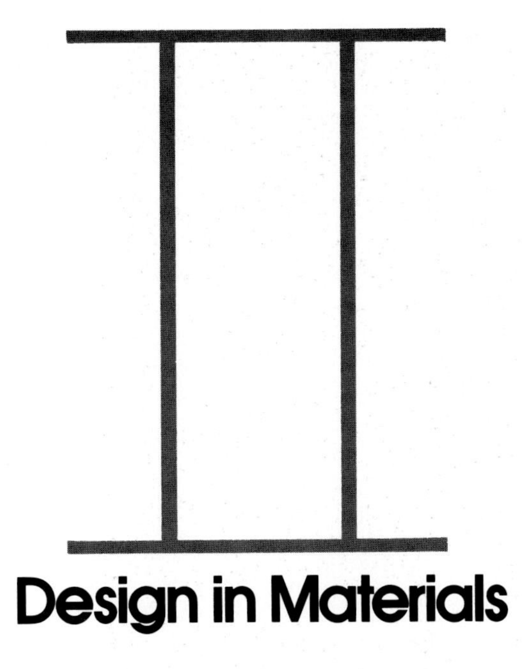

Design in Materials

12 Wood

Of all the materials used in design, wood is among the most basic. From weapons to ceremonial and religious objects, from the structure of the home and its contents to the fire on the hearth, wood has served humanity faithfully for thousands of years (Fig. 241). Besides meeting essential human needs, wood has the capacity to endow any object with its natural beauty. Each piece of wood is unique, having its own peculiarities of growth and cut (Fig. 242). Grain offers so much diversity that sections of wood taken from the same trunk may have quite different patterns, while retaining the general grain qualities that belong to the species.

Characteristics of Wood

The growth pattern of trees determines the grain of wood. Each year, in temperate zones, trees produce two rings of growth. The early or spring wood is lighter in color than the late or summer wood, so the rings alternate between light and dark to form a definite grain pattern. When a tree trunk is cut through, it is possible to estimate its age by counting the number of rings. Grain will also be affected by the

below: 241. Tsimshian clan headdress, collected at Kitkatla, British Columbia, 1895–1901. Painted wood with seashell teeth and bear canines, height 17″. National Museums of Canada, Ottawa.

right: 242. Cedric Wright. *Junipers at Timberline.* Photograph.

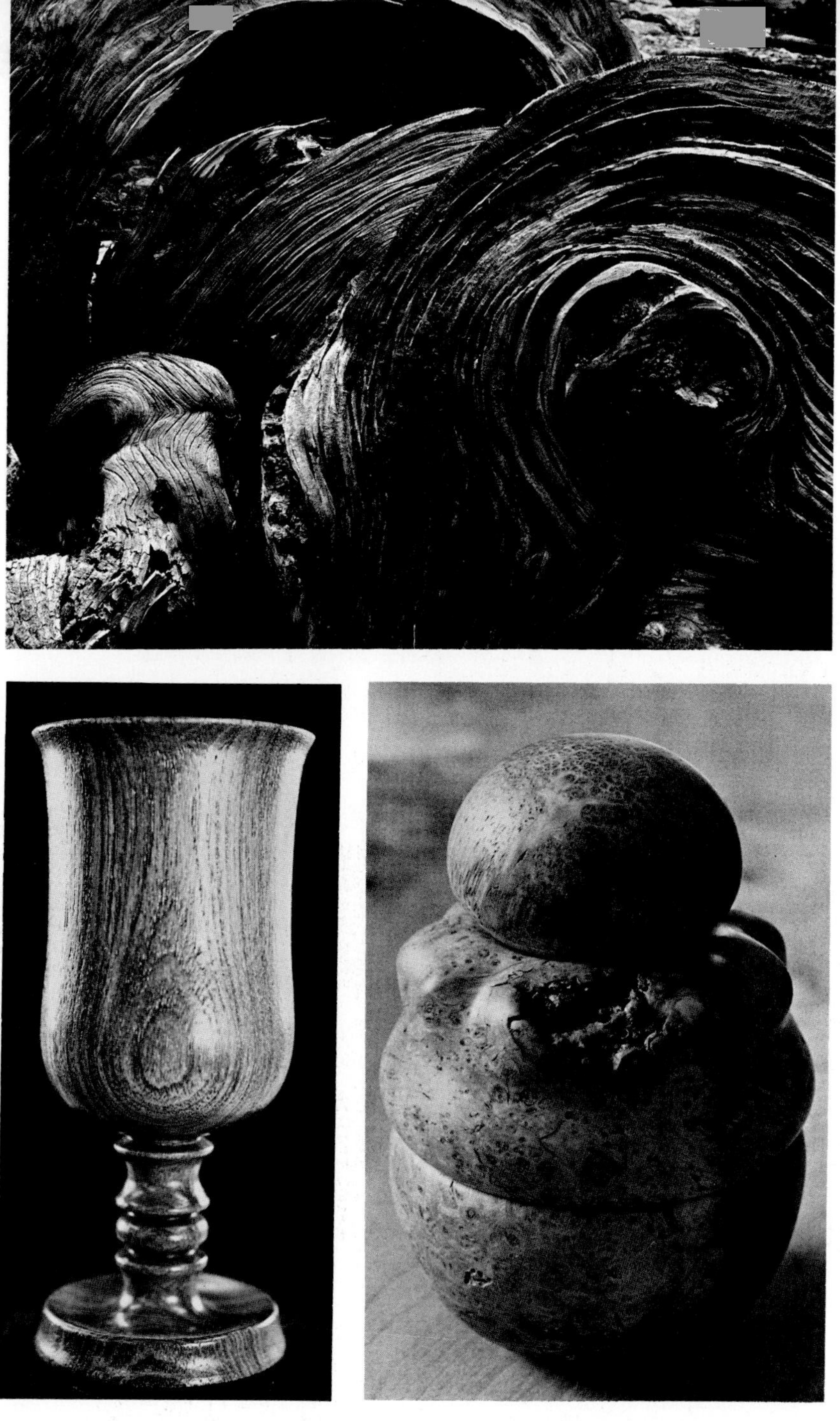

right: 243. John Habbersett. Goblet. 1974. Teak, height 5″. Courtesy the artist.

far right: 244. Mark Lindquist. Covered jar. 1975. Wild cherry burl, turned and carved; height 7″. Courtesy the artist.

branching characteristics of a tree. Where a tree forks, the grain will be wavy and irregular. Knots form where a branch begins, so a tree with many branches, such as pine, will produce knotty lumber.

The method of sawing lumber has a great deal to do with the way grain shows up. Wood from the same tree will look quite different if it is sawed parallel to the axis (or lengthwise line) of the trunk or across the axis. But either way, each type of tree presents its special grain pattern (Fig. 243).

There are two general categories of trees. *Deciduous* trees have broad leaves which they shed annually, while *coniferous* or cone-bearing trees have narrow leaves or needles that they retain the year round. Wood is classified as either *hard* (from deciduous trees) or *soft* (from coniferous trees). These terms refer to the cellular structure rather than the actual hardness, although most hardwoods are harder than most softwoods.

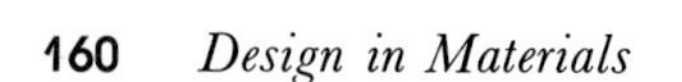

The hardwoods include maple, oak, walnut, hickory, and mahogany. They tend to have a finer and often more interesting grain pattern than softwoods and to respond well to finishes. Hardwoods are, of course, more difficult to carve, but they will take very fine details. The less expensive softwoods, including pine, cedar, and redwood, are easier to shape than hardwoods. In a special subcategory are fruitwoods and nutwoods, which are classed as hard. The fruitwoods, such as cherry, pear, and lemon, have attractive colors and grain patterns and sometimes *burls,* or sections of unusual growth. Most fruitwoods carve beautifully (Fig. 244).

The designer who works in wood learns to treasure each variety for its particular qualities, even each piece for its own personality. The names alone have the power to inspire creative expression—chestnut, rosewood, satinwood, tulip, amaranth, lemon, birch, holly, harewood. Each implies a special—perhaps exotic—nature.

Common Varieties of Wood

Walnut is a highly versatile wood. An ideal cabinet material, it is outstanding for its rich color, durability, and beauty. Walnut can be *turned*—that is, shaped on a rapidly turning lathe to produce round forms. It has long been a favorite wood for carving. Contemporary designers use it for its rich grain and color in many kinds of objects, from sculpture to furniture. As a very hard, strong wood that resists warpage, it proves suitable for meticulously balanced objects, like a spinning wheel (Fig. 245).

Mahogany comes from the jungles of central and South America, the West Indies, and Africa. It is an expensive and rather "formal" wood, distinguished by its interesting grain. Mahogany was a favorite wood of 18th-century cabinetmakers, who embellished it with inlay, turning, and fine carving. It retained its popularity in fine furniture during the 19th century, when elegant pieces came from the workshops of master designers (Fig. 246).

Oak has long been associated with floors and furniture because of its hardness and resistance to wear. At the turn of this century oak was

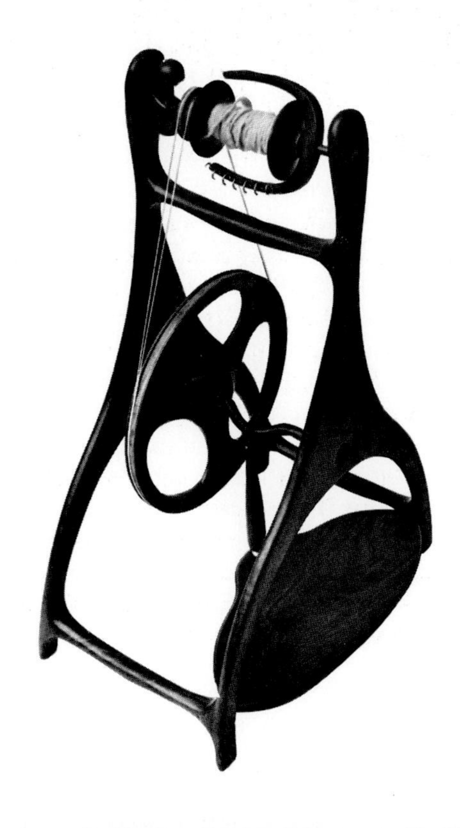

left: 245. Stephen A. Foley. Spinning wheel. 1974. Walnut, height 34″. National Collection of Fine Arts, Smithsonian Institution, Washington, D.C.

above: 246. Upholstered side chair from New York. c. 1830. Mahogany. Metropolitan Museum of Art, New York (Edgar J. Kaufmann Charitable Foundation Fund, 1968).

left: 247. Gustav Stickley. Suite of Craftsman furniture. 1898–1905. Oak. Collection Ethel and Terence Leichti.

below: 248. Chair from "The Pine Line," designed by Thonet Industries, Inc. Pine planks and urethane cubes, height 24″.

below left: 249. Erasmus Grasser. *A Morris Dancer.* 1480. Painted wood, height c. 25″. München Stadtmuseum, Germany.

in great demand for common furniture, taking the place that pine holds now (Fig. 247). White oak was given the popular "golden oak" finish. Today oak tables, desks, and washstands are among the most sought-after items at country auctions. There is a solidity about oak that evokes the security and tradition of the past.

Pine was the most common wood during the American Colonial period and remains so today. Like a master actor whose face is unfamiliar because he sinks so thoroughly into his roles, pine can assume endless different personalities, depending on the way it is handled. Pine can be painted, stained, or simply waxed and buffed to a soft *patina*—the term used for the mellowing of surface texture and color. Because of its low cost and light weight, as well as the fact that it warps little, lumber from white and yellow pine is important in building construction. A modern approach to pine lets the honest, natural wood show through, with simple shapes and joinings (Fig. 248).

250. Henry Moore. *Reclining Figure.* 1945–46. Elmwood, length 6′3″. Private collection, Italy.

Redwood comes from the Pacific Coast of the United States. Its special property is a very high resistance to rot, decay, and insects. In fact, when redwood is left outdoors to weather, its natural reddish-brown color softens to an attractive warm gray. For this reason redwood has been extremely popular for outdoor furniture, decks, and architectural siding. However in recent years a growing concern for the redwoods as *trees* rather than as lumber has restricted the availability of this wood.

Teak, a tropical wood of marked strength and durability, has become one of the most favored woods for contemporary furniture and artifacts (Fig. 243). Teak comes from Southeast Asia, where for centuries it has provided material for the construction of ships and temples. The wood has a somewhat lighter color than walnut and responds beautifully to oils, which bring out the grain and give the surface a soft luster. Since the 1940s Scandinavian designers have made teak their special material.

Structural Design

The methods of working wood have changed very little over several thousand years. Like clay, wood permits two basic kinds of shaping—a *subtractive* process, in which material is gradually taken away to reveal a form; and an *additive* process, in which portions of the material are joined together.

The subtractive processes include carving, sawing, and turning. Artisans of 14th- and 15th-century Europe carved splendid figures in wood, often with lifelike and intricate details (Fig. 249). Usually these statues were *polychromed,* or painted in many colors. Except for traces, most of the paint has disappeared, but the structural integrity of the figure remains. A few contemporary sculptors have carved in wood, notably Henry Moore (Fig. 250). The tendency, however, is to stress the pure, natural quality of the wood, with no artificial finish.

The additive processes in wood include joining, laminating, and inlay. *Joining* may mean nothing more than hammering pieces of wood

left: 251. Mario Ceroli. *A Modulo Ondulatorio.* 1968. Wood, each section 6′2$\frac{1}{8}$″ x 2′3$\frac{1}{4}$″ x 1′5$\frac{1}{2}$″. Galleria d'Arte del Naviglio, Milan.

below left: 252. Eduardo Chillida. *Abesti Gogora III.* 1962–64. Oak, 6′9$\frac{5}{8}$″ x 11′4$\frac{3}{8}$″. Art Institute of Chicago (Grant J. Pick Purchase Fund).

below: 253. H. C. Westermann. *The Big Change.* 1963. Laminated plywood, height 4′8″. Private Collection, New York.

254. Francesco di Giorgio of Siena. Room from the Ducal Palace, Gubbio, Italy. 15th century. Walnut, oak, beech, rosewood, and fruitwood inlay. Metropolitan Museum of Art, New York (Rogers Fund, 1939).

together as for architectural construction. The aesthetic appeal of planks of wood nailed in a regular pattern has encouraged sculptors to utilize the methods of building and furniture construction for pure visual effect (Fig. 251). In contemporary sculpture joining can also mean assembling pieces of wood to create new, dynamic forms, but forms that still express the solidity of lumber (Fig. 252).

Laminating is a technique of gluing thin sheets of wood together. The resulting "sandwich" can be molded very freely to achieve shapes that would be impossible in flat planks, but the wood retains its warmth and grain quality. The sculpture in Figure 253, by H. C. Westermann, uses laminated layers of different-colored woods to create a whorl pattern reminiscent of the natural whorls in some trees.

The Westermann sculpture is actually made of *plywood,* which is in itself a form of laminated wood. Plywood results when thin sheets of wood—usually three or five, but any odd number—are glued together with the grain of each layer at right angles to that of the adjoining layers. The product is much stronger and much less resistant to warpage than a single board of the same thickness could be. When the outside or visible layer is made of finer wood than the others, as in much furniture, the technique is called *veneer.* Veneer also serves for wood paneling, which is manufactured in a great variety of finishes.

The ancient art of *inlay* calls for small pieces of wood, shaped and generally in different colors, to be set into a framework according to a particular pattern. Most of us are familiar with *parquetry* from parquet flooring, in which the wood is laid in geometric designs. In previous centuries much more elaborate inlay was done, as Figure 254 shows.

This work is truly astonishing in its complexity. Although the wood is laid in a completely flat surface, it gives the effect of three-dimensional design. Clever placement of the curved and square fragments of wood create a *trompe-l'oeil* (fool-the-eye) sense of perspective and deep space.

One final example of structural design in wood does not really fall into either the additive or the subtractive category. *Bentwood,* a means

above: 255. John Cederquist. *Tera's Chair.* 1974. Laminated cherry wood and leather, height 31″. Courtesy the artist.

left: 256. Varujan Boghosian. *November.* 1973. Pine, basswood, and walnut, height 4′. Courtesy Cordier-Ekstrom, Inc., New York.

of shaping wood by applications of steam, was invented in the 1830s. The flowing, curvilinear forms that bentwood is capable of assuming have made it a fixture of rocking chairs from that period up to the present (Fig. 255).

Decorative Design

The exquisite natural patterns of wood grain are frequently all the decoration anyone needs. For certain purposes, however, designers may wish to enhance the quality of the wood with various decorative techniques, especially since wood adapts so well to a range of finishes. Perhaps the simplest way to create more interest is in combining different woods, which gives a variety of colors, textures, and grain patterns (Fig. 256). Painted or polychromed wood has already been mentioned in connection with wood sculpture of the medieval and Renaissance periods, but there are numerous modern interpretations of this decorative method (Pl. 20, p. 144). Actually, the unique "coffee table" in Plate 20 combines many techniques, including carving, gluing, and joinery, with the whole painted in acrylic colors.

Carving in wood is a decorative process that cuts across all centuries, all cultures, and all parts of the world (Fig. 257). Because the tools needed for woodcarving can be simple, even quite primitive cultures have made ornate wood carvings.

257. Door panel, from New Caledonia, Melanesia. Carved wood, height 6′10$\frac{1}{4}$″. Museum für Völkerkunde, Berlin.

In certain geographical regions it has been fashionable to decorate architecture with intricate carved patterns, particularly along the rooflines. Among the best examples are those found in old Russian wood churches and houses (Fig. 258). Here the overlapping carved segments of wood combine with an architectural mode that is in itself a delightful fantasy to yield a wonderfully rich effect. This type of architecture is no longer built, but there are a great many remarkable examples still standing.

Designing in Wood

Wood is such a versatile material that effective design depends largely on which characteristics are chosen to be emphasized. If the designer is most interested in the wood's grain, this aspect may be played up, perhaps by varying the pattern of the grain lines for an interesting

left: 258. Church of the Transfiguration, Kizhi (Russia), U.S.S.R. 1714.

below: 259. Hugh Townley. *O Western Wind When Wilt Thou Blow.* 1972. Mahogany, 24¼" x 18". Courtesy the artist.

left: 260. Rennie MacKintosh. "Willow 2," chair designed for the Willow Tearooms Dining Room. 1904. Dark stained oak with rush seat. Reproduced by Cascina S.p.A.

right: 261. Jens Kugle and Bent Kodesen. *Workchair.* 1975. Laminated wood. Courtesy ITL–Design, Randers, Denmark.

surface (Fig. 259). Of the design elements, line obviously is important to the work in Figure 259—both the grain line of the wood itself and the strong lines of overlapping slats. Texture is also crucial to this design. The heavy texture of the overlapping slats contrasts with smoother (although still rich) textures in the inset pieces at the center.

One very practical quality of wood is its *tensile strength,* which means its resistance to breakage under bending or pulling forces. Designers can take advantage of this property in many kinds of structures. Tensile strength permits the spanning of great distances with wooden beams in architecture. It also allows for *cantilevered* constructions—horizontal projections from a vertical surface.

Some designers will wish to emphasize the solid, blocky nature of wood-as-lumber (Fig. 248). Others achieve a sense of lightness within the framework of sawed pieces. The oak ladder-back chair in Figure 260, with its absolutely squared lines, seems almost delicate because of the carefully drawn spaces. On the other hand, the sinuous, organic quality of wood may be the point of departure for another designer (Fig. 261). The "workchair" illustrated, a Danish design, demonstrates the cantilever principle dramatically, with the seat jutting out from a slender, curving back. This piece focuses attention on the interplay of form and space, as well as achieving a unique balance.

The two chairs just discussed really sum up the endless scope of design in wood. Both are intended to hold the seated human figure and both are made from wood. Yet how different they are! One is absolutely straightforward in its use of the material, the other playful and inventive. Although wood is one of the oldest design materials on earth, its potential has barely been tapped.

13 Metal

From thumb tacks to spacecraft, from wedding rings to skyscrapers, metal plays a central role in human activity. Modern industry could not exist without metal, nor could modern transportation, for metal moves along the highways in automobiles, crisscrosses the land in railroads, plies the sea in ships, and fills the air lanes with jet planes that bridge continents at almost unimaginable speeds. The first foreign object to set down on the Moon was made of metal, as was the first vehicle to plumb the ocean's depths. But with all these new applications for metal, the oldest ones still remain. The tools we use in everyday life for cutting and pounding are made of metal, just as were similar tools used by Bronze-Age peoples more than five thousand years ago. Not only implements but also works of art were fabricated in metal as early as 1500 B.C. (Fig. 267), and contemporary sculptors have continued this tradition. Here, however, the physical resemblance is less telling, for the bold, machined works of the 20th century speak eloquently of our own era (Fig. 262).

Characteristics of Metal

Metal possesses several important characteristics that make it valuable to the designer. The most outstanding, perhaps, is its *tensile strength,* which means that it resists breakage under pulling or bending forces. It is tensile strength that allows metal to span great distances without underlying support at the center, as in much contemporary architecture and especially in suspension bridges (Fig. 263). Steel cables on a bridge may sustain a roadbed well over a mile long, yet the cables are so small in diameter that from a distance they resemble spun wires.

Unusual *formability* is another notable quality of metal. The various metals can be hammered, cut, drawn out, welded, joined with rivets, melted down and cast, or shaped by any number of industrial processes. One aspect of this, *malleability,* refers to the capacity of metal for being shaped or extended under great pressure. The term comes from the Latin word for mallet. No other material can be hammered so thoroughly without cracking or breaking. Gold, the most malleable of the metals, can be hammered into gold leaf—sheets thinner than the finest tissue paper. This method of working gold was well known to the

left: 262. Robert Bart. *Untitled.* 1965. Cast aluminum, $12\frac{3}{4} \times 17\frac{3}{4} \times 17\frac{1}{2}''$. Courtesy Leo Castelli Gallery, New York.

above: 263. John Roebling and Washington Roebling. Brooklyn Bridge, New York. 1869–83. Cables woven of steel wire hung from two Gothic-style towers. (Compare Fig. 212.)

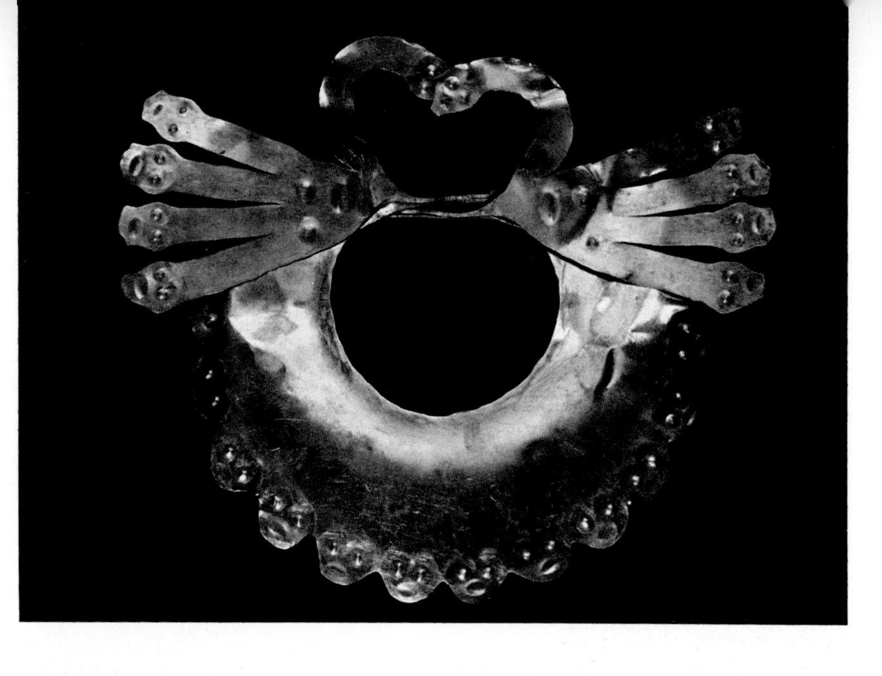

264. Mouth mask, from Peru. Naxca Period (A.D. 100–400). Sheet gold, width c. 9″. American Museum of Natural History, New York.

native peoples of ancient Peru—possibly the greatest goldsmiths of all time (Fig. 264).

Ductility is the characteristic of metal that permits it to be drawn out into fine wires. Platinum has been reduced to wire that is 1/20,000 of a millimeter in thickness, and it is said that a single ounce of gold can be drawn into a wire 60 miles long.

Metals do not rot, decay, mildew, or attract insects, and this makes them exceptionally *durable.* The great majority of artifacts that have survived from early civilizations are those fabricated from metal (Figs. 264, 267). Of course, many metals do rust, but today we have methods of preventing or treating this problem.

One final characteristic of metal explains its widespread use in industrial and architectural applications. This is *conductivity*—the ability to transmit heat, cold, or electricity. Metal wires create an elaborate network—usually unseen, but sometimes all too visible—throughout our technological world. Most cooking utensils today are of metal, and the material is indispensible for heating, cooling, and lighting our homes. It is possible to conceive of modern civilization without clay, wood, or even glass, but not without metal.

Methods of Working Metal

In order to describe fully the various methods by which metal can be shaped, we would almost have to add together the forming techniques of all the other materials—and then add a few. Metal lends itself to both *additive* and *subtractive* shaping; that is, it can be formed by building up or paring down. The one thing one can*not* do with metal is carve it, but beyond that the possibilities are limitless.

Hammering, one of the oldest ways of treating metal, is still much used. The softer metals, such as gold or tin, can be hammered cold, for which there are several variations. *Raising* is the commonest method of creating objects from a sheet of metal. The metalworker repeatedly strikes the flat sheet with hammers, working from the back and sometimes over a mold, until it "rises" into a curved or hollowed shape, such as a bowl or saucer. *Beating down* reverses the process of raising. In this technique the metalworker places the flat sheet over a recessed area and then hammers the metal into the depression.

Harder metals such as iron must be hot-hammered or *forged.* A hundred years ago the blacksmith and the ironmonger were as ordinary as the corner grocer, but the development of industrial forming methods and the advent of the automobile have combined to put them virtually out of business. Today the smithy is found only in very rural areas, but many sculptors and metalworkers still use the forge. In simplest terms, forging calls for a piece of metal to be heated in a furnace until it is red hot (sometimes white hot), then held on an anvil with tongs and pounded with hammers. Several stages of heating and pounding may be required until the piece takes on the desired shape. Examples of *wrought iron* tools, weathervanes, and other artifacts so common in the American Colonial period were made by forging (Fig. 265).

Spinning is the technique by which rounded objects are formed on a revolving lathe, a process similar to *turning* in wood (Fig. 243). Flat sheets of soft metal are pressed over wooden forms that turn on the lathe to create the round shapes of pitchers, goblets, vases, and sometimes jewelry (Fig. 266).

One of the most flexible methods of molding metal is by *casting,* which is at the same time a very ancient and an ultramodern technique. It consists of nothing more than pouring molten metal into some kind of mold and allowing it to harden. Chinese craftsmen of the Shang Dynasty (the second millenium B.C.) cast their remarkable bronze vessels in intricate molds probably made from clay (Fig. 267). Archaeological sites near An-Yang in the central plains of China have provided a wealth of these vessels ornamented with incredibly detailed abstract designs. On close examination the intertwined motifs are seen to be parts of animal bodies stylized to an extreme degree. It is likely that the vessels were used for ritual or ceremonial purposes.

right: 265. Skewer holder and skewers, American. Early 18th century. Forged wrought iron, 15¾ x 5¼″. National Museum of History and Technology, Smithsonian Institution, Washington, D.C.

below left: 266. Wendy Ramshaw. Set of five turned "Pillar Rings." 1971. Silver, amethyst, green carnelian, and agate. Courtesy the artist.

below right: 267. Footed vessel, from China. Shang Dynasty, 12th century B.C. Cast bronze, height 9¾″. Freer Gallery of Art, Smithsonian Institution, Washington, D.C.

For centuries artists have had their works cast in metal by the lost-wax process (see Chap. 19), and today many sculptors and jewelers have explored new applications for casting (Fig. 262). Industrial casting procedures are behind most of the metal appliances in our homes, such as typewriters, irons, and vacuum cleaners.

A much newer procedure, not unrelated to casting, is *electroforming.* This technique makes use of a pattern or *matrix,* usually of wax, that duplicates the final shape the metal work is to assume. By a complex electrochemical process particles of metal floating in an acid bath are deposited on the matrix, after which the wax is melted out. Electroformed pieces tend to be free-form, since the process makes it easy to create irregular shapes that would be difficult to obtain otherwise (Fig. 268). They are also surprisingly light in weight.

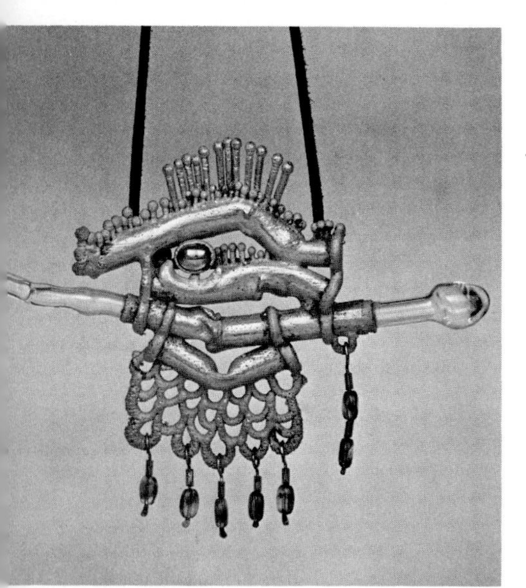

Besides casting, industrial forming methods include *pressing* metal sheets with dies or patterns, as most flatware is made; *injecting* fluid metal into molds; and *rolling* out sheets of metal to be used either in that form or subjected to a later shaping process.

Welding is a technique very much of the 20th century. In essence it consists of applying a torch to a piece of metal so that the material will melt and flow at the point of application, making it possible to join two pieces permanently. Until the late 1940s welding was generally restricted to industrial purposes. However, in the period after World War II the American sculptor David Smith, intrigued with the absolute freedom of construction he could obtain from torch techniques, began to experiment with metal forms that were cut, welded, and otherwise joined. Others soon followed his lead, and within a few years the entire concept of sculpture had been altered forever (Fig. 269). Today, little more than a quarter century later, we take for granted

above: 268. Lee Barnes Peck. Pendant. 1971. Copper electroformed, with plating of 24k gold and blown glass; width $5\frac{1}{4}''$. Courtesy the artist.

right: 269. David Smith. *Zig IV.* 1961. Steel, painted yellow-gold; $7'9\frac{3}{8}'' \times 7'\frac{1}{4}'' \times 6'4''$. Lincoln Center for the Performing Arts, New York.

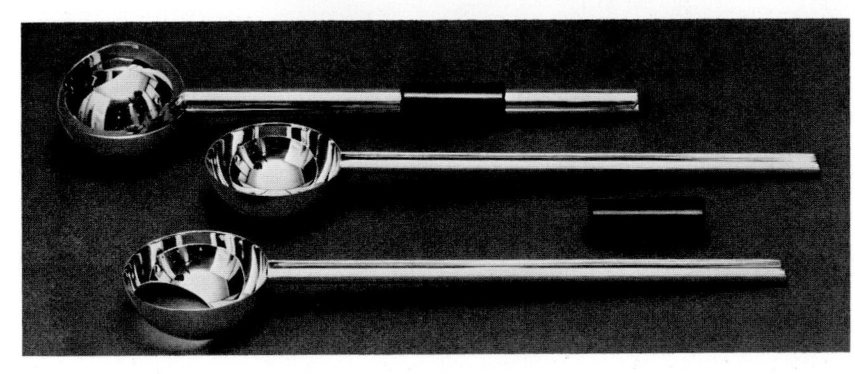

above: 270. Earl Krentzin. *Circus Train.* 1969. Sterling silver and gold on burnt walnut base, height 8″. Courtesy Kennedy Galleries, Inc., New York.

left: 271. Lino Sabattini, for Argenteria Sabattini, Italy. Set of ladles. Silver-plated metal, each $11\frac{5}{16}$″ long. One ladle has a hole for serving vegetables; the two can be held together with a black melamine tube.

huge metal sculptures that—with their bolts and rivets and gleaming surfaces—suggest the body of a machine but spring from the mind and soul of the artist (Fig. 262).

Varieties of Metal

Gold has been considered the most precious of metals throughout recorded history and in every part of the world. Even in regions where gold was relatively plentiful, such as the mountains of Peru in the pre-Columbian period, it was reserved for precious objects and articles of adornment (Fig. 264). Scarcity accounts largely for the preciousness of gold but does not explain it entirely; for this we must take account of the metal's beautiful soft luster and color. Gold was the most treasured substance for jewelry in the oldest civilizations—those of Egypt and Mesopotamia—and it has remained so ever since.

In its pure state gold is not hard enough for use in plate, jewelry, or coinage, and so it must be *alloyed*—combined in a fluid state—with another metal or metals, usually with silver and copper. The same is true of *silver* itself. Sterling silver, for example, is actually 92.5 percent silver and 7.5 percent copper. Silver is not so scarce as gold, but still its comparative rarity helps to make it precious. Beyond this, it is valued for its luster, permanence, and great pliability. Silver and gold are natural foils for each other, since their colors contrast yet blend so beautifully. The *Circus Train* shown in Figure 270, which combines the two, represents a contemporary trend for casting in precious metals.

For many years the technology has existed to *plate* metals on top of one another—that is, to deposit a thin layer of one metal on the surface of another. The procedure is similar to electroforming. Objects plated in gold or silver have sustained a fairly bad reputation, because the practice often has led to "decorating" inferior metals in cheap jewelry and artifacts. Sensitive designers today have begun to change that image. The ladles shown in Figure 271 are not cheap imitations of

above left: 272. Thomas Danforth, III. Covered sugar bowl. American, late 18th century. Pewter, height $3\frac{7}{8}''$. Metropolitan Museum of Art, New York (gift of Mrs. J. Insley Blair, 1941).

above right: 273. Weather vane. American, from Ohio, c. 1860. Copper with traces of gilt, height 20″. Courtesy George E. Schoellkopf Gallery, New York.

left: 274. Saul Baizerman. *Sun Worshiper.* 1940–49. Hammered copper, height $37\frac{1}{2}''$. Courtesy Zabriskie Gallery, New York.

anything, nor do they masquerade as something they are not. These pure forms are honest, sturdy metal objects that have been given a gleaming surface treatment—a plating of silver.

Pewter, an alloy of tin with various other metals, originated as a substitute for silver. Although similar in color, it is cheaper, softer, and less shiny. In Colonial America few families could afford silver, but most had a supply of pewter utensils. The sugar bowl in Figure 272 dates from the late 18th century. Clearly visible at the top of the bowl itself are the *hallmarks,* stamped insignia that identify the maker, the place of origin, and the purity of the metal. Hallmarks on silver first appeared in the 14th century and gradually became standardized. Today they serve as invaluable guides for collectors of antique silver and pewter.

Copper may have been the first metal used by primitive civilizations. It is an excellent conductor of heat and is highly resistant to corrosion—both of which qualities place it in great demand for electrical and plumbing equipment. Moreover, since copper spreads heat evenly across its surface, it has been a standard for fine cooking pots since the 17th century. But the fact that such pots are seldom shut away in cupboards and instead are left hanging on display points to the most appealing characteristic of copper: its warm, reddish color. This factor has made copper a favorite material for artisans and artists the world over, from the makers of whimsical weather vanes (Fig. 273) to modern sculptors (Fig. 274). Outdoor sculptures in particular

Plate 21. Barbara Chase-Riboud. *The Cape*. 1973. Multicolored bronze, hemp, and copper; 8′1½″ x 4′10½″ x 4′10½″. Courtesy the artist.

above: Plate 22. Kenneth Price. *Untitled.* 1974. Porcelain, in two parts; height 4″. Courtesy Willard Gallery, New York.

left: Plate 23. William J. Burke. *Royal Carriage #2.* 1974. Stoneware with lusters, flocking, and china paints, glazed; height 12″. Courtesy the artist.

benefit from the use of copper, since the metal does not rust but oxidizes to an attractive green surface color. Sometimes other metals, such as pewter, are applied in a wash over copper to achieve an attractive combination of silvery and reddish tones.

Brass and *bronze* are both alloys of copper, the first with zinc, the second with tin and sometimes other metals. Brass has a long history, especially in China, Persia, India, and the Middle East, where the manufacture of brass objects has been an important industry for centuries. Typically these items are incised with elaborate designs, and they may be inlaid with enamel or other contrasting materials. Brass has a yellower color than copper, and it takes a high polish. Common products are musical instruments, ceremonial pieces for churches, and decorative hardware, such as doorknobs and locks. The octant in Figure 275 serves as an example of one traditional use for brass—in ships' fittings and precision instruments.

Bronze is darker, harder, and longer lasting than brass. Its rich brownish-red color makes it popular for such items as desk accessories and medals. Most bells are cast from bronze, with the metal providing not only durability but the potential for a rich tone. In addition, bronze is the primary metal for cast sculptures—including the large statues that decorate parks and plazas around the world (Fig. 276).

Aluminum, one of the lightest and most plentiful of metals, can be treated in a variety of ways to produce practical, inexpensive, and attractive utensils. It neither tarnishes nor rusts and has high conductivity of heat and electricity, so it has become popular for cooking pots. Aluminum's conductivity also makes it useful in industrial applications, such as the pistons of internal combustion engines, high-tension power transmittors, nuclear reactors, and aircraft. This hard-working image seems to make aluminum particularly appropriate for certain

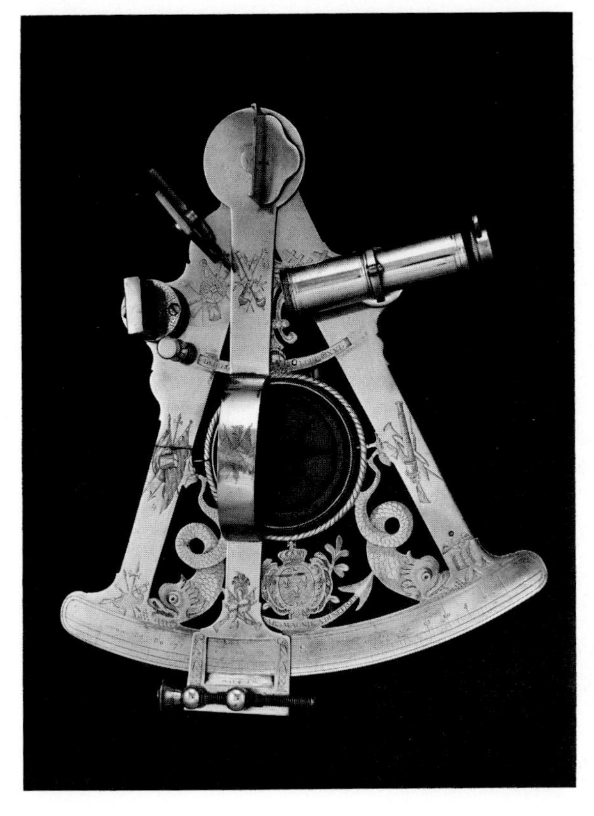

left: 275. Octant (*Hadley's Quadrant*). French, c. 1786. Brass. Peabody Museum of Salem, Mass.

right: 276. Augustus Saint-Gaudens. *William Tecumseh Sherman.* 1903. Bronze, over lifesize. Grand Army Plaza, New York.

above: 277. Eduardo Paolozzi. *Akapotic Rose.* 1969. Welded aluminum, height 9′1″. Private collection, New York.

below: 279. Doorhinge. German, 15th century. Wrought and incised iron. Metropolitan Museum of Art, New York (gift of Henry G. Marquand, 1887).

below: 278. J. Kraus. *Tin Man.* c. 1894: made for the West End Sheet Metal and Roofing Works, Brooklyn. Tin, height 5′8″. Collection Mr. and Mrs. Eugene Cooper, New York.

modern sculptures that celebrate the technological age in both form and perfectly machined surfaces (Fig. 277).

Tin is, surprisingly enough, one of the most expensive of all metals. It has many applications beyond the so-called "tin can"—which has always contained more zinc than tin and in which the tin is now being replaced entirely by other metals. Sheets of tin are soft and easy to work with simple tools, so the metal has earned its place in decorative accessories such as trays, lighting fixtures, mirror frames, and ornamental boxes. The word "tin" almost invariably evokes a picture of animated figures, from the classic tin soldier to the Tin Woodsman in "The Wizard of Oz." In this tradition is the "Tin Man" trade sign used by a 19th-century metalworks in Brooklyn (Fig. 278).

Iron is so prevalent a structural material that we sometimes lose sight of its history and potential for decorative design (Fig. 287). Wrought iron, a combination of high-purity iron and iron silicate, has been used since Biblical times. Tools more than five thousand years old have been found in Egyptian pyramids and under the base of the Sphinx at Karnak. Although present methods of making wrought iron are far different from those developed in ancient times, many of the products are similar. Medieval blacksmiths forged iron over open fires in creating architectural accessories such as locks and doorknockers, as well as agricultural tools. The results of their efforts are still visible on old castles and churches, where heavy oak doors are embellished with elaborate hardware (Fig. 279).

Wrought iron has traditionally been important in Spain and in regions of Spanish influence, including the South and the Southwest of the United States. In these areas the accents of ornate wrought iron balconies and grilles provide a uniquely rich surface detailing on the pastel-colored buildings (Fig. 280). The craftsmen of Colonial America also created a distinctive style in wrought iron in the process of providing useful objects such as weather vanes, lighting fixtures, and cooking utensils (Fig. 265).

Steel is basically an alloy of iron and carbon with an admixture of other elements, but it is manufactured in thousands of different types

above: 280. Cast-iron balcony on Royal Street, New Orleans. c. 1837.

below: 281. Dining table and chairs from the Belmont Dining Group. Steel tubing, glass, and upholstery. Designed by Paul Tuttle for Landes Manufacturing Company.

and in different compositions to serve specific purposes. The alloy of stainless steel contains about 12 percent chromium and often a small percentage of nickel to prevent corrosion. This quality makes stainless steel perfect for inexpensive, tarnish-free tableware, which is frequently similar in design to silver flatware. Almost no home built today could be entirely without steel, for it appears in structural members, plumbing fixtures, sinks, countertops, appliances, and an infinite number of other places. Nor have the aesthetic aspects of steel been ignored, as we can see from the wide variety of sleek, clean-lined furniture (Fig. 281). The extreme durability and easy maintenance of these pieces alone would make them practical, but the gleaming metal finish, set usually against padded upholstery, offers a contemporary design statement.

Structural Design

The designer in metal should avoid all preconceived ideas. It is true that metal carries an image of strength and unyielding solidity—an image created by its association with skyscrapers, bridges, airplanes, and industrial plants. Some designers, in fact, have exploited this quality. The sculptor Alexander Calder has his giant *stabiles* (or fixed

282. Alexander Calder. *The Eagle.* 1974. Steel stabile, height 40′. Plaza, Fort Worth National Bank, Tex.

objects, as opposed to *mobiles*) fabricated out of heavy-duty steel riveted together by industrial methods. *The Eagle* (Fig. 282), a work weighing 16 tons, complements the 37-story skyscraper in front of which it stands. Despite the size and heaviness of the sculpture, it has a kind of airiness, an upward sweep that gives the impression of energy poised for flight—a fitting antidote to the solidity of the building itself.

One example of an instance in which designers used metal to make the building itself seem light and airy can be found in the Detroit & Northern Savings & Loan Association building in Hancock, Michigan (Fig. 283). Although only eight stories high, this structure is the tallest building in little Hancock. If it had been made of conventional masonry, steel, and glass, it might have seemed overwhelming. Instead, the shimmering surfaces give it the appearance of a giant tinselly Christmas package set down amid the town. The rectangular main structure, supported by steel framing, is sheathed in gold-tinted reflective glass, but the "silo" elevator tower—a reference to the agricultural heritage of the land—rises in a column of gleaming copper-bonded stainless steel. Design in this instance has combined two of the major qualities of metal—strength and potential shine.

At the opposite extreme from the heavy architectural constructions, we can find works of great delicacy fabricated in metal. The inherent strength of the material makes it self-sustaining even in very thin constructions, such as Ibram Lassaw's *Enactment* (Fig. 284). Here the fine, almost organic tracery of forms and lines was created by depositing layer upon layer of molten metal with the torch. The work perches delicately on just a few supports.

above left: 283. Tarapata/MacMahon/Paulson Corp. Detroit & Northern Building, Hancock, Mich. 1973.

above right: 284. Ibram Lassaw. *Enactment.* 1961. Steel and bronze alloys, welded; 25 x 20 x 12″. Whitney Museum of American Art, New York (gift of Mrs. Howard Lipman).

A combination of metal with other materials expands the possibilities for structural design. We are accustomed to seeing partnerships of metal and glass, even metal and wood, but the pairing of a hard, inorganic substance with softer materials offers new challenge to the designer. Works that join metal with fiber are the special province of sculptor Barbara Chase-Riboud, whose *Time Womb* appears in Figure 285. Here polished aluminum, tooled and welded, flows into a cascade of wrapped silk yarns, setting the gleam of the metal against the lush texture of the fiber. Harmony in form is achieved partly through the predominantly vertical movement, partly through the similarity in warm color. A particularly vibrant, glowing tone marks Chase-Riboud's *The Cape* (Pl. 21, p. 177), a sculpture in multicolored bronze and copper with braided strands of hemp.

Effective structural design in metal depends to a very great extent on awareness of what the materials—and especially the forming processes—can do. A thorough grounding in both hand and industrial techniques frees the designer to exploit the possibilities of metal.

Decorative Design

The bright, mirrorlike surface of some metals is one form of decorative treatment; the "satin finish" on certain metals such as pewter is another. Still other metals, notably bronze, thrive on adverse natural conditions like dampness and temperature extremes, developing a rich, mellow, subtly colored surface film called a *patina.* Metals can be polished or buffed to almost any degree of smoothness. Gold and silver especially benefit from this type of handling, since they are inherently lustrous. But even precious metals can gain surface interest through a variety of decorative procedures.

right: 285. Barbara Chase-Riboud. *Time Womb (Version II).* 1971. Aluminum and silk, height 4′8″. Courtesy Betty Parsons Gallery, New York.

Chasing and *repoussé* are perhaps the commonest methods of working metal surfaces (Fig. 286). Both are accomplished with rounded tools held against the metal and struck with hammers, so that a depression is formed. In chasing, the work is usually done from the face or outside; thus, a *recessed* design appears on the finished piece. Repoussé, from the French to "push again," is done from the back, and therefore the lines or images are *raised* on the surface.

Engraving and *etching* both developed as methods of embellishing medieval armor and goldwork. Fine lines *incised* or cut into the surface are the result of each technique. In the case of engraving, the work is done with a sharp tool that cuts directly into the metal. Etching relies on the cutting action of acid. To etch metal the craftsman first covers, or *stops out,* portions of the surface that are not to be cut with an acid-resistant substance, such as wax. Then the acid is applied and allowed to eat into the metal to the desired depth, but only in the exposed areas. Sometimes incised lines are filled with a black material called *nigellum* to create color contrast. This is known as *niello.*

Contemporary methods of giving surface interest to metal include *torch texturing,* which is exactly what the name implies. The welder's torch is held against the metal at a certain point until the surface melts and begins to flow. Very rich, mottled textures can be obtained in this manner. Simple hammering, worked on solid rather than molten metal, can give similar results (Fig. 274).

Designing in Metal

Some of the most exciting design in metal gains its effect from the surprising, the unexpected, the tongue-in-cheek. Bart's giant aluminum sculpture (Fig. 262), for instance, cannot help but remind us of a piece of fruit, perhaps a melon, from which a wedge has been cut. Our eye is caught by this familiar form, translated into unfamiliar scale in an unfamiliar material. This work makes dramatic use of form and space, or more specifically of positive and negative form, since the cutout portion functions just as strongly where it is *not* as where it *is.* We keep mentally putting it back in place, through an instinctive desire to complete the perfect sphere.

In the case of David Smith's *Zig IV* (Fig. 269) the unexpected quality is the balance. The steel projection at right seems almost to

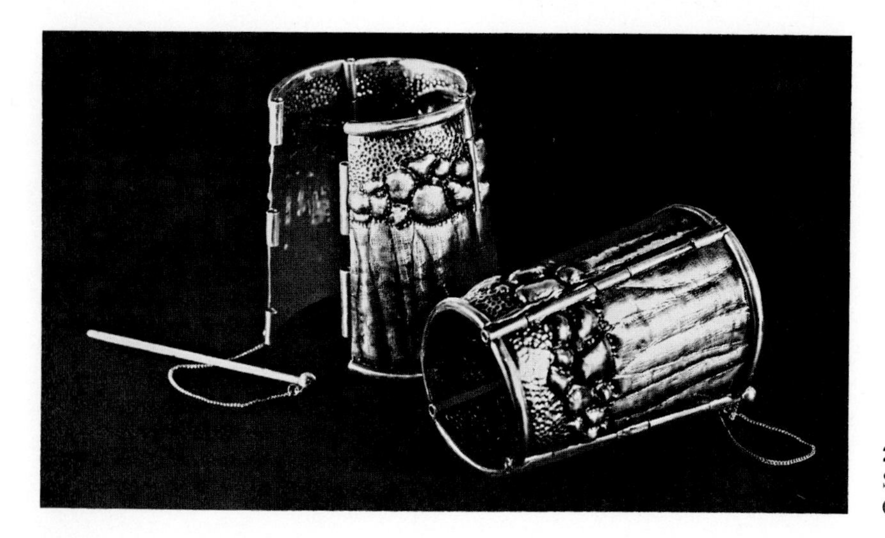

286. Anne Echelman. Cuff bracelets. 1975. Silver, with repoussé and chased decoration. Courtesy the artist.

hover in the air, with only the merest connection to the rest of the sculpture. Few materials except metal could maintain this precarious physical balance, and yet the piece as a whole is *visually* balanced, with the focus of attention on the flat disk near the top.

The Spanish architect and sculptor Antoni Gaudí was a master of the surprise element. His fantastic forms are always organic, asymmetrical, and delightful in their free play of imagination. Gaudí's "El Drac" gate for the Güell Pavilions in Barcelona is a wonderfully bizarre dragon conceived in iron, with wire mesh for the wings (Fig. 287). The dragon's wide-open mouth, plus one terrible scaly claw, jut out from the gate to balance the great swooping curve of the body and tail at the other end. In every way this gate is a virtuoso performance in iron.

Many designers choose metal for its quality of strength and solidity. There is a sense of security to be felt from being encased in a protective shell of metal, whether it be the four walls of a building, an automobile or airplane, or a military tank.

It does not stretch the imagination overly to consider medieval suits of armor as being the forerunners of the modern tank (Fig. 288). By the 15th century the suit of armor had become an elaborate head-to-toe affair. Typical armor worn by a German knight in this period weighed about 60 pounds, the partial armor for his horse another 60 pounds, plus some 20 pounds of chain mail for the unshielded areas of the horse's body. So unwieldy was this rig that, except when he was actually in the saddle, the knight was quite helpless. He could not even mount the horse unaided. Yet how secure he must have felt in his portable "tank," knowing that a sword could not penetrate anywhere. This brings to focus an aspect of design that is too often overlooked—the way it makes people *feel.* Designs in metal can make us feel secure, rich (in the case of jewelry), or sometimes threatened and overwhelmed, depending upon the designer's intent and the success of the design.

left: 287. Antoni Gaudí. *El Drac,* entrance gate to the Güell Pavilions, Barcelona. 1885. Laminated, cast, and wrought iron with wire mesh for the dragon's wings.

right: 288. War harnesses, for knight and his horse. South German, c. 1480. Steel. Wallace Collection, London.

14 Clay

Clay is the material of pottery and dinnerware, of bricks and tiles, of sculpture and artifacts. This amazingly versatile medium affords endless creative opportunities for the designer. Regardless of the final product, clay always is formed while it is wet, either in a moist, *plastic* state or as a semiliquid. Then the resultant piece is allowed to dry, after which it is *fired* in a kiln or oven of some kind. Firing changes the chemical composition of the clay so that it can never be returned to its plastic condition. The application of heat also makes a clay object hard and relatively waterproof. Often a *glaze*—a glassy coating—will be applied to the clay walls, and then the piece is fired again to fuse the clay and glaze together.

Clay is the very substance of the earth itself, a result of the weathering and decomposition of granite and similar rocks. Many people confuse it with soil, but actually soil is a combination of several ingredients, including clay, sand, and decayed vegetable matter. Where deposits of relatively pure clay occur—in hillsides and along riverbanks, for example—the material can be dug for use in making ceramic wares.

Clay deposits are widely distributed throughout the world, and nearly every ancient civilization developed ceramic techniques (Fig.

289. Tripod cooking vessel. Neolithic, 2nd millenium B.C. Earthenware, height $5\frac{3}{4}$". Collection Dr. Paul Singer, Summit, N.J.

289). It seems likely that the first step in this process was the daubing of baskets with damp clay to make them more effective containers. If at some point one of these clay-encrusted baskets dropped accidentally into the cooking fire, it would have been observed that the clay became much harder. The next step probably consisted of shaping a vessel from clay alone and putting it into the fire. These discoveries were made independently in various parts of the world.

Ceramic objects are breakable, but the material itself does not decompose. For this reason, pots and clay fragments comprise a large portion of the remains we have from earlier cultures. Pottery played a major role in ancient life, holding grain or olive oil, carrying water or wine, and storing the ashes of the dead. In Egypt archaeologists have found shards of pottery bearing messages that translate into personal notes among family members or excuses for workers not to report to their jobs. Paintings on vases from ancient Greece and Rome tell us much about these classical cultures from which our own derives. To a great extent, the history of human civilization can be traced back through the hands of potters.

The Nature of Clay

Clay is composed of alumina, silica, and various other elements, frequently including minerals that give it color. Geologically there are two types. *Residual* clay has remained in the same place where it was formed. *Sedimentary* clay, however, has been carried by the action of wind and water to be deposited in new locations. In its movement sedimentary clay picks up impurities and also breaks down in particle size. The impurities contribute color, while a finer particle size means the clay will be more plastic—a quality that indicates ease of molding and ability to hold a shape.

Rarely does one single clay offer all the characteristics desirable for ceramic design. Most often clays are mixed to yield a *clay body,* and these can be classified into three basic types according to the temperatures at which they are fired.

Earthenware fires in the lowest temperature range, at around 2000°F. A rather coarse, porous ware, earthenware is usually reddish and never completely waterproof except when glazed. Unglazed

above: 290. Honoré Daumier. *Le Fardeau* (*The Burden*). Before 1852. Terra cotta, height $13\frac{3}{8}''$. Walters Art Gallery, Baltimore.

right: 291. Camel. Chinese, T'ang Dynasty (A.D. 676–908). Glazed terra cotta, height $34\frac{3}{4}''$. Los Angeles County Museum of Art (William Randolph Hearst Collection).

earthenware pots are the standard material for planters, because the ware permits water to "sweat" through the walls. The Italian term for earthenware, *terra cotta* or "baked earth," most often is applied to sculptures and red clay tiles. Sculptors frequently use terra cotta as the medium for studies and models that are later to be translated into another material, such as bronze (Fig. 290). However, finished terra cotta sculptures—with clay as the final medium—have been popular since early times and in many cultures (Fig. 291). These may be *polychromed,* or glazed in bright colors for a brilliant effect. The glazes that fire in the low heat range tend to be bright and shiny, in contrast to the more subtle glazes typical of high-fire ware. Recent years have brought a new popularity for the bolder-colored earthenware forms for nonfunctional ceramics (Pl. 22, p. 178), especially in works of a whimsical or satirical nature.

Stoneware fires in the middle range of temperatures. The clay is usually light gray or tan, and the glazes, whether glossy or mat, tend to have softer colors. Because it is relatively durable and has such a warm, earthy quality, stoneware is the most popular choice for functional pots, planters, and dinnerware (Fig. 292). Most commercial dinnerware today, except for fine china, is made of stoneware.

The highest-fired ware of all is *porcelain,* made from a very pure and usually white clay. In firing, porcelain becomes extremely hard and vitreous; therefore, it can be molded into remarkably thin, actually translucent forms. The most elegant commercial dinnerware and figurines from Europe and China are made of porcelain. Because the clay body may be less plastic and workable than earthenware or stoneware, hand potters have not historically done much work in porcelain. However, with the new expansion in all the crafts, the artist-craftsman in clay is beginning to experiment with this pristine ware (Fig. 293).

China is a designation of the commercial manufacturer rather than the craftsman. It refers to a white ware, similar to porcelain but firing at a slightly lower temperature, used for dinnerware and figurines. For design purposes, china and porcelain can be considered synonymous.

Forming Methods

The many ways by which clay can be shaped fall into three general categories: *hand-building, throwing,* and *production molding.* The first two

below: 292. Ray Finch. Selection of functional stoneware pots.

right: 293. Pat Probst Gilman. *Dragon Covered Urn.* 1975. Porcelain, thrown and assembled by hand, with incised decoration; height 23″. Courtesy the artist.

left: 294. Zuñi potter working in the coil technique, New Mexico.

below: 295. Bruno LaVerdiere. *Arch.* 1975. Clay with sawdust and grog, coil-built; 7′3″ x 4′. Courtesy the artist.

relate to the artist-craftsman, the third to commercial manufacturers. Hand-building further breaks down into several different methods, which include pinching, coiling, slab construction, and carving.

Pinching is just what the name implies, a process of pressing the clay between the fingers to form a hollow vessel. No doubt the earliest clay objects were formed in this way, and today the "pinch pot" is usually the first project undertaken by a beginning ceramist. Pinching requires no tools—just the lump of clay and the potter's hands. However, it remains a limited technique, because it is so slow.

Coiling affords many possibilities for all kinds of shapes, whether rounded or asymmetrical. The potter begins with a flat slab of clay for the base, then gradually builds up ropes of clay upon this base to form the walls of the piece. The walls can be smoothed or left to show the

296. Anthony Caro. *Con-Can Tablet.* 1975. Stoneware, 28 x 18 x 16″. Courtesy the artist.

ridges of the coils (Fig. 294). While also time-consuming, the coiling technique is among the most versatile of the hand methods. There are no limitations of shape or even of size, as there are in wheel-throwing. Ceramic sculptor Bruno LaVerdiere has built structures more than 7 feet high from clay coils (Fig. 295).

Slab construction, another versatile technique, consists of rolling out flat sheets of clay, cutting them to size, and joining the slabs. Box shapes are the most obvious application for the slab technique. However, slabs can be joined, curved, bent, and distorted in any number of ways. Marilyn Levine's *Knapsack* (Fig. 45), Sandra McKenzie-Schmitt's *My Grandmother's House* (Fig. 302), and Anthony Caro's *Con-Can Tablet* (Fig. 296) were all built with slab construction.

The *carving* procedure really covers a general technique of building up and cutting away the clay, with the hands and with simple tools. This is the method used by sculptors in constructing models (Fig. 290), because it approximates the effects one can obtain in carving marble or wood, for example, yet the clay permits much faster and easier adjustments in the planning stage. Carved and molded pieces can also be fired as final works, but the building procedures then become more complicated. A solid (as opposed to hollow) form in clay cannot be fired, because it would almost certainly explode in the kiln. When a carved piece is to be fired, the sculptor will generally mold it over some internal support, such as wadded newspapers or plastic. The support is removed before or during the firing.

297. Throwing on the potter's wheel.

Throwing on the potter's wheel provides the most efficient means of creating round, symmetrical objects such as bowls, plates, mugs, and vases. This is a highly skilled technique requiring months—perhaps years—of practice to achieve complete control (Fig. 297). A single form emerging from the basic cylinder often goes through many transformations as the potter experiments and rejects different ideas before settling on the most effective shape. During the throwing process, various devices can be employed to provide texture, including a comb, fork, or the potter's fingertips. Wheel throwing has a special rhythm. It relates the artist and the materials in an intimate way, so that the two are virtually united during the creative process.

Wheel-thrown pieces display an absolute perfection and symmetry that, for many designers, brings one of the greatest satisfactions in working with clay (Fig. 298). However, once removed from the wheel, thrown forms can be cut, molded, and distorted as long as the clay remains plastic. For some craftsmen, the thrown form is only the point of departure.

Casting and *press forming* are two of the several methods used by industry to produce a large quantity of identical objects. In casting, a semiliquid mixture of clay called *slip* is poured into a plaster mold and allowed to harden. Press forming depends on the action of large mechanical press molds that force plastic clay into a predetermined shape. All production methods, of course, begin with a *prototype* model of the piece to be made, and this is usually hand-built by a designer at the factory. The range of possible shapes, especially with casting, is almost limitless.

While industrial methods lack the touch of originality and the imprint of the potter's hands, they do permit the fabrication of large

above left: 298. Ruth Gowdy McKinley. Double-lidded tobacco jar. 1973. Porcelain, hand-thrown; 8 x 6″. Courtesy the artist.

above right: 299. BLT dinnerware, intended for "breakfast, lunch, and tea"; designed by Nils Refsgaard, for Dansk International Designs.

right: 300. Paul Cardew. Lidded container. 1972. Earthenware clay, slip-cast, molded, and glazed; height $8\frac{3}{4}$″. Courtesy the artist.

301. Kim Bruce. Tea set. 1975. Stoneware. Courtesy the artist.

quantities of ceramic objects at relatively low cost. The functional quality—and the aesthetic quality as well—may be quite high (Fig. 299).

The increasing refinement of commercial techniques has led a number of studio potters to investigate them. Slip casting, for example, has the great advantage of permitting forms of a size or complexity that would be difficult to attain using conventional hand methods. There is no reason why a mold cannot be made for a single, one-of-a-kind piece, as opposed to thousands of identical items. Paul Cardew's lidded container (Fig. 300) illustrates a form that *could* have been created by laborious hand processes but no doubt was realized much faster by slip casting. The goal of the designer is *form,* and all avenues to its creation should be explored.

Structural Design

There are two major considerations in structural design for clay. First, will the piece be functional or nonfunctional? Second, will it be a one-of-a-kind item or intended for mass production? These factors govern shape to a high degree.

Many potters are concerned with the design of practical forms: jars with lids that fit tightly, pitchers that pour without dripping, handles that are well balanced and comfortable to hold, teapots with elements that relate well to one another. These are very real concerns, and the studio potter is better equipped to deal with them than the commercial manufacturer. If the studio potter makes a pitcher that does not "work," that pours milk onto the table, the buyer can go directly back and complain. Thus, the potter has immediate "feedback" and can alter the design. However, the consumer of a commercial pitcher would be lucky to reach a person in authority in a large commercial factory, and even if the complaint were heeded, it might take months to retool the equipment so that the pitcher would not leak. It seems obvious, then, that the designer of solid, functional pottery will find a responsive audience (Fig. 301).

Nonfunctional, sculptural pieces present no restrictions whatever. The artist-craftsman who works in clay has as much freedom as any sculptor, given (as always) the limitations of the material. Sandra McKenzie-Schmitt has created a series of Victorian buildings with

right: 302. Sandra McKenzie-Schmitt. *My Grandmother's House.* 1975. Stoneware, height 13″. Courtesy The Farmhouse.

below: 303. Ceramic tile bathroom, designed by Country Floors.

people in them (Fig. 302). The plasticity of clay seems to express particularly well the "gingerbread" quality of these structures. David Furman's series of little environments featuring his dog Molly (Fig. 210) give the same effect of charming miniaturization. Once the designer has fully understood what clay can and cannot do, there is no limit to structural design for sculpture.

The designer responsible for the creation of a prototype in mass production has two important considerations that must be borne in mind. Will the piece be acceptable to a broad range of people, rather than just a sophisticated elite? And will it be moldable on standard machinery? No design can be considered practical if its manufacture requires expensive retooling of the plant's equipment or, even worse, a certain amount of hand work. The designers of ceramic tiles (Fig. 303) have less of a problem in this regard, because at least the objects are always flat. Dinnerware and other household items require more planning, to ensure that the design is compatible with the machinery.

In between the creation of one-of-a-kind objects and commercial mass production lies the world of *limited production,* which has enabled many studio potters to survive. Limited production means that every piece is hand-built, but on an assembly line system. For instance, the potter who is making cups might throw a score of cups all at once, then make a score of handles, and so forth. Naturally, this program would be applied to designs that have proved successful. Here again the studio potter benefits from the direct relationship with the consumer.

Decorative Design

To many people, decorative design in ceramics means a glaze. However, this is only the beginning. While a glaze may be the only decoration a ceramic piece needs, there are many other possibilities.

304. *Mihrab* (mosque niche), from the Madrasa Imami, Isfahan, Iran. Founded 1354. Glazed ceramic tiles, height of niche 11′3″. Metropolitan Museum of Art, New York (Harris Brisbane Dick Fund).

A glaze is a superficial layer of molten material—of a composition resembling glass—that is fused onto a clay body. The glaze makes the object not only more attractive, but also more durable and waterproof.

Glazes can be mat or shiny; transparent, translucent, or opaque; brilliantly colored or subdued. As mentioned earlier, glazes that fire in the low range, usually on earthenware bodies, tend to be brighter and rely more on primary colors. The colors of Kenneth Price's abstract cup (Pl. 22, p. 178) resemble oil or acrylic paints in their smooth, shiny quality. Colorful effects also are to be found in the famed Persian wall tiles (Fig. 304), which offer a riot of hue and design complexity. Among the most important examples of bright glazes are Italian *majolica* (an imitation of Chinese porcelain), and the more ornate *faience,* which includes gold as well as colors.

305. Tom Turner. Bottle vase. 1976. Blue porcelain with salt glaze, height 8″. Courtesy the artist.

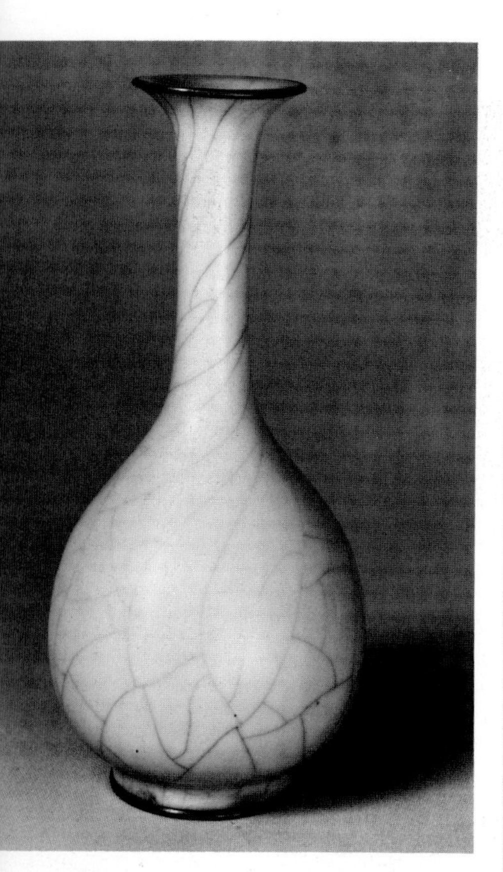

A number of special effects are possible with glazes. The *salt glaze,* which has a rough, pebbled texture (Fig. 305), is produced by literally throwing salt into the kiln during the glaze fire. It was a favorite decorative technique of Early American potters, and today the characteristically blue salt-glazed jugs are prized as collectors' items.

Crackle glazes result when the rate of expansion or contraction in the glaze and the clay body of a particular piece are different. The Chinese of the Sung Dynasty (A.D. 10th–11th century), perhaps the master potters of all time, calculated the effects of the crackle glaze precisely, so that they could predict to a high degree what pattern would appear

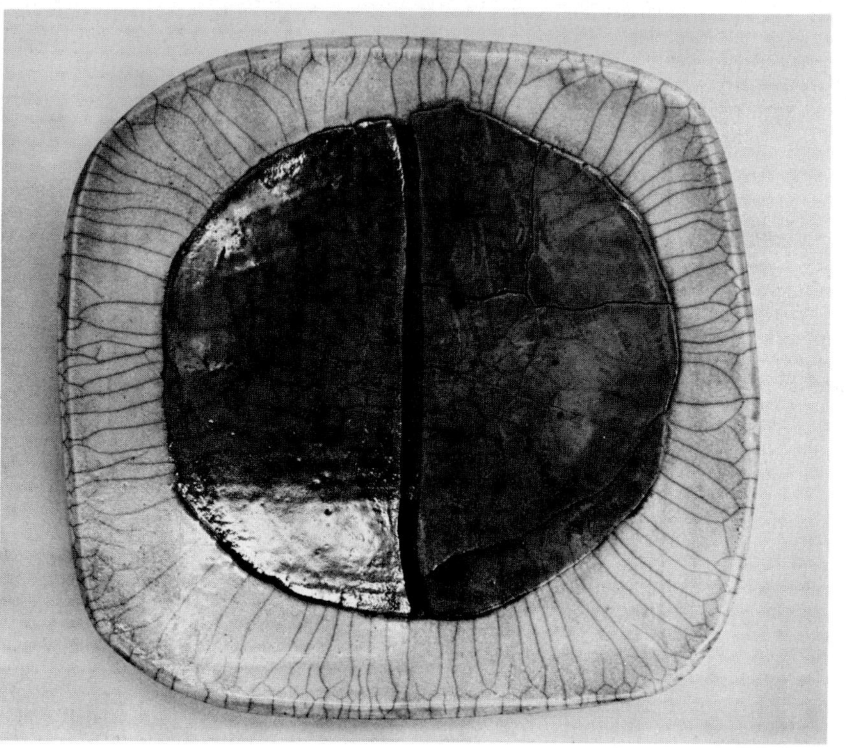

above: 306. *Kuan* vase. Chinese, Sung Dynasty, A.D. 10th–11th century. Blue-gray crackle glaze with copper rims at foot and mouth, height 7″. Percival David Foundation of Chinese Art, London.

right: 307. Barbara Segal. *Shattered Sun.* 1975. Raku-fired clay with amber luster and white crackle glaze, diameter 14″. Courtesy the artist.

on the finished object (Fig. 306). The intricate network of lines visible in a crackle glaze seems particularly appropriate for a classic form such as this.

Raku is a Japanese technique that contradicts every principle of ceramic procedure. Most ceramic pieces are heated *very* slowly in the kiln and then allowed to cool just as slowly, for otherwise they might crack. Raku works, by contrast, are plunged suddenly into the hot kiln, removed with tongs as soon as they have reached a glowing red heat, then dipped abruptly into sawdust, leaves, or similar material. The coarse, porous clay body protects against breakage. The attraction of raku pottery lies in its accidental quality, for the potter can never be quite sure of the colors and textures that will result. The act of making raku ware is always dramatic—a combination of glowing furnace, red-hot clay, smoking ashes, and unpredictable results.

Barbara Segal's *Shattered Sun* (Fig. 307) combines the effects of a crackle glaze with a raku technique. This plate form also makes use of a *luster glaze,* which includes gold or silver for an even richer quality. The complex decorative design works because it is beautifully integrated with the simple form.

Many types of decorative design are accomplished during the forming process without the use of glazes. Patterns can be scratched into clay that is *leather hard*—in other words, clay that has dried enough to hold its shape and takes on the consistency of leather. *Millefiore,* or "thousand-flower" effects are an adaptation of an ancient type of glass design. In a millefiore piece many coils of different-colored clay are assembled and attached together. The act of slicing through these multicolored rings at right angles creates an exciting surface design (Fig. 308).

Millefiore construction illustrates one important fact about decorative design in clay. The clay itself may provide wonderfully varied textures and color that satisfy the need for decoration. On the other hand, there is no limit to the techniques a ceramist may call upon to achieve a particular effect. The *Royal Carriage* by William J. Burke (Pl. 23, p. 178) is a fantastic vision of decorative design that integrates lusters, decals, and overglazes, with applied motifs, onto a complex thrown and hand-built form. Surely this vehicle could float, fly, or drive King and Queen Pig wherever they might wish to go.

308. Jane Peiser. Planter. 1976. Porcelain, hand-built in the millefiore technique, with salt glaze and overglaze; height 15½″. Courtesy the artist.

Designing in Clay

Design in clay begins when the artist first picks up a lump of plastic material and begins to mold it. The urge to shape, pinch, pat, and form the clay is almost irresistible. Few other materials offer such immediate response to the fingers. In clay, one's creative impulses can be transformed instantly into reality.

Many ceramic designers work from preliminary drawings and sketches. However, the real creative process takes place when the clay itself is shaped by hand. As we mentioned earlier, even industrial designers will hand-build a model to discover just how the clay will behave. Some artists who work in metal never actually touch the material. Rather, they will draw up specifications to be sent to a foundry or mill, and the finished work is delivered to them. This method of designing seems inconceivable in relation to clay. Design in clay indicates a particularly intimate relationship between the artist and the materials.

15 Glass

Glass is among the most naturally beautiful of all materials. Simply molded, colorless, and unadorned, it provides a fascinating study in its very essence (Fig. 309). Designers treasure glass for the qualities associated with this pure form—transparency, fluidity, and sparkle. We think of glass as being very fragile, which makes it seem all the more precious. Yet these aspects of glass only begin to suggest the facets of its personality and its potential for design. Much glass, rather than being transparent, is merely translucent or even opaque; some has no noticeable sparkle, and many special types are as hard and durable as steel.

We can find numerous parallels between design in glass and design in nature. Probably the most obvious comparison is with ice or water. A frozen pond, a glacier, or a large body of water on a calm day will often be likened to "a sheet of glass." Trees and brush that have been covered with frost, when the sun hits them resemble a glass landscape. Designers often exploit the crystalline qualities of water and ice in working with glass.

It should not surprise us that form in glass often mimics form in nature, because molten glass readily assumes organic shapes. The delicate, flowerlike structure shown in Figure 310 is actually a model,

blown in glass, of a tiny sea creature. Another possible reason for the affinity of glass with natural forms is its identity as an "earth" material. Like clay and wood, glass is used in a state very close to that in which it occurs naturally.

above left: 309. Willem Heesen. Cut and polished crystal cylinders. 1974. Glasrormcentrum, Leerdam.

above right: 310. Blown-glass model of *Trypanosphaera transformata,* a minute sea creature. American Museum of Natural History, New York.

Composition of Glass

Sand is the chief raw material in glass—specifically silica sand in its purest possible state. Most glass must be manufactured, but in special circumstances it will form naturally. The commonest type of natural glass is *obsidian,* a shiny black substance created by volcanic action. This was the earliest glass and was used as long ago as 75,000 B.C. Primitive peoples carved it into flints, arrowheads, and simple tools. Obsidian is similar in chemical analysis to some bottle glass manufactured today.

Basically, glass consists of silicon dioxide fused with metallic oxides; when cooled, this substance becomes a brittle solid. Various other materials can be added to produce the qualities desirable for different uses. There are literally thousands of types of glass, but they fall generally into six broad categories.

Lead glass is the aristocrat of glasses. A complex of potassium-lead silicate, lead glass, often known as *crystal,* is the most important to the designer. Its high refractive index makes it useful for lenses and prisms, and, because of its brilliance when cut, it serves for fine table crystal, decorative cut glass, and reflective chandeliers (Fig. 311).

Windows, lighting fixtures, table glasses, bottles, and other common glass products are made from *soda-lime glass,* which is inexpensive and easy to form. This type works well in situations where the minimum number of qualities are needed; that is, when the product does not require extra strength or brilliance.

Borosilicate glass has the special property of being highly resistant to heat and temperature changes. It therefore goes into such hardworking products as Pyrex cooking utensils, laboratory equipment, and aircraft windows.

Fused silica, 96 percent silica glass, and *aluminosilicate glass* are all remarkably tough materials that have been developed for scientific

below: 311. Cut-crystal chandelier designed by Pioggia. Courtesy Venini, Ltd., New York.

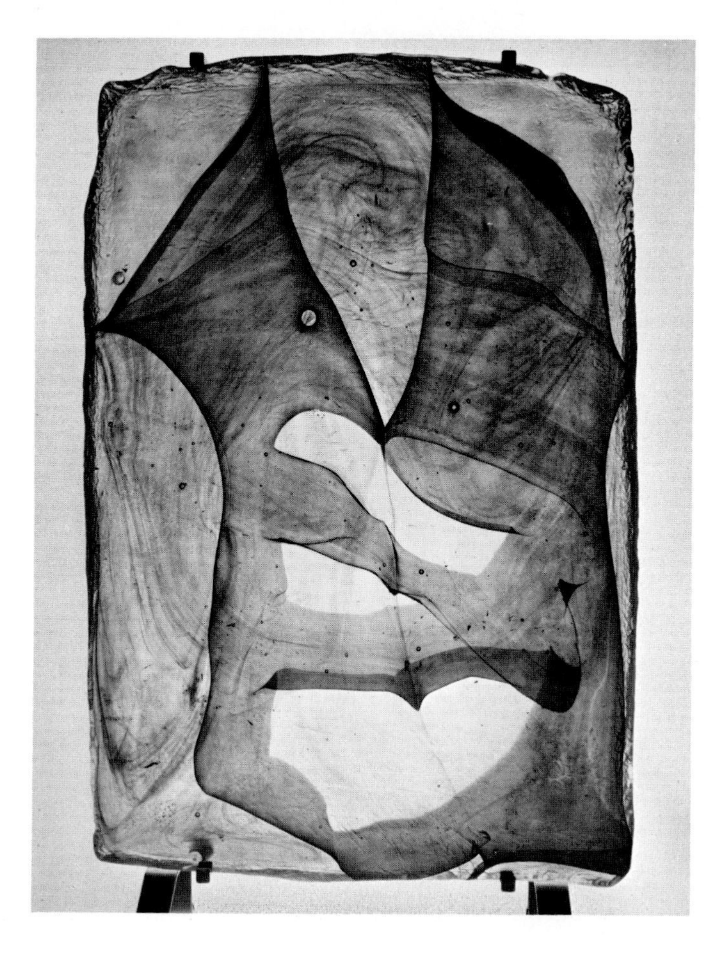

312. Dominick Labino. *Anatomie Surrealiste.* 1970. Hot-cast panel, 18 x 14". Courtesy the artist.

and industrial applications. They function in such demanding places as missile nose cones, laser beam reflectors, and space vehicle windows. The Apollo astronauts peered through windows of these special glasses in docking with their lunar landing vehicles and with the Russian cosmonauts.

Various compounds are added to molten glass in order to color or decolorize it, to improve its texture, and to lessen its tendency to form bubbles. Iron oxides, often present as impurities, give glass an undesirable greenish or brownish cast, so decolorizers must be included in the mixture. Coloring agents, on the other hand, give the jeweled tones that distinguish stained glass and glass mosaics, as well as the various hues that can be seen in tableware. For example, cobalt salts will produce blue, selenium and cadmium a ruby red.

Forming Methods

Glass is one of the few materials that must be worked in a state too hot to handle. This means that the designer or artist can never actually touch the glass while it is being shaped. Furthermore, the molten glass cools and hardens very quickly, so the forming must be done in a short time and with a sure hand. Mistakes can be corrected only by remelting the glass and starting afresh. There are five basic methods for forming glass.

The oldest forming technique is *pressing,* in which semifluid glass is taken from the melting pot and worked into shape by means of paddles or other tools. Ancient Egyptian potters discovered that the glazes they put on their wares could be made to stand alone, and by 1500 B.C. this process had been applied to making glass beads and jewels, as well as containers for cosmetics. Today machine-operated presses force the glass into molds that shape the outsides of objects, while plungers are inserted to smooth the insides.

Casting resembles pressing, except that no pressure is applied. The glassmaker simply pours the molten material into a mold to the desired thickness and allows it to cool until it hardens. The creative process of design takes place largely in the planning and construction of the mold (Fig. 312).

One of the most fascinating methods of working glass is the ancient art of *blowing,* believed to have been invented in the 1st century B.C. The blowpipe is a hollow metal rod about 4 feet long with a mouthpiece at one end. The glassblower dips up a small amount of molten material with the opposite end, rolls or presses it against a paddle or metal plate to form a rough cylinder, then blows into the mouthpiece, producing a bubble of glass (Fig. 313). While the blowing is in progress, form can be controlled by twisting the pipe, rolling with a paddle, cutting, shaping with a caliper, or adding more molten glass. The finished piece is broken away from the pipe, then reheated and trimmed with shears. Glassblowing is an exciting process to watch, because the glow of the furnace, the slashing of the shears, the sizzling vats of fluid, the crash of abandoned material, and the ever-present threat of disaster all provide drama.

For the past several centuries most glassblowing has been done in molds; the designer, then, plans the mold, and the glassblower contributes only lung power and general skill in handling the material. However, in the last two decades there has been a strong revival of

313. Bob Held and Marvin Lipofsky blowing glass at the World Crafts Council Conference, Toronto, 1974.

314. Larry Bell. *Garst's Mind #2.* 1971. Vaporous layers of silver alloy on glass plates, each panel 8 x 6′. Courtesy the artist.

freehand glassblowing, largely through the efforts of Harvey K. Littleton (Fig. 316) and Dominick Labino (Fig. 312). This has reunited the two functions—design and execution—in one individual, the artist-craftsman. Wonderfully free effects can emerge from the blowpipe in the hands of a sensitive designer.

Rods and cylinders, as well as fibers and some window glass, are made by a process known as *drawing.* This method calls for the molten glass to be actually pulled from the furnace by some device that controls its shape, such as a core for tubes or a long, narrow trough for sheets. Drawing can also be done by hand. The glob of hot glass might be affixed between two blowpipes, and the craftsmen holding them gradually move apart.

The last forming method, known as *rolling,* produces uniform sheets of glass, such as are needed for plate window glass or mirrors. Rolling is a factory technique and therefore of importance primarily for industrial designers (Fig. 318), but some artists have explored the potential of sheet-glass constructions (Fig. 314).

After a glass piece has been formed, it generally will be subjected to one or more finishing processes. Nearly always it must be *annealed,* or

left: 315. Michael Boehm. Set of tumblers. Blown glass, hand-formed while hot. Courtesy Rosenthal Studiohaus.

right: 316. Harvey K. Littleton. *Amber Loops.* 1974. Drawn glass, largest form $9\frac{1}{2} \times 7\frac{1}{2} \times 2\frac{1}{2}''$. Courtesy the artist.

reheated and cooled slowly, to relieve the stresses that develop because of uneven cooling in the formation. Most glass work will also be ground, buffed, and polished.

Structural Design

As the illustrations in this chapter show, glass can be made to assume an extraordinary range of shapes. We are most accustomed to seeing it in everyday objects such as table glasses, but even here the designer has broad scope in creating distinctive effects. The protruding striated band on the tumblers in Figure 315 is not mere decoration, but performs two functional services. First, it places the weight toward the bottom of the glasses so they will not topple so easily; second, it makes a convenient and sure grip for the hand.

A number of artists have experimented with innovative structural design in glass. Harvey K. Littleton, for instance, shapes freely blown glass into curved forms that typify the molten purity of the material (Fig. 316). The forms seem "classic" in their very simplicity, even though they do not remind us of any familiar shape. The viewer's impression of Littleton's work comes largely from the way in which heated glass was made to flow during the creative process and the point at which this flow was interrupted. We can compare this effect to the Labino piece in Figure 312, which gives the illusion of eternally flowing liquid within a form that we know to be static. Littleton's work often takes advantage of the "controlled accident," with free-blown rods or cylinders of glass that appear to be splaying out or falling but that have been stopped in their movement.

Structural design on a grand scale has been possible in glass ever since sheet glass became practical and relatively inexpensive. Modern cities are filled with soaring towers of glass, and we take them very much for granted. But the most extraordinary glass structure of all was built more than a hundred years ago in London's Hyde Park—the famous "Crystal Palace" (Fig. 317). This fantasy creation was the winning plan of Joseph Paxton, a designer of greenhouses, to contain the "Great Exhibition" of 1851. All details of the exhibition were under the direct control of Prince Albert, consort of Queen Victoria. Its purpose was to bring together under one roof the "Works of Industry of All Nations." Today the exhibit features have generally been superseded by later inventions, but the splendid "roof" that Paxton conceived has never been equalled.

In sheer physical terms the Crystal Palace was a wondrous thing. It was 1851 feet wide (symbolic of the year), 108 feet high, and contained 18,000 individual panes of glass mounted on an iron structure. On the day of the opening ceremonies the building comfortably held 250,000 visitors. The brilliance of Paxton's design lay not only in its beauty and daring, but in the degree to which it was thought out in advance. An ingenious system of prefabrication enabled the entire structure to be assembled in the incredibly short time of sixteen weeks, and all of the 18,000 panes of glass were set in place by eighty workmen in a single week.

By all reports Prince Albert was delighted with the structure, as were most of its visitors. We must remember that in Victorian times people were accustomed to heavy, ponderous buildings overfilled with heavy, ponderous furnishings. The Crystal Palace, by comparison, must have seemed like a fairyland. Long, open vistas carried the eye to infinity, with no solid walls to interrupt the view to the outside. Within, live trees growing to ceiling height gave the breathtaking

317. Joseph Paxton. Interior, Crystal Palace, London. 1851. Cast iron and glass, width 1851′. (Lithograph from *The Builder* of January 4, 1851.) Science & Technology Research Center, New York Public Library (Astor, Lenox, and Tilden Foundations).

impression of the "outdoors-indoors." Paxton wisely left his design free of any applied ornamentation; the bare structure of iron and glass speaks magnificently for itself.

Architects still are fascinated by the possibilities of glass in structural design, but new ways of living call for a new design approach. Glass offers many functional advantages. Except for plastics, which appeared only in this century, glass is the one material that combines transparency—for light and view—with protection from the elements. These practical considerations do not limit the potential for creative design in building glass, as architects Kevin Roche and John Dinkeloo have proved. The office complex of the College Life Insurance Company (Fig. 318), near Indianapolis, was conceived as three (eventually nine) pyramid-shape structures each having one wall of almost solid glass. Because this wall is sloped sharply backward, the outer face of the glass reflects the sky, thus bringing a wonderful lightness to these bold forms jutting up from the flat terrain. On the inside, the sloping glass permits much more light to enter the offices than would be possible with conventional upright windows. The College Life Insurance buildings stand as deceptively simple but ingenious design in glass; they exaggerate its natural qualities for a fresh result.

Decorative Design

Many interesting types of surface decoration lend themselves especially well to glass. Delicate designs seem to "float" on the transparent material and become even more attractive when light shines through them. Decorative techniques that call for adding glass appendages to the basic form may increase the sense of fluidity. Below are described some of the various decorative methods that have been applied to glass throughout history and in contemporary work.

Laid-on designs consist of separate shapes of glass applied to the principal form. In the past the additions were often of contrasting colors and sometimes were gilded for a luxurious effect. The artist-craftsman today takes a free approach to laid-on ornamentation. Fritz Dreisbach's *10th Anniversary Cup* has sinuous organic shapes applied to the basic goblet form (Fig. 319).

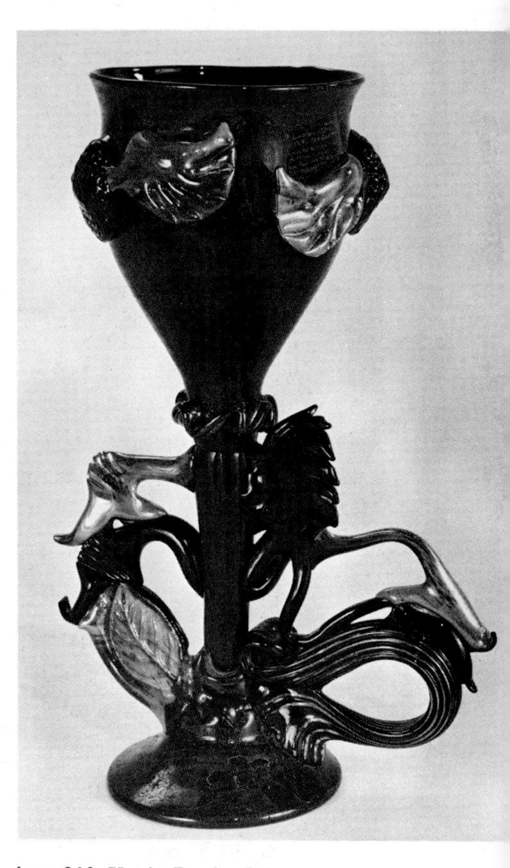

top: 318. Kevin Roche John Dinkeloo Associates. College Life Insurance Company headquarters, Indianapolis. 1973–74.

above: 319. Fritz Dreisbach. *10th Anniversary Cup.* 1972. Blown glass, engraved, with applied decoration; height $13\frac{3}{8}''$. Toledo Museum of Art, Ohio.

320. Ann Wärff. *Give and Get.* 1973. Sandblasted and etched plate, diameter $19\frac{1}{2}''$. Courtesy the artist.

Etching creates a frosted texture on the surface of glass. It may replace engraving or cutting in less expensive tableware; however, the subtle quality of etching can be used for great design effect (Fig. 320). To etch glass the craftsman first coats areas that are to remain undecorated with wax, or else coats the entire surface and scratches through the wax to reveal the design portions. This is called *stopping out.* Then, the glass is submerged in hydrofluoric acid, which eats into the exposed glass.

Heavy crystal may be ornamented by *cutting* (Fig. 311), a method of decoration that reached considerable popularity in past eras, especially around the turn of this century. Today most cutting is done by diamond wheels.

Engraving is perhaps the most adaptable of the decorative processes for glass, because it enhances the surface without detracting from its inherent qualities of brilliance and clarity. Rapidly turning copper or diamond wheels engrave the glass that is pressed against them. Since the process is painstaking, however, it usually is limited to the finest crystal.

A number of decorative techniques that are rare or unknown today were extremely important in the past. The ancient Romans developed a technique that combines decorative and structural design. *Millefiori* or "thousand-flower" glass is made from narrow rods of glass in many colors, which are bundled together, partially fused, then sliced into discs for mounting in the base material. The original rods appear in the finished piece as little dots or rings of color, like so many flowers in a field (Fig. 321). Today, craftsmen are adapting this method to ceramic design (Fig. 308), as well as to glass.

Perhaps the most highly prized of all historical glass is that manufactured in Venice from the late 15th through the 17th century. Venetian glassmakers of this period made great technical strides in the introduction of new colors and especially in surface decoration. Glass vessels were painted, gilded, covered with swirls of opaque white glass, and *crackled*—that is, made by controlled heating and cooling to have an overall pattern of fine lines. The goblet in Figure 322 is richly *enameled* in brilliant colors. A contemporary adaptation of this technique, the glass sculpture in Figure 323 is also painted, but this time with acrylic lacquers. The piece was assembled from blown sections, then sandblasted, painted, and lustered. As with the Venetian goblet, the blown glass form becomes a point of departure for creative decorative design, and the transparent sparkle we associate with glass is underplayed.

Many contemporary glassworkers have experimented with *color trailing*, a method whereby swirls or patterns of color are set against clear glass or glass of a contrasting color (Fig. 324). This kind of decoration leaves the glass still transparent and sparkling, yet creates a fascinating visual texture. In the example shown the trailed design heightens the fluid quality of the glass.

below left: 321. Millefiori glass bowl. Roman, 1st century B.C. Metropolitan Museum of Art, New York (gift of Henry J. Marquand, 1881).

below: 322. Angelo Beroviero (?). Goblet showing *Triumph of Fame*. c. 1475. Glass with enamel work and gold ornamentation, height 7½″. Toledo Museum of Art, Ohio (gift of Edward Drummond Libbey, 1940).

below: 323. Jon F. Clark. Glass form from the series *Delaware Valley Span*. 1974. Blown glass with platinum luster, polyester resin, and acrylic lacquer; length 24″. Collection Portnoy Ltd., New York.

right: 324. William Bernstein. Pitcher. 1976. Blown glass, color trailed; height 11″. Courtesy the artist.

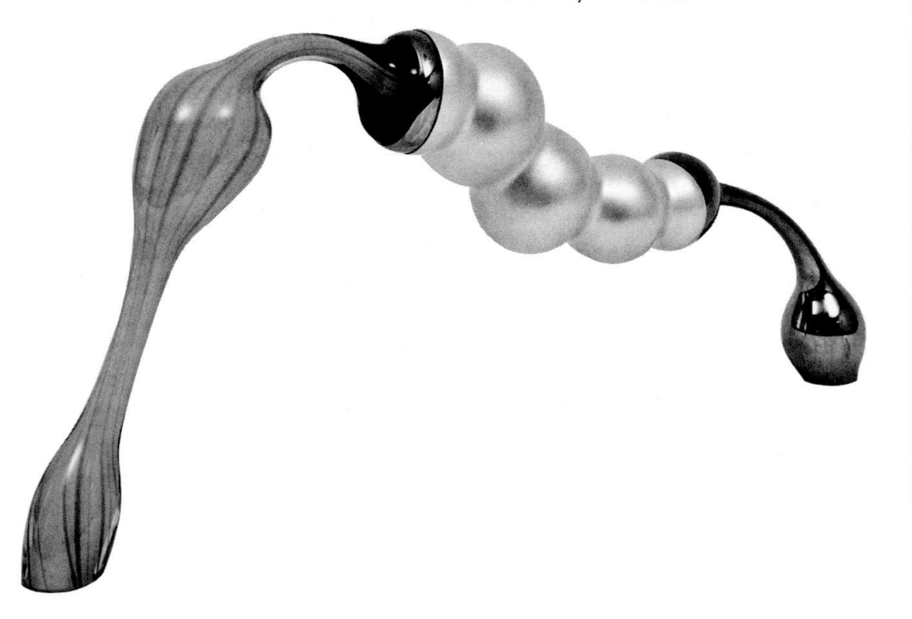

325. Lucas Samaras. *Room #2.* 1966. Wood and mirrors, 8 x 8 x 10′. Albright-Knox Art Gallery, Buffalo, N.Y. (gift of Seymour H. Knox).

Designing in Glass

We might say that the most important element in glass design is space, since a large portion of all glass objects *define* a segment of space while at the same time revealing it through the transparency of the material. Designed space was certainly a major accomplishment of the Crystal Palace (Fig. 317). Light is also crucial, since the nature of glass is to transmit and/or reflect light to a higher degree than any other substance. The buildings shown in Figure 318, which might otherwise be stolid and heavy, gain an airy lightness from the soaring glass wall, especially since they reflect the blue sky and passing clouds.

These elements take on an even greater dimension in mirrored glass. Lucas Samaras' *Room #2* (Fig. 325), a construction in wood and mirrors, is only 10 feet deep, but it seems to be a never-ending landscape of shimmering planes and angles. Light bounces from one surface to another in an infinite progression, so that everywhere one looks there is brilliance.

The shape of a glass object usually comes directly from the forming method. Blown pieces tend to be rounded and organic, rolled pieces thin and flat. Casting and pressing, however, provide the means for an endless variety of shapes, especially with the new superstrength glasses.

In some glass objects line may all but disappear, so gossamer is the material. But most often there is the external line of the object (Fig. 316) and possibly the line created by surface decoration, as in engraving and color trailing (Fig. 324). Texture can be controlled to any degree, from the smooth quality of pure glass, through frosted decoration, to the aggressive textures of laid-on designs (Fig. 319).

Related Glass Techniques

Stained Glass

Stained glass derives its effect from variations in the light that strikes and shines through it. Once stained glass has been illumined by natural or artificial light, it glows with a gemlike iridescence.

One shared element unites the art of stained glass with the various glassforming techniques described above—their common material. In other respects stained glass more closely resembles painting or assemblage. Basically, stained glass is made by cutting or pouring bits of colored glass into preplanned shapes, then joining the individual pieces with separating strips, usually of lead (hence the term *leaded glass*). Stained glass works always are mounted so that light can penetrate them, for their effect depends less upon the substance of the glass itself than on the patterns of multicolored light that are created when rays of the sun or of artificial illumination pass through. Naturally, this makes stained glass ideal for windows and lampshades.

Gothic cathedrals present the most splendid array of stained glass ever created. These magnificent windows were meant to illustrate for a largely illiterate congregation the moral teachings of the Bible and the Christian tradition, with historical episodes interwoven. Thus, the windows became "the gospel of the illiterate." Yet at the same time the stained glass windows in cathedrals played another role—the creation of an atmosphere within an enclosure. Patterns of flickering, rainbow-hued light, changing slowly with the daily movement of the sun, filled the vast interiors of the churches. This play of color transformed massive walls of stone into a mystical, ever-expanding space.

Similar—but secular—concerns motivated Louis Comfort Tiffany, the Art Nouveau artist whose name has become almost synonymous with decorated glass lampshades. Tiffany's work, like that of the other Art Nouveau proponents, was based on natural forms, specifically plant forms. Lines curve, swell, and intertwine in a decorative manner.

Tiffany's glass, especially the stained-glass windows in which he was most interested (Pl. 24, p. 211), catered to the tastes of wealthy clients in New York and other urban areas. The residents of a house in New York or Newark or Philadelphia could retreat behind their Tiffany stained glass into a world that was pastoral and benign, in contrast to the urban ugliness growing up around them. Tiffany's products included many opaque elements—such as mottled and marbled glass segments—to screen unpleasant views.

Contemporary work in stained glass still emphasizes windows and lampshades, because the close association with light is so natural, but inventive craftsmen have also experimented with new applications. The stained-glass clock in Figure 326 is illuminated from within to make the colors glow. It refers back to an age of lavish decoration, yet the approach to design is totally fresh. Increasingly today designers are exploring old techniques and translating them into modern terms.

326. Fred Varney. Clock. 1974. Opalescent glass, copper foil, tin/lead solder, and wire; height 24″. Private collection, Boston.

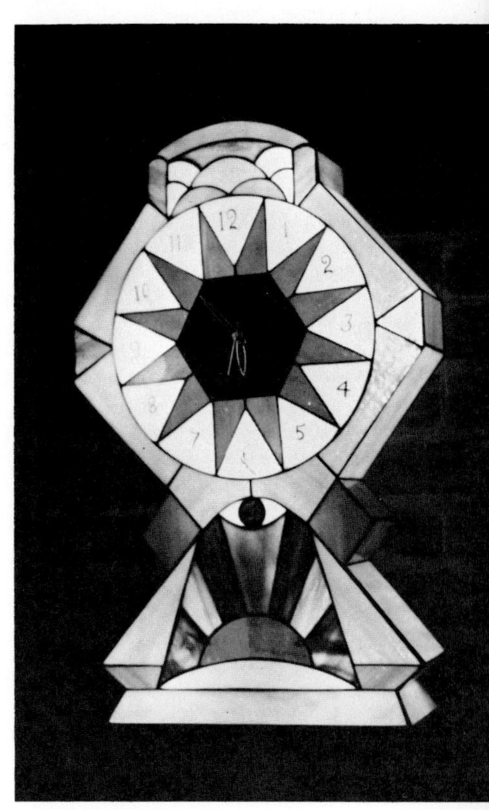

Mosaic

The renewal of interest in stained glass has been paralleled by a revival of mosaic—an art in which small pieces of material called *tesserae* are embedded in wet mortar to form a pattern or figurative image. Often mosaics are made of colored stones or small (usually glazed) ceramic tiles. However, tiny pieces of glass can also be formed into mosaics.

327. *Crucifixion,* mosaic in the Monastery Church at Daphnē, Greece. 11th century.

As enthusiasm has increased for the integration of decorative design with architecture, mosaic has come to hold a place no other art can fill. The color, sparkle, and texture produced by a panel or wall of mosaic cannot be obtained in either painting or sculpture. Furthermore, mosaic is durable and easy to maintain, often outlasting the structure to which it is applied. Many examples of ancient Roman mosaics found in the past several hundred years have been uncovered from the debris of crumbled walls.

There are two methods of making mosaics, the *direct* and the *indirect.* In the direct method the tesserae are inlaid directly into the mortar. The designer works with the realization that irregularities of surface will add to the interest of the finished composition, catching the light, casting shadows, and making a tapestrylike pattern. In the indirect method, the work is done from a full-scale drawing or *cartoon* that is a representation of the design in reverse. The tesserae are placed on the paper with a special paste, and much of the mosaic composition is completed before the mortar is applied to the base. When the mortar is ready, the paper-backed mosaic is set face down against it and pressed into the mortar. After the paper has dried, it is peeled off. Grout can be added to fill in the crevices between tesserae.

The early mosaics of the Greeks and Romans were of pebbles, clay tiles, or marble fragments, but under the Eastern Empire established by Constantine in A.D. 323 interest shifted to more reflective colored glass. Mosaic as an art form reached unprecedented heights in the Byzantine wall decorations of buildings, especially in Daphnē, Constantinople, and Ravenna (Fig. 327). Glittering jewel tones of glass are

above: Plate 24. Louis C. Tiffany, and Tiffany Studios. *Triptych: Landscape.* c. 1910–19. Stained glass window, 4′2″ x 7′7½″. Art Museum, Princeton University, N.J.

right: Plate 25. Simon Rodia (Rodilla). Watts Towers, Los Angeles, detail. c. 1921–54 (now partially destroyed).

above: Plate 26. Carol Maree Hoffman. *Helical Rainbow.* 1976. Crocheted, hand-dyed jute; 36 x 24 x 18″. Courtesy the artist.

right: Plate 27. Risa Goldman. *Untitled.* 1974. Gum bichromate and pigment on muslin and cotton, hand and machine stitched; 8′2″ x 6′. Copyright American Crafts Council, *Your Portable Museum.*

328. Joan Curtis. Antelope pendant. 1976. Cloisonné enamel set in silver, height 1½″. Collection Betsy Krieger, Washington, D.C.

combined with a lavish use of metallic gold to produce an effect of richness suitable for the high intellectual and artistic level of the designs themselves.

Mosaic is an art of *assemblage,* which is to say that the artist assembles individual units into a new and coherent whole. Nothing could better typify this aspect of the art than the fabulous Watts Towers in Los Angeles (Pl. 25, p. 211). The towers were built over a period of thirty years by Simon Rodia, an Italian immigrant tile setter. Although totally untrained in art or design, Rodia obviously drew upon an intuitive feeling for form, line, color, and rhythm. His materials included broken pieces of bottle glass, mirrors, shells, shattered dishes, and other castoffs, all on a frame of concrete and wire mesh. In closeup we can identify specific elements, but from a distance the effect is one of overall richness in color and pattern. While they are an isolated example, the Watts Towers do suggest the enormous potential for mosaic art in contemporary expression.

Enameling

Enamel is related to glass in composition and to ceramics in technique. The raw material of enamel actually consists of ground glass particles that are applied—either dry or in a liquid, pastelike state—to a metal ground, after which the entire piece is fired in a kiln. Firing causes the glass particles to melt, forming a smooth, lustrous coating on the metal. Any metal that will fuse with the enamel—for example, copper, silver, or gold—can serve as the ground.

There are several different kinds of enamel work. In *cloisonné* or "partitioned" enameling, the craftsman affixes tiny flat metal wires known as *cloisons* to a metal base according to the desired pattern, then applies the enamel between the cloisons. Firing causes the enamels to fuse with both the cloisons and the base. Cloisonné enamels usually show a delicate, weblike structure, with the enamel contributing color, the cloisons fine linear detail (Fig. 328).

Plique-à-jour enamel resembles stained glass, because the metal base material is removed after firing to leave only the cloisonné wires and the enamel. The result is a transparent or translucent colored shell interspersed with the fine lines of the wires.

When no separators or cloisons are involved, the enamelist can literally "paint" with enamel colors to obtain effects as varied as in oil painting. This technique is called *Limoges,* after the French city where it originated. An offshoot of this is *grisaille,* which utilizes layers of white enamel against a dark background to create a subtle shaded quality. Few contemporary enamelists work in grisaille, but Harold B. Helwig has made the process uniquely his own. Helwig's works (Fig. 329) often feature lushly decorative layered effects, which are made all the more complex because of the shaded grisaille effect.

Quite a different style is evident in the work of Ellamarie Woolley, whose *Child's Play* is illustrated in Figure 330. This large enamel piece shows no surface textural interest, no shaded colors and tones, no real reflective quality. Instead, the work consists of broad geometric areas of absolutely flat color. Wooley uses enamels in the same manner that contemporary painters use the new acrylics—as a means of obtaining flat, pure, saturated colors. Her main interest is form, in this case the illusionistic forms of boxes that appear to be cubic and bent at angles to one another. *Child's Play* demonstrates that enamels, like other forms of glasswork, can be adapted to new modes of expression.

The range of illustrations in this chapter should begin to suggest the amazing versatility of glass as a design material. While many designers are still attracted by the qualities traditionally associated with the material, others have found in glass creative possibilities that were undreamed of less than a century ago.

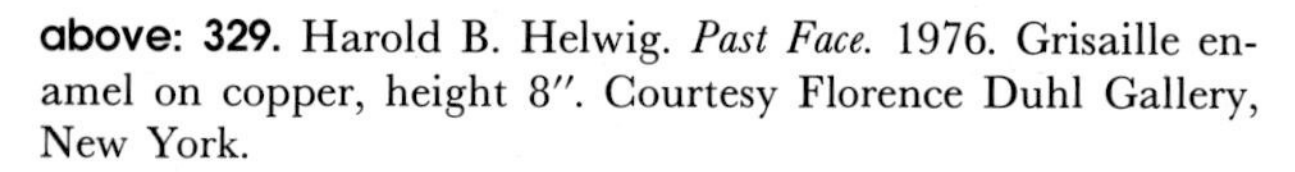

above: 329. Harold B. Helwig. *Past Face.* 1976. Grisaille enamel on copper, height 8″. Courtesy Florence Duhl Gallery, New York.

right: 330. Ellamarie Woolley. *Child's Play.* 1971. Enamel on copper, $22\frac{1}{2} \times 15\frac{1}{2}$″. Courtesy the artist.

16 Fiber

By definition, a fiber is a thread, or something capable of being spun into a thread. Until this century fibers were limited to organic materials—the products of plants (cotton, jute, sisal, linen, and others) or of animals (wool, silk, and specialty furs). The introduction of nylon in 1940 vastly increased the vocabulary of fibers, and today fibers of endlessly different qualities are made from such ingredients as wood pulp, chemicals, and petroleum.

Like clay, fiber is a very ancient medium. The earliest settled cultures wove baskets to contain the seeds needed for agriculture or the grain for the herds. In nomadic societies, fiber gave the means for constructing shelters that were either portable or readily left behind.

Today the range of fibers has expanded to fill every area of life, from upholstery in the home to space suits on the Moon. In the field of design, some of the most exciting and innovative work during the 1970s has been in fiber. The advantages of this medium are obvious: unlimited color, shape, texture, moldability, and (as we shall see) size. Added to this is the special warmth, the responsive quality of the material.

No single chapter could possibly cover the scope of design in fiber, nor could even a whole book. Hundreds of books appear each year dealing with various aspects of the subject. It is the purpose of this chapter, then, to try to show the enormous potential for creative design in fiber and some of the many ways in which it has been realized.

Structural Design

Structural design in fiber can be divided loosely into three categories: *interlacing* techniques, *sewing* techniques, and *pressure* techniques, in which the fibers are bonded together by matting or pounding. Of the three, interlacing techniques are by far the most widespread.

Interlacing Techniques

Weaving is an elaboration of *basketry,* a process in which reeds or grasses are interlaced by working them in an up-and-down pattern. Basketry was among the earliest techniques developed by primitive cultures and, as was mentioned in Chapter 14, probably served as the stimulus to ceramic construction. No tools except the fingers are required to make a basket, so that the craftsman has a direct relationship with the material. Today, the Indian tribes throughout the Americas still weave baskets, and sophisticated craftsmen, following the same procedures, create works of art that would not seem out of place in a manor house. The Japanese use baskets as packaging (Fig. 331). Few consumers would deny that this is more appealing than the plastic bubble-wrap that is standard in many Western countries.

Reeds can be worked just as they are. However, the more common natural fibers—cotton and wool—must be spun into yarn in order to make them practical for any construction. *Spinning* is a process whereby fibers are twisted together into a long, unbroken strand, a *yarn.* To an overwhelming degree, machines accomplish this process today, but before the Industrial Revolution of the late 18th and early 19th centuries, all spinning was done by hand. In the early history of the United States, spinning was a vital part of every household's routine.

331. Salt basket, from the Kagoshima Prefecture, Kyushu, Japan. Woven bamboo and vine. From *How to Wrap Five More Eggs,* by Hideyuki Oka.

High-speed spinning machines now make the work of these early spinners seem tedious, but it must be remembered that the product of machines is always standard. Many artists who work in fiber have sought a more controlled, "designed" effect. To a large extent, this has revived the craft of handspinning. Susan Weitzman, for instance, builds wall hangings of straight, unwoven yarn. The wonderful textural and color effects result from the yarns that Weitzman handspins (Fig. 332). Handspinning can introduce designed thick-and-thin areas, as well as many other special qualities.

In *weaving* two sets of yarns, arranged at right angles to each other, are interlaced. Ted Hallman's *Rondel* (Fig. 333) shows this relationship clearly. The basic instrument for weaving is the *loom,* on which the lengthwise yarns (the *warp*) are held rigid, while the intersecting crosswise yarns (the *weft* or *woof* or *filling*) move back and forth to create a *web,* or fabric. Modern looms look tremendously complicated, but they all depend on a few simple principles. First of all, the warp must be kept under tension. Second, there must be some device to raise selective warp yarns, creating a *shed* for the weft to move through. In *plain weave,* for example, the weft is supposed to move over one yarn and under the next, evenly across the fabric, so the shed would be one-up-one-down throughout. Third, it is necessary to pack each weft

left: 332. Susan Weitzman. *To Shyam.* 1973. Handspun linen, unwoven; 9′11″ x 3′11½″. Courtesy International Biennial of Tapestries, Lausanne, 1973.

below: 333. Ted Hallman. *Rainbow Weave Rondel.* 1974. Silk, cotton, and linen; diameter 5½″. Courtesy the artist.

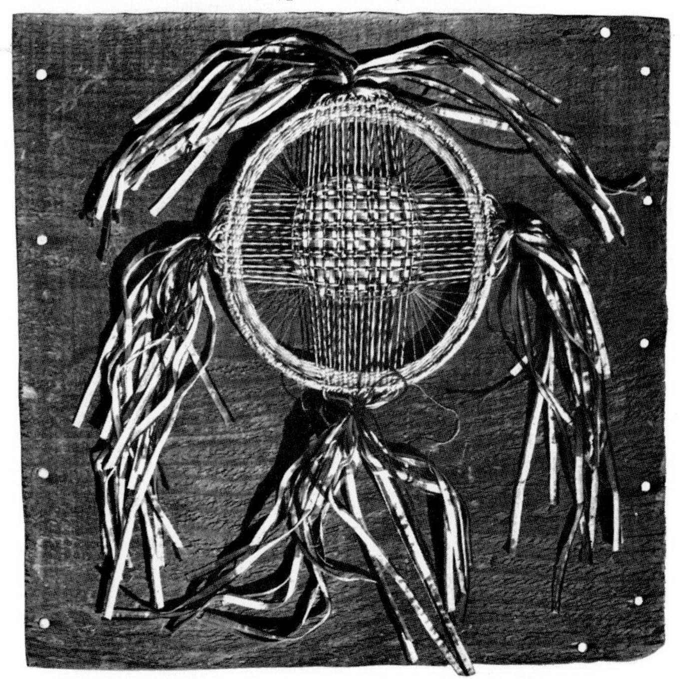

yarn into position in the cloth, a task that is accomplished by a *beater.* Further refinements to the loom are convenient but inessential.

Plain weave is the simplest of constructions, yet so many variables present themselves—color, texture, thickness, composition of yarn—that the design potential is unlimited. Sheila Hicks' *White Letter* (Fig. 334) was woven from yarns that are uniform in color and material. Only the texture, the thickness of the yarns in certain places, has a role

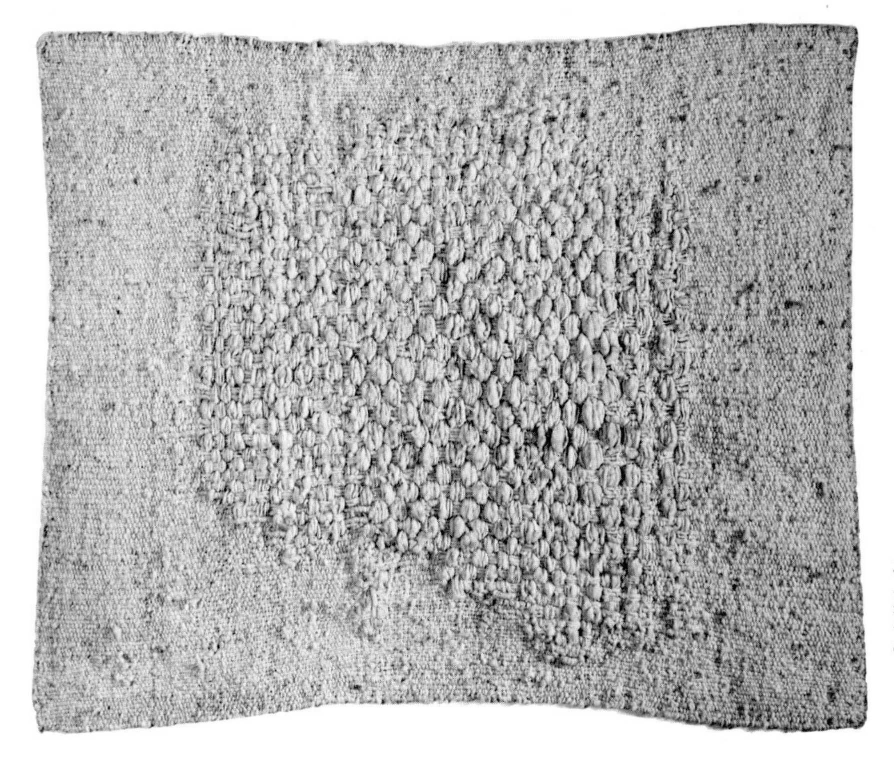

334. Sheila Hicks. *White Letter.* 1962. Wool, plain weave in white yarns; 3′2″ x 3′11½″. Museum of Modern Art, New York (gift of Knoll Associates).

left: 335. Daniel Graffin. *Indigo Quadrangulaire.* 1975. Knotted, stuffed, and woven, $17'10\frac{1}{2}''$ x $18'2\frac{3}{8}''$. Courtesy International Biennial of Tapestries, Lausanne, 1975.

right: 336. Double cloth tapestry of cotton from Central Coast, Peru. c. A.D. 1000–1450. American Museum of Natural History, New York (Bandelier Collection, 1901).

in creating the subtle, elegant design. Even though a single weaver could never begin to explore the possibilities of plain weave, there are hundreds of other combinations, all dependent on raising certain warp yarns on the loom. These range from the intricate figure weaves of Early American coverlets to the classic patterns of Scots tartans.

One of the most important breakthroughs in contemporary fiber design has been the conquest of scale. Daniel Graffin's *Indigo Quadrangulaire* (Fig. 335) is a huge work about 18 feet high. Obviously, no ordinary loom could handle a structure this large. The weaver today has shown tremendous ingenuity in developing methods to satisfy the creative impulse.

Tapestry is a specialized form of weaving in which weft yarns are hand-controlled. Rarely does a single weft yarn move completely across the fabric. Instead, yarns of a particular color or texture appear and disappear on the surface of the web as the pattern demands.

The Indians of ancient Peru—in addition to being supreme potters and goldsmiths—created abstract-design tapestries of astonishing complexity (Fig. 336). We can only wonder at their skill—considering the primitive equipment, the limitations of natural dyes, and the simple materials available.

The "golden age" of tapestry came in the 15th and 16th centuries in Europe. Weavers trained in a rigorous apprenticeship program and working from detailed *cartoons* (or scale drawings) created amazingly complex figural tapestries—like paintings in cloth. Among the most famous is a series depicting a subject steeped in mythology: *The Hunt of the Unicorn* (Fig. 337). These tapestries were woven about 1500, probably in Flanders.

Some contemporary handweavers utilize the tapestry technique to create effects of surprise, delight, and mystery. Janet Roush Taylor's *Exit* (Fig. 338) builds a splendid *trompe l'oeil* image (not unlike the marquetry in Figure 254) with just two pieces of fabric, one bent at the floorline. We can study this work patiently, to see how the artist has deceived us into seeing the third dimension, but we never completely sort out the composition.

To the standard warp and weft of flat weaving, pile weaves add a third element—a standup yarn called a *pile.* This surface yarn is evident in velvets, carpets, and terry-cloth toweling. It adds a quality of warmth, sensuousness, and above all luxury to any fabric. *Shag* rugs, which have a very long pile, have enjoyed considerable popularity because of these characteristics.

Designers can exploit this quality of warmth and sensuality even in a work that is not actually walked upon. The tactile textures translate

left: 337. *The Unicorn in Captivity,* from *The Hunt of the Unicorn.* Franco-Flemish, c. 1500. Tapestry weave, 12′ x 8′3″. Metropolitan Museum of Art, New York (gift of John D. Rockefeller, Jr., 1937).

right: 338. Janet Roush Taylor. *Exit.* 1971. Tapestry weave in linen, wool, mohair and rayon, two panels; 7′11″ x 3′3″ and 11′8½″ x 3′3″. Courtesy International Biennial of Tapestries, Lausanne, 1973.

339. Madeleine Bosscher. *5 Banen.* 1971. Transparent plastic film, 8′2″ x 13′1″. Executed by Atelier Kortelaan 29. Courtesy International Biennial of Tapestries, Lausanne, 1973.

into visual ones. Madeleine Bosscher's *5 Bahnen* (Fig. 339), a pile-weave tapestry made of transparent plastic film, seems lush and comfortable because of the textured pile.

In *knotting* techniques, the yarns are not merely interlaced but tied—together or to each other. Most knotting methods involve only a single set of yarns oriented in the same direction, rather than the crossing yarns of weaving.

Knotted patterns have been used to create all manner of fabrics, from the functional to the exquisite, from sailors' nets to altar hangings. The knotted design in Figure 340 is a form of *macramé,* which results from combinations of certain knots. Here the artist has worked delicate macramé patterns around a base of copper for an intriguing neck pendant.

On a dramatically different scale, the large knotted rope work in Figure 341 duplicates the pleasure of a jungle gym. One can climb upon, swing through, and dangle from any portion of this room-size construction. It pays tribute to the new openness in sculpture, the freedom to touch and experience.

The art of *wrapping* yarns around one another came into its own as a design medium during the late 1960s and early 1970s. This technique avoids any real interlacing or knotting, and rather concentrates on the sheer beauty of fiber yarns laid next to each other. David Kaye's *Bound Linen and Five Loops* (Fig. 342) is such a perfect, satisfying form that it seems to make other fiber techniques superfluous. We are reminded of a skein of yarn as it looks when sold—yet a skein elevated to a harmonious, liquid flow of lines.

Sometimes wrapped yarns are made to curl, spring, or spread out. Barbara Chase-Riboud combines wrapping with metal forms in an

above: 340. Chris Yarborough. *Necklace II.* 1973. Knotted wool, linen, and copper; 3½ x 5½″. North Carolina Museum of Art, Raleigh.

above right: 341. Wilhelm and Eva Heer. *Spielwildnis* (detail). 1973. Knotted rope, 13′1″ x 13′1″ x 9′10″. Courtesy International Biennial of Tapestries, Lausanne, 1973.

right: 342. David Kaye. *Bound Linen and Five Loops.* 1972. Linen blocking cord, knotted and sewn; length 22″. Collection Mr. and Mrs. Lee Howard, Willowdale, Ontario.

intimate blend of soft and inert materials (Pl. 21, p. 177; Fig. 285). Fiber wrapping appears to be simple, but this impression is deceptive. Success depends upon a thorough understanding of the material, a direct connection with the fiber.

Knitting and *crocheting* both rely upon a method of pulling successive loops of yarn through one another to construct fabric. Long relegated to the world of baby sweaters and afghans, these crafts have begun to be explored by serious artists for their design potential. Carol Hoffman's "tapestry" in Plate 26 (p. 212) is actually a 3-foot-wide, three-dimensional crocheted work that seems to have run riot in its colors, textures, and designs. The balloonlike shapes of which it is composed echo the basic construction loops to make a harmonious overall design.

There are a number of other interlacing techniques not illustrated here that the designer might call upon to achieve a particular effect, either for a whole work or for a small section. These include netting, braiding, sprang (twisting), lacemaking, plaiting, and twining. With this wide repertoire of construction methods, one has tremendous flexibility in structural design. However, should the creative needs of a particular work still not be met, there is no reason why the designer could not invent yet another technique to meet the situation. Designers in fiber are continually experimenting with new combinations.

Sewing Techniques

In a sense, sewing construction techniques are an outgrowth of interlacing methods, because the designer is always working with prewoven fabric. Usually, although not always, this fabric will be machine made. However, the composition of the designed piece in this instance is created by sewing the fabric in a special way. Structural design depends upon how the *fabric* is manipulated.

A very old sewing technique, *quilting* reached a high point in the Colonial American period and continued to evolve through the 19th century. The original stimulus for making quilts no doubt was the need for warmth. A layered, quilted fabric is warmer than a single piece of material of the same thickness because of the trapped air between the layers. From this point of departure early quilters developed an art form with designs of wonderful complexity and beauty. Many of the patterns became traditional and were given names, such as "Sunbursts" or "Festoon and Bowknot." The most intricate of these quilts have found their way into museum collections.

A revival of interest in historical quilts during the mid-20th century has stimulated modern designers to interpret the craft in a new idiom. Risa Goldman's muslin and cotton quilt (Pl. 27, p. 212) presents a gallery of faces, familiar and unfamiliar, including one cat. While the underlying structure is traditional, the treatment is strikingly contemporary.

Stuffed dolls, toys, and pillows have been around for a long time. Nearly every child today has had a Teddy bear or Raggedy Ann doll, and many primitive cultures have made stuffed toys for their children. Recently, a number of designers have begun to explore the potential of *stuffing-and-sewing* as an art form (Fig. 343). A large portion of the work is figural, but these stuffed people are not of the sort a child would cuddle. The content may be satirical, even morbid, or may make a statement about contemporary society. Such works are unusually expressive, evoking a direct response in the viewer.

Pressure Techniques

One of the oldest methods for making fabrics was by compressing or pounding fibrous materials. In the cold regions of the world early cultures developed *felting,* in which loose fibers are bonded together by a combination of heat, moisture, and pressure. In warmer climates fabric was made by pounding the bark of the paper mulberry tree. The result was *tapa cloth,* a brittle, warm-hued material often decorated with geometric designs (Fig. 344). Color variations result from dyeing the bark with natural dyes or from pressing in dried leaves and flowers. We find examples of tapa in South America, Africa, and Southeast

above: 343. Paul Harris. *Norissa Rushing.* 1972. Stuffed cloth on wood and metal frame, height 7′1″. Courtesy Poindexter Gallery, New York.

above right: 344. Fragment of tapa-cloth skirt from the Futuna Islands. Collected c. 1932. Bernice P. Bishop Museum, Honolulu.

right: 345. Mildred Fischer. *Legend.* 1973. Handmade paper of colored kozo and linen fibers; 26⅛ x 16¾″. Collection Harold and Caroline Porter, Cincinnati.

Asia, but the material is most closely associated with Hawaii and the South Sea Islands.

A contemporary artist, Mildred Fischer, uses papermaking techniques to create unique hangings with rich textural effects. *Legend* (Fig. 345) includes both colored kozo (paper mulberry) and linen fibers pressed into a handmade paper. The loose configuration of the strands seems perfectly expressive of the fiber medium.

Some types of structural design in fiber defy classification. This is certainly true of recent works by Magdalena Abakanowicz, an inter-

346. Magdalena Abakanowicz. *Human Structure Images,* from the cycle *Alteration.* 1974–75. Linen, thread, and glue; approximately life size. Courtesy the artist.

nationally known weaver who until recently has been identified with huge environmental hangings. In 1975 the artist exhibited *Alteration* (Fig. 346), a series of fourteen male figures molded from burlap, sisal, and glue. These figures, which are disturbing in their headless, looming presence, represent Abakanowicz' comment upon the dehumanization of industrial society. Her work demonstrates that fiber has taken its place as a fully realized artistic medium.

Decorative Design

Decorative design in fiber most often imparts color, texture, or pattern. We can divide the various types into two broad categories: *fiber techniques* and *printing techniques.*

Fiber Techniques

Fiber techniques of decorative design include all the methods that call for a yarn or thread to be worked through the fabric. Under the heading of *stitchery* come the crafts in which fabric is completely covered by decorative yarns, such as crewel and needlepoint. Helen Bitar's pillow in Plate 28 (p. 229) shows a lavish assembly of stitches in bright tones reminiscent of Joseph's "coat of many colors." The gay, brightly colored yarns add not only hue but areas of pattern and texture to the work.

Embroidery is actually a specialized form of stitchery in which the individual stitches themselves are highly decorative. Embroidery may or may not cover the entire surface of the fabric. Its particular appeal lies in the unique personalities of the stitches and the ways they are combined. Many books have been written to codify the large vocabulary of forms. The charming 17th-century embroidered piece in Figure 347 shows Adam and Eve in the Garden of Eden, curiously accompanied by the King and Queen of England. This naïve transport through time and space was intended to show the maker's devoted loyalty to King Charles and his consort. The arrangement of four figures also provides a balanced composition, made all the more decorative by the lush display of vegetation around the figures.

The technique of *appliqué* concentrates less on the stitches themselves than on what they hold together. In appliqué, pieces of some material, usually fabric, are applied to a fabric background by sewing all around. The purpose is to add pattern or contrasting color but may also have the effect of making the fabric more three-dimensional. Figure 348 shows a hanging from Africa, in which stylized figures of men and a bird have been appliquéd to a cotton backing. Its theme is the hunt of a giant bird come to prey upon the village. No attempt has been made to relate position to the natural world. The various forms, instead, have been designed and arranged for purely decorative and symbolic value.

Printing Techniques

Printing is used to apply color to a fabric according to a particular pattern. There are several different methods. In *silk-screen* printing a mesh screen is prepared in such a way that all the areas through which the designer does not want dye to pass are *stopped-out* or blocked with a substance to close the pores in the screen. Then the screen is laid over the fabric to be printed, and dye is forced through the open areas of the screen. A separate screen must be made for each color to be printed, with only the specific design area for that color left open. Silk-screen prints tend to be large, bold, and brightly colored (Fig. 349), although the technique could be applied to any type of pattern.

Batik and *tie-dye* are both *resist* printing methods, which means that some device prevents color from penetrating the fabric where it is not wanted. In batik, nonprinting areas are covered with a wax coating, and then the fabric is dipped in dye. Only the unwaxed areas of the cloth will accept color. When the dye has dried sufficiently, the wax can be melted off and reapplied in other portions of the fabric for the

left: 347. *Adam and Eve and King and Queen.* Mid-17th century. Embroidery in silk on canvas, 19¼ x 20¾". Metropolitan Museum of Art, New York (Irwin Untermeyer Collection).

above: 348. *Bird Hunt,* contemporary appliqué on fabric, from Abomey, Dahomey, West Africa. Collection Dr. Regina A. Perry, Richmond, Va.

printing of the next color. In *tie-dye,* the nonprinting sections for a particular color are twisted and tied very tightly to retard color absorption. This method is not as "hard-edged" as batik, for some color will bleed around the knots, giving the characteristically soft, blurred quality of tie-dye. Marian Clayden's silk (Pl. 29, p. 229) employs a unique clamp-resist method for a stunning display of color and pattern in the fabric.

Finally, images and patterns can be *photoprinted* onto fabric using the techniques of photography. Catherine Jansen's *Blue Room* (Fig. 350) is a whole environment of stuffed and stitched forms that have been photoprinted to create, among other things, the figures on the bed, the mirror image, and the television screen. The effect of a totally soft world, with flattened people, makes us look at familiar objects in a completely new light. The confusion of imagery—between two and three dimensions—provides a fascinating experience of space.

Not too long ago, works in fiber were concentrated primarily on weaving or needlework. The renewed interest in fiber as a material carrying its own fascination has expanded the potential for design to virtually unlimited horizons.

left: 349. Walter B. Broderick for Schumacher. Floral screen print on cotton. Introduced 1975.

below: 350. Catherine Jansen. *Blue Room.* 1972. Photoblueprint on cotton and vinyl, 9 x 12′. Courtesy the artist.

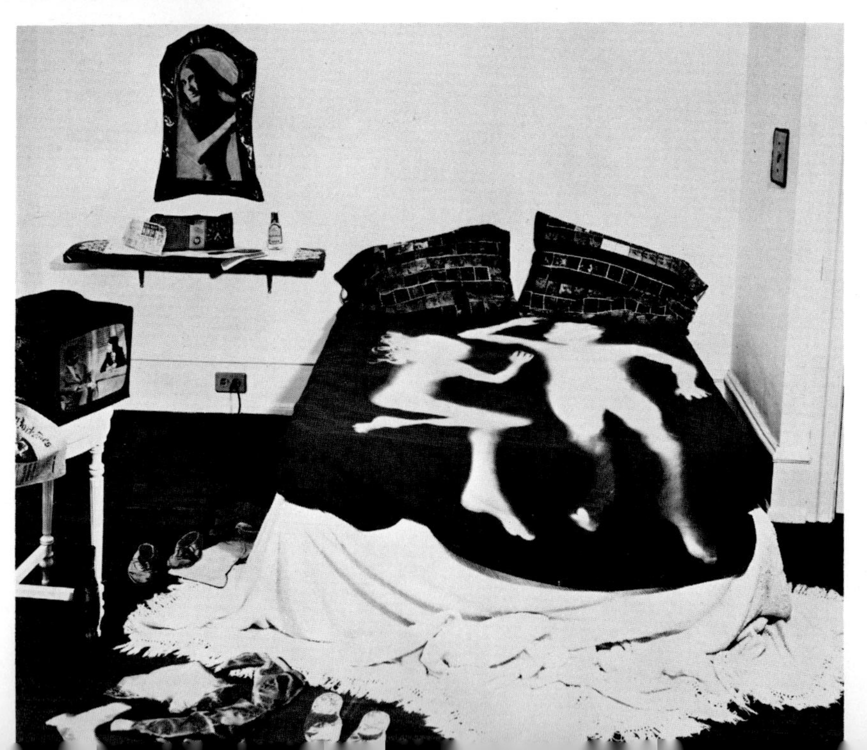

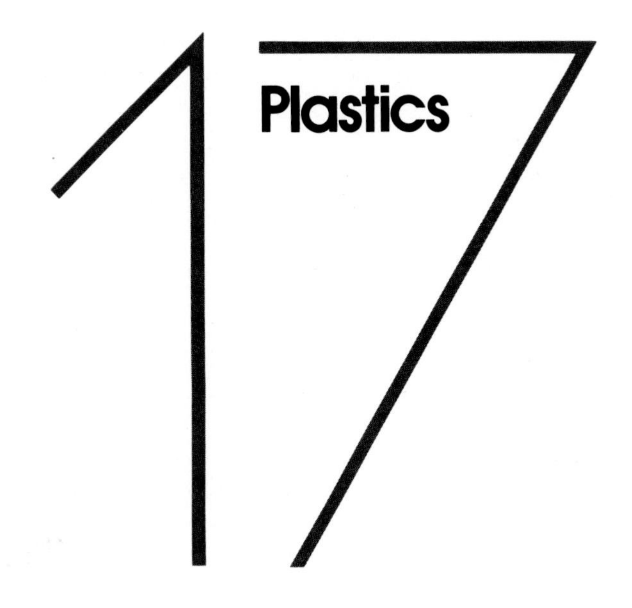

17 Plastics

The most contemporary of all design materials are the varied and versatile substances that we categorize as plastics. Traditionally, the term "plastic" has referred to ease of manipulation, in the sense that easily modeled clay is plastic. The materials designated by 20th-century usage of the word all possess this trait (Fig. 351). No other substance is so readily shaped or handled. Molding, rolling into sheets, forming with dies, pouring as liquids, spraying as foams, carving, casting, laminating, joining—these are only some of the possible methods for shaping objects from plastics.

The layman tends to refer to "plastic" in the singular, to say that something is "made of plastic." This is an oversimplification, for the world of plastics includes a vast and growing range of materials that differ in color, texture, transparency, strength, and methods of handling and molding.

All plastics do share one basic trait: They are composed principally of carbon compounds in long molecular chains. Each type of plastic on the market today has been developed by polymer chemists to have a specific molecular structure, which in turn offers a definite combination of properties.

Because plastics are synthesized in the laboratory, their properties are subject to maximum control. The designer can select a plastic

above: 351. Lynda Benglis. *Adhesive Products.* 1971. Nine individual configurations of iron oxide and black pigmented polyurethane, 13′6″ x 80′ x 15′. Walker Art Center, Minneapolis.

right: 352. Steven Weiss. "Infinity" table. Plexiglas. The cut edges actually conduct light, because of the nature of the material.

suitable for the precise application intended, and if such a plastic does not exist, there is a good possibility that one can be specially developed through chemical modification. The broad range of potential properties is the overriding virtue of plastics for the designer.

The designer working in wood, metal, clay, glass, or fiber must necessarily plan within the context of known constraints in the material. With plastics, however, one can design freely and, after the design process is complete, seek the most appropriate type. Occasionally it will be necessary to make concessions to the material, but these are seldom major.

A knowledge of polymer engineering is of course helpful in order to make the best choice of a plastic for a particular design. When an object proves unsatisfactory in use, the owner often lays the blame on its being "only plastic." More likely the problem arose not because the item was made of plastic but because it was made of the *wrong* plastic.

The visual similarity of some plastics to glass, as well as their substitution for glass in such things as drinking vessels, has encouraged us to think of plastics as being transparent. And indeed, many plastics do show a luminous, liquid transparency (Fig. 352). Others, however, are merely translucent or completely opaque. Examples of the latter can be found in melamine countertops and dinnerware (Fig. 356).

Although we associate plastics with the 20th century, their origin goes back fifty years earlier to the discovery of nitrocellulose, which

above: Plate 28. Helen Bitar. Pillow. 1967. Stitchery in satin and wool yarns, c. 14 x 8″. Copyright American Crafts Council, *Your Portable Museum.*

right: Plate 29. Marian Clayden. *Untitled.* 1974. Silk twill, clamp resist; 4′2″ x 3′4″. From the exhibition "The Dyer's Art," 1976, Museum of Contemporary Crafts of the American Crafts Council.

Plate 30. John Chamberlain. *Untitled.* 1970. Metal-coated Plexiglas, 2′3″ x 4′ x 3′9″. Courtesy Leo Castelli Gallery, New York.

353. Louise Nevelson. *Model for Atmosphere and Environment: Ice Palace I.* 1967. Clear Lucite, 24 x 26 x 12″. Courtesy Pace Gallery, New York.

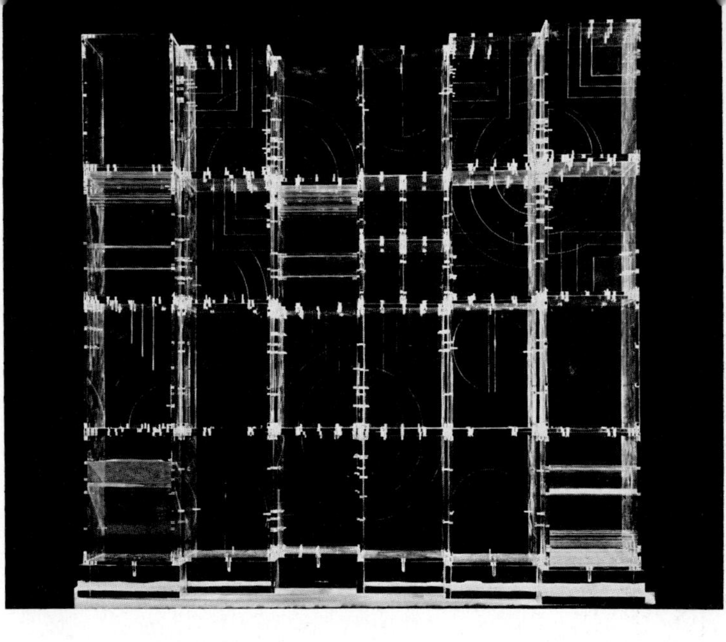

was developed more or less simultaneously in England and the United States. Part of the stimulus for the American inventor was a contest to find a new material for billiard balls, since the elephant herds supplying the traditional ivory were being decimated. The result of both experiments was Celluloid.

The next major development, around the turn of the century, was the introduction of Bakelite, the first plastic material composed of a giant molecular structure built up by chemical reactions between small molecular units. This structure became the basis for many of today's plastics. The expansion of the plastics industry was facilitated by two world wars, which established new needs and caused shortages of familiar materials.

Plastics now make up an intrinsic part of industrial society, and they appear in nearly every category of objects we use. The conquest of space probably would not have been possible without plastics. In recent years the concern with shortages of energy has brought questions about plastics production, since plastics chemicals originate with crude petroleum. Scientists are working to overcome these problems.

Types of Plastics

The chemistry and technical aspects involved in plastics are so complex that they can be touched upon only lightly in a chapter dealing with design. However, anyone interested in working with plastics should have some idea of the various types and their distinguishing characteristics.

The main division in plastics categories is the distinction between thermoplastic and thermosetting materials. *Thermoplastic* substances can be softened and resoftened indefinitely by the application of heat and pressure, provided the heat is not enough to cause decomposition. While changing their shape, the materials will not lose their molecular cohesion. *Thermosetting* plastics, on the other hand, undergo a chemical change during the curing process; after that change takes place, the shape becomes set and cannot usefully be modified again when exposed to heat and/or pressure.

Although plastics materials now number in the hundreds, they can be categorized into several general "families."

Acrylics are thermoplastic materials with outstanding brilliance and transparency (Fig. 353). In the United States they are made under

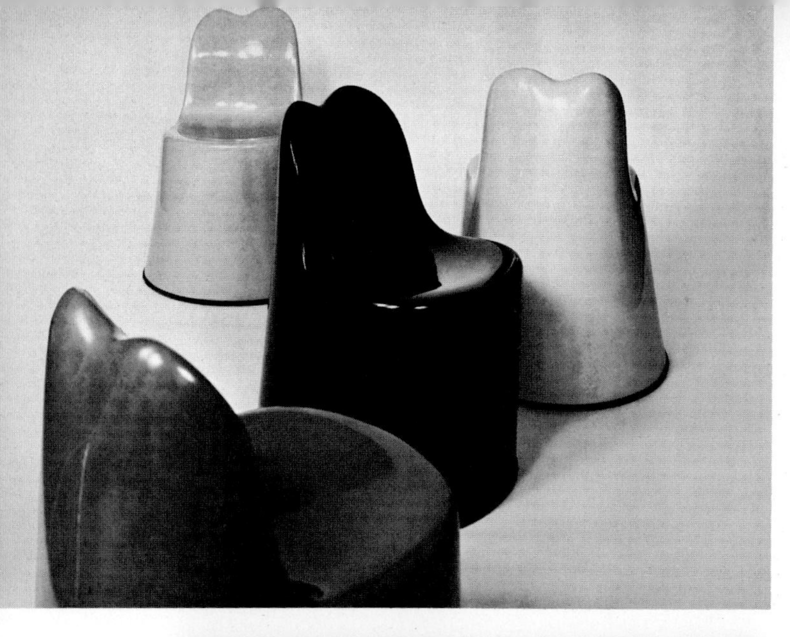

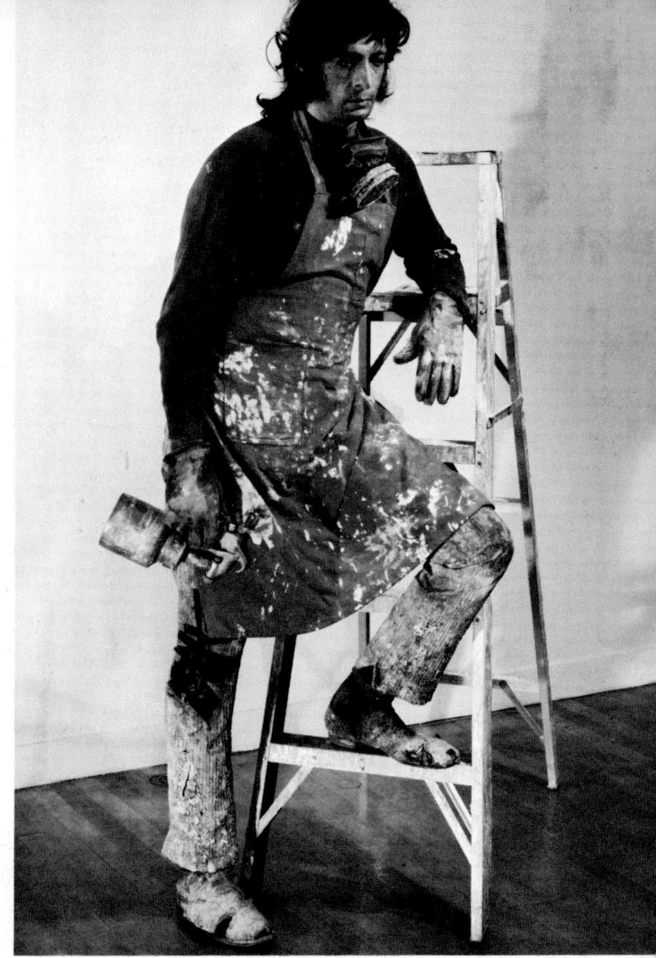

top left: 354. Wendell Castle. Side chairs. FRP. Courtesy the artist.

above: 355. Duane Hanson. *Artist with Ladder.* 1972. Polyester and fiberglass, lifesize.

left: 356. Massimo Vignelli for Heller Designs, Inc. Stacking dishes of Melamine.

below: 357. Frei Otto and Günter Behnisch. Olympic Stadium, Munich. 1972. Plexiglas sheets on aluminum and steel frame, c. 90 yards square.

such trade names as Plexiglas, Lucite, Perspex, and Acrylite. Because they can be molded into large, unshatterable shapes, are readily carved, withstand weather and hard use, and accept a high polish, acrylics have become popular with sculptors and jewelers. One drawback is a tendency to scratch easily, but acrylic often can be restored by buffing. Acrylic-base paints are among the most popular artists' media today (Pl. 35, p. 250).

Epoxy, another thermoset plastic that is popular with designers, resembles polyester in many ways. This resin costs more than polyester resin (see below), but it does not have the shrinkage factor associated with polyester castings. As a result, epoxy is used widely for cast prototype shapes. When combined with metal powders, epoxy can yield a cold-cast metal very similar in appearance to foundry-cast metal. Epoxy can be cast in the design studio without elaborate equipment, because it will cure at room temperature after the components of the system have been mixed.

FRP, or *fiberglass-reinforced plastic,* is literally a plastic with which fiberglass has been combined for added strength. It appears in molded and laminated furniture (Fig. 354), boat hulls, and automobile bodies. These plastics are weather-resistant, and they can be colored as desired. Artists use polyester reinforced with fiberglass as a sculpture medium, because of the great freedom it provides in modeling. When this material is applied to figural sculptures, the results can be amazingly lifelike (Fig. 355).

Melamines are exceptionally hard and durable plastics that have become a staple in kitchen countertops and casual dinnerware (Fig. 356). The common trade names are Formica, Micarta, and Melmac. Depending upon composition, these plastics can be transparent, translucent, or opaque, and they are available in many colors.

Polyester is a thermoset plastic commonly used by designers. It is available as several different chemical types. In fabric form, polyester can make a huge, unbroken sheet, such as the tent shell for the 1972 Olympic Stadium at Munich (Fig. 357). When reinforced with fiberglass, laminating polyester offers the artist a highly expressive working medium, often characterized by intense colors (Fig. 358). Also, clear, unsaturated polyester works excellently for clear casting or embedding.

358. Ron Davis. *Large L.* 1969. Polyester resin and fiberglass, 4′8½″x11′10″. Collection Mr. & Mrs. William S. Ehrlich, New York.

359. Otto Piene. *Manned Helium Sculpture* from *Citything Sky Ballet.* 1970. Helium-filled polyethylene tubing. Courtesy the artist.

Polyethylenes may be flexible, semirigid, or rigid in form. A waxy surface identifies them in such products as squeeze bottles and freezer containers. Polyethylenes are resistant to breakage, weather, and extremes of temperature, which makes them ideal for outdoor sculptures (Fig. 359).

Urethanes are especially valued by artists and architects because of their ability to foam. This permits them to be sprayed onto a limitless variety of forms, whereupon they assume a rigid or semirigid structure. Urethanes will bond to almost any surface. In architectural construction, a spray coating of polyurethane on a frame will simultaneously provide the shell and the insulation of the building (Fig. 360). By these means shapes undreamed of in conventional construction methods can be realized. Sculptors, too, make use of this exceptional flexibility of form (Fig. 361). It should be noted, however, that the ingredients for

360. Stan Nord Connolly. "Igloo" house. Built 1969. Plastic foam sprayed over balloons.

urethane foam are highly toxic, and the foam itself is dangerously flammable.

Vinyls are tough, lightweight plastics best known in their applications to fabric or floor and wall coverings. Designs can be printed onto vinyl fabric, either commercially or as an edition piece created by an artist (Fig. 362). The flexible, shiny, "wet" look of vinyl appeals to many contemporary sculptors, and the material has become a fixture in the work of Claes Oldenburg (Fig. 363).

right: 361. Steve Urry. Works in progress. 1976. Expanded polyurethane. Courtesy the artist.

below left: 362. Roy Lichtenstein. *Moonscape.* 1965. Serigraph on moiré-patterned vinyl, 22 x 28″. Courtesy Leo Castelli Gallery, New York.

below right: 363. Claes Oldenburg. *Soft Washstand.* 1966. Vinyl. Collection Dr. Hubert Peeters, Bruges.

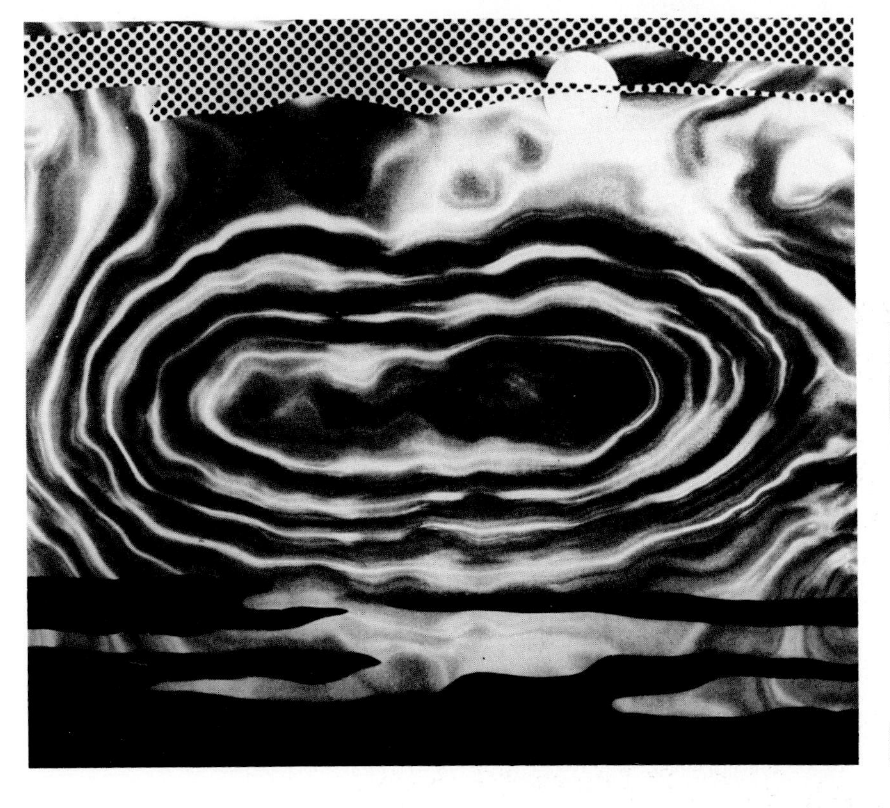

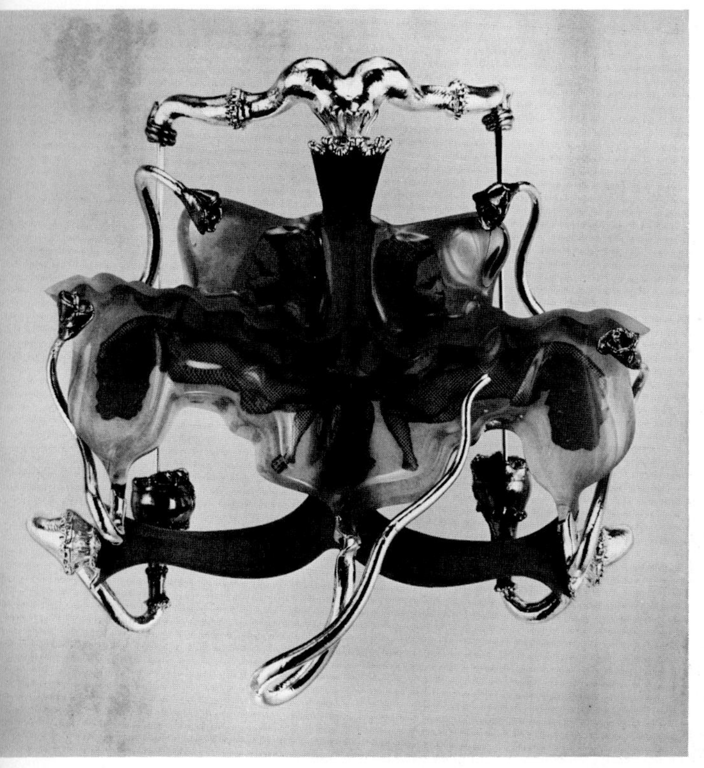

above: 364. Stanley Lechtzin. *Cameo Brooch.* 1976. Cast acrylic resin and electroformed silver-gilt. Courtesy the artist.

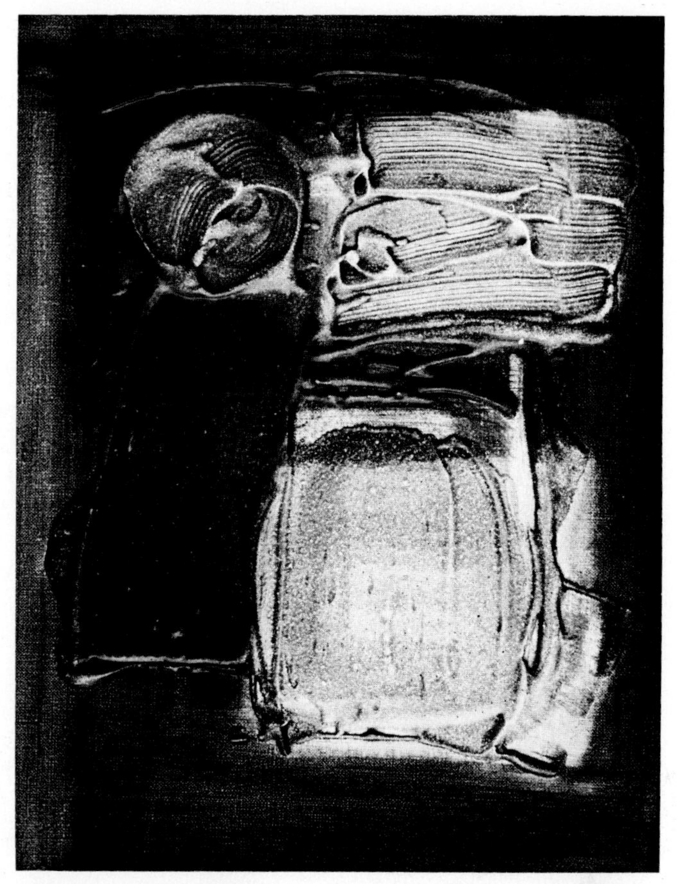

above: 365. Yannis Maltezos. *Space Construction.* 1962. Painting of polyvinyl and marble powder with oil colors added; 4 x 3′. Courtesy the artist.

left: 366. David Watkins. Bracelets. 1974. Silver with white acrylic. Courtesy the artist.

This list of plastics families is not complete. It does, however, identify some of the materials most popular with artists and industrial designers. Those involved in production molding will need to become familiar with many other varieties.

Structural Design

As mentioned at the beginning of this chapter, plastics lend themselves to an unprecedented range of shaping techniques—more by far than any other material. It does not stretch the point too much to say that nearly anything one can do with every other material can be done with plastics, although in some cases the cost will not be justified. We will mention and illustrate some of the structural design methods, but the artist who intends to work extensively with plastics should explore all the possibilities.

Casting is perhaps the most common process for molding plastics. Thermoset plastics usually come in liquid form and harden when the two or three parts of the chemical system are mixed together. Thermoplastics are supplied as pellets that must be melted. The materials flow easily, will readily assume just about any shape, and will hold that shape without breaking or cracking. In working properties, plastics for casting resemble bronze. They flow as easily as molten bronze in the fluid state, and when they solidify certain plastics may be almost as hard as bronze. However, plastics are often easier and cheaper to work with. The resultant form is much lighter than cast bronze, and both color and texture can be controlled, whereas with bronze one is limited by the color of the metal. Jewelry made of cast plastics, alone or combined with other materials, has a uniquely contemporary look (Fig. 364). Plastics also, incidentally, make superior molds for casting other materials, such as plaster or clay.

Modeling can be done with any plastic paste or putty that does not require extreme heat to soften it. The sculptor can make a modeling paste from polyester or epoxy resin, combined with a filler. These materials are modeled in the manner of clay, sometimes with a wire armature or metal screen for support. The finished piece does not require firing and has high strength. For the work shown in Figure 365, Yannis Maltezos used a polyvinyl acetate binder and fine sand to build up thick impasto effects and textures.

Fabricating is a general term that covers any method of working with preformed plastic shapes, cutting and joining them together by means of heat or adhesives. Louise Nevelson's *Ice Palace I* (Fig. 353) depends on fabricating, as do many similar works. The technique permits a combination of plastics with other materials. David Watkins' bracelets (Fig. 366) join acrylic with silver. Manufacturers offer plastics in such a wide variety of shapes, colors, and textures, that one could scarcely exhaust the possibilities of design in preshaped materials. Most firms provide information about suitable adhesives for a particular plastic. In other cases the designer will utilize local applications of heat in the manner of welding metal. For all practical purposes, the bond formed by heat-joining or adhesive is permanent.

Spraying of plastics has become extremely popular, for the possibilities in size and shape are limitless (Fig. 360). Any form the designer can build from support materials can be sprayed with a coating of plastics. After the plastic sheath has solidified, the framework may remain or be removed. The resulting plastic shell will be strong, usually rigid, and impervious to weather and wear. Spraying does require fairly sophisticated equipment. Care must be taken to control the release of toxic fumes.

Laminating is a process of bonding together thin sheets of plastic material or fabric. This permits the embedding of other objects or substances. Collectors use lamination to mount specimens, such as leaves, drawings, stamps, and butterflies.

The designer can purchase plastics in many forms, including liquids, pastes, pellets, foams, emulsions, rods, sheets, strips, tubes, fibers, and molding powders. Structural design, therefore, is limited only by the nature of each plastic and the ingenuity of the designer.

Decorative Design

To a large extent, decorative design in plastics takes place at the formative stage, when the material is being processed. Superficial decorative design is less common in plastics than in most materials.

Pigments and dyes can be added to a plastic before polymerization, by either the manufacturer or the user (depending upon the specific plastic). Nearly any color can be produced, and once introduced, the colors are wedded chemically to the material. The colors in plastic thus are more stable than colors applied to other materials, such as fiber. They resist fading, bleeding, or yellowing, even over a long period of time. The clear, bright, luminous colors of plastics have fascinated designers in the same way that gems fascinate the eye with their rich hues (Pl. 30, p. 230). In handcraft jewelry, colored plastics represent a 20th-century challenge to rubies and emeralds.

The surface of a plastic object, once formed, usually stands on its own. It exhibits certain qualities of sheen, color, and texture that motivated the designer to choose it in the first place. However, many decorative techniques can be added, as the expressive intent requires. Hanson's *Artist with Ladder* (Fig. 355), for example, was painted in oil colors for the Photorealism effect the artist wanted. Other works could be engraved, textured, gilded, polished, or covered completely. There is also the possibility of combining plastics with other materials or forces. Les Levine's *Slip Cover* (Fig. 367) is conceived as a "room" of Mylar and Butyrate, in which lights and air create a total environment of pulsation. It would be difficult to imagine this effect resulting from any material other than plastics.

Plastics have a brief history, an exciting present, and a challenging future. Any material invented by human ingenuity can be modified by human ingenuity. The designer who works in plastics controls not only form but substance as well, making the creative possibilities of this material virtually limitless.

367. Les Levine. *Slipcover* (interior). 1965. Mirrorized Mylar and Butyrate, with slide projections, closed-circuit video projections, and audio sound track; 31 x 31 x 10′. Courtesy Museum of Mott Art, Inc., New York.

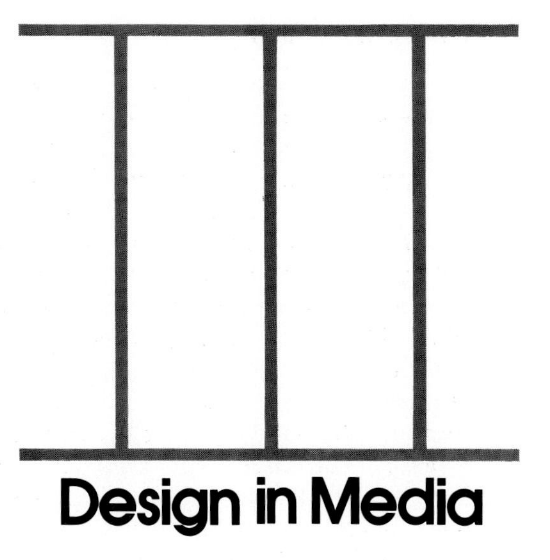
Design in Media

18 Painting

The relationship between painting and design has been the subject of discussion and controversy for centuries. Artists and critics who wished to make a negative comment about certain works—perhaps because they were either highly decorative or highly simplified—have been inclined to dismiss these works as "mere design." This type of designation insults both painting *and* design.

As we have tried to stress throughout this book, design is the underlying structural basis for all forms of visual expression. Regardless of the content or artistic aims a painting may have, it still can be analyzed in terms of lines, spaces, shapes, colors, and textures, as well as the ways in which these are related—the principles of design.

Many people today have difficulty understanding modern painting and would find some of the illustrations in this chapter incomprehensible in context of the work of Rembrandt, Michelangelo, or Leonardo da Vinci. To the individual schooled in the notion of "pictures," such as Leonardo's *Mona Lisa* (Fig. 368), a work like Robert Rauschenberg's *Mona Lisa* (Fig. 369) seems chaotic, disrespectful, and somehow unfair in its borrowing from Leonardo's masterpiece of evocative representation. The problem lies in a misconception about the nature of painting.

368. Leonardo da Vinci. *Mona Lisa.* c. 1503–05. Oil on panel, $30\frac{1}{4}$ x 21". Louvre, Paris.

In some periods during the history of art, artists had as their goal the absolute simulation of "reality" on canvas. Yet a painting is *not* natural reality—not flesh and bone and trees and rocks, but an arrangement of pigments on a two-dimensional surface. The artist is not copying natural reality but creating a new reality on canvas, a reality that consists of paints and ground. In this respect, then, the two versions of *Mona Lisa* have much more in common with each other than either has with the physical world.

Leonardo's *Mona Lisa* is no more an attempt merely to capture the physical appearance of a particular woman than is Rauschenberg's. Leonardo's misty landscape, invented and not a real place, adds to the mystery of the woman and becomes a part of her character as we perceive it. For Rauschenberg, the image of Mona Lisa is part of a mental landscape made up of fragmentary images and dreamlike shapes that, while not explicit, are highly suggestive. Thus, both artists use the image of a woman as part of a subjective reality, created and communicated to the viewer by means of design.

Painting Media

Before exploring the design factors in various types of painting, it will be helpful to understand the materials that artists use. The material for any work of art is called the *medium.* (This term can be somewhat confusing, since it also is applied to a particular category, such as painting or sculpture or graphic arts, as well as to means of mass communication. However, it will be understood in context.)

In painting the medium is determined by the *binder,* the vehicle that holds the particles of pigment in suspension and makes it possible to spread pigment as paint on a *support,* such as canvas. (Sometimes a preliminary coating—a *ground*—is applied first.) It is the medium, therefore, that enables the painter to use pigment plastically, whether painting with a brush, a knife, or some other implement.

The oldest type of painting medium appears to have been *encaustic,* a mixture of hot beeswax and pigment perfected by the ancient Greeks. The mixture is applied to wood with a brush or a metal instrument known as a *cauterium.* As the wax cools, the cauterium is heated, and successive layers are applied, making possible considerable plasticity and intricate modeling. Encaustic has provided a challenge to contemporary artists in their search for expressive effects.

Tempera generally has egg yolk as a binder, although animal and vegetable glues also can be used. It is most often applied to a ground of *gesso* (plaster or gypsum with glue) built up on wood panels but also can be worked on canvas (Fig. 370). *Casein,* with a binder of milk curd, is water soluble and can be applied to gesso panels, cardboard, paper,

369. Robert Rauschenberg. *Mona Lisa.* 1958. Mixed media on paper, $22\frac{3}{4}$ x $28\frac{3}{4}$". Collection Ethel Scull, New York.

left: 370. Andrew Wyeth. *Ground Hog Day.* 1959. Egg tempera on board, 31″ square. Philadelphia Museum of Art (given by Henry F. duPont and Mrs. John Wintersteen).

below: 371. Vincent van Gogh. *Cypresses.* 1889. Oil on canvas, $36\frac{3}{4} \times 29\frac{1}{8}$″. Metropolitan Museum of Art, New York (Rogers Fund, 1949). (See also Fig. 147.)

and other surfaces. Since ancient times wall paintings have been executed on lime plaster. A painting on wet plaster is called *fresco,* one on dry plaster, *secco.* For tempera, casein, and fresco, water serves as the thinning agent.

Oil paint came into general use in the 15th century. Pigment is ground and mixed with a binder of linseed oil, which dries slowly but permits precise manipulation. The artist must wait for each layer of paint to dry adequately to prevent the paint film from cracking. However, the flexibility of oil paint allows the creation of either an opaque or a translucent film and also permits overpainting in areas the artist wants to change. Oil paint can be applied in a single, thick coating, or built up in successive transparent layers or *glazes.* The latter method accounts for much of the soft modeling in the work of the old masters.

As mentioned previously, *impasto* refers to a technique in which paint is applied so thickly, often with a palette knife, that its texture assumes an expressive role all its own (Fig. 371; compare Fig. 147). Impasto exploits the quality of paint as a plastic medium, a quality not always revealed with the brush. The supports for oil paint generally are canvas, Masonite, or wood.

Watercolor is bound by gum arabic, while *gouache,* an opaque watercolor, contains in addition a paste of zinc oxide. Both dissolve in water and lend themselves to rapid painting. Used on specially prepared paper, transparent watercolor has a clarity and sparkle that sets it apart as a medium of freshness and spontaneity.

Among recently developed media, pigments bound with *acrylic* polymer emulsion have gained wide popularity (Pl. 35, p. 250). The ingredients of this binder are entirely synthesized (see Chap. 17). Acrylic paints are favored for their durability and quick drying properties. Different acrylics dissolve in water and stronger solvents, so the artist can use them to paint "thick" or "thin." One can add glaze upon glaze in an almost immediate succession, knowing the layers will dry promptly, to create a paint film of extraordinary inner glow and brilliance. On the other hand, it is possible to build up thick layers of paint at once without danger of peeling, since the film created is porous and allows moisture to pass through to the surface without cracking the paint.

Thick acrylic paste or a paste of polyester applied to a ground can provide the surface for a collage. Artists today press paper, fabric, wood, wire netting, and any number of other materials into this sort of medium to make the most of its adhesive powers and achieve unique effects (Fig. 372). Experimentation leads to new uses for established materials, as well as to exciting combinations of the old and the new.

372. Arman. *Frozen Civilization #2.* 1971. Compressed garbage in Plexiglas, 4′ x 3′ x 4¾″. Courtesy Andrew Crispo Gallery, Inc., New York.

Attributes of Painting

Traditionally, three attributes have been associated with painting: *subject, form,* and *content.* In any work of art the three will be closely intertwined and interdependent. It is almost as difficult to discuss them separately as it would be to convey the quality of "green" by analyzing blue and yellow. However, to approach an understanding of the design concepts involved, we will explore each of these aspects independently.

In John Singer Sargent's *Daughters of Edward Darley Boit* (Fig. 373), the *subject* obviously is four young girls posed in a quiet moment,

373. John Singer Sargent. *The Daughters of Edward Darley Boit.* 1882. Oil on canvas, 7′3⅝″ square. Museum of Fine Arts, Boston.

perhaps in respite from studies or play. The *form* of this painting also is clear. It is a rectangle in which certain shapes representing recognizable things—four girls, a rug, architectural elements, and two large vases—have been arranged by the artist in a particular *composition.* Sargent's composition is elegantly balanced and unified through placement of the figures and other elements. Two of the girls stand in perfectly vertical poses, while a third creates a gentle diagonal against the vase shape. The two strong groupings of standing figures are balanced by the seated child. Our eyes are led to the child by the downward sweep in the aprons on her older sisters. Finally, the lightstruck area to the right of the canvas, and the bit of vase just visible, complete the composition's balance. The lights and darks in the composition show a graceful rhythm that contributes to an overall sense of unity.

The *content* of the Sargent painting, while more subtle and intuitive, comes through plainly. It is the innocence, the purity, the shy naïveté of childhood, as well as, perhaps, the emotional ties of sisters. Content, then, is the essential meaning or underlying idea in a work of art—that which it communicates to the viewer.

It may be interesting to perform the same exercise on a contemporary nonrepresentational work, such as Barnett Newman's *Dionysius* (Pl. 31, p. 247). This painting has a straightforward form—three rectangles masterfully balanced against one another and separated by two narrow stripes. But what are the subject and content? A great many people would argue that a work such as this has no subject, yet in one sense *color* is the subject. It is a painting about color, a "painting about painting." Similarly, the content of this work is the intense experience of green, the response to pure, vivid color that exists entirely for its own sake.

Plate 31. Barnett Newman. *Dionysius.* 1949. Oil on canvas, 5′9″ x 4′. Collection Annalee Newman, New York.

above: Plate 32. Willem de Kooning. *Two Women in the Country.* 1954. Oil, enamel, and charcoal on canvas; 46⅛ x 40⅞″. Joseph H. Hirshhorn Museum and Sculpture Garden, Smithsonian Institution, Washington, D.C.

left: Plate 33. Tom Wesselmann. *The Great American Nude, 2.* 1961. Gesso, enamel, oil, and collage on plywood; 4′11⅝″ x 3′11½″. Museum of Modern Art, New York (Larry Aldrich Foundation Fund).

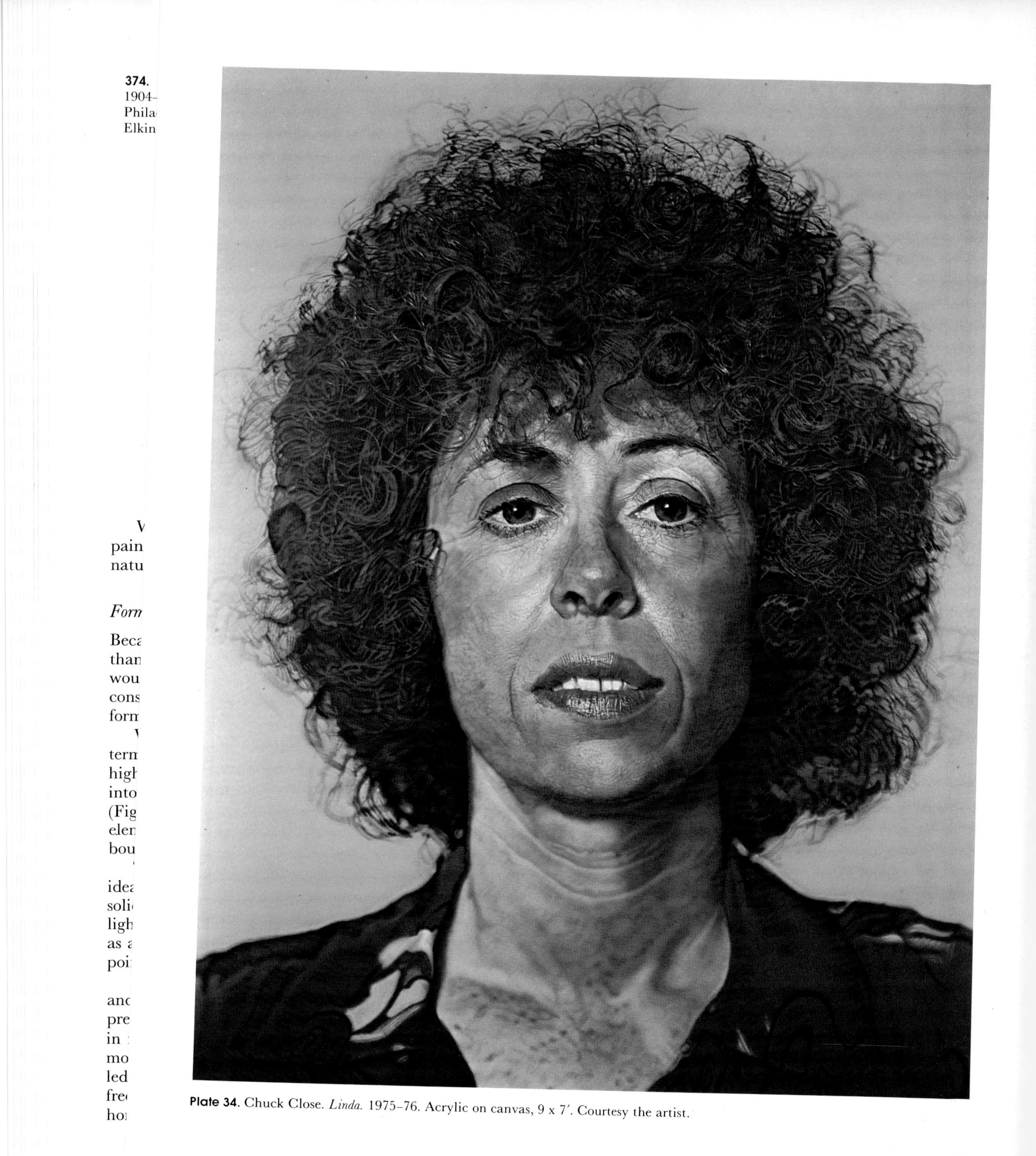

Plate 34. Chuck Close. *Linda.* 1975–76. Acrylic on canvas, 9 x 7′. Courtesy the artist.

Plate 37. Nicolas Schöffer. View of the artist's studio. Courtesy the artist.

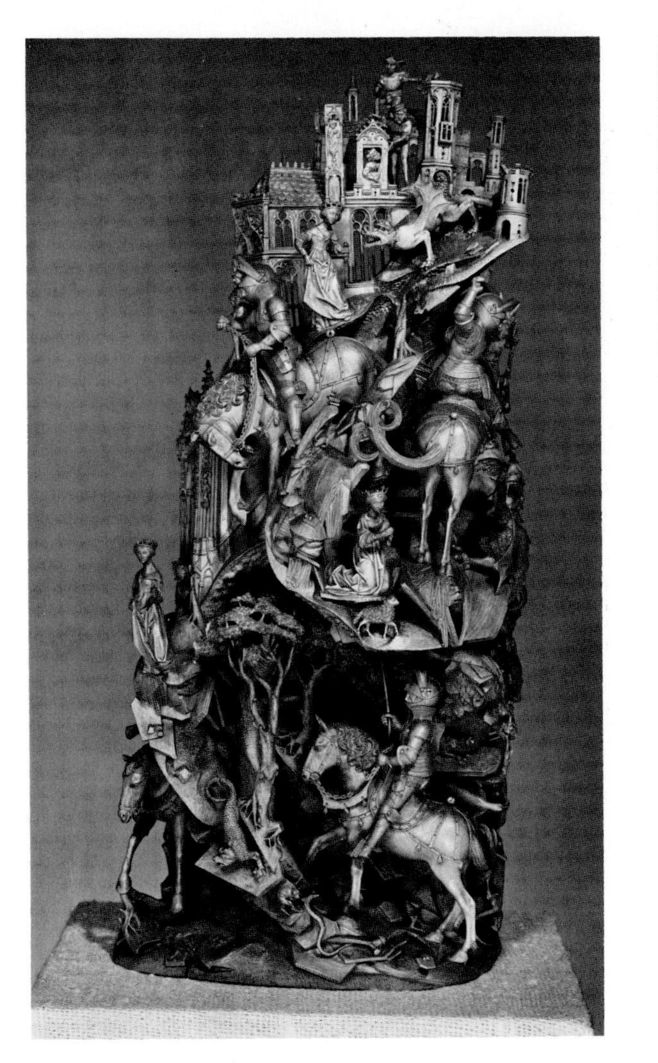

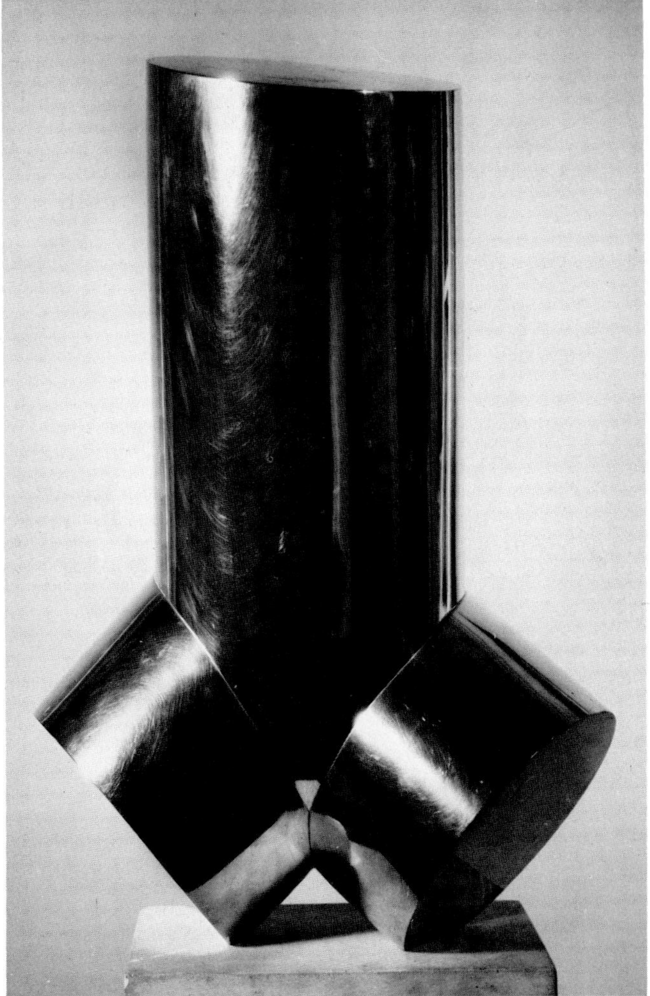

position. The viewer thus has limited points of observation, so that in a sense one relates to the work as one would to a painting.

The carved wooden piece shown in Figure 397 has forms sculpted in very high relief. (While this photograph shows it mounted on a freestanding pedestal, the work actually is meant to rest against the wall, and the back is plain.) The figures of knights, horses, dragons, ladies, buildings, and trees are carved almost completely in the round, with minimum attachment to the central form. The viewer would wish to move around this piece to the extent possible, but rather than relating broadly to the spaces and forms, as one does with the Şugarman sculpture, one *examines* these intriguing figures. The fascinating hollows and projections lend themselves to close study. As with any miniature, our view of this work is a close and leisurely one.

If time and space add dimension to our understanding of sculptures, so too does the ability to touch. One seldom considers touching paintings, since our perception of them is mainly visual. But many sculptures are meant to be touched, despite the reluctance of museums to permit this. Our experience of a sculpture is heightened immeasurably by a tactile knowledge of its surface textures, its major forms and movements, its molded details. The sleek, machined purity of polished metal offers a special tactile experience unique to 20th-century sculpture (Fig. 398).

left: 397. *Scenes from the Legend of St. George.* Franco-Flemish, late 15th–early 16th century. Carved boxwood, height 13⅜″. Victoria & Albert Museum, London.

right: 398. Constantin Brancusi. *Torso of a Young Man.* 1925. Brass, height 18″. Hirshhorn Museum and Sculpture Garden, Smithsonian Institution, Washington, D.C.

left: 399. Richard Stankiewicz. *Untitled.* 1964. Welded found objects, height 4′1″. Collection Mr. and Mrs. Arthur Mones, New York.

right: 400. Arman. *Venu$.* 1970. Dollar bills in polyester form, height 35″. Courtesy Andrew Crispo Gallery, Inc., New York.

Sculptural Methods

The sculptor has two basic ways of approaching a work: the *subtractive* and the *additive.* In the subtractive method, one begins with a mass of material in which the form is visualized and gradually cuts away the material until this form emerges. Carving and cutting are the major processes involved, and the material may be wood, stone, clay, wax, plaster, metal, or plastic. Size and shape are limited by the initial mass.

The additive method is more flexible. In this process, the sculptor gradually adds or joins material to build up a form. All the materials used subtractively also can serve for the additive technique with the possible exception of stone—although even stones can be bolted together or assembled without joining. This process enables the sculptor to build up, tear down, change, and modify without danger of ruining the finished work. Often, materials such as clay, wax, or plaster will be built up on an *armature,* or support, of metal, cardboard, wood, or some other material.

Many sculptures result from a combination of the two methods. The artist who works in clay, for instance, can add or remove material freely as the form emerges. Metal works frequently derive from both cutting and joining (Fig. 399).

Casting is a technique that really falls into neither category. Essentially, casting involves pouring molten material into a mold and then allowing the material to harden. Various materials can be cast, including wax, plaster, and clay, but the most common are metal and plastics (Fig. 400). The overriding advantage of casting is that it permits the sculptor to create form in soft, malleable materials such as clay or wax and then translate this freely conceived form into a durable, permanent medium.

The mold for casting can be a simple depression into which material is poured. Plaster, wax, and some plastics may be cast solid, but a hollow cast involving only a thin layer of material is preferred for metal and clay to avoid the danger of cracking as well as excessive weight. Hollow casting necessitates a mold composed of at least two sections—one for the outer surface and one for the inside. The classic method for hollow casting metal, especially bronze, is the *cire-perdue,* or lost-wax technique.

In cire-perdue casting, the sculptor builds a model of wax around a core of some nonmelting material, such as clay. Next, an outer mold usually of clay is applied to the wax model, conforming to it in every detail. To make the cast, the wax is melted out and replaced with molten metal. Several identical sculptures can be produced from the same mold. Furthermore, the sculptor is not confined to the compact form required for materials that could break easily, but is free to make extensions into space as the design requires. Most of the monumental bronze sculptures in parks and plazas were made by the cire-perdue method (Fig. 276).

Another popular casting method depends on molds made of damp sand, which is solid enough to hold a shape but will release the cast material after it has hardened. Bronze, plaster, plastics, and concrete are the materials often cast by this technique, and the surface texture resulting from sand particles adhering can be left or smoothed. Panels for exterior walls of buildings can be relief cast by pouring wet concrete into flat sand molds modeled in reverse (Fig. 401).

Within the last quarter century or so, the repertoire of the sculptor has broadened tremendously in terms of both material and process. Plastics have come into common use, and the welding torch now is standard equipment in many a sculpture studio. Some sculptors comb junkyards and dumps for interesting castoffs and use them as ingredients for new forms without reference to their original purpose. Today, virtually any material offers possibilities for sculpture (Fig. 407).

401. Constantino Nivola. Mural façade of Covenant Mutual Insurance Building, Hartford, Conn. 1958. Sand-cast concrete relief, 30 x 110′.

below: 402. Antoni Gaudí. Casa Battló, Barcelona (detail of roof). 1905–07.

right: 403. Gargoyles on the face of Washington Cathedral, Mount St. Alban, Washington, D.C.

The Role of Sculpture

Like any other work of art, a sculpture need have no purpose except to *be.* It is an object that expresses the aesthetic impulse of the artist and may evoke some aesthetic response in the viewer. Nevertheless, in the long history of art, many pieces that we consider sculptures have assumed additional roles. The totem pole or ancestor figure (Figs. 18, 219) had a definite religious significance for its maker, as do Christian statues. The carved amulet was meant for warding off evil spirits.

Sculpture always has maintained a close relationship with architecture, and some buildings actually could be thought of as overgrown sculptures (Fig. 402). The practice of embellishing public buildings, especially temples and churches, with wonderful sculptures carved in high relief dates back at least to ancient Egypt and still prevails today (Fig. 403). Such works exist on two levels—for their own sake and for the lively surface they contribute to the architecture.

The association with architecture affects sculptural design in several ways. First, it emphasizes large forms that can be viewed from afar with no loss of detail and that are in keeping with the scale of the building. Second, the high placement of the sculpture necessitates certain refinements to accommodate the lower eye level of the viewer. In the sculpted friezes on ancient Greek temples, for example, the upper portions projected farther from the background than the lower ones, so the forms would catch the most favorable effects of light and shadow. Third, true integration of sculpture with architecture indicates a degree of harmony in style.

Most of our public sculptures today are freestanding (Fig. 414). In a sense, then, they do not so much embellish architecture as humanize it, creating a transition in scale and purpose between towering skyscrapers and people. A monumental work like King's relates to architecture in scale and material, to pedestrians in aesthetic response, so that human beings and their megastructures still maintain a basic relationship.

Attributes of Sculpture

As with painting, three attributes generally are applied to sculpture: form, subject, and content. The form refers to both the actual physical shape of the piece and its composition, which in sculpture may be called *organization.* The subject is what the sculpture is or represents, and the content its aesthetic or emotional impact.

The possibilities for form in sculpture are infinite, limited only by the nature of the materials and the technique used. However, it is possible to make some broad generalizations about form, based on the overall characteristics of a particular piece. A work such as Lipton's *Sanctuary* (Fig. 404) could be described as a *closed form.* Although it is irregular, its overall outline suggests a sphere, or some other enclosed mass. The major impact of the form is inward, toward its center, and there are virtually no extensions into space.

In contrast to the Lipton, Antonio Canova's *Hercules and Lycas* (Fig. 405) might be described as an *open form.* The thrust of the work is outward, both in the powerful diagonal carried through the body of Hercules and in the implied movement of Lycas being thrown over his shoulder. This energetic form pushes out into space in several directions, but predominantly on the angle of the strongest diagonal.

above: 404. Seymour Lipton. *Sanctuary.* 1953. Nickel silver over steel, height 29¼″. Museum of Modern Art, New York (Blanchette Rockefeller Fund).

right: 405. Antonio Canova. *Hercules and Lycas.* 1812–15 (original 1796). Marble, height 11′5¾″. Galleria Nazionale d'Arte Moderna, Rome.

Another method of categorizing sculptural form is by its internal form or organization. The Bamenda mask shown in Figure 406 has a formal, stylized organization. It depends upon almost perfect bilateral symmetry, and the careful detailing of parallel lines adds to the overall feeling of controlled organization. At the other extreme, Robert Morris' untitled work illustrated in Figure 407 shows an extremely informal organization. A loose pile of thread, felt, steel, and miscellaneous junk, the work seems to have random organization, almost as though it were the aftermath of an accident. This, too, is a kind of composition—the composition of happenstance.

The subject matter of a sculpture may be obvious or illusive. Throughout the history of the art, one of the most frequent sculptural subjects has been the human figure. In order to consider the questions of subject and content in sculpture, we might compare three different works: the Stone Age figurine called *Venus of Willendorf* (Fig. 408), a *Woman* by George Segal (Fig. 409), and Duane Hanson's *Sunbather* (Fig. 410). Each of these sculptures has as its subject the human female.

left: 406. Dance mask from West Bamileke, Banga-Djang region, Africa. Late 19th–early 20th century. Wood, height 26½″. Rietberg Museum, Zurich (Von der Heydt Collection).

below: 407. Robert Morris. *Untitled* (study; later destroyed). 1968. Thread, mirrors, aluminum, asphalt, copper, felt, steel, and lead; 30′ square. Courtesy Leo Castelli Gallery, New York.

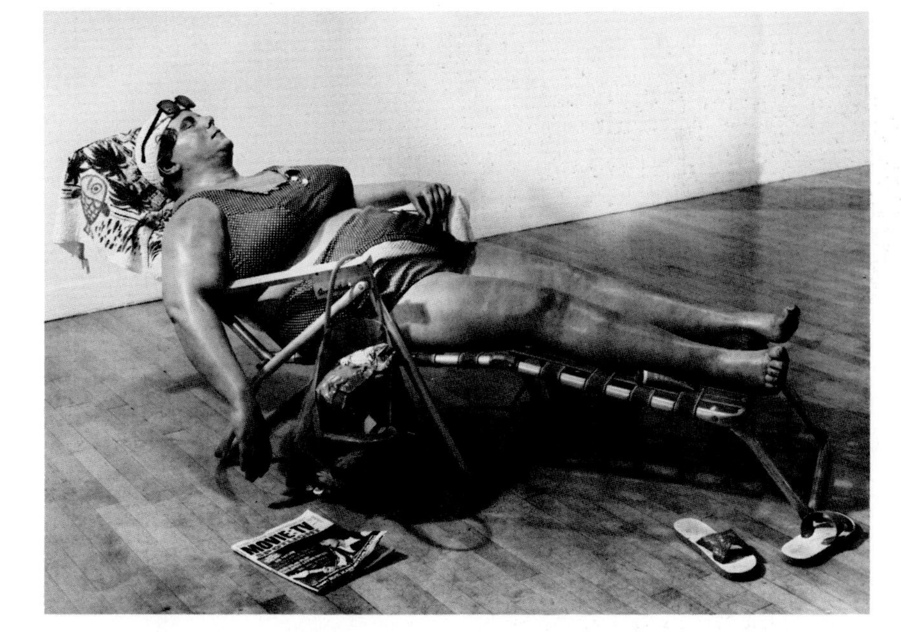

above left: 408. *Venus of Willendorf.* c. 15,000–10,000 B.C. Stone, height $4\frac{3}{8}$″. Museum of Natural History, Vienna.

above right: 409. George Segal. *Woman Standing in Bathtub.* 1963. Plaster cast figure, linoleum tile, and porcelain tub; 5′4″ x $5'4\frac{1}{2}$″. Collection Mrs. Robert B. Meyer, Chicago.

right: 410. Duane Hanson. *Woman at Beach on Lounge Chair,* or *Sunbather.* 1971. Polyester and fiberglass, polychromed; lifesize. Private collection.

However, the content of the three works is drastically different. It is assumed that the Venus of Willendorf was intended as a fertility figure. Her enormous breasts and protruding bulbous forms suggest ripeness and fecundity. This statuette could stand as Woman personified, but it is woman in the procreative sense.

George Segal's *Woman* (Fig. 409), cast in plaster, is faceless, colorless, devoid of expression. She represents a kind of depersonalization of the human being, a ghost of a woman—impassive, stolid, oblivious to her surroundings. In direct contrast, Duane Hanson's *Sunbather* (Fig. 410), a representative of the New Realism, is almost more lifelike than life. The artist recreates every detail of the body, however unappealing, with merciless fidelity. This figure, then, can be seen as Hanson's cynical comment upon the cruder aspects of our society. His woman symbolizes the dissolute 20th-century individual—overfed, underdressed, overindulged, and understimulated. Thus, we have three sculptures in which the subject is a woman and the content is, respectively, fertility, alienation, and flaccidity of mind and body.

above: 411. Jasper Johns. *Painted Bronze (Ale Cans).* 1964. Painted bronze, $5\frac{1}{2}$ x 8 x $4\frac{1}{2}$″. Courtesy Leo Castelli Gallery, New York.

below: 412. David Smith. *Royal Bird.* 1948. Stainless steel, 1′$9\frac{3}{4}$″ x 4′11″ x 9″. Walker Art Center, Minneapolis (T. B. Walker Foundation Acquisition, 1952).

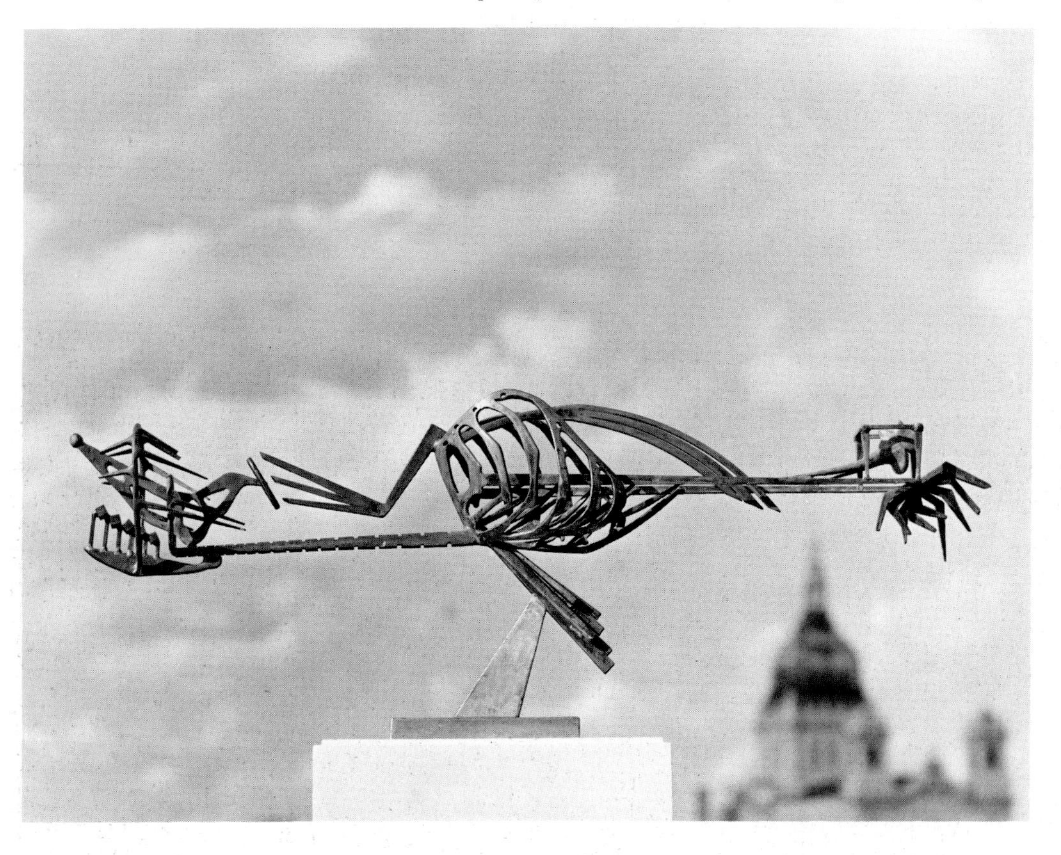

Jasper Johns' bronze sculpture of ale cans (Fig. 411) also has recognizable subject matter, but its content is more elusive. The viewer must supply a personal response. Content could derive either from the symmetry of the spatial relationships established or from the wit implicit in a commercial form meticulously rendered in a traditional sculpture material. We could even consider these bronze ale cans to be emblems of our society.

Contemporary Trends

The sculpture of the 20th century is an international art movement in which form, subject, and content are directed by contemporary society and by new materials that make possible an expression suggestive of our age. Color and light have achieved new importance as elements of sculptural design, and there is a marked tendency toward a synthesis of art and technology, art and science, sculpture and painting.

One of the major influences on modern sculpture was the work of David Smith, who in the late 1940s began cutting and welding metal shapes to build machined forms with a quality directly expressive of 20th-century society (Figs. 269, 412). Smith's development of the direct metal construction technique not only expanded the possibilities for work in this medium, but also conditioned sculptors to think in terms of direct building for other materials, such as plastics.

A number of the movements that we identified in painting appeared also in the work of sculptors. Certainly there has been Pop sculpture, with which we could associate the soft constructions of Claes Oldenburg (Fig. 363). Minimalism in sculpture developed more or less concurrently with the same aesthetic in painting, and its goals are similar: to reduce the sculptural elements to an absolute minimum—mass, size, and perhaps color. Usually, Minimal sculptures are geometric, and no surface treatment interrupts their pure forms (Fig. 413). In many contemporary sculptural compositions, space—or negative form—actually becomes more important than positive form.

Despite such trends, the figure always has been important in sculpture and remains so today. Perhaps this is because the three-dimensionality of sculpture relates closely to solid forms in the natural world, including the human form. Contemporary versions of the

413. Ronald Bladen. *Untitled.* 1967. Painted aluminum (after a 1965 version in wood), in three sections; each 8 x 4′. Museum of Modern Art, New York (James Thrall Soby Fund).

left: 414. William King. *Amité.* 1976. Stainless steel, height 24′. State University of New York at Plattsburg, courtesy Terry Dintenfass, Inc., New York.

right: 415. Magdalena Abakanowicz. *Bois Le Duc* (environmental hanging). 1970–71. Sisal and wool, 24 x 71′. State Building, North Brabant, Hertogenbosch, The Netherlands.

figure, however, may depart radically from the conceptions of 19th-century academicians. The witty constructions of William King (Fig. 414), with their paper-doll flattening and giant scale, turn the human body into environmental sculpture, making the same transitions between cityscape and people that Sugarman's works do (Pl. 36, p. 267).

Materials for sculpture today encompass the entire range of moldable substances. During the decade of the seventies, fiber has taken on a new role as a sculpture medium, and a pioneer in this field was Magdalena Abakanowicz. Removed from the strictures of the conventional loom, fibers and yarns have begun to assume free sculptural shapes, sometimes of a size impossible in traditional materials. Abakanowicz' work has included both huge environmental sculptures (Fig. 415) and eerie molded lifesize figures (Fig. 346).

The use of light as an element of design has resulted in an entire new area known as *luminal art,* or luminal sculpture. This broad category includes such phenomena as beams of light moving in ever-changing patterns, as well as more permanent compositions made of Lucite and Plexiglas, painted metal, or batteries of colored lights. Lights may be placed under, behind, or inside a sculptural form to create an illumination that is integral with the form itself (Pl. 37, p. 268). They may change constantly or remain fixed.

Among the newest materials for sculpture are electronic devices—cathode tubes, transistors, and photoelectric cells. From these elements are fashioned strange and intriguing constructions that speak eloquently of a technological age. Lights flash, noises rumble, and electronic music sets up an interaction with radar. These machinelike forms have as their sole function an expression of their involvement with human inventions.

Finally, one of the most startling aspects of contemporary art is the phenomenon known as *conceptual art.* It is somewhat misleading to classify this type of endeavor with sculpture, yet it falls into other aesthetic categories even less well. As the name implies, conceptual art calls for the carrying out of a concept, which could mean stringing a giant curtain across a gorge (Fig. 10); digging a long trench, photographing it, then filling it in again; or taking a journey and plotting the points visited on a map. Nancy Holt's conceptual work *Hydra's Head* (Fig. 416) consists of six concrete pipes buried in the ground and filled with water. The pipes are arranged in an area 28 by 62 feet above the Niagara River, according to the positions of the six stars in the head of the constellation Hydra. The diameter of each pool and the water it contains depends upon the light magnitude of the particular star it represents. Obviously, the *idea* behind such a work is more significant than its physical appearance. The viewer must have an understanding of the concept involved in order to appreciate its expression. The medium of *Hydra's Head* is not so much pipes and water as the earth (or for that matter, the universe) itself. Conceptual art takes its cue from nature and acts directly upon nature.

Much of the sculpture we see today is pure experimentation, an appropriate expression of a society preoccupied with technology, mobility, and disposability. In works of this nature, the sculptor's grasp of the underlying principles of design may well provide the primary basis for understanding any individual work.

416. Nancy Holt. *Hydra's Head.* 1975. Six pools of water based on the positions of the six stars in the head of constellation Hydra. Located along the Niagara River, Artpark, Lewiston, N.Y.

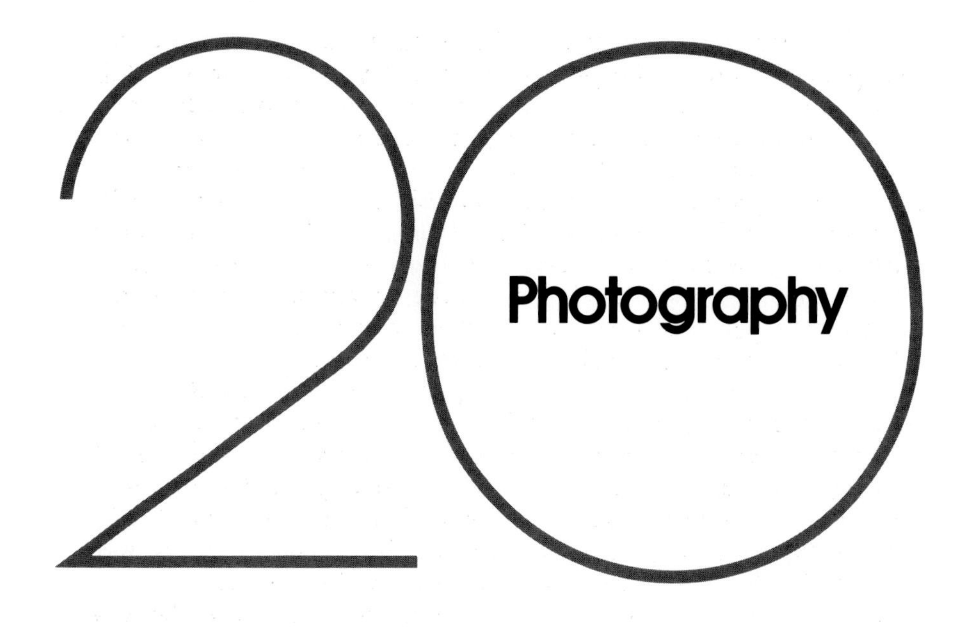

20 Photography

The invention of photography is generally attributed to the Frenchman Louis Jacques Mandé Daguerre, although many other people had contributed to the underlying technology. In 1837 Daguerre succeeded in recording on a sheet of copper the image of a corner of his studio, and more important in *fixing* that image so it would not fade. Thus was born the *daguerreotype,* a popular 19th-century portrait medium and the precursor of all modern photographs.

One of the major stimuli for the invention of photography was a perceived weakness on the part of painting: its inefficiency in recording the way things "really" look. A painter could do a portrait, a landscape, or a historical scene to record appearances for posterity, but many things could interfere with the creation of a "true" image. For one thing, the painter's skill might be insufficient. For another, the painter could select and interpret, could introduce personal biases into the work. Goya's paintings of the Spanish royal family in the early 19th century have become famous not because of their accurate representation of physical attributes, but because the artist subtly conveyed the corrupt and venal characters of his sitters. It was felt that a photograph would be a much more factual picture of reality.

Subsequent developments in photography have proved this reasoning to be faulty. The photographer today has almost as much freedom to manipulate imagery as does the painter, and in some cases possibly more freedom. Myriad choices must be made before the camera is even pointed—choices of subject matter, lighting, distance, camera angle, focus, shutter speed, possibly color—and all these will seriously affect the final image. The moment at which the shutter is clicked will have much to do with the result. Finally, modern equipment and techniques allow for considerable manipulation in the developing and printing stages, so that the image recorded on film may be only the starting point for the ultimate work of art.

It is ironic to think that, just at the point when many painters have returned to a faithful depiction of the natural world with Photorealism (Fig. 385), photography has moved farther than ever from the original conception of its role. Still, one of the most important qualities of photography is its immediacy. A photograph of corpses on a battlefield has much greater impact than would a painting of the same scene, just as a televised report of the battle hits us more directly than a reconstructed feature film. Seeing the photograph, we know beyond doubt that the corpses were really people and that they were really there.

Photography is an art form very much of our own era. It offers at the same time great directness and enormous potential for creation. Before considering the various ways in which designers exploit that potential, we will look briefly at the technical aspects of photography.

The Camera

In simplest form, the camera is a light-tight box with an opening at one end to admit light and a receptive ground at the other to take the image. The diagram in Figure 417 shows the essential features of all cameras. Light enters the camera through the *aperture.* The amount of light entering can be controlled by the *diaphragm,* which regulates the size of the aperture, and the *shutter,* which determines the amount of time during which light may enter. A *lens* gathers and refracts the light, throwing it onto the light-sensitive field at the back of the camera—the film.

Differences in cameras result mainly from the quality of their lenses and from the distance between the lens and the film (the *focal length*). The most sophisticated equipment is that which allows the photographer maximum control in distance, shutter speed, and diaphragm openings. Special lenses permit photographs of very broad vistas (*wide-angle* lenses), of subjects that are very far away (*telephoto* lenses) or very close to the camera.

After a photograph has been exposed, the film is removed from the camera, developed, and—except for transparencies—printed on special paper. It is in these steps that recent developments have given the photographer unprecedented latitude for creation.

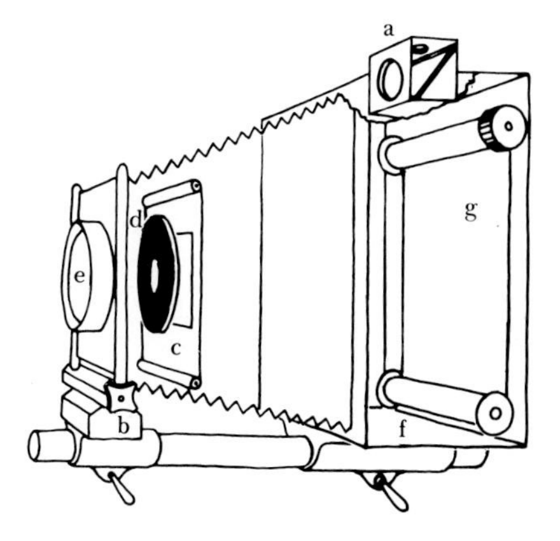

417. Diagram of the essential parts of a camera: *a* viewfinder; *b* focusing system; *c* shutter; *d* aperture with diaphragm; *e* lens; *f* light-tight box; *g* film.

Subject Matter in Photography

All photographs begin with some subject matter, even though, when translated by the creative eye of the photographer, that subject matter may become an abstraction. A photograph of a child, for example, may be a portrait of a particular child, a symbol of childhood, a commentary upon innocence or impishness, a contrast in light and

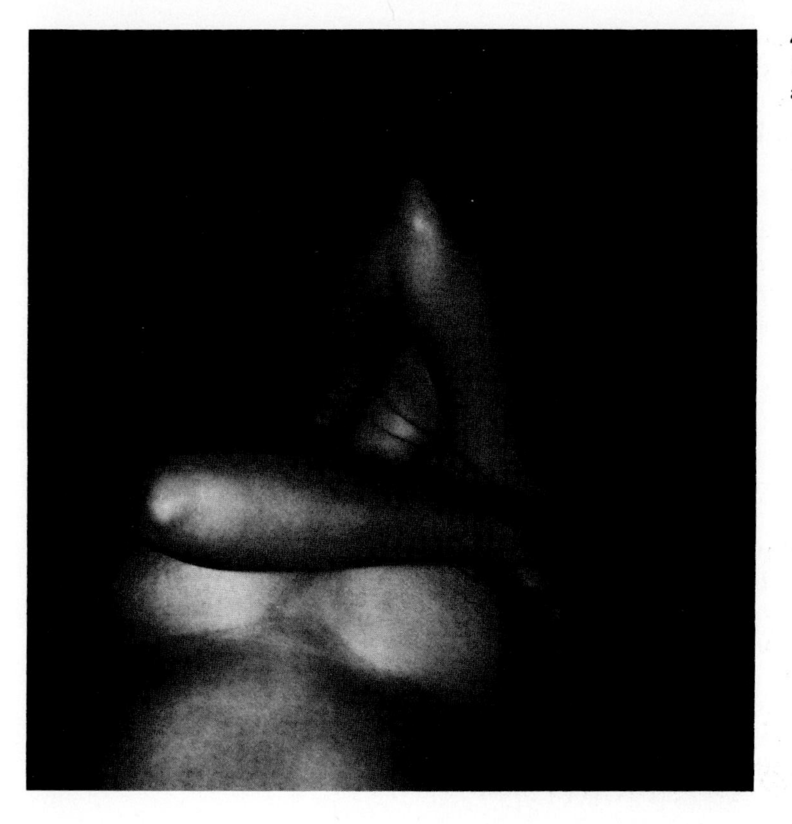

418. Harry Callahan. *Eleanor.* 1948. Photograph. Courtesy the artist.

shadow, a study of form—or conceivably all of these at once. Nevertheless, we can classify photographs according to their subject matter, bearing in mind that the actual *content* may vary tremendously.

People

Over a period of many years Harry Callahan has taken thousands of photographs of his wife Eleanor (Fig. 418). Few of these, however, could be described as portraits. For Callahan, Eleanor serves as a symbol of womanhood, of the essential life force, of fertility and richness. She is the center of his life, and he makes her the center of the world, the standard against which all other things are measured and all forces react.

As Callahan with his Eleanor sought the essence, the archetypical, Diane Arbus specialized in photographs of people who were *a*typical, who, because of occupation, appearance, sexual orientation, or some other characteristic, were unusual. A portfolio of her photographs runs the gamut of eccentricity in human nature. Arbus' subjects included giants, transvestites, nudists, sword swallowers, burlesque queens, and families of curiously mismatched individuals (Fig. 419). The photographs are disturbing, but at the same time often poignant—a combination of qualities that can be attributed to Arbus' special rapport with her subjects.

Nature

Since the early history of photography, many practitioners have turned to the natural landscape for subject matter. For some, the intent has been quasipolitical, an attempt to show us the beauties of our natural world in the hope of preventing further destruction by rampaging industrial society. Others simply delight in the wonder of natural forms as they are. Yet others find in nature the source of abstract compositions of form and space, line and texture, value differences of light and shade.

Minor White's photograph *Capitol Reef, Utah* (Fig. 420) clearly depicts a natural form, but the viewer is not certain what that form might be. Is it wood or rock or earth? Are we above it, below it, or facing it? Are these small forms seen up close or monumental ones in the distance? We cannot know, yet we are fascinated by the interplay of shapes and textures, of dark and light surfaces arranged in a way that seems to shift and move. Again, the subject matter is a simple one but the content of the photograph goes far beyond it.

Motion

The ability of the camera to capture and freeze motion is one of its most appealing characteristics for many photographers. In fact, the origin of the motion picture is traced to a series of still photographs taken by Eadweard Muybridge in 1873 of a horse at full gallop.

Today sophisticated lenses, films, and camera settings enable the photographer to depict motion in a single still picture. There are two basic ways to do this: with the subject moving and with the camera moving. The first is illustrated in Figure 54, a time-lapse photograph

below: 419. Diane Arbus. *A Young Brooklyn Family Going for a Sunday Outing, New York City.* 1966. Photograph.

right: 420. Minor White. *Capitol Reef, Utah.* 1962. Photograph. Museum of Modern Art, New York.

above: 421. Yale Joel. *Illusion of Speed.* 1965. Photograph taken with panning camera.

right: 422. Philip L. Molten. *Cast-Off Machinery, Wawona, California.* 1971. Photograph. Courtesy the artist.

of a helicopter landing. Figure 421 shows the reverse situation, in which a girl appears to be racing along on a motorcycle. In fact, she was motionless when the picture was taken, but the camera was rotated on a tripod during the exposure. This effect should dispel the illusion that what we see in a photograph is what actually happened.

Still Life

Few photographers today would be interested in making an arrangement of fruit, vegetables, and crockery on a table. Nevertheless, composed still-life photographs can be exciting, and there are endless subjects to choose from. Philip Molten's photo of cast-off machinery (Fig. 422) shows the potential of found objects in photographic com-

Plate 38. Charles Swedlund. *Untitled.* 1975. Dye transfer print. Courtesy the artist.

Plate 39. Lucas Samaras. *Photo-Transformation.* 1974. Polaroid SX-70 manipulation of photoemulsion pigments, 3″ square. Courtesy Pace Gallery, New York.

423. Sam Shere. *Explosion of the Hindenburg, Lakehurst, New Jersey.* 1937. Photograph.

position. Such objects, under the eye of the photographer, lose their original identities and become abstract shapes and forms, just as isolated portions of the natural world can do.

Purposes of Photography

Beyond the goal of creating a striking image, many photographs have a definite purpose. As mentioned above, some nature photographers hope to encourage a restoration of sound ecological principles in dealing with the environment. Other purposes may include illustration (as of fashion), portraiture, advertising, or what is known as documentary photography.

The documentary photograph is almost as old as the art itself. During the 1860s a number of photographers, of whom Matthew Brady was the most famous, followed the two armies through the Civil War, thus establishing the genre of photojournalism. One of the most famous documentary photographs of all time is one taken by Sam Shere showing the exploding dirigible *Hindenburg* as it was preparing to land in New Jersey in 1937 (Fig. 423). This photo was essentially an accident. Shere and many other photographers were poised, their cameras ready, waiting to shoot a routine landing of the ship. The *Hindenburg* itself provided the drama by conveniently exploding before their eyes. Other photographers have deliberately sought drama and have gone out with their cameras to find it.

During the Depression, the Works Progress Administration and various other agencies sent photographers out through the United States—partly to document the hardships across the land, and partly to keep the photographers from starving. The pictures that emerged

424. Russell Lee. *Tenant Purchase Clients at Home, Hidalgo County, Texas.* 1939. Photograph. Library of Congress.

from this assignment stand as some of the most poignant records of human poverty and hopelessness (Fig. 424).

The plight of the Depression victims could only be recorded; little could be done immediately to relieve their suffering. This was not the situation, however, with a special group of photographs taken by W. Eugene Smith and Aileen M. Smith in Japan. The Smiths took their cameras to the fishing town of Minamata in southern Japan to document the unspeakable mutilation that was taking place among the population as a result of industrial pollution. A nearby chemical plant had for years been dumping mercury wastes into the water from which the village took much of its food supply. The result was paralysis, brain damage, loss of hearing, and horrible disfigurement, especially in the children (Fig. 425). The Smiths' aim was to make the chemical firm recognize its liability, and their photographs were meant to bring Minamata to the attention of the world. As a result of his intervention, W. Eugene Smith was severely beaten by thugs connected with the plant and was blinded. The photographs, however, received wide publicity and eventually were collected in a book, so that the plight of Minamata could no longer be concealed.

425. W. Eugene Smith. Victim of "Minamata disease." 1974. Photograph. Courtesy the artist.

left: 426. Jerry Uelsmann. *Poet's House* (first version). 1965. Multiple-image photograph. Courtesy the artist.

above: 427. Harry Callahan. *Chicago.* 1954. Photograph. Courtesy the artist.

Special Effects in Photography

The photographer may undertake special effects in order to create a mood, an abstraction, or a distortion. Sometimes this is done through multiple exposure or multiple printing. Jerry Uelsmann's *Poet's House* (Fig. 426) consists of several images, photographed separately, and printed on the same paper. The result is a romantic, surrealistic quality that seems especially evocative of a poet's home.

Uelsmann's technique brings together several images to create a unified effect, but multiple imagery can also work with contrasting subjects that seem out of place together or that reinforce one another. Harry Callahan's photo of *Chicago* (Fig. 427) is such a work. In this combined photograph, two nudes seem to be standing on the side of a skyscraper. The Garden of Eden quality of the figures meeting seems especially disturbing against the shabby façade of the building, as though Callahan is showing us how much of the simple life we have lost in letting the cities overtake us.

Not all multiple images are superimposed. Tetsu Okuhara's "expanded photograph" is actually assembled from 112 individual prints to create a stunning visual montage (Fig. 428). Duane Michals' "photostories" are serial arrangements of still photographs that tell

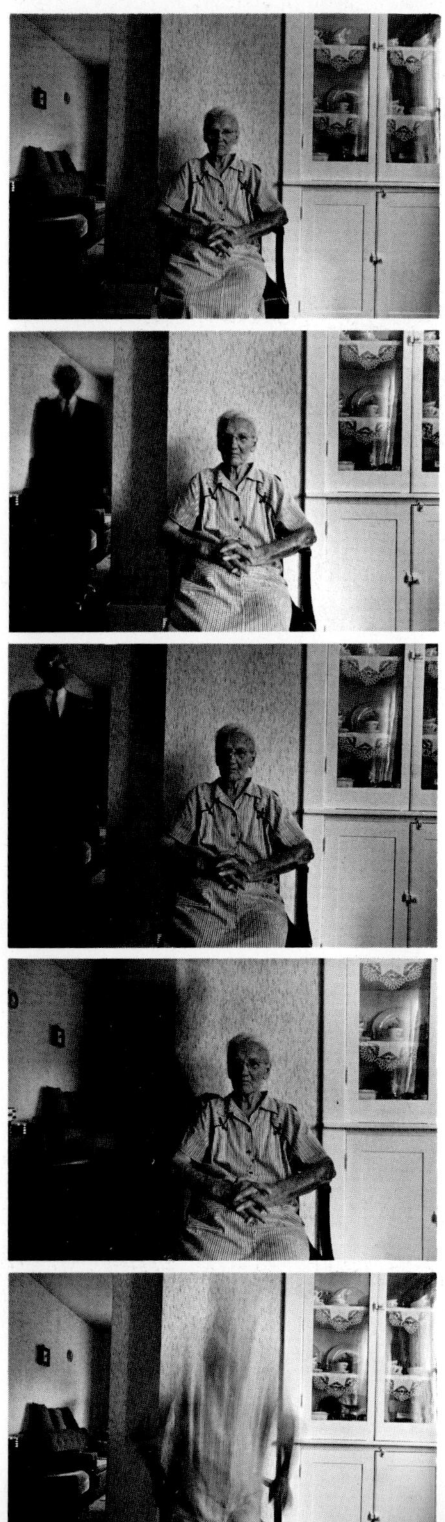

above: 428. Tetsu Okuhara. *Winter's Head.* 1971. Expanded photograph assembled from 112 separate prints, mounted on Masonite; $2'1/2''$ x 8'. Courtesy the artist.

left: 429. Duane Michals. *Death Comes to the Old Lady.* 1969. Serial photograph. Courtesy the artist.

little vignettes, tiny stories that are meant to be read in sequence. In *Death Comes to the Old Lady* (Fig. 429), a series of five photographs, we see an old woman seated rigidly in a chair, and then the gradual approach of a death figure, followed by the partial vaporization of the woman. Clearly this sequence is posed—some would say contrived. But it is no more contrived than a painter's act in posing a model. Michals' serial images should not be read as attempts at motion. *Death Comes to the Old Lady* must be viewed as a succession of five separate events that are related in time.

Beyond the combination of images, special effects can also be obtained by "pure" means—that is, with just the usual single-shot exposures. Two of the most common devices for achieving unique qualities are lighting and viewpoint. Lighting effects can be obtained in several ways. The photographer can set up artificial lights to a particular specification; can control natural lighting by means of filters, camera setting, and film; or can simply exploit the special qualities of natural light that may occur. The third option allowed Philip Molten to shoot the eerie photograph in Figure 430, which shows a portion of the California Palace of the Legion of Honor bathed in San Francisco's famous fog. The mysterious presence of the mist, combined with a stark composition, make this modern structure as timeless as the monoliths at Stonehenge (Fig. 101).

The photographer's viewpoint can have a substantial effect on the ultimate result. A photo taken from great distance, for example, may isolate the subject matter and give it a timeless quality. Extreme closeups, on the other hand, tend to foster abstraction. In Edward Weston's photograph *Neil, Nude* (Fig. 431) the nude male figure is brought so close to the camera that all fleshy quality disappears, and there is nothing remotely erotic about the image. The male torso might as easily have been carved from marble, so pure and pristine are its outlines. We read the figure as an abstract composition of planes, with small hollows and depressions.

It should be noted that all the so-called "special effects" illustrated here could be obtained with the simplest camera. Except for Jerry Uelsmann's *Poet's House,* which would require the intervention of the photographer in the developing stage, any of these photographs could have been taken with normal equipment and no special manipulation.

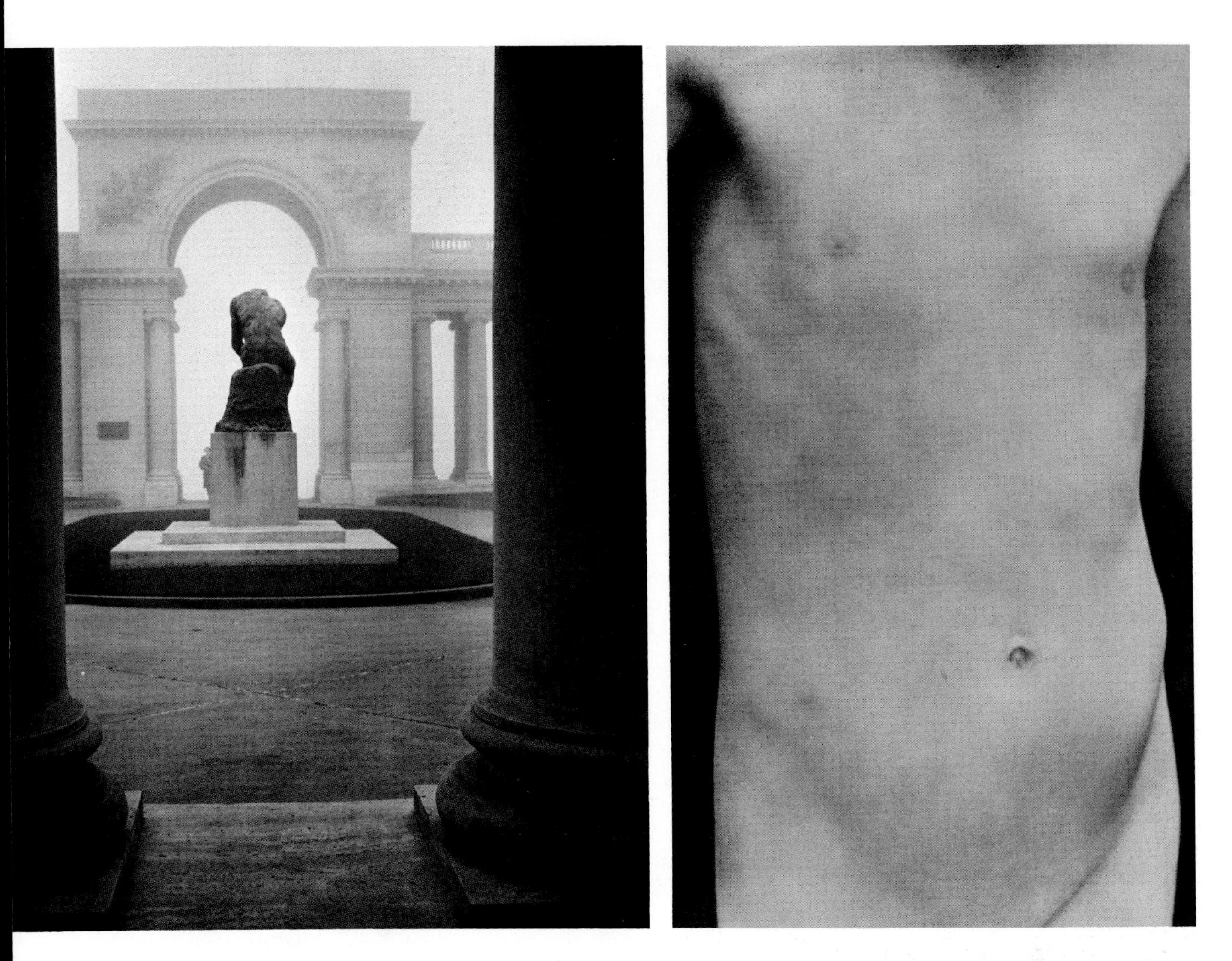

We turn now to a consideration of pictures that *do* need special photographic gear or an extreme control of the developing process.

Special Techniques

The photograph of New York in Figure 432 was taken with a Zoomar camera, which records a complete 360-degree image in one exposure. The approaches to the Brooklyn Bridge swoop and bend like dancers moving to an unheard tune. Special cameras and lenses can do

above left: 430. Philip L. Molten. *California Palace of the Legion of Honor.* 1960. Photograph. Courtesy the artist.

above right: 431. Edward Weston. *Neil, Nude.* 1925. Photograph. Museum of Modern Art, New York.

below: 432. *The Brooklyn Bridge.* Photograph taken with the Zoomar 360° Panoramic camera. Courtesy Zoomar, Inc., New York.

433. Charles Swedlund. Girl on a swing. 1973. Widelux photograph. Courtesy the artist.

marvelous things. Charles Swedlund used a Widelux camera to make the image in Figure 433, which shows a child on a swing. The Widelux has a lens that actually swings from left to right during the exposure. This action reinforces the movement of the swinging figure to yield a unique quality of energetic motion.

A few special techniques are accomplished with no camera at all. During the 1920s there was a vogue for the *photogram,* in which objects were placed directly on photographic paper and exposed for a brief period. The objects could be leaves or other plant forms, found objects, bolts, nuts, keys, kitchen utensils, or almost anything else. After exposure, the paper was developed and printed. Keeping up with the times, a modern adaptation of this process is the *xerograph,* which employs conventional Xerox equipment. As with the photogram, objects are placed directly on the exposure surface and photographed as one would copy a business letter, except that the duration of the exposure is controlled. The results are soft-edged, intricate, and fascinating (Fig. 434).

Some of the most exciting effects in contemporary photography are obtained not in the camera but in the darkroom. Charles Swedlund's color photograph in Plate 38 (p. 285) was made with three separate exposures of the subject on individual pieces of black-and-white film using blue, green, and red filters. After exposure, the three color negatives were printed by means of a dye-transfer method. Lucas Samaras' *Photo-Transformations* (Pl. 39, p. 286) depend upon a technique of actually stirring the color granules on a piece of Polaroid film after the exposure has been made. In both of these techniques, the resultant colors are fabulous and other-worldly.

Finally, the art of photography has refused to confine itself to the two-dimensional image. Our notions of a photograph may be shattered by such works as Dale Quarterman's *Peace Baby* (Fig. 435), a sculptural construction of styrofoam and photographic prints. However, since photography is a unique *reproductive* process, there is no reason why this reproduction cannot move into the third dimension. The photographic image is as fresh and innovative as the brain behind the camera.

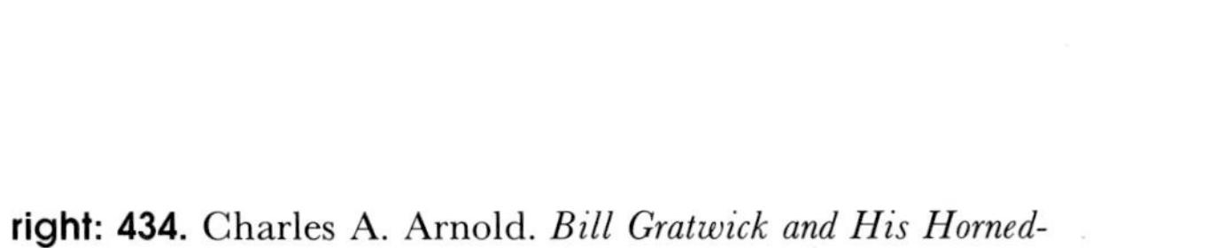

right: 434. Charles A. Arnold. *Bill Gratwick and His Horned-Dorset Ram.* 1976. Xerograph. Courtesy the artist.

below: 435. Dale Quarterman. *Peace Baby.* 1974. Bent and molded photographs on built-up styrofoam, enclosed in wooden boxes with Plexiglas; 20 x 28 x 2½″. Collection First and Merchants Bank, Richmond, Va.

21 Prints

A print is an original work of art created by an indirect transfer method. Rather than making an image directly on a ground, as in painting, the artist works on a "master" surface, with the image usually in reverse. From this master, many impressions can be made on paper. The principle involved is identical to that of the common rubber stamp.

Because it is general practice to strike a number of impressions from a single master, prints often are referred to as *multiples.* The artist will create an image on a plate, stone, screen, or other surface, then supervise the printing or perhaps undertake it personally. The number of impressions, known as the *edition,* possible from a single original will vary with the material. A linoleum cut, for example, yields relatively few prints before the soft material begins to wear and the quality of the impressions diminishes. A steel-faced metal plate, on the other hand, is capable of striking many thousands of fine-quality prints. As a rule, prints are numbered as they come from the press, with the earlier impressions being the finest and therefore the most desirable. The artist will hand sign each print that meets with his or her approval.

Art prints should not be confused with reproductions. A *reproduction* is just that—a copy of a work done in some other medium, usually a painting. While good-quality reproductions may be suitable for educational purposes, they can in no sense be considered works of art, since the artist had nothing to do with them. A print, on the other hand, is an original that may happen to exist in several versions. It resembles, in this sense, a bronze sculpture for which there may be a number of castings from the mold. Sometimes the printmaker will vary the image between impressions, so that each print is a bit different from the others.

Within the last two or three decades the price of paintings and sculptures has skyrocketed, to the point that only the very rich can afford such a work by a known artist. Collectors therefore have turned to prints, which, while certainly not cheap (with some ranging into the thousands of dollars), are still within an acceptable price category. Artists, too, have newly discovered prints. Recent technical improvements and innovations have enormously broadened the creative potential for printmaking.

Printmaking derives ultimately from two historical sources: the early woodblock prints used for illustrating books, playing cards, and religious images (Fig. 436); and the medieval practice of decorating metal, such as armor, with incised designs. Today most techniques fall into one of four categories: relief, intaglio, lithography, and serigraphy. However, there are many variations, with considerable overlapping.

Relief

Relief describes any process in which the image to be printed is *raised* from the background on the printing surface and takes the ink directly. The inked image is then transferred to the paper by pressure. The oldest printmaking processes are the relief methods. In their most typical form relief prints preserve the qualities of the material from which they are made, translating these qualities into an artistic expression. The most common methods are *woodcut, linocut,* and *engraving* on wood or plastic.

436. Illustration from *The History of Sir Richard Whittington Thrice Lord Mayor of London.* 18th century. Woodcut. British Library, London.

left: 437. Heinrich Campendonk. *Nude by a Farmyard* (*Frauenakt vor Bauerhof*). 1920–21. Woodcut, $8\frac{9}{16}$ x $8\frac{5}{8}$". Brooklyn Museum, New York.

above: 438. Henri Matisse. *Seated Nude.* 1906. Linoleum cut, $18\frac{3}{4}$ x 15". Museum of Modern Art, New York (gift of Mr. and Mrs. R. Kirk Askew, Jr.).

Woodcut

Woodcuts have a forthright charm that has never been surpassed. The basic technique is simple. The image to be printed is projected or sketched on the side of a block of even-grained wood, then the areas that are *not* to be printed are cut away with knives or gouges. The block is inked and the image transferred to paper by pressing or rubbing. Because they are cut primarily *with* the grain, woodcuts have a hand-hewn look that emphasizes the feeling of the wood itself (Fig. 437). Sometimes knots are left in the wood to become a part of the design. In any case, a woodcut possesses characteristics that cannot be imitated in any other medium.

Linocut

In place of wood, some artists use heavy linoleum blocks, generally made by gluing thick linoleum to plywood (Fig. 438). The technique is the same as for a woodcut, but the actual cutting may be easier, because the smooth linoleum has no resistant grain. The resulting print may have fine smooth lines or may be rough to approximate the effect of wood. Plate 40 (p. 303) shows Picasso's first linocut, a work marked by very rich colors. Color prints involve several blocks, each planned for a single hue. In printing, the various blocks are *registered* or lined up, so that they print in exactly the right image area. This technique is also possible with woodcut.

Stone Cuts

The Eskimo printmakers of Cape Dorset, on west Baffin Island in Hudson Bay near the Arctic Ocean, have perfected a number of unique processes, including a type of print from stone reliefs (Fig. 439). For their stone cuts, these artists polish a large stone, trace an image upon it, then carve away the background areas from the stone. After the raised portion of the stone has been inked, they lay a sheet of paper on it and rub with the fingers or a sealskin pad, thus transferring the image. Contemporary Eskimo artists are receiving increasing recognition for their bold, stylized, and charming prints.

Wood Engraving

Wood engravings differ from woodcuts in that they are cut from the *end grain* of the wood. A fine steel tool called a *burin* allows for finer lines and greater detail than is usual in woodcuts. The process is still relief, because the fine lines show white against the dark background that is inked and printed (Fig. 440). Lucite sometimes replaces wood, again making for smoother cutting.

left: 439. Mungituk. *Man Carried to the Moon.* 1959. Stone relief print, $19\frac{1}{8}$ x 15″. Brooklyn Museum, New York (Dick S. Ramsay Fund).

above: 440. Rockwell Kent. *Voyages.* 1924. Chiaroscuro wood engraving on maple, 6″ square. National Gallery of Art, Washington, D.C. (Rosenwald Collection).

Rubbings

Strictly speaking, rubbings are not art prints, since the "printmaker" was not involved in creating the master image. Rubbings are impressions taken from preexisting relief surfaces. Popular subjects have included gravestones, manhole covers, metal doors, and similar reliefs (Fig. 441).

In making a rubbing, one fixes a piece of paper over the relief surface and rubs across it with charcoal or some other soft drawing material. Only the raised surfaces take an impression from the charcoal, with the depressed areas remaining white. Rubbings have great value in providing a reproduceable record of works that may be difficult to photograph or that will wear with time. Quite apart from this, they offer a splendid introduction to the potentialities of the relief process. It could even be argued that rubbings *are* original works of art, since they imply a creative act that was not envisioned by the artist who made the relief. The overall effect of the rubbing is quite different from that of the stone or metal original.

Variations

Contemporary artists frequently build up their relief blocks instead of cutting out the design. Various materials are used, including acrylic gesso or white glue, cardboard, wire mesh, and other textured surfaces. Sometimes the surface of a block of wood is coated with shellac and imprinted with paper clips or coins or other objects before the glue has dried. This sort of experimentation has unlimited possibilities. It provides the first example of overlapping in print techniques, since it resembles the collagraph print discussed under intaglio methods.

Intaglio

The term *intaglio* comes from the Italian word meaning "to incise." It describes a printing process that is, in essence, just the reverse of relief, in that the parts to be printed are etched *into* the plate and are lower than the surface. Ink is retained in the incised areas rather than on a raised surface. Intaglio hand processes include metal engraving, drypoint, etching, aquatint, and mezzotint.

Engraving

Metal engravings are executed with sharp tools (*burins* or *gravers*) on sheets of copper, zinc, or steel. Whereas the wood engraving prints an inked background from which white lines have been cut, the metal engraving is basically a composition of dark lines that have been incised and then inked, with the plate surface wiped clean to provide a white background. Metal engravings thus have a quality not unlike ink drawings (Fig. 442).

In making an engraving, the V-shaped burin is pushed into the surface of the metal plate to gouge out the lines of the design, after which ink is rubbed into these grooves. The artist then wipes the surface clean, places it face up on the bed of a press, lays dampened paper on the inked plate, covers the paper with a felt blanket, and applies pressure with a heavy roller. The roller forces the paper into the grooves, and the ink is transferred to the paper.

left: 441. *Sir Reginald Malyns and Wives.* c. 1385. Rubbing of sepulchral brass at Chinnor, Oxon, England. British Museum, London.

below: 442. Martin Schongauer. *St. Michael.* c. 1480–91. Engraving, 6⅜ x 4½″. British Museum, London.

Before the invention of the camera, engravings were widely used to reproduce paintings and print book illustrations. Copper engraving is still employed for seals on official documents, postage stamps, paper money, and fine stationery.

Drypoint

The process for drypoint is much the same as that for engraving except in the preparation of the plate. Drypoints generally are executed on copper plates with needlelike instruments that have steel or diamond points. The resulting lines differ in effect from those made by the burin (Fig. 443). Instead of being pushed into the surface, the tool is drawn across the plate to raise a *burr* or tiny curl of metal along the edges of the lines. When the plate is inked, this burr retains the ink, so that the printed image has a velvety appearance recalling the darker accents in a fine pencil drawing.

Etching

The term etching comes from the German word meaning "to eat." In this process the lines of the image are eaten into the metal plate with acid, rather than being gouged out with tools.

To produce an etching the artist coats a polished metal plate with a protective film of waxlike substance called the *ground.* The lines of the drawing are then scratched into the ground with a blunt needle,

right: 443. Egon Schiele. *Portrait of Franz Hauer.* 1914. Drypoint, $5\frac{1}{8} \times 4\frac{1}{4}''$. Courtesy Fischer Fine Art Ltd., London.

below: 444. Jim Dine. *Five Paintbrushes.* 1972. Etching, 30 x 40". Courtesy Petersburg Press, London.

exposing the metal in the areas that are meant to print. The plate is immersed in an acid bath, and the acid eats into the exposed lines, etching them permanently. Finally, the plate is inked and printed in the same manner as an engraved plate. Used originally for decorating metal, such as armor, the etching technique came into use as a method of illustrating books in the 16th century. Etchings generally are characterized by a somewhat softer line than engravings (Fig. 444). It is said that in place of a sketchbook Rembrandt carried a metal plate with him, making his sketches with an etching needle and then inking and printing the plates when he returned to his studio.

Aquatint

Aquatint is a process that creates subtle tones in an intaglio plate. The artist covers a metal plate with a powdered resinous substance and then heats the plate, causing the resin particles to harden and adhere to the metal. Next, the plate is immersed in an acid bath, and the acid eats into the metal around the resin particles to create a soft allover texture. The light-to-dark tones are controlled by the amount of etching. This process can be repeated several times, with certain areas being stopped-out with acid-resistant varnish to produce gradations of light and dark. The resulting print has a soft and beautiful tonal quality that can be compared to an ink wash (Fig. 445).

445. Mary Cassatt. *In the Omnibus.* 1891. Color aquatint with drypoint and soft-ground, $14\frac{5}{16} \times 10\frac{1}{2}''$. Cleveland Museum of Art (bequest of Charles T. Brooks).

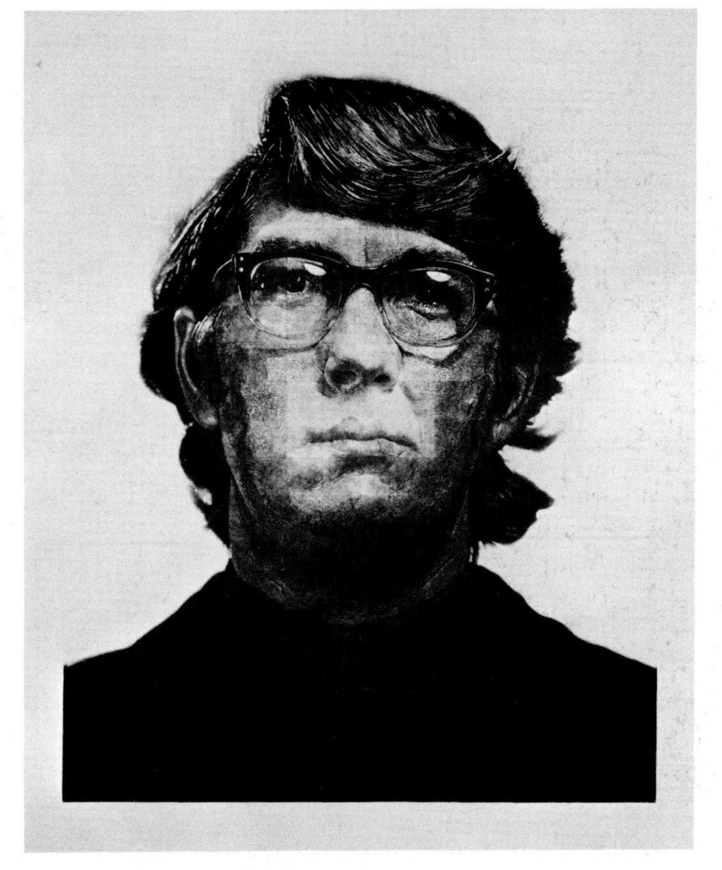

446. Chuck Close. *Keith.* 1972. Mezzotint, 4′4″ x 3′6″. Courtesy Parasol Press, New York.

Mezzotint

A velvety tone characterizes mezzotint, another variation on the etching technique. Here the artist first works over the entire plate with a *rocker,* a tool with many sharp cutting teeth, to dig up the surface and produce an allover covering of burrs. If the plate were printed at this stage, the burrs would create a uniform black tone. To build intermediate tones the artist partially removes the burrs with a *scraper;* highlights result from smoothing away the burrs completely. Mezzotint prints usually have a dark, rich, brooding quality (Fig. 446).

Collagraphy

Collagraphy is the name given to a printmaking process based on *collage,* or "pasted-on" techniques (Fig. 447). The artist builds up the plate from a variety of materials glued onto a rigid base—usually Masonite, hardboard, or plywood—maintaining a uniform thickness. The distinctive quality of the collagraph comes from the use of everyday materials, such as metal foil, newsprint, nylon net, plastic wrap, paper doilies, and the whole range of contact tapes. Of fundamental importance is the fact that all surfaces must be coated, so they will be nonporous. Thus, the ink will not be absorbed into the material but will remain in crevices and hollows, printing a clear-cut image.

Found objects—such as coins, buttons, or metal plates—and natural materials (leaves, grasses, pods) can be applied to the plate if they are flat enough. If not, they can be imprinted into a gel or plastic coating on the plate, thus incorporating the imprint into the design

right: Plate 40. Pablo Picasso. *Bust of a Woman after Cranach the Younger.* 1958. Color linoleum cut, 25⅝ x 21⅛". Collection Norton Simon, Los Angeles.

below: Plate 41. Frank Stella. *York Factory II.* 1973. Screen print in 53 colors, 18 7/16" x 44' 7 7/16". © Gemini G.E.L., Los Angeles.

Plate 42. James Rosenquist. *Horse Blinders: East.* 1972. Lithograph and silk screen, 3′¼″ x 5′8″. Courtesy Multiples, Inc., New York.

left: 447. Michael Ponce de Leon. *Nude.* 1970. Collagraph, $24 \times 21\frac{1}{2}''$. Courtesy the artist.

right: 448. Willem de Kooning. *Untitled.* 1960. Lithograph, $45\frac{5}{16} \times 31\frac{13}{16}''$. Museum of Modern Art, New York (gift of Mrs. Bliss Parkinson).

rather than the object itself. Ink is applied and wiped off as in other intaglio techniques, and the plate is printed under pressure.

It is possible to use the collagraph as a relief plate, building up a surface to be inked and printed. Frequently the relief and intaglio techniques are combined in a single print. The contemporary artist adopts traditional techniques not so much as established methods of working but rather as springboards from which to discover new methods and unprecedented effects.

Lithography

Lithography is known as a *planographic* process because it employs a flat surface with neither raised areas nor depressions. The main printing medium is the basic *lithograph,* but *monoprints* are also considered planographic. The invention of lithography is credited to the German Alois Senefelder, who used a special limestone in his native Bavaria for drawing images, thus introducing a new printing process based on chemical rather than physical properties (Fig. 448).

The lithographic process depends on the mutual antipathy of grease and water. The artist draws on a stone with a grease pencil or with a brush dipped in a greasy paintlike substance. Next, the stone is treated with a solution of gum arabic to which a small amount of nitric acid has been added. Finally, after excess drawing substance has been removed, the stone is moistened with water, then inked with a roller. The areas treated with gum arabic accept the water; the greasy image areas accept the greasy ink. Thus, when ink is rolled onto the

above left: 449. Edgar Degas. *The Bath (Le Bain)*. c. 1880. Monotype, $8\frac{3}{8} \times 6\frac{7}{16}''$. Den Kongelige Kobberstiksamling, Statens Museum for Kunst, Copenhagen.

above right: 450. Andy Warhol. *Hand Colored Flowers,* detail from a portfolio of ten. 1974. Silk screen and watercolor, $41 \times 21''$. Courtesy Castelli Graphics and Multiples, Inc., New York.

surface of the stone, it is retained by the drawn areas but does not adhere to the wet surfaces. The artist places damp paper onto the stone and applies pressure, thereby transferring the image to paper. Bavarian limestone remains the classic ground for lithographs. In recent years, however, many lithographers have used zinc plates to make their prints, resulting in unique textural characteristics.

Each of the printmaking techniques described in this chapter has its counterpart in commercial photomechanical reproduction—the means of printing books, magazines, newspapers, posters, and so forth. The corresponding planographic process is *offset lithography,* or simply *offset.* The text and illustrations for this book were offset printed.

451. John Baeder with Madeleine-Claude Jobrack, platemaker and printer. *Empire Diner.* 1976. Photoetching, $8\frac{5}{8} \times 13\frac{5}{8}''$. Courtesy the artist.

Monoprint

A monoprint or *monotype* is made by painting on a flat surface of metal or glass with either paint or ink. The printing paper is pressed onto the colored surface and then peeled off, resulting in a slightly different effect than could have been achieved by painting directly on the paper (Fig. 449). While it is theoretically possible to take more than one impression, the monoprint, as the name implies, usually creates a single work.

Serigraphy

Serigraphy or *screen printing* is a stencil technique, which means that an image is transferred to a ground by applying color or tone around or inside a pattern. Except for its application to paper rather than cloth, the technique of serigraphy for art prints differs not at all from the fabric screen printing described in Chapter 16.

The term serigraphy means literally "writing on silk," and silk is the traditional material for this process, although others, such as nylon, have come into use. Because color printing is relatively easy, screen prints usually are characterized by bright, multiple colors (Pl. 11, p. 90; Pl. 41, p. 303).

To make a print, the artist first stops out on the screen mesh all the areas that are not to print in a particular color. Next, ink or dye in that color is forced, with a squeegee or roller, through the open areas of the screen onto the paper. Each color requires a separate screen and individual inking action. There is no limit to the number of colors that can be printed on a single sheet, provided the different screens are registered properly. Many artists have discovered that screen printing offers a fertile area for exploration. The basic process easily combines with oil painting, watercolor, drawing, and other techniques (Fig. 450).

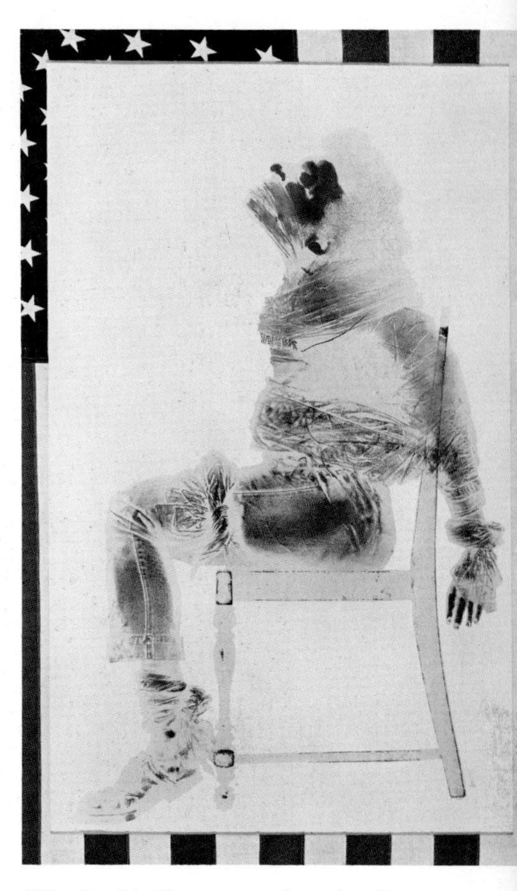

452. David Hammons. *Injustice Case.* 1970. Mixed media body print, 5′3″ x 3′4½″. Los Angeles County Museum of Art (Museum Purchase Fund).

Contemporary Design in Printmaking

In the second half of the 20th century printmaking has made enormous strides in both technical and expressive development. In aesthetic terms much contemporary work mirrors the trends in painting, such as Photorealism (Fig. 451).

Some of the most exciting technical innovations come from combining two or more techniques. James Rosenquist's *Horse Blinders* (Pl. 42, p. 304) was hand printed in 66 colors from 29 aluminum plates, one stone, and 27 silk screens. The result is an extraordinarily lush color image. Another characteristic of many prints today is great size, made possible by experimental printing mechanisms. Huge mural-size prints have been made, often incorporating areas of actual relief—that is, with portions jutting out from or depressed below the print surface.

The implements used for making an image also have broken free of tradition. Plastics and slate may take the place of woodblocks, and dentists' drills serve as burins. All manner of objects and materials are either adhered to the plate or pressed directly upon the printing surface. David Hammons, for example, specializes in "body prints" (Fig. 452), for which he applies his own margarine-coated body to the printing paper and then inks the resultant image. The scope of possibilities for printmaking has never been wider.

22 Graphic Design

The word graphic, in its broadest sense, refers to anything written, drawn, or engraved. Under this definition the term *graphic design* could apply to any of the visual arts, especially those that involve a two-dimensional surface. Drawing and printmaking, in particular, often are described as graphic arts. However, the goals of a painter or draftsman and those of an advertising designer are quite different, as are the problems encountered. Therefore, a more specific and generally accepted categorization limits the term graphic design to work intended for commercial reproduction.

For our purposes we will define graphic design as the selection and arrangement of elements for a printed format. The elements are words and images, which in design terms are called *type* (letters and words), *halftones* (photographs), and *line art* (drawings). Usually graphic design has some definite purpose, for instance to sell a product or an idea, to make a book readable and attractive, or to call attention to something. Printed advertising, package design, and the design of such things as television commercials, books, magazines, and record jackets all are examples of today's graphic design.

A significant difference between graphic design and most other forms of design is the audience to which it is directed. The painter, the sculptor, the photographer, and the craftsman can aim their designs at a limited and usually sophisticated market. However, the graphic designer must be concerned with reaching out and influencing great numbers of people. Except for the limited-edition collector's book, every other design medium discussed in this chapter will be expected to have a mass audience. Every creation of the graphic designer is meant to sell something—either itself or another product. Thus, the graphic designer must be very much aware of how people react to shapes, sizes, lines, textures, colors—and ideas.

As suggested above, graphic design is essentially a two-dimensional medium. Even when the actual product takes on a third dimension, as in packaging or books, the design will be conceived in planar terms. This is because every design must be *printed* by commercial methods and thus must run through a press. Regardless of how the final product may be assembled, the basic design unit is flat.

In this chapter we will discuss the design of books, magazines, record jackets, and advertising materials, including packaging and television commercials. Many designers work interchangeably in these various fields, moving freely back and forth from one to another. While the basic character of each may be different, the manner of applying the elements and principles of design is quite similar.

Books

A fine book holds a unique place among the world's treasures. Not only can it provide a record of great ideas and literary composition, but it may also be a work of art in itself. A combination of beautiful papers, ink, type, illustrations, binding, and cover can produce an aesthetic expression worthy of the most noble content.

Books have a history almost as old as civilization. The ancient Egyptians threaded their hieroglyphs through their paintings as a running commentary, using the thick stem fibers of the papyrus plant to make scrolls. After the beginning of the Christian era, the practice of creasing parchment scrolls into flat sheets led to the development of the *codex,* the predecessor of the bound book. During the Middle Ages devoted monks kept western culture alive by painstakingly copying and recopying the texts of Christianity, as well as those of ancient Greece and Rome. These manuscripts often were *illuminated,* or hand-painted, with intricate pictures and designs. The custom of illuminating manuscripts was also practiced in the Far East.

In the New World elaborate and colorful codices were made by the Miztec and Aztec cultures in Mexico (Pl. 43, p. 321). While the gods depicted can be identified readily, archaeologists are still deciphering the episodes and their meanings. Only eight of these codices survive from the pre-Columbian era, because the conquering Spaniards, considering their writings to be "heathen," destroyed the remainder.

The modern book evolved largely because of the development of printing technology and photography. Ideally, a book should be an entity in which format, text, and illustrations—in other words, form and content—are sensitively coordinated to achieve a unified whole. Generally, the graphic designer has little control over the text, and often he or she has no choice in the selection of illustrations. Both may be presented as the "given," around which the designer must create.

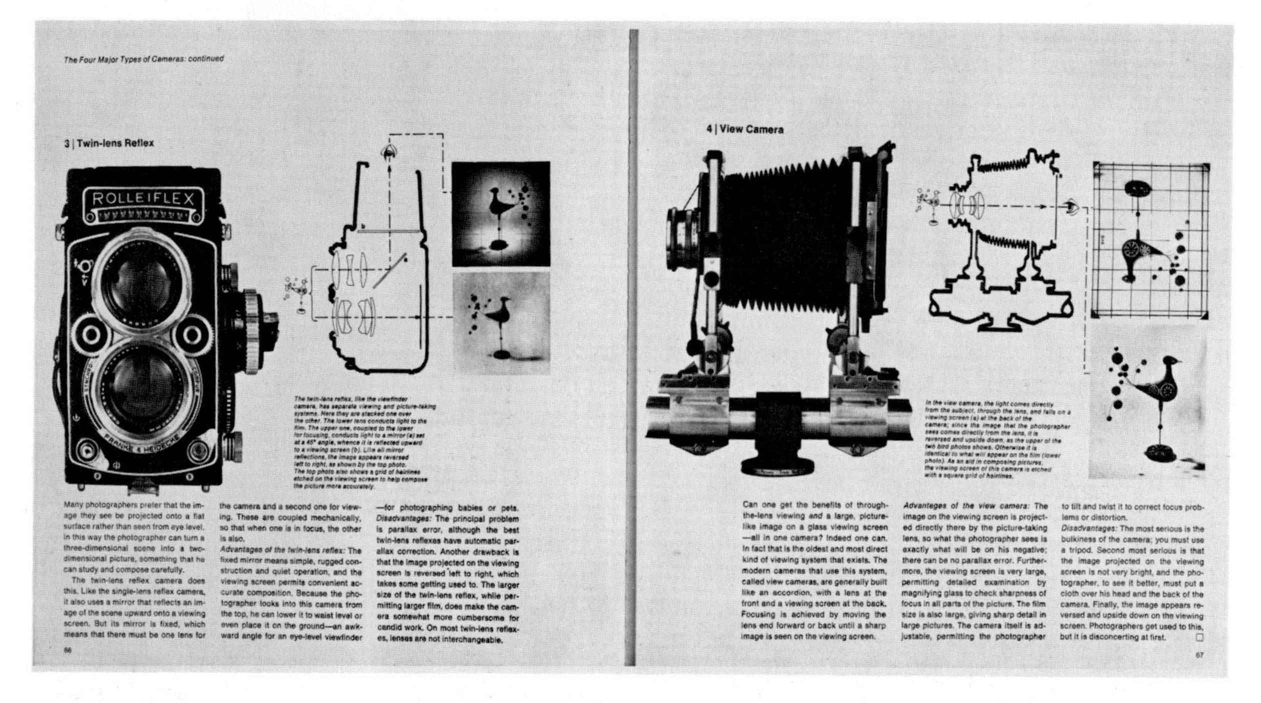

The Four Major Types of Cameras: continued

3 | Twin-lens Reflex

The twin-lens reflex, like the viewfinder camera, has separate viewing and picture-taking systems. Here they are stacked one over the other. The lower lens conducts light to the film. The upper one, coupled to the lower for focusing, conducts light to a mirror (a) set at a 45° angle, whence it is reflected upward to a viewing screen (b). Like all mirror reflections, the image appears reversed left to right, as shown by the top photo. The top photo also shows a grid of hairlines etched on the viewing screen to help compose the picture more accurately.

Many photographers prefer that the image they see be projected onto a flat surface rather than seen from eye level. In this way the photographer can turn a three-dimensional scene into a two-dimensional picture, something that he can study and compose carefully.

The twin-lens reflex camera does this. Like the single-lens reflex camera, it also uses a mirror that reflects an image of the scene upward onto a viewing screen. But its mirror is fixed, which means that there must be one lens for the camera and a second one for viewing. These are coupled mechanically, so that when one is in focus, the other is also.

Advantages of the twin-lens reflex: The fixed mirror means simple, rugged construction and quiet operation, and the viewing screen permits convenient accurate composition. Because the photographer looks into this camera from the top, he can lower it to waist level or even place it on the ground—an awkward angle for an eye-level viewfinder—for photographing babies or pets.

Disadvantages: The principal problem is parallax error, although the best twin-lens reflexes have automatic parallax correction. Another drawback is that the image projected on the viewing screen is reversed left to right, which takes some getting used to. The larger size of the twin-lens reflex, while permitting larger film, does make the camera somewhat more cumbersome for candid work. On most twin-lens reflexes, lenses are not interchangeable.

66

4 | View Camera

In the view camera, the light comes directly from the subject, through the lens, and falls on a viewing screen (a) at the back of the camera; since the image that the photographer sees comes directly from the lens, it is reversed and upside down, as the upper of the two bird photos shows. Otherwise it is identical to what will appear on the film (lower photo). As an aid in composing pictures, the viewing screen of this camera is etched with a square grid of hairlines.

Can one get the benefits of through-the-lens viewing *and* a large, picture-like image on a glass viewing screen—all in one camera? Indeed one can. In fact that is the oldest and most direct kind of viewing system that exists. The modern cameras that use this system, called view cameras, are generally built like an accordion, with a lens at the front and a viewing screen at the back. Focusing is achieved by moving the lens end forward or back until a sharp image is seen on the viewing screen.

Advantages of the view camera: The image on the viewing screen is projected directly there by the picture-taking lens, so what the photographer sees is exactly what will be on his negative; there can be no parallax error. Furthermore, the viewing screen is very large, permitting detailed examination by magnifying glass to check sharpness of focus in all parts of the picture. The film size is also large, giving sharp detail in large pictures. The camera itself is adjustable, permitting the photographer to tilt and twist it to correct focus problems or distortion.

Disadvantages: The most serious is the bulkiness of the camera; you must use a tripod. Second most serious is that the image projected on the viewing screen is not very bright, and the photographer, to see it better, must put a cloth over his head and the back of the camera. Finally, the image appears reversed and upside down on the viewing screen. Photographers get used to this, but it is disconcerting at first. □

67

453. Two-page spread layout from *The Camera,* a volume in the *Time-Life Library of Photography* published by Time-Life Books, © Time Inc. Photographs by Ken Kay and Harold Zipkowitz. This complex spread shows an elegant balance of text, captions, half-tones, and line illustrations.

The task, then, becomes one of interpreting the written material and finding the most effective physical means of presenting the book's contents. To do this, the designer manipulates text design, layout, paper, and cover (Fig. 453).

Text Design

While nearly everyone can see the underlying ideas behind a cover or dust jacket design, the layman often has some difficulty understanding text or internal design of a book. One has a tendency to think that the only concern is to have the words printed clearly. However, text design actually can be quite complicated. The designer must choose a *type face* and its size, a *display type face* for such things as chapter titles and headings, perhaps a decorative numeral or initial letter. The size and shape of the page, the margins all around on each page, and the space between various elements must be determined. If the book has illustrations, either line drawings or halftones, these and their captions must be integrated into the total design. At best, all these elements work together to create a coherent "look."

Type faces have developed considerably since Gutenberg invented movable type in the 15th century, and today the range of possible faces is extraordinary (Fig. 454). Standard book design makes use of only a dozen or so, however, with somewhat more flexibility in the display faces. This text is printed in a type face called "Baskerville," with the chapter titles and principal headings in "Avant Garde."

Type design must be consistent with the overall design of the book and appropriate to its content. Closely related to the choice of a type face is the question of *layout.* Design of the title page is crucial, for it usually provides the reader's first impression of the book itself (Figs. 77, 78, 197). The layout of every page is likewise important. The arrangement of text and illustrations, titles and subtitles, and the spacing of lines within the text all play a part in the book's visual attractiveness. As discussed in Part I of this book, the designer is actually working with shapes, spaces, and proportions to create a unified visual effect.

right: 454. There are thousands of different type faces available today. Illustrated here are (*top to bottom*): Baskerville (a larger size of the type used for this text); Prisma capitals; Swinger Shadow; Andrich Minerva italic; LSC Manhattan; and Helvetica.

below: 455. Cover design by Dennis Cash Stockmann for *Urban Spaces,* published by New York Graphic Society Ltd.

Design
Through
Discovery

Design
Through
Discovery

Cover Design

The first thing one notices about a book is its "package"—the dust jacket or paper cover that encloses the book. The main purpose of exterior design is to attract the attention of the potential buyer and to make the book's contents seem interesting. In the highly competitive field of book merchandising, covers and jackets are planned to be as conspicuous as possible when placed on the crowded shelves and display racks of bookstores.

The cover designer's primary task is to interpret the book's content in an effective manner. There are several possibilities. The designer may choose a literal or symbolic representation of the contents (Fig. 455), an abstract design that alludes to the contents, or a striking combination of type alone, with no imagery. Cover design is vital to a book's success, for if one is never stimulated to pick up the book, one may never discover the treasures it contains.

Children's Books

A special category of books are those designed for children, which usually feature colorful and fanciful illustrations (Fig. 456). The typical book for young children has a limited text and stresses the pictures as much as or more than the words. Since the book will be aimed at novice readers or those who do not read at all, the designer must strive for immediate visual impact to engage the young audience. All design considerations are planned around the illustrations, although, as always, the various elements—type, page size, margins, and so forth—must be joined in a coherent whole.

top: 456. Illustrations by John Lawrence for *Rabbit and Pork,* a children's book about Cockney rhyming slang published by Hamish Hamilton, Ltd. The illustrations were executed as wood engravings.

right: 457. Yasuo Ihara. *Jimi Hendrix.* 1976. Batik on rice paper, 20 x 15″. Courtesy the artist.

After you've razed the turkey...

[illegible]fter you've chomped your way through *any* great holiday [illegible]eal, do you bravely march on to the minces, the [illegible]uddings, the pies, the fruitcake with hard sauce? [illegible]f they're too much, too rich, why do it? Make [illegible]*offee* your dessert. Highly satisfied, you won't [illegible]eave the table feeling glutted and gorged.

The easiest and least painful way to have dessert is to get right on with the coffee and post-dinner drinks. Begin with good café noir, either double strength or espresso. Then give the cup some snap with a jigger or a generous pouring of Cognac, liqueur (anisette, Sambuca, Kahlúa or Tia Maria, Amaretto, crème de cacao) or a shot of dark rum. But if you crave more of a dessert-rich flavor, add a sweetener—white or brown sugar or honey. Or add sweet hot chocolate (made with the cinnamon-rich Mexican kind, below right) to replace half the coffee. For added texture, try bits or gratings of chocolate (even a crumbled Hershey bar). Whipped cream is a natural topping, which you can flavor subtly with almond, vanilla or a few dashes of Galliano. Garnish to suit your fancy—grated nutmeg, cloves, coconut, mint, fruit-rind spirals or peels, crushed hard candies. A cinnamon stick makes a perfect spoon, one to savor long after the dessert coffee has warmed your belly.

To get you started, here are a number of specific formulas, spirited finales for any holiday gathering:

Coffee Amaretto: Combine ½ teaspoon dark brown sugar and a jigger Chocolate Amaretto liqueur. Fill cup ¾ full with hot espresso. Stir and top with whipped cream, shaved [illegible]eet chocolate and a sprinkling of [illegible]ushed toasted almonds.

[illegible]ffee Cointreau: Combine a teaspoon [illegible]ated lemon peel with a teaspoon hon[illegible]. Add hot double-strength coffee to ¾ [illegible]. Add a jigger Cointreau, stir with cin[illegible]mon stick. Top with whipped cream.

[illegible]ffee Golden Top: Combine a jigger an[illegible]tte with a jigger Cognac or brandy. Fill cup [illegible] full with double-strength coffee. Float a tea[illegible]oon honey over the top and add whipped cream [illegible]avored with Galliano. Stir with a licorice stick.

Bajan Snap: Combine a teaspoon dark brown sugar with a jig[illegible] [illegible]. Add hot double-strength coffee to ¾ full. Stir and top with whipped cream. Garnish with grated lime rind.

Coffee Alfredo: Combine a teaspoon sugar, one whole clove, a pinch cinnamon and a jigger each dark rum and Cognac. Fill cup ¾ full with hot espresso. Put a dollop of butter on top and garnish with an orange or lemon spiral.

Photographed by Jerry Friedman/Compiled by Marilyn Kaytor

left: 458. Two-page spread layout from *Esquire.* Photograph by Jerry Friedman.

Magazines and Periodicals

The magazine designer works with the same elements as does the book designer—type, illustrations, shapes and spaces. There are, however, certain differences between the two media. For one thing, the magazine designer usually has much more control over the choice of illustrations and may be able to commission a photographer or illustrator for a particular article (Fig. 457). The visual appearance of the page will therefore be endlessly flexible. Another difference between magazines and books is one of "tone." Magazine design tends to be more casual, more flamboyant, more colorful. The designer can follow styles and fashions closely without fear of obsolescence, because the magazine, unlike the book, will probably be thrown away in a few weeks.

below: 459. Cover from *Holiday* designed by Mark Patterson.

A magazine by its very nature is meant to be read in odd moments and in spurts—in the dentist's office, under the hair dryer, or while dinner cooks. Thus, the layout will be designed in such a way that one's eye is caught and then moved along from place to place (Fig. 458). Except for scholarly magazines and the like, the visual design should be striking enough to exist alone, so that one can scan the illustrations and ignore the text.

The cover of a magazine must be even more attention-getting than that of a book (Fig. 459). As a rule, people decide quickly about which magazine they will buy—while rushing to catch a train or checking out at the supermarket, for example. The vast display of publications vying for attention makes the choice extremely difficult, so the designer must capture attention immediately with a smashing cover.

Magazines rely heavily on illustration as a design element. There is one realm of illustration, however, associated with magazines and newspapers, that exists in a class all by itself. That is the *cartoon*—encompassing the political satire cartoon, the humorous cartoon, and the comic strip. Many different styles of cartoon illustration exist, and there have been changing fashions over the years. Recently, one of the most popular styles has been the simple outline drawing, in which characterizations are created by the most basic means. The classic example of this type is "Peanuts" (Fig. 460).

Record Jackets

The covers for record albums perform much the same task as book covers and dust jackets: they attract the consumer's attention. Buying recorded music is usually a pleasure, and this enjoyment can be heightened by looking through a file of attractive albums. If a person does not have a specific selection or a certain artist in mind, the design of the jacket can influence the purchase. Although photography plays an important part in album design, it is an interpretive photography, and many albums show stunning use of the photographic medium (Fig. 461). Others feature bold and colorful illustration. Often the album cover will be a visual interpretation of the music involved and thus becomes a high form of evocative graphic design (Fig. 462). Like book covers, album jackets have a longer life than the typical "package," so the design prevails as a source of visual pleasure playing its part in the daily life of the consumer.

Advertising

Advertising art has existed since about 3000 B.C., when the Sumerians employed pictures to advertise their wares. The elaborate wrought-iron signs still hanging over shops along many medieval streets in Europe were essentially an advertisement of the goods or services to be found within.

460. "Peanuts" by Charles M. Schulz. © 1968 by United Feature Syndicate.

Advertising is related to production, for only when goods are plentiful is it necessary to seek buyers for them. The advertising industry, then, is a natural outgrowth of the Industrial Revolution with its mass production of all kinds of objects. The earliest known advertising agency opened its doors in England in 1812, and within a mere century and a half the advertising industry has grown into a giant multimillion-dollar business.

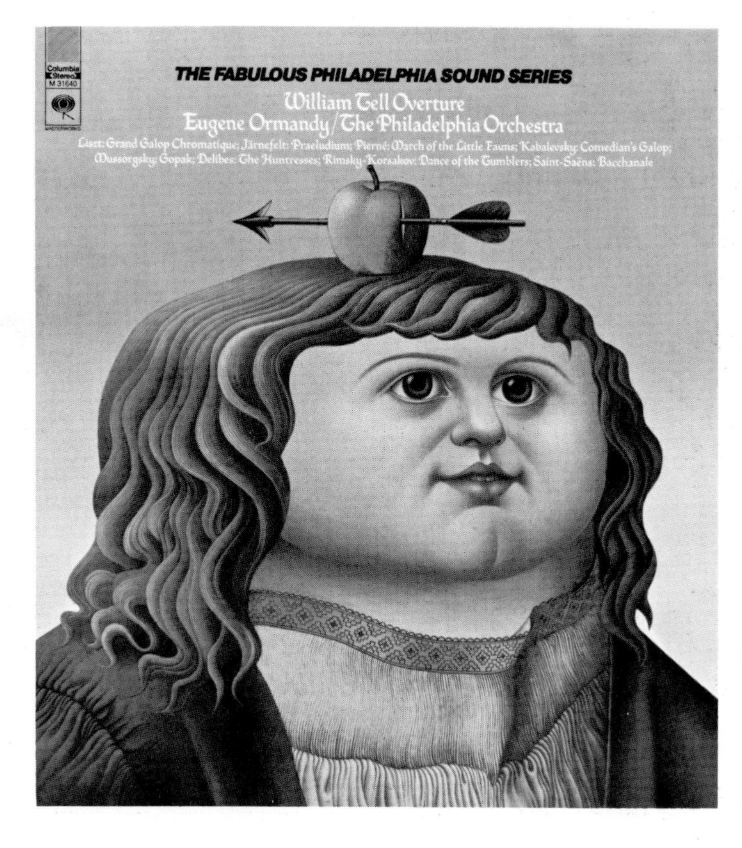

top: 461. Front and back jacket for the record album *Chicago,* designed by John Berg for Columbia Records, division of CBS Inc.

right: 462. Jacket for the Philadelphia Orchestra's recording of the William Tell Overture, designed by Teresa Alfieri for Columbia Records, division of CBS Inc.

above: 463. Advertisement for Clinique skin care products. Photograph by Irving Penn for Clinique.

below: 464. Advertisement for Blackglama furs. Courtesy Blackglama, and Peter Rogers Associates, Inc., New York.

Until well into the 20th century, foodstuffs and other goods were marketed in barrels, tubs, or sacks with no indication of the source of supply as far as the consumer was concerned. The trademark (Figs. 233–236) was developed as a kind of reward for products of excellent quality and a means by which the buyer could be assured of purchasing goods of similar quality in the future. Actually, the trademark became a stepping stone for manufacturers developing their own businesses, for it quickly established their identities and provided them with an opportunity to extend their reputations.

Most advertisements consist of two elements—the words or *copy* and the illustration. The role of the graphic designer is to arouse curiosity or interest to the point that a reader will stop to examine the copy (Fig. 463). It is vital that the ad be addressed to specific people, to fill specific needs or interests, or to help achieve specific goals. The most compelling reason for spending money is the conviction that the object or service to be purchased is more necessary than the money itself. Amounts of money spent for the necessities of everyday living are usually fairly fixed, yet the actual selection of varieties and brands provides wide scope for advertising.

Consumers engage in two kinds of spending: spending for *basic* necessities and *discretionary* spending, which means the purchase of items that make life more comfortable, satisfying, or attractive. An effective ad has little trouble in convincing the average person that many items in this category are actually needed in order to live as one wishes or deserves. To design an ad that will touch the vulnerable spot closest to the consumer's dreams requires an exploration of the motives to which those dreams are geared. There are many kinds of motives: the desire to create or build, to protect or conserve, to acquire property, to achieve power, to move up the social scale (Fig. 464).

Kinds of Advertising

The public is exposed daily to at least two specific kinds of advertising: direct and indirect. *Direct* advertising is used when the seller expects immediate returns. Department stores, supermarkets, and other retail outlets take this approach, especially when they have special sales. *Indirect* advertising, on the other hand, is effective for building a reputation and establishing the desirability of a product or service, with an emphasis on future as well as immediate results. A subcategory of indirect advertising is the *institutional ad,* which has as its aim the creation of goodwill for a particular firm or organization. This approach may take the form of a short documentary showing company operations and products or a series of television commercials that demonstrate the company's efforts at improving the environment. A subtle form of institutional advertising is the sponsorship of some artistic endeavor—drama, art, or music, for example—along with advertisements that quietly mention the company's participation (Fig. 465).

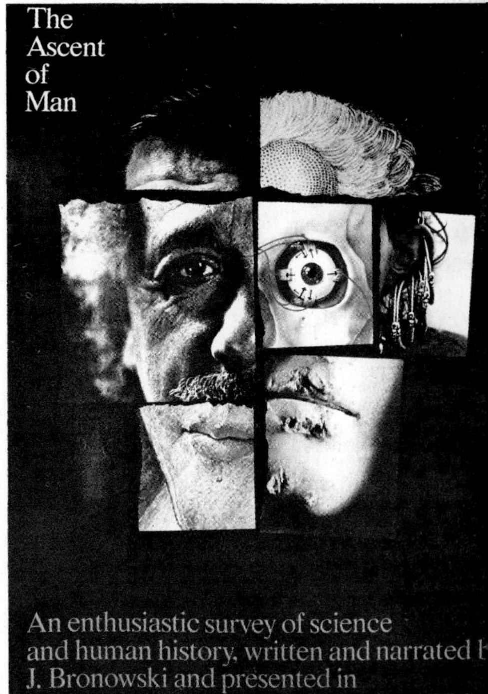

465. Institutional advertisement for the Mobil Oil Corporation, designed by Ivan Chermayeff of Chermayeff & Geismar Associates.

Designing the Advertisement

When the designer is presented with a product or service to be advertised, the process of decision-making begins. With the type of consumer in mind, one must first of all determine the kind of approach most likely to be effective. In general, there are two broad categories of approach: factual and imaginative.

The *factual* approach usually proves best in reaching the no-nonsense individual or in promoting a product with a serious mission. Visual design usually focuses on a realistic representation of the product, but this can be done in many ways. For example, a product can be depicted alone, in a decorative setting, in actual use, or in combination with the results it is supposed to yield.

The *imaginative* approach may feature something totally unrelated to the product, with the ad serving mainly as an attention-getting

left: 466. Poster for New York's Metropolitan Transportation Authority, designed by Howard York of Howard York & Associates, under the direction of Michael Bosniak of MTA.

right: 467. Packaging for L'eggs pantyhose, by Dancer Fitzgerald Sample, Inc.

device to introduce the product's name. It can also rely on imagination to convey that purchase of a product will bring rich rewards in social satisfaction and prestige.

In either instance, the advertisement begins with a layout, which means the total design of the ad—illustrations, blocks of type, display type, white areas, the entire composition. Many ads depend on a provocative headline in large, bold type to capture attention (Figs. 463, 464). Others strive for a point of identification, something that will trigger an association in the viewer's mind (Pl. 2, p. 53). Color may be very important to the success of an ad, although its use is not always possible because of the limitations of advertising budgets. The ad shown in Plate 2 is meant to be reproduced in either black and white or color, depending upon the periodical in which it is inserted.

The principles of design apply to every aspect of design graphics. Type and illustrations must be in proportion to one another, and colors and shapes should be arranged for a sense of total balance. Variety in type size and style as well as in visual textures adds to the overall effect. Unity is, of course, of the utmost importance in focusing the viewer's attention on the primary object—the product advertised.

Advertising Media

Newspapers and magazines, along with television, carry the greatest burden in presenting advertised products to the consumer, but sometimes other outlets may be more suitable for a particular situation. Outdoor advertising—including billboards, spectacular lighting displays, and wall signs—are a challenge to the designer. The viewer is on the move, frequently in a hurry, and the idea must be concise and presented clearly to achieve an impact.

Buses, trains, and terminals sell advertising space for the placement of posters. The poster requires a design that will attract immediate attention, with clear lettering and usually with bright colors or some appealing image (Fig. 466). Unlike most other types of advertisements, posters may be collected by individuals to decorate their homes. The graphic design therefore exists on two levels: it sells the product and then becomes a "work of art."

The television commercial has the potential of reaching 11 million homes in the United States during the average minute of evening programming. The designer, thus, can bring a personality into the family living room with as much persuasion as a salesman who may come to the door—but with the added enticements of attractive settings and often color. Since television is most effective in *showing* what is to be sold, the designer bears most responsibility for the advertising. All the advantages of association and symbolism used in magazine advertising adapt even more readily to television, with the bonuses of dramatization, action, music, and characterization. Besides the usual principles of graphic design, the designer must have some knowledge of film techniques in order to create effectively. A new dimension has been added to commercial advertising now that color television is so common, and a well-conceived commercial may be more entertaining than the programs it supports (Pl. 44, p. 321).

Packaging

The widespread practice of self-service shopping makes package design as important as advertising. A customer faced with a shelf of similar products tends, in spite of advertising, to select the one whose package seems most attractive. The design of a package performs several functions. First, it helps to sell the merchandise by identifying it and distinguishing it from competing articles. It also facilitates a better display, making it easier for the merchant to put the article before the public. Occasionally, an innovative packaging design will be integrated with special display racks, which serve the dual purpose of setting off the merchandise from its competitors and making stock maintenance easy for the shopkeeper (Fig. 467). Packaging may also improve the appearance of the merchandise and help to keep it clean.

The packaging designer must keep several factors in mind in creating a new design. A successful package must above all serve the needs of the product, protecting the contents while at the same time being easy to handle. A group of packages should stack easily with no loss of space, so that a merchant will be predisposed to giving them a visible display.

From an advertising point of view, the package must immediately attract the customer's attention. The best way to start a new design is to gather together all the competing products and analyze their packaging. This will make clear the similarities, the weaknesses, and the good qualities to be surpassed. A color not previously used may attract attention; a totally new concept can make a product stand out.

Layout is vital to package design. The name of the product must be clear, preferably in print that contrasts with its background. Shapes and illustrations on the package should relate to the contents in some way. For example, in the packaging of household products, the stress is usually on health and cleanliness, whereas containers for foodstuffs may emphasize the "natural" origins of the food (Fig. 468).

468. Packaging for Erewhon rice, designed by Rod Williams, Fred Ribeck, and John Evans of A. R. Williams & Associates, South Lynnfield, Mass.

A practical consideration in package design is ease of opening. Too many designers invent fancy openings that turn out to be more trouble than the conventional ones.

Total Design

One of the most fascinating and challenging assignments for the graphic designer is the task of designing a "corporate image" (Fig. 469). This involves creating a visual impression that carries through every aspect of a company's business, with integrated designs for packaging, shipping materials, advertising, labels, stationery, brochures, warranties—even to the decor of the corporate headquarters. The designer who takes such an assignment knows that the entire consumer market—perhaps millions of people—will learn to associate the company with that particular design. Such a responsibility can be a designer's dream come true, for in a single design lies total control of the visual aspects of a company's operation.

469. Corporate identity and packaging program designed for Tom's Natural Soap by A. R. Williams & Associates, South Lynnfield, Mass. The total design concept includes letterhead and shipping cartons (Rod Williams, designer); a poster (Rod Williams, Frederick Pickel, and John Evans, designers); and packaging (Rod Williams, Fred Ribeck, Fred Pickel, and John Evans, designers).

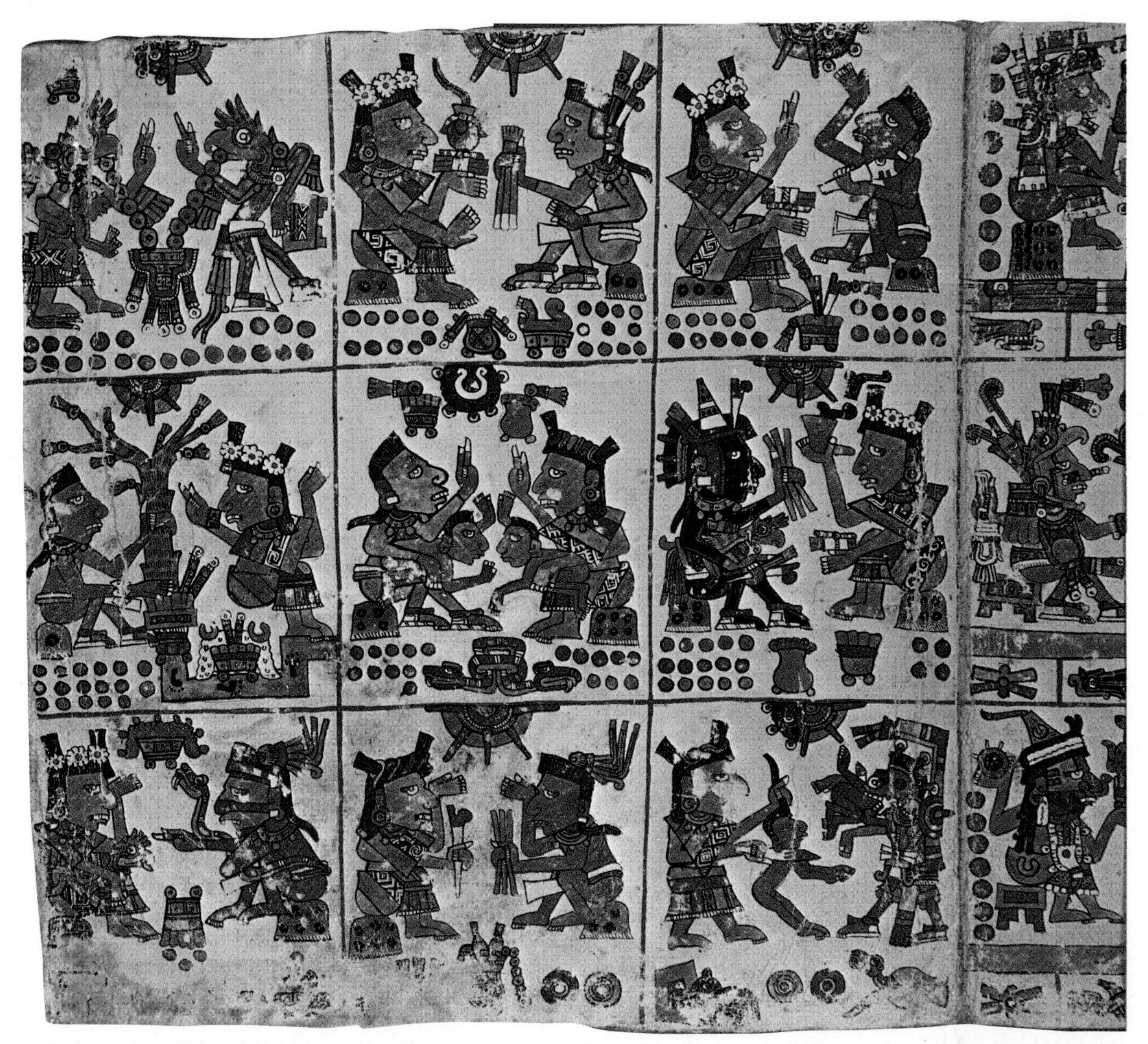

Plate 43. *Nine Pairs of Divinities,* codex from the Mixtec culture, Mexico. 14th–16th century. Vatican Library, Rome.

Plate 44. Segment of the television commercial "Bubbles," for 7UP, the "Uncola," designed by Robert Ebel and Robert Taylor for J. Walter Thompson Company, Chicago.

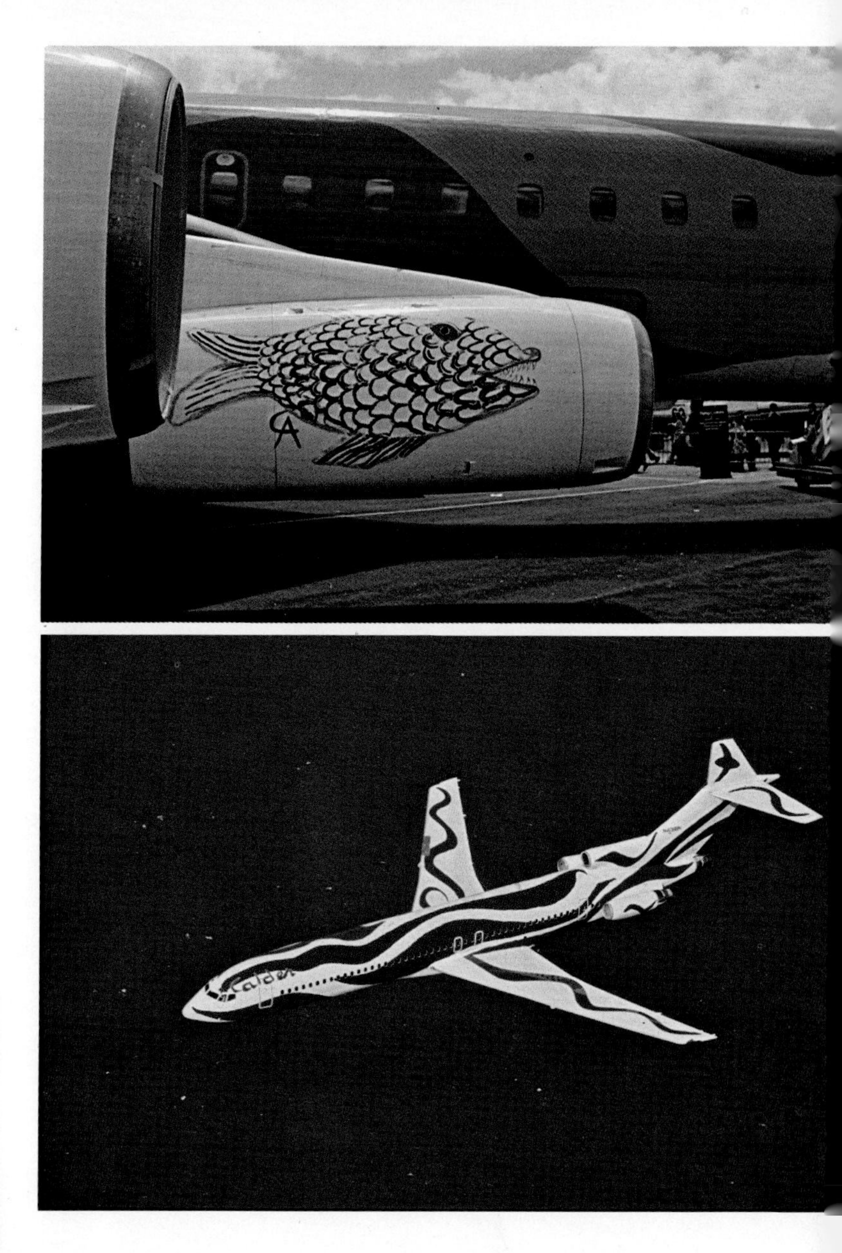

right: Plate 45. Alexander Calder. *Flying Colors.* (*above right*) Braniff International's South American jet, 1972; (*right*) Braniff International's Bicentennial Flagship, the 727-200 jet, 1975.

below: Plate 46. Janet Lipkin. *Bird Coat.* 1972. Crocheted. Courtesy Julie: Artisan's Gallery, Inc.

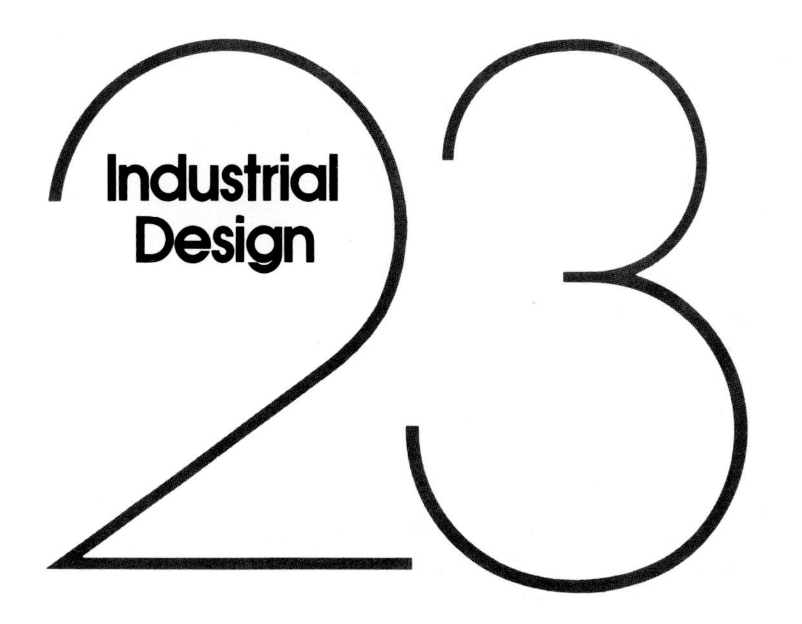

Industrial design is that field which creates products for mass manufacture. With a discussion of its characteristics, we move back into the realm of *functional design* mentioned in Chapter 1. The objects for which an industrial designer is responsible must do more than be visually attractive. They must also *work,* or in other words perform some particular task. Whether that task is to mix a cake, to move people from place to place, to plow a field, or to drill a tooth, the product's user will expect it to operate efficiently. If the product also has a pleasing appearance, then the two criteria of successful industrial design have been satisfied.

The origins of industrial design are traditionally dated to the late 19th century, with the philosophy of William Morris and the Arts and Crafts Movement. But, of course, production design reaches back to the beginnings of the industrial revolution and beyond, with roots in the medieval European craft guilds. Even before the coming of the machine, goods were manufactured in more or less standardized forms. The craftsman who made a pot or a silver pitcher or a wooden object would not immediately scrap the design but would make many different versions of the same form. Each would show slight irregularities of hand construction, but the essential design remained the same. The craft guilds that flourished in Europe from about the 12th century set rigidly high standards for the goods produced under their auspices.

The Industrial Revolution of the late 18th century had drastic implications for design. Perhaps the most negative result of machine production was the extraordinary increase in ornamentation on all consumer goods. The machines could stamp out in moments elaborate effects that would have taken a handcraftsman days or weeks to create. In furnishings, household objects, and artifacts, the manufacturers strove constantly to outdo one another in lavish decoration.

Another problem in the early phases of mass production was that design tended to be in the hands of the manufacturers. The people responsible for the machines decided what they would make, with the result that individuals having no experience in design became the arbiters of taste. Meanwhile, the craftsmen who had devoted their lives to making beautiful objects were suddenly reduced to pulling levers or tying threads in the factories. Standards in both visual and functional design declined rapidly.

The first voice to speak out seriously against this situation was that of the Englishman William Morris. Morris was associated with the Arts and Crafts Movement active in both the United States and England during the late 19th century. He wrote and lectured widely on the need for honesty and sound functionalism in design. Through his firm, Morris & Co., he produced textiles, wallpaper, and household furnishings that embodied his high standards for design.

Morris no doubt would have preferred to wipe out all the machines entirely. It was not until the Bauhaus, established in 1919, that a deliberate attempt was made to work *with* the new technological systems (Fig. 470). The Bauhaus program established the principle of trained designers working alongside skilled engineers, so that each could make a contribution. With that modest beginning, the profession of industrial designer gradually took root. Today it is the rule rather than the exception for large manufacturers to either have professional designers on staff or to call in outside consultants. Two conditions fostered this change: a general disgust with shoddy mer-

left: 470. Ludwig Miës van der Rohe. "Barcelona" chair. 1929. Steel and leather.

above: 471. Citizens' Band radio, by Publicom I. 1976. Courtesy Lafayette Radio Electronics, New York.

chandise and the increasing competition among producers. In order to capture the attention of the mass consumer, a manufacturer must maintain high standards in performance and visual appeal. The industrial designer helps to make this possible.

Characteristics of Industrial Design

Industrial design differs from other design fields discussed in this book in several important ways. For one thing, the industrial designer rarely works as an individual. Usually, a whole production team handles the various aspects of a planned design, from consumer research to the final merchandising. Only occasionally does a specific designer receive credit for a work. Moreover, a chain of decisions may be involved before the problem ever reaches the designer. Most designers—the craftsman, the painter, the printmaker, the sculptor—work from the end to the means. They decide what they want to make and then figure out how to make it. Industrial designers, on the other hand, often have the means severely restricted by available machinery. They must devise ways to make a product within that context.

Another important difference between industrial design and other areas is the gap between the producer and the consumer. In the craft communities, the artist knew exactly what the buying public wanted and furthermore knew immediately whether a particular object had satisfied the need. However, with huge concentrations of manufacturers serving many types of people all over the world, it can be extremely difficult to establish communication.

In their way consumers are as close to a product as the designer is; the general public feels entirely competent to criticize industrial design. A person who might stand indecisively before a painting or a sculpture, apologizing for a lack of background to appreciate it, speaks out emphatically about the power saw or the refrigerator.

Price may be a more compelling factor in industrial design than in any other field. Whereas a weaver or a potter will produce a work and then put an appropriate price on it, the industrial designer must know from the beginning what kind of price each product should bring and design it accordingly, taking into consideration the material, the processes, the tools, or the expense of retooling.

With increasing competition among manufacturers and a relatively high standard of living, a new aspect has entered the realm of industrial design: the generation of need. Before industrialization, the consumer knew basically what his or her needs were: furnishings, eating utensils, clothing, and so forth. Today's industrial designer, however, has gone far beyond this, inventing new products that have never before existed. When this happens, industry must first create a *desire* on the part of the consumer for that product, and then translate desire into *need.* For example, until a short time ago the general public had never heard of the Citizens' Band radio (Fig. 471). When manufacturers developed the radio to the point where it could be produced for a reasonable price, they set out to instill a desire for it in the public. Newspaper and magazine attention gradually increased interest, but the highly visible nature of the product helped as well. The automobile driver, seeing more and more antennas sprouting on passing cars, gradually became convinced of the radio's practicality. Thus, a product that was unknown a few years ago becomes a luxury and then a "necessity."

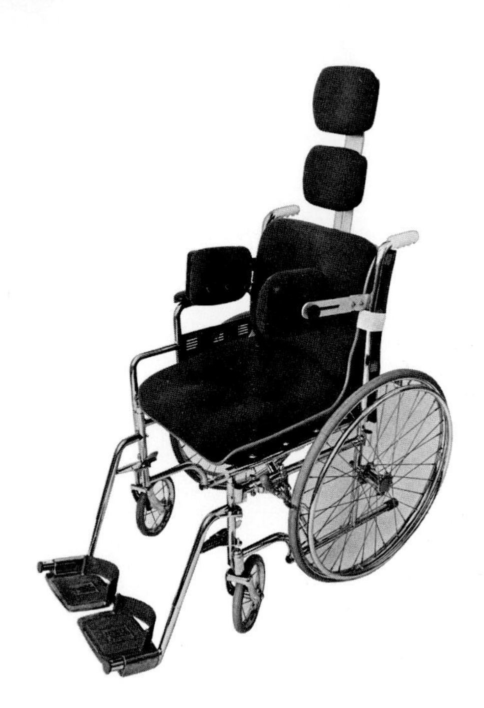

At its best industrial design can answer genuine needs. Some of the most effective designs result from someone's having thought, "Why can't they make a . . ." This was the incentive behind the creation of the wheelchair shown in Figure 472. In the United States alone, hundreds of thousands of people are chronically confined to wheelchairs. Until now, the two major problems have been balance (especially when the lower anatomy is paralyzed) and pressures that result from staying in the same position. Painful skin ulcers were the least of the difficulties that might arise with improperly fitted equipment. At worst, the pressures could result in amputations or even death. A team of designers researched the problem and came up with the chair shown, which provides for custom-adapting the contours to each patient. Although function is the primary concern, the wheelchair is also more attractive than previous models.

Categories of Industrial Design

The world of industrial design becomes increasingly diverse. Individual products designed for mass production could easily number in the millions. All, however, fall into one of four broad categories.

Consumer products are the objects that people use in their homes and their recreational activities. They include electrical and other appliances, plumbing fixtures, lighting equipment, garden implements, radios and television sets, stereo components (Fig. 473), luggage, furniture, sports gear (Fig. 474), toys, and children's vehicles.

Commercial and service equipment encompasses the fixtures for stores and offices, gas stations, shops, restaurants, soda fountains, barber and beauty shops, and similar enterprises. The items range from desks to scales and cash registers, data processing equipment, and typewriters (Fig. 475). Quite remarkable design changes have been made in some of these products since their introduction (Fig. 476).

Durable goods are such things as heavy equipment and machine tools, agricultural machinery and equipment, industrial furnaces, and power generators.

Transportation design embraces all the aspects of travel from airliners to sailboats and yachts. Included here is automotive design from the practical family car to the racing machine (Fig. 477).

top: 472. Frank Low and Robert Burridge, for Contourpedic. Custom wheelchair. 1975. Chair was designed with plastic bags filled with foam beads to conform to the contours of the body. Courtesy Contourpedic Corporation.

right: 473. David Gammon. Turntable. 1964. Aluminum and acrylic, height $6\frac{3}{4}''$. Museum of Modern Art, New York (gift of Transcriptors).

left: 474. Super Swallowtail (SST), designed by Chris Price, Chris Wills, and Bob Wills for Wills Wing, Inc.; manufactured by Sport Kites.

below left: 475. Olivetti Lexikon 82 typewriter. Courtesy Olivetti Corporation of America.

below: 476. Blickensderfer electric typewriter. 1902. Courtesy British Typewriter Museum, Bournemouth, England.

bottom: 477. Mercedes 300 SL, Gullwing. 1954. Courtesy Mercedes-Benz of North America, Inc.

The Industrial Designer

Industrial designers have a certain advantage over designers in other fields: the broad exposure of their work. While painters, sculptors, potters, and weavers might hope that a few hundred people will be touched by their creations, the industrial designer always faces the dizzying prospect that *millions* may use and enjoy a particular design. For example, the designer of a telephone could within reason expect that virtually every person in the United States will at some point pick up that telephone and talk into it—perhaps several times a day. Our very concept of what a telephone is could be shaped by the output of one person's creativeness. The person who designs a soft-drink bottle, a bicycle, or a toothbrush might see that design exported around the world to serve literally billions of people.

The industrial designer must be, first, a balanced combination of the creative and the practical. To original ideas must be joined the technological knowledge to facilitate putting those ideas into large-scale production. A designer should be familiar with all the standard processes of manufacture and be able to see ways of improving a product within the framework of the present machinery and practices of the manufacturer.

Sometimes the designer will be a member of the manufacturer's staff, but there are also many independent designers who take commissions from firms needing their services. An independent designer can build up a reputation for a certain type of product through past successes, but many people have established reputations for widely varied design or for total design concepts. Occasionally, a commercial firm will seek to present to the public a truly unique image. Braniff Airlines showed remarkable corporate daring in commissioning the artist Alexander Calder to custom design patterns and images for the exteriors of two of their jetcraft (Pl. 45, p. 322). Intrigued with the idea, Calder did much of the actual painting himself.

The Design Process

Industrial design follows a logical process much like that described in Chapter 2, except that there are many more considerations involved. Usually the first step will be an extensive research program to determine whether a given product would be successful. Mass production requires such an enormous outlay in tools, machinery, labor, materials, and marketing, that the manufacturer can afford few mistakes. An independent craftsman who has a design failure can simply discard the product and start again. The mass producer who markets a product people will not buy may be facing bankruptcy. For this reason, extensive research will attempt to answer many questions before any other money is committed to design: Who would buy the product? Why do they want it? What features would be most popular? How much will the consumer pay? Can the product be made commercially successful at that cost? What features does the competitor's product have, and can one improve upon them?

Even the best research will not be infallible, for consumers are notoriously unpredictable as a group. In 1958 the Ford Motor Company unveiled the culmination of a gigantic research effort that had sought to discover precisely what the American driver wanted in an automobile—the best engineering features, the most comfortable

478. Ford Edsel, 1958. Courtesy Ford Motor Company.

interior, the most attractive exterior design. The result was a classic failure of industrial design: the Edsel (Fig. 478).

After research, the next step is analysis of the problem. This phase will consider all aspects of materials, color, structure, production, cost, and marketing. The merchandising requirements of a particular product often have a significant effect on its design. Perhaps it will be decided that a certain product will appeal only to affluent people and should therefore be advertised in expensive magazines. This may expand the possibilities for pricing and thus for materials and design.

Once the general characteristics of a product have been established, the more concrete design process can begin. The designer will usually start with sketches, proceed through several stages of models in clay or some working material, and finally develop a *prototype* of the finished product. The prototype is a trial run for both the product and the process of manufacture. It could be made in cheaper materials than the final piece, but it will be exactly the same in all other details. Flaws of shape, structure, engineering, and manufacturing can be eliminated at this stage.

Materials and Techniques

All the materials discussed in Part II of this book appear in some phase of industrial design. In this century, however, metal and plastics have assumed a dominant role in all types of mass-produced products, because they lend themselves so easily to machine shaping.

The techniques used in industrial production are so sophisticated and so varied that it is almost impossible to generalize about them. They do, however, fall into several broad categories. *Casting* in molds is among the most common. *Extrusion* calls for a molten material to be forced through shaped openings, after which it hardens upon cooling. *Stamping* is a fully automatic process in which material, usually metal, is cut, shaped, and combined into the desired form. *Lamination* and *fabrication* in industrial terms resemble the processes as they apply to plastics (see Chap. 17). The industrial designer cannot hope to make intelligent decisions without becoming totally familiar with the range of manufacturing processes possible for the object to be designed.

Current Trends in Industrial Design

The myriad products available today are so diverse in appearance and function that we cannot isolate a particular "style." But there are certain trends visible in many areas of industrial design. A general

above 479. Telephone design from 1876 to 1976: Liquid Telephone, 1876; The Butterstamp, 1877; The Blake Transmitter, 1880; Common Battery, 1900; Desk Set, 1910; Desk Set, 1928; "500" Type Desk Set, 1949; Trimline, 1976. Courtesy American Telephone and Telegraph Company.

below: 480. Torre kitchen unit, designed by Piero Batini for Eda Urbani, Italy, incorporates sink, electric stove, dishwasher, and rubbish disposal unit.

bottom: 481. Nick Roericht. Stacking Tableware. 1963. Porcelain. Manufactured by Rosenthal China Corporation, Thomas Division, Germany. Museum of Modern Art, New York (gift of the manufacturer).

tendency toward streamlining and *simplification* can be seen if we trace a given product over the last century (Fig. 479). Forms are smoother, more compact, more geometric. *Compactness,* in particular, has become important as our world becomes increasingly crowded. Tools and appliances that perform several different functions on the same motor save both space and money. A kitchen unit that combines all the standard fixtures in a single compact design could solve many problems for the small apartment or vacation house (Fig. 480).

Another trend is toward *modular* design, composed of repetitive units that fit together or can be interchanged. Cups and dishes that stack neatly not only save space but also lessen the possibility of breakage (Fig. 481). A design that has many interlocking parts can be used in many ways, for flexibility as needs change (Fig. 482).

Until recently it was considered desirable for all working parts in machinery or appliances to be concealed behind a façade that might have nothing to do with function. An example of this would be the television set within a "French Provincial" cabinet. Today, however, the tendency is toward greater *visibility* of mechanisms. The ability to watch things work adds an extra dimension to industrial design. The coffee grinder shown in Figure 483 has transparent compartments so that the owner can see the ground particles coming out. An ultimate extension of this effect is a transparent television set (Fig. 484).

Industrial Design and the Environment

The designer who creates something beautiful may find it difficult to contemplate that object's destruction, but most things outlive their usefulness sooner or latter. At a time when we are much concerned about assaults on the environment, it becomes necessary to plan ahead for the disposal of products even while they are being designed. For craftsmen who work in one-of-a-kind objects, the problem is not so acute, but it assumes tremendous proportions when multiplied by the thousands or millions of units that may result from industrial design. Each year the United States manufactures 60 tons of products that

have no recycle value. Such colossal output results in 3.5 billion tons of waste annually that must somehow be absorbed into the landscape. The first disposable drinking cup was marketed in 1910, but it was only in the 1950s that the term "disposable" came into general use. Now, a mere quarter of a century later, we realize that the word is inaccurate. "Disposable" objects rarely disappear; they simply convert into clutter. One of the most disturbing problems of the American landscape is the piles of junk cars that stretch across the countryside. It has even been suggested that later civilizations will identify

below: 482. Fabio Lenci, for Bernini. Table and chair set. 1970 Polyurethane and metal, diameter of table 59".

right: 483. Coffee grinder, designed by Braun A.G., Germany. 1965. Plastic and metal housing, height 7½″. Museum of Modern Art, New York (gift of the manufacturer).

below right: 484. Marco Zanuso and Richard Sapper, for Brionvega. Television set with transparent casing.

as the one characteristic artifact of our culture the metal pull top from a soft drink can. Thus to our standards of function and attractiveness in industrial design we should add one other criterion of success: the ability of an object to go away quietly when its time has passed. While this quality could be considered desirable in any material object, the overwhelming presence of mass-produced items in contemporary culture makes it an imperative consideration in industrial design.

24 Apparel

There are some areas in which every individual, of necessity, becomes a designer. One is in the home, or the portion of a home one occupies. Another may be in one's office or part of a working space. A third, inevitable, design realm is apparel. Every person, in dressing to meet the world, creates a façade that speaks of his or her personality. Even if an individual dresses always in blue jeans and tee shirts, this represents a decision about one's walking "shell." By the design of one's apparel, one can set out to be obvious or inconspicuous, conventional or eccentric, even attractive or ugly. The choice of particular apparel means a choice, conscious or unconscious, of presenting a certain appearance to the world.

On another level, a multimillion-dollar industry has grown up around people whose profession is the design of clothing for others. Their goal is either to anticipate or to influence the type of garments large numbers of people will select to wear. Most apparel designers are motivated by a genuine love of the human body as a medium, are fascinated by the interaction between cloth and flesh, line and line. The clothing designer uses the body as a painter uses a canvas, arranging lines, shapes, spaces, colors, textures, and patterns to achieve the most satisfying result.

It seems fairly sure that human beings have worn clothing, in some form, for at least seven thousand years, and probably much longer. Incredible as it may be, it is really only in the last two centuries, out of seventy or more, that people have been able to buy readymade clothing. Before that time, with some exceptions, clothing had to be either made in the home or ordered specially from a dressmaker or tailor. The luxury of being able to walk into a store, buy a garment, and wear it immediately did not exist.

In order to analyze the design considerations that apply to apparel, we should first consider the various purposes that clothing serves—power, status, warmth, protection, modesty, sexual attraction, and simple adornment. Next we will examine the ways in which clothing design reflects the elements and principles of design enumerated in Part I of this text.

Purposes of Clothing

Power

The book of Genesis teaches that clothing was invented when Adam and Eve, having eaten of the Tree of Knowledge, saw that they were naked and felt shame. Most archaeologists, on the other hand, believe that the first stimulus for wearing clothing was the desire for power—against one's enemies or one's prey. Perhaps the earliest manifestation of this came in body painting and tattooing (Fig. 485). Colors and designs either applied to or injected under the skin might have any one of several purposes: to frighten the enemy, to protect the warrior in battle, to indicate rank in the community, to identify with a particular god, to gain ascendancy over an animal one hoped to kill. All these are indicators of power in some form.

Today we might find equivalents of clothing that celebrates power in the uniforms of the police or military personnel. Also, such accessories as boots, leather jackets, helmets, chains, and the like all stand as symbolic attributes of physical power (Fig. 486). This power may be real or imagined, but the apparel nevertheless creates a certain effect.

left: 485. Karaja Indian of the Amazon River area, Brazil, with tattooed face and body painting.

right: 486. Articles of clothing associated with the motorcycle culture may convey an image of physical power.

Status

Status may imply power, in the sense that a tribal chieftain, a reigning monarch, or a President of the United States has both. But in many cases status means rank alone, without any physical or political power being attached. A religious habit, for instance, marks the wearer as having a certain status, as do a judge's robes or academic attire.

Status clothing can operate on several different levels, depending upon one's location and social group. In Western countries, and among others who have adopted Western styles, the "rules" often change from month to month or from week to week. In one group status may depend upon wearing jeans or boots from a particular manufacturer. More durable, reliable status symbols have been, for men, the Brooks Brothers suit or custom-tailored English tweeds; for women, the Chanel suit or, more recently, the Halston dress (Fig. 487). The fact that such clothing acts as a status indicator depends upon two implied statements of the wearer: First, "I have enough money to buy this clothing." Second, "I am well-enough informed to know that this clothing is correct." Since material wealth and knowledge are among the major indicators of status in our culture, clothing has the ability to convey these things even before the wearer says or does anything.

Warmth and Protection

Nearly all members of the animal kingdom are admirably equipped by nature for protection from the elements. Dogs, cats, bears, raccoons, and hundreds of other animals have heavy fur coats that protect equally well against winter snows and summer sun. Fish have an outer coating ideally suited to swimming and to their watery habitat. Some

above left: 487. For many people, the Halston-designed garment acts as a status symbol.

below: 488. John James Audubon. *Rock Ptarmigan,* from *The Birds of America.* 1836–37. Watercolor and oil on paper, $13\frac{7}{8} \times 21\frac{1}{4}''$. New York Historical Society, New York.

species even change the character of their body covering according to the seasons. The bird shown in Figure 488, a rock ptarmigan, assumes white plumage in winter, varicolored in summer, so that it blends with the coloring in the landscape, thus acquiring excellent camouflage from predators.

Human beings, having lost their protective covering of body hair millenia ago, must adapt their *clothing* to the changing needs of climate. A dog goes out nonchalantly in all kinds of weather, dressed in the same attire, but to walk the dog in winter its owner may don as many as twelve separate articles of clothing. In cooler regions, a warm coat is essential in winter, and oftentimes its design will mimic the coat of furred animals (Fig. 489). Extreme atmospheric conditions may demand even more protection for the body. An entirely new field of apparel design opened up with the era of space exploration (Fig. 490). Here designers had to take into consideration protection against very severe heat, cold, and pressure; to provide for self-contained breathing, communications, and eliminatory apparatus; and still allow for light weight and maneuverability. The designer of clothing for space travel or other specialized purposes must put function above all, with little or no consideration for style, fashion, and visual appeal.

Modesty

Standards of modesty have varied from time to time and from place to place ever since Adam and Eve, according to tradition, donned the first apparel of fig leaves. In many tropical cultures clothing has been deemed adequate if it covers the genitals, and no thought is given to concealing a woman's breasts. The early missionaries in Hawaii and the South Sea Islands caused a major upheaval among the native people in urging the women to wear "muu-muus," in place of the standard half-sarong.

Possibly the most rigid standards of modesty ever known prevailed in England and the United States during the middle and late 19th century—the Victorian era. For a period of several decades it was unthinkable for a woman to show an ankle, much less a leg—or even to mention the words in public. Gowns were designed on a hoop or bustle superstructure that completely denied the form underneath, so that a woman's torso appeared to be floating along on a wheeled cart.

Much has changed in less than a hundred years. Today our standards of decency are a great deal more relaxed. If the watchword is not yet "anything goes," it may be "anything can be tried." To be sure, in some Moslem countries the women still wear veils covering their bodies and faces, but this is changing rapidly.

The criteria for modesty can vary even in the same place at the same time. A woman in a bikini or a man who is shirtless would seem out of place and "immodest" on a city street, whereas they would pass unnoticed on the beach. Beachwear, in fact, has all but abolished the role of clothing for modesty. The introduction of Rudi Gernreich's notorious "topless" swimsuit in 1964 launched an era of increasing

above right: 489. Fake fur of modacrylic fiber, by Collins & Aikman.

right: 490. Astronaut Walter Cunningham, wearing a space pressure suit, 1964. Courtesy NASA.

nudity in bathing apparel (Fig. 491). The nonfunctional strap on the Gernreich suit actually emphasizes the wearer's exposed bosom, thus creating a greater impression of nudity than would the wearing of only a bikini bottom. Of course, in most situations, people usually prefer to be reasonably covered. This illustration shows, however, that while clothing has much to do with modesty, its influence may be either negative or positive.

Sexual Attraction and Adornment

For the last 150 years or so, the fashion industry has catered primarily to women, but in the full context of history the emphasis on female dress can be seen as a relatively recent development. Nature has always been more lavish in her adornment of the male; traditionally, it has been the male who sought by his appearance and behavior to attract the attention of the opposite sex. This is apparent in the plumage of birds. The gay feathers of the male are fundamental to the ritual of mating, while the female's neutral coloration aids in the protective function she performs for her brood. Until the 19th century the human male took his cue from nature. The Georgian man spent at least five times more on clothing than his wife did. Fine laces, furs, brocades, satins, velvets, and ribbons were all part of masculine embellishment from the time of the 16th century. This elaborate style reached the pinnacle of elegance during the reign of Louis XIV in France (Fig. 492).

491. Topless bathing suit introduced by Rudi Gernreich, 1964.

During the 19th and early 20th centuries men in Western societies were overshadowed by the more decorative women. Male clothing remained conservative in color, cut, and fabric. The classic example of this could be found at a formal party or ball, where the men would be dressed identically in black dinner clothes, while the women fought to outdo one another in lavish gowns, opulent fabrics, precious gems, and bright colors.

The recent popularity of so-called "unisex" clothing may represent a temporary leveling trend in the swing back and forward between elaborate female dress and elaborate male dress (Fig. 493). Today men and women wear identical jeans, trousers, shirts, overalls, boots, and even high heels. With longer hairstyles for men, it has become difficult sometimes to tell if a person is male or female simply from apparel. This situation has never before occurred in the history of Western civilization. Sociologists and psychologists will make what they can of it, but clothing designers can delight in the freedom to design, without restrictions, for men and women alike.

Elements and Principles in Apparel Design

All of the various elements and principles of design apply to apparel as well as to any other medium, although some—line and rhythm, for example—may assume greater importance in the context of the body.

The *line* of a garment must be considered in relation to the line of the body that will be under it. In this area line has two meanings: the overall line of the garment and the internal lines that may be part of its design. A garment with vertical lines tends to make the body seem taller and slimmer (Fig. 494), whereas one having predominantly horizontal lines will create a shorter, broader impression. Designers often use horizontal lines to shorten a long waist, give fullness to a thin

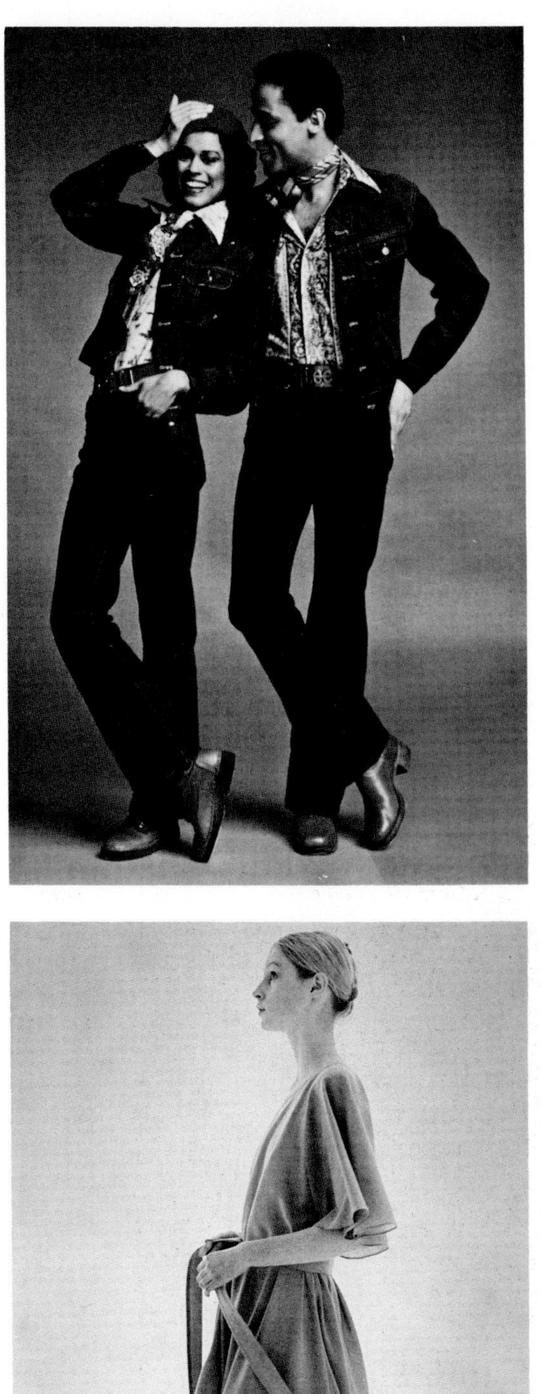

above left: 492. Hyacinthe Rigaud. *Louis XIV.* 1701. Oil on canvas, 9′½″ x 6′⅝″. Louvre, Paris.

above right: 493. "Unisex" jeans and jackets. Courtesy The Lee Company.

right: 494. "Perhonen" dress, designed by Vuokko Eskolin-Nurmesniemi for Ateljee Max Petrelius, Helsinki, 1973.

above: 495. "The Great Sweater Dress," designed by Kimberly Knits.

below: 496. "Sandstripe" maillot and skirt by Rose Marie Reid, fabric by E. I. DuPont de Nemours & Company.

neck, or widen too-narrow shoulders (Fig. 495). The impression of virility in a male figure may be enhanced by broadening the shoulders and slimming the hips. Diagonal lines may establish a rhythm moving around the body to heighten the effect of its rhythmic movements (Fig. 496).

Shape can be surprisingly varied in apparel design, considering that it is inevitably based on clothing the human figure. A garment may hug the body, fall from the shoulder, or billow out in a form all its own that ignores the outlines of the body underneath (Fig. 497). Although today's designs have their full share of variety in size and shape, they are characterized by an honesty and comfort not always experienced in the past. Overemphasis on tiny waists and feet or on overlarge bosoms has given way to a sense of practicality that, on the whole, allows the human form a natural appearance and freedom of movement.

Texture and *pattern* in clothing design relate primarily to fabric construction, although other elements can participate in creating them. Actual textures can range from the sleekness of a nylon swimsuit to the deep pile of a shaggy fur coat, whereas visual textures emerge from the myriad textile patterns available, as well as from such trim as braid, lace, sequins, ruffles, and beading.

Unity and *variety* are, as in every other field, the overriding principles of apparel design. A woman's costume may be composed of blouse and skirt or dress, belt, hat, stockings, shoes, purse, scarf, jewelry, and coat, while a man's can have just as many elements. Some unifying idea should pull all these diverse items together so that the total effect is harmonious. This unity may be in color, fabric, pattern, "style," or a number of other things. The Yves St. Laurent costume in Figure 498 assembles many diverse elements—many colors, fabrics, shapes, and patterns. All these elements blend because of the underlying theme of ornate peasantry, a kind of ethnic opulence.

Balance is a particularly interesting principle in apparel design, because the designer always is working with a "support" that is basically symmetrical. The overwhelming majority of Western garments today mirror this symmetry, so that most of our clothing is formally balanced. This is not true of other cultures, however, the notable exceptions being in the Indian sari and the tropical sarong.

Because they are unusual, asymmetrical garments attract attention and often seem particularly striking. An asymmetrical balance in the clothing sets up a dynamic relationship with the symmetrical body. In the last few years there has been a revival of one-shoulder dresses. The one shown in Figure 499 has been masterfully balanced by the long curl of a bracelet on the naked arm and shoulder.

The *emphasis* in apparel design is usually on the wearer's face, toward which all adornment directs attention. Even though one may be tempted by beautiful materials and colorful patterns, the designer should remember that the purpose of clothing is to enhance a person, not to dominate the personality.

Proportion comes into play in designing for a particular person or in choosing and combining apparel for oneself, because apparel is automatically in *scale* with the body. Generally speaking, large, tall people can better carry oversize garments or large-scale designs (Fig. 500), whereas small people would be overwhelmed by them. Conversely, a large person might seem ridiculous wearing a dainty, ruffled dress.

Color has always been an intrinsic part of apparel design, and this was never more true than today. As recently as two decades ago,

above left: 497. Evening dresses designed by Paco Rabanne for his 1976–77 winter collection. The dresses combine chain mail with tiered silk taffeta.

above right: 498. Jacket, tartan dress, and wool shawl designed by Yves St. Laurent for his 1976–77 winter collection.

left: 499. Two designers join forces to create a costume of asymmetrical balance. Dress by Rudi Gernreich, Inc.; arm sculpture by Brewer-Den Blaker Designs.

right: 500. "Keinuva dress, designed by Vuokko Eskolin-Nurmesniemi.

certain color combinations—such as blue with green or red with pink—were considered unthinkable. Now rules no longer exist. Designers happily mix all the colors of the fabric dyer's palette, and the consumer has complete freedom in assembling a costume. To some extent colors vary with styles and with seasons, but the available range is so broad as to permit options to anyone. The stern heritage of the Puritan blacks and grays has been replaced with a vivid spectrum of hues (Pl. 46, p. 322).

right: 501. Silver anklets and chopins, part of the traditional adornment for women in North Africa. Collection Traphagen School of Fashion, New York.

below: 502. Denim overalls by Town Set, Division of Country Set, fabric by E. I. DuPont de Nemours & Company.

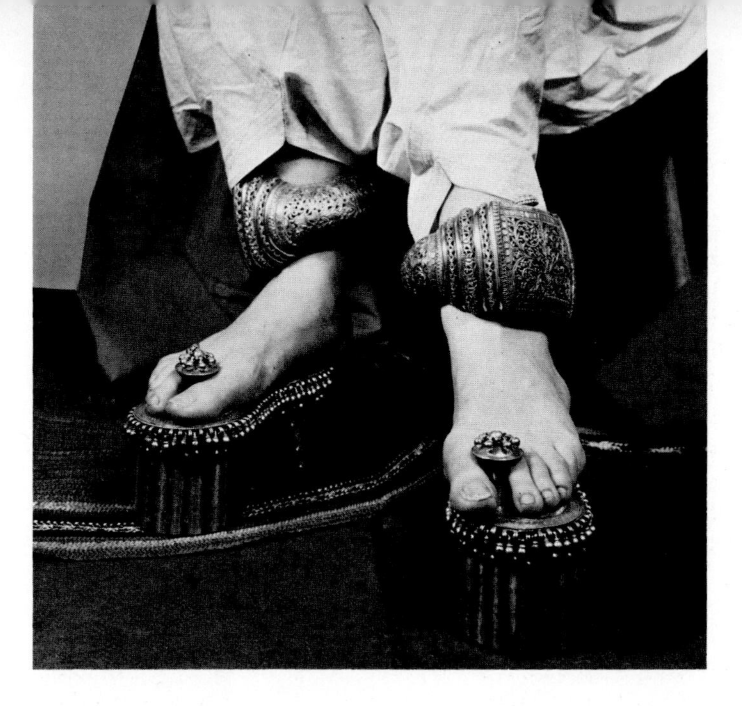

Apparel and Life Style

In the not-too-distant past, North African and Oriental women of good family wore *chopins* or platform shoes like those shown in Figure 501, which made it difficult for them to walk, much less run. This type of accessory helped to emphasize a woman's station in life. She could be waited on hand and foot and need do nothing for herself, so her costume flaunted this helplessness.

Western women today lead busy, energetic lives that would not permit such constraint of clothing. Even the hoop skirts of a century ago would seem ludicrous in a world that includes active sports, automobiles, mass transportation, and theater concerts (rock or classical). One has only to imagine a hoop-skirted Southern belle attempting to board a commercial jetliner to understand how drastically our mode of living influences apparel.

Today's woman can adopt the occupation and life style that suits her best, and whatever her choice there will be clothing appropriate to that way of life. Some will prefer the hardworking, no-nonsense approach of blue jeans and overalls (Fig. 502), others the comfort of free-and-easy nonclinging apparel (Fig. 503). For those who wish a more voluptuous, "feminine" image, this possibility remains open (Fig. 498).

Relaxed living has influenced men's apparel as well as women's. Fifty years ago, a gentleman—whatever his occupation, whatever the season of the year—wore a jacket, shirt with starched collar, and cravat. Today the business suit still predominates in city offices, but new materials have made it more comfortable. Moreover, the popularity of blue jeans, leisure suits, and even caftans for men has infinitely expanded the possibilities in apparel.

Influences on Clothing Design

Any designer striving for an individual touch must have many resources from which to draw. A thorough knowledge of the history of costume is essential to a fashion designer. For example, the ancient Greek *chiton* was revived in Napoleon's day, becoming the basis for the Empire waistline that reappears frequently in modern fashions for evening wear and lingerie. The full skirt of European courts was translated into the hoop skirt of the antebellum South, and variations can still be seen in bridal gowns and ball dresses. Styles derived from a South Sea Island or the Italian countryside turn up on patios in suburbs across the United States. Oriental influence can be found in slit skirts, frogged openings, and mandarin collars. The enthusiasm for boots and fur hats indicates a response to Russian styles. Fabric design has been affected by East Indian and Persian colors and designs.

In introducing his revolutionary fall 1976 collection (Fig. 498), Yves St. Laurent said the clothing "incorporated all my dreams—all my heroines in the novels, the operas, the paintings." Furthermore, the dresses were "derived from the typical clothes of Austria, Morocco, Czechoslovakia, Russia." A master designer will assimilate all kinds of impressions and then pull them all together in a new, unique style.

The advent of mass communication—film and television especially—has had a vital impact on apparel design today. No one can predict when a certain film will set off a wave of popularity for clothing styles that resemble the costumes designed for the film. After the premiere of *The Great Gatsby,* for instance, designers rushed to their drawing boards to create a line of F. Scott Fitzgerald fashions in soft, pastel colors (Fig. 504). The film received mixed notices, but the clothing was a tremendous success.

As can be seen from the illustrations in this chapter, the world of apparel design has never been more eclectic. New fabrics and new construction methods have greatly expanded the designer's repertoire. Clothing design is of the utmost importance to every individual, since it influences and reflects the way we feel about ourselves.

left: 503. "Pujahdus" ensemble designed by Vuokko Eskolin-Nurmesniemi, 1975.

right: 504. Mia Farrow and Robert Redford in a scene from, *The Great Gatsby.* Paramount Pictures Corporation.

The performing arts are those associated with acting and music: theater, film, television, dance, opera, and all types of musical expression. The people most prominent in such productions—those who speak the words, interpret the movements or the music—often are referred to as "artists." However, the *visual* artists involved may never appear before an audience, even though their roles are crucial to the success of the production. Nearly all performances take place in some kind of set, which raises the question of how the performers will relate to that set. Often, too, the performers are costumed. Depending upon the type of production, many different people could be concerned with its visual design, including director, choreographer, stage manager, camera technician, set designer, lighting designer, costume designer, and producer. In this chapter we will show some of the ways these people exert their influence on the visual effect of a performance.

Set Design

There are some types of performances that require no special setting or from which an elaborate set would detract. For example, the intricately related melodic lines of a string quartet could be appreciated just as well on a bare stage, in an empty loft, or in a pleasant meadow (Fig. 505). The art of mime traditionally is practiced on an empty stage with no props, and with the performer made up in whiteface (Fig. 506). Because the effect of mime depends largely upon the viewer's imagination, an excess of visual cues would be destructive of the intent. All meaning derives from the mime's postures and facial expressions.

Today, Shakespearean plays often are mounted in very elaborate settings, but of course in Elizabethan times the sets were quite simple. Two doors at the rear of the stage allowed for exits and entrances, and probably there would be some screened area, called the "discovery space," in which people could be discovered or revealed for dramatic effect. A trapdoor in the stage allowed for the appearance of ghosts and similar manifestations. Apparently, in Shakespeare's time, more emphasis was placed on the power of the words than on "realism." Costumes were elaborate versions of contemporary dress, rather than evocations of the period in which the play was set. Young boys played all the female roles (it being unseemly for women to appear on stage), so the audience devoted most of their attention to the drama, not the trappings.

Much the same was true of the heritage from which all modern drama derives—the classical Greek theater. Plays were performed outdoors in an open amphitheater, with no real sets at all (Fig. 507).

left: 505. A string quartet practicing in a meadow.

above: 506. The mime Marcel Marceau in "Bip as a Street Musician."

below: 507. The theater at Epidaurus staging its festival of classical Greek drama.

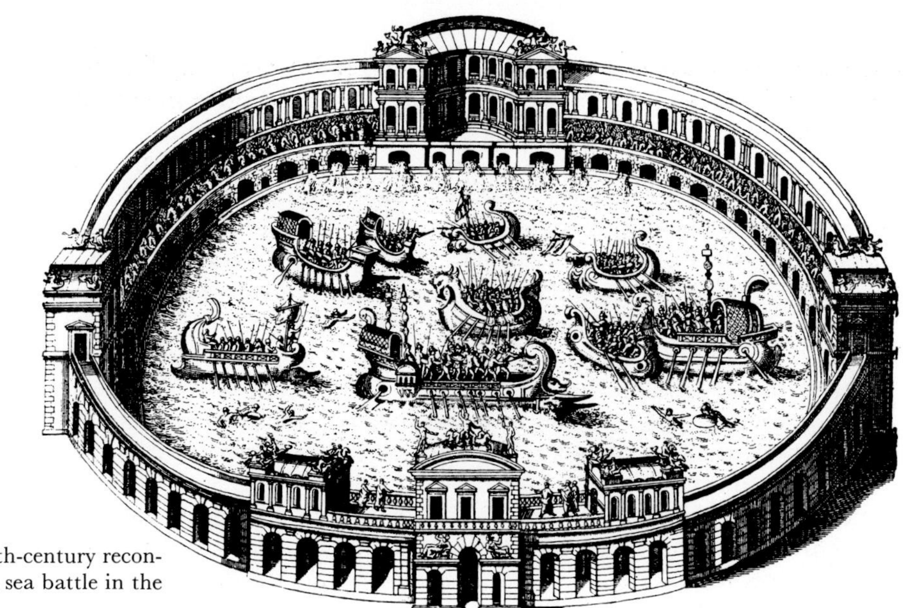

508. A whimsical 19th-century reconstruction of a staged sea battle in the Roman Colosseum.

Authorities generally agree that the same formal backdrop served for all the various plays. The opposite approach, however, marked the theatrical spectacles of the Romans, who actually flooded the Colosseum on special occasions in order to stage realistic sea battles (Fig. 508).

Designers of sets in the 20th century have options embracing these two extremes and everything in between. There are basically two requirements for an effective set. First of all, it must be expressive of the spirit of the production—its mood, historical period, locale, social stratum, and season. Beyond these details, expressiveness results from the designer's ability to suggest the emotional tone of the work. Second, a set must be practical, meeting the needs of the production and the performers. This means doors that are wide enough to permit the passage of costumes and props, bannisters strong enough for leaping over or sliding down, balconies that will support whatever action must take place on them. A particular play or musical may require unusual effects in the set. For example, in *Peter Pan* Peter must be able to fly through the air, preferably without bashing into anything. Finally, the set should lend itself to rapid construction, be easy to shift and store, and stand up under continued use.

As in all areas of visual design, the basic elements and principles play an important role in the creation of sets. *Balance* must consider the action that takes place and the movements of the performers. *Shape* and *mass* are elements that change continually as the action develops. In the dance, the choreographer is dealing constantly with changes of shape and mass within a given space (Fig. 515). These in turn will relate to the design of the set.

The size of a stage is established, but *proportion* and *scale* can be subject to much control on the part of the designer. A witch at a small pot is less ominous than one dwarfed by an immense vat. A huge tree stretching stark branches across the top of a stage provides an element of menace.

Symbolism is important in all phases of design, but nowhere does it become so basic and so natural as in the performing arts. Theater, film, opera, dance, television—all are symbols of life. The situations and experiences take place only symbolically. It follows, then, that the use of symbolism can be the set designer's most effective means of communication.

Symbolism in set design can serve many specific purposes. One is identification, as in the primary set for *Sesame Street* (Fig. 509). The brownstone stoop featured in the program each time serves as a kind of "home base" for the viewing children. Audience involvement may be another goal of the set designer. In the Chelsea Theatre Centre production of *Candide* part of the audience actually sits in the middle of the set (Fig. 510), so there can be considerable interaction between performers and viewers.

The set designer has an extraordinary opportunity to create visual drama in schematic approaches such as that used for a production of *Parsifal* (Fig. 511). Here the simple but impressive set lends itself to choreographed arrangements of the performers, with the visual pattern flowing continually. Each movement of the singers forms a new abstract composition on the stage, operating as a counterpoint to the progressions of the music.

above: 509. Big Bird, Susan (Loretta Long), and Bob (Bob McGrath) in front of the brownstone set for *Sesame Street.* Courtesy Children's Television Workshop.

above right: 510. A scene from the Hal Prince/Chelsea Theatre Center production of *Candide* at the Broadway Theatre.

right: 511. Wieland Wagner's production of Richard Wagner's *Parsifal,* staged in Bayreuth, Germany.

512. A scene from Michael Powell and Emeric Pressburger's 1948 film, *The Red Shoes.* Courtesy Janus Films.

The question of set design becomes especially interesting when a certain work is translated from one medium into another, as in the common situation of a stage play or musical being made into a film. Since the play usually precedes the movie, the movie's set designer must respond to whatever setting was created for the stage production. Space, of course, is highly constricted on the stage, and an entire play may be set in one room or building, whereas the filmmaker has unlimited scope. The film's director and set designer must decide whether there is any real advantage to broadening the arena of activity, whether it would serve a dramatic purpose for the characters to move outdoors. If outdoor shots are included simply because the camera is capable of recording them, then some quality of the original drama—such as intimacy or claustrophobia—may be lost.

Such a challenge occurred in *The Red Shoes,* a film about the ballet. The film includes many full-scale ballet productions. Because of the flexibility of the camera, the set designer could have taken great liberties with the appearance of the stage, using extravagant and complicated scenery. Instead, the film preserved a sense of realism by having the sets limited to what might actually appear on the ballet stage. The backdrops are stark, schematic flats that evoke a mood and create an experience, rather than describing reality (Fig. 512).

Lighting Design

Even the most skillful of set designs would be rendered ineffectual without the reinforcement of lighting. A play that has no set at all can be made visually dramatic through the stunning use of light.

There are two overall kinds of lighting on a set: *general illumination,* which makes it possible for the audience to see the action; and *specific illumination,* which molds and models to create dramatic effect or control audience reaction. Lighting can serve a variety of purposes.

Although it is important that the audience see the performance comfortably, it need not always see everything equally well. Visibility must be focused on the action and, when the stage is empty, on that segment of the set that is significant at the moment. Sometimes a set will have several rooms or areas, with action taking place sequentially in different spots. Selective lighting then helps to build the sequence.

Seasons, weather, and localities are all subject to individual lighting effects. The harsh light of the tropics is quite different from the hazy light of London in the fog. Shadows are cast in late afternoon and in moonlight, while the hot light of noon comes from directly overhead. With no verbal clues at all, lighting can create an atmosphere that sets us in a particular time and place and climate.

The true artistry of the designer takes form in the use of light to create a living composition that changes with every movement of the performers. Light in this sense is the means of breathing life into a set, of giving form to the work and bestowing unity upon the whole.

As with music, light can manipulate an audience without the viewers being consciously aware of it. A flooding with warm, rosy light raises the spirits and anticipates gaiety, whereas a dimly lit setting may suggest the sinister or the supernatural. A sudden flooding of light predicts a moment of triumph. Shadows set the mood for violence.

Designers today have the capability for many special lighting effects. The strident, brilliant lights that often accompany a rock concert (Pl. 10, p. 90) envelop the listeners in a world of sensory experience. In the film *Barry Lyndon,* director Stanley Kubrick made use of sophisticated equipment to set many scenes under natural light, even the dim illumination of a candlelit interior (Pl. 47, p. 355). By these means he created an almost eerie sense of naturalism.

Costume Design

The costume designer is immensely influential in establishing the visual and emotional qualities of a work. Before the first word is spoken or the first note of music played, the audience gains an impression from the actors' clothing.

Sometimes the goal of the costume designer is meticulous historical accuracy, as for a classical play set in 16th-century France or a television drama recreating World War I England (Fig. 513). At the other extreme, costumes sometimes are meant to have a jarring, unsettling effect. In large part the surreal quality of a scene from Fellini's *Juliet of the Spirits* (Fig. 514) derives from the visual shock of seeing a young woman dressed halfway between a bride and a chorus girl dancing with an old

left: 513. Hudson (Gordon Jackson) and Rose (Jean Marsh) in a scene from the television production *Upstairs-Downstairs.*

right: 514. A scene from Federico Fellini's 1965 film, *Juliet of the Spirits.*

above left: 515. Judith Jamison, one of the performers in Alvin Ailey's American Dance Theater in a sequence from *Cry.*

above: 516. Maurice Béjart's Ballet of the 20th Century performs the Petrouchka segment from *Nijinsky: Clown of God.*

left: 517. The "Small House of Uncle Thomas" sequence from the Twentieth Century-Fox film production of *The King and I.*

below: 518. The "Ascot Gavotte" number from the Broadway production of *My Fair Lady.*

519. The Nikolais Dance Theatre production of *Grotto,* premiered in February 1973 at the Brooklyn Academy of Music. Choreography, costumes, and lighting by Alwin Nikolais.

man in a black cape. In the first instance, the audience "believes" the play because the costumes are *right;* in the second, the audience reacts because the costumes are *wrong.*

Costumes for the dance can be exceedingly useful in creating visual patterns and shapes as they swirl around the dancer's moving body (Fig. 515). Costumes also serve the vital purpose of helping to establish characterizations in a medium that relies largely on visual cues to tell a story (Fig. 516).

Costume may in some circumstances go beyond its usual role to become something else entirely. In the "Small House of Uncle Thomas" sequence from *The King and I* (Fig. 517), the long flowing scarves held by the performers serve as a kind of set for the playlet.

Finally, a coordinated ensemble of costumes can function as a dramatic visual composition, almost like a painting within a play. This was true of the costumes Cecil Beaton designed for the famous Ascot Gavotte number from *My Fair Lady* (Fig. 518). All the performers were dressed in combinations of black and white, which made a witty commentary upon the sameness and boredom of upper-class amusements during the period in which the play was set. The starkness of the costumes, together with the stilted movements of the actors, created a stunning tableau.

The Overall Production

Visual design in the performing arts reaches a peak when the entire production is controlled in such a way as to yield a unified result. One good example of this is in the offerings of the Alwin Nikolais Dance Theatre (Fig. 519). For these presentations, every aspect, visual and musical, is coordinated with every other aspect. The costumes blend with the sets, with both often being masses of stretchy fabric. The movements of the dancers are choreographed so as to exploit the visual qualities of the costumes. Such a performance springs from a total concept of the performing arts, rather than from individual ingredients made to blend.

In some ways, the planning of a rock concert follows the same approach. Brilliant costumes, programed movements by the performers, dizzying lights and reflections—all these reinforce the effect of the deafening, pulsating music so that the audience and the musicians become engulfed in a total experience that blocks out any interference (Pl. 10, p. 90). Many performers are identified as closely with movements and facial expressions as with their music (Fig. 520).

520. Janis Joplin in concert.

A number of films made in Hollywood from the 1930s through the 1950s reached for visual effects that put the Roman sea battles to shame. A good example can be found in any of the watery musical extravaganzas featuring Esther Williams (Fig. 521). Amazingly intricate water ballets spiced with lights, colored smoke, and elaborate mechanical devices to introduce and remove the star made these productions a visual feast in special effects.

Total design is no more evident than in a production by Maurice Béjart's Ballet of the 20th Century set to the music of Beethoven's Ninth Symphony (Fig. 522). Even without the dancers, Beethoven's composition allowed for a massive production involving orchestra, chorus, and soloists. The choreography introduces many new elements, including movement, visual rhythms, setting, costumes, and relationships among the groups of performers.

Design for the performing arts is one of the most exciting and glamorous of all the many design realms. While it is based upon the identical elements and principles that underlie other fields, the designer here has the exhilarating experience of delving into make-believe, as well as the heady reward of applause.

right: 521. A scene from Metro-Goldwyn-Mayer's *Million Dollar Mermaid,* starring Esther Williams.

below right: 522. Maurice Béjart's Ballet of the 20th Century in a production of Beethoven's Ninth Symphony.

Design for Living

26 Interiors

Most people spend by far the greatest portion of their lives within enclosures. Except for the relatively few individuals who have outside jobs, we pass the bulk of each day indoors, in a home, a school, an office, a factory, or some other building. The design of interior spaces is therefore of the most immediate importance to everyone. It is what we see more than anything else.

The interior design over which we have the greatest control is that of the home. Only rarely can individuals affect, to any degree, the character of their working spaces, but nearly everyone lives somewhere. For this reason we will concentrate in this chapter on interior design for the home, using the term "home" in the broadest sense to encompass the apartment, the camper, the dormitory room, or whatever serves as a "living space."

Interior design gives everyone the opportunity to create, to experiment with the elements and principles of design. To be sure, some interior design costs a great deal of money, but dramatic design effects can also be introduced with such inexpensive ingredients as plants, flowers, paint, wallpaper, and simple artifacts.

A home reflects the special personality of its owner, and for this reason the interior design of a home can be the most intimate and personal of all design activities. Conversely, the design of an interior contributes immeasurably to the creation of a way of life that is unique. The setting in which we find a sense of home affects our outlook, moods, and total personality.

In addition to the close connection between interiors and people, there are several other interactions that bear heavily on the design of interior space. These are the relationships between interiors and architecture, interiors and landscape, furnishings and space. Architecture and interior design are so closely related that, in essence, they perform the same function. Together they represent the culmination of a creative effort that attempts to compose an effective space. Landscape is important, because a home does not exist in a vacuum. Rather, it is part of a greater environment, whether its surroundings be a pastoral field or the inner city. Some designs will attempt to shut out the environment altogether, to build a peaceful island into which the world cannot intrude. Others will seek to expand the interior spaces to spill out into the world beyond, to include the natural setting. Finally, the relationship between furnishings and space is a vital consideration, because furniture acts as a transition between architecture and people.

Relationships in Interior Design

The photographs in Figures 523 to 525 show three different views of the same house. The structure, a one-family house overlooking San Francisco Bay, shows especially well how all the various elements—landscape, architecture, interior spaces, and furnishings—can be integrated to achieve a composition of satisfying unity. In the first view (Fig. 523) we see how the house nestles into the cliffside, with trees and

523–525. A house in Belvedere, California, designed by Callister Payne & Bischoff, shows sensitive integration of landscape, architecture, and interior spaces.

523. View toward the house from the pool.

above: Plate 47. Scene from Stanley Kubrick's production, *Barry Lyndon.*

right: Plate 48. Ralph Bisdale. Lighting design for a loft-residence, New York City. Courtesy the artist.

left: Plate 49. Luis Barragán, with Andrés Casillas. San Cristobal: residence, swimming pool, stable, and horse pool of Mr. and Mrs. Folke Egerstrom, near Mexico City. 1967–68.

below: Plate 50. Gene Davis. *Franklin's Footpath.* 1972. Epoxy, 80 x 414′. Photograph courtesy Philadelphia Museum of Art.

above: 524. The atrium, or enclosed inner courtyard.

right: 525. The main living area.

plantings making a natural transition between the building and the terrain. A long, narrow swimming pool adjacent to the approach leads the eye along the edge of the cliff to the house itself. Indoor-outdoor harmony is carried through in the atrium (Fig. 524), an enclosed courtyard within the house, partially walled by a glassed-in gallery. Potted plants in the gallery blend with plantings in the atrium to create a natural landscape that brings the outdoors indoors. The main living area of the house (Fig. 525) is lit by a huge skylight running the entire length of the room. This effect further emphasizes the close relationship between landscape and interior space. Furnishings in this room have deliberately been kept close to the floor level, in order not to break up the impression of a wide, unhampered vista. The low furniture, covered with soft, colorful cushions, helps to enhance the quality of leisure and comfort that pervades this entire house.

Obviously, the planners of this house exercised maximum control over the three relationships mentioned above. The house was built into that particular landscape, the inside and outside were carefully balanced, and furniture was chosen to fill the exact needs of a space. Most people do not have that kind of freedom in designing an interior. The majority of us move into spaces planned by others and can have minimum impact on the broader relationships. Everyone, though, can determine the interaction between furnishings and space. For some this will mean the arrangement of furniture already owned. Others enjoy the flexibility of *modular* furnishings that can be moved from home to home and rearranged as the space dictates.

A relatively new concept, modular furniture means pieces that have been designed according to a repeated pattern and that can be interlocked or fitted together in various ways. The modular unit shown in Figure 526 offers a good example. This piece consists of a desk, bookcase, chest of drawers, closet, and miscellaneous storage space, with a bunk bed overhead. Exposed bolts provide a decorative touch, but when they are removed the unit can be disassembled and set up in different ways. Other sections can be added as the owner's needs and available space may change.

In planning interior space, the elements and principles of design are surprisingly easy to manipulate. We have already seen, from illustrations elsewhere in this book (Figs. 85, 87, 145, 146, 194), how the elements of space, texture, and proportion play important roles in interior design.

Elements and Principles in Interior Design

Soaring vertical *lines* have been built into the interior structure of the house shown in Figure 527. The rising line of the broken fireplace wall is, however, counteracted by horizontal bookshelves behind it and the horizontals of low furniture in the main living area. The diagonal pitch of the roof (barely visible in this photograph) completes the masterful composition of directional lines. A bentwood rocker in the foreground gives just the right curvilinear relief to the otherwise straight-edged geometry. We might speculate that the great popularity of bentwood furniture, especially rocking chairs, in recent years stems from a need for curves in our generally angular spaces.

The element of *space* is nowhere more important than in interior design. The walls, roof, and floor of a home mold space in a particular way—a way that may be open or constricting, sedate or free, geometric or irregular. Few houses today are built on the old boxes-in-a-box plan that characterized architecture until the middle of this century. Even

left: 526. KD6 modular furniture bolts together in many different combinations, depending upon the owner's needs and available space. Courtesy John Adden Furniture, Boston.

right: 527. Rodney Friedman's design for a house in Belvedere, California, includes a soaring pure white fireplace wall—a strong vertical line.

528. An ingenious painted design breaks up the blocky effect of a kitchen wall in a house designed by William Turnbull of MLTW/Turnbull Associates.

before that time, of course, rooms might be irregular. Victorian houses often had round or octagonal rooms that mirrored the exuberant exterior architecture. Still, these rooms would be carefully enclosed all around, with limited access to adjacent spaces. The reasons for this were largely practical. Central heating did not exist to any real degree in the United States until about the turn of this century and was relatively uncommon in Europe until after World War II. Rooms of great height or with many open spaces meant heat loss. The converse was true in warm climates, where thick enclosing walls kept heat *out* of the rooms.

Today, with modern heating, air conditioning, and insulation we can afford more open, dramatic, and irregular spaces. As the homes illustrated in this chapter show, the trend now is toward wide-open spaces, areas instead of rooms, and easy communication among parts of a structure. Interior design has changed greatly to respond to these new kinds of spaces. More than ever designers must consider how various functional and decorative pieces will mold the space and define it. In the house shown in Figure 527, for example, the designer chose to let the lofty space stand on its own. A long vertical hanging might have emphasized it but might also have given too much of a sense of height so that the space seemed overwhelming. Instead, with most of the furnishings very low, we have a feeling of close-to-the-ground security. The space therefore exhilarates but does not intimidate human beings.

Shape and *mass* are elements many people feel they cannot control in their homes, because relatively few can afford to custom design and build a house. However, as the illustration in Figure 528 shows, shape does sometimes bend before the simplest devices. Part of the kitchen wall in this house has been painted in sharply contrasting broad stripes that carve out dramatic masses from what might have been an ordinary box. The optical illusion of fascinating space is quite strong here. A new freedom in the use of paint has encouraged many people to experiment with changing shapes, and similar effects can be achieved inexpensively with wood, wallpaper, or sheets of plastic.

Color in interiors is much subject to fashion. In some eras the style has decreed all soft pastels, in others the predominance of dark, somber hues with much wood paneling. Today there is no prevailing fashion in interior design. Instead, the designer has many different styles to choose from or to combine. Designers can select from an infinite realm of colors in paint, wallpaper, carpeting, furnishings, and accessories. As with other areas of design, however, certain characteristics of color should be borne in mind.

Warm, bright colors (red, orange, and yellow) seem to advance; they make things seem larger and nearer. Cool colors, mainly the blues and greens, seem to recede and make things look farther away. Warm colors tend to be stimulating and uplifting. Many people would have difficulty falling asleep in a bedroom done in bright red and orange,

left: 529. Architect Mark Mills designed a beautifully composed study in textures for this California house.

right: 530. A collection of antique artifacts and kitchen utensils illustrates the principles of unity and variety in this New York loft-apartment.

but these colors might be quite appropriate for a room in which parties are to be given. Some research has shown that red and orange, as "hot" colors, actually create a sensation of thirst (which may be why they often appear in the decor of bars!). Cool blues and greens, on the other hand, usually have a soothing effect. They are staples in doctors' offices and hospitals. Of course, we are simplifying in attaching such qualities to colors. An electric blue could be far more exciting than a dull, grayed red such as a maroon. Moreover, combinations of colors can change the effect of each color. Green alone may be peaceful, but green side-by-side with red often seems vibrant, since the two complementaries reinforce one another. Red with gold is a favorite combination for creating an atmosphere of opulence and drama.

In interior design color must always be considered in relation to lighting, for different-colored lights can seriously influence both colors and moods. Generally speaking, warm-hued lights that cast a soft glow in a room flatter the occupants, whereas a green- or blue-tinted light can make the healthiest person look sickly. For special effects, however, designers have increasingly turned to brilliantly colored lights, which can transform a mere room into an event (Pl. 48, p. 355).

A combination of *textures* can be one of the most exciting aspects of interior design. The photograph in Figure 529 shows a deliberately composed area of texture—an entryway in which the smooth planes of wood have been beautifully set off by a large, feathery plant. This arrangement is almost Japanese in its studied simplicity. It offers a classic introduction to the mingling of textures in the home. Walls, ceilings, floors, and most furnishings contribute smooth textures; upholstery and carpeting give an intermediate soft texture; and plants, rough stonework, or shag textiles bring the roughest textures. The designer can combine these in any degree to achieve the desired effect. The more that smooth textures tend to prevail, the more pristine and "cold" a room will be, while a dominance of rough textures will tend to make a room seem warmer. Excessively rough textures may even give a crude impression. Most designs strive for a balance between the two extremes. Figure 533 shows a room with the entire range of textures, from the rough stone-and-concrete fireplace and the fake-fur rugs, to the smooth flooring and built-in furniture.

The principles of *unity* and *variety* in the home can be demonstrated in microcosm by the wall display shown in Figure 530. In this kitchen alcove many diverse elements have been arranged to create a pleasant composition. The grouping works as a unit because of several factors: a similarity of size (or proportion); the repetition of different forms; the regular spacing of various pieces; and the pattern effect that results. The same principles can be applied to the arrangement of a whole room or interior space. Furnishings will work together if they are in suitable proportion to one another. A repetition of forms—whether of similar pieces or merely similar shapes—will make a space coherent. Placement of individual elements in relation to each other and to the space as a whole brings a unity to the composition.

Pattern in interior design can be literally the patterns in rugs, wallpaper, or upholstery. It also can be the pattern of pictures or other elements arranged on a wall (Fig. 530). Light entering through windows or provided by artificial illumination can create a pattern to enliven the interior space.

Certain elements in the home naturally serve as points of *emphasis,* or focal points. The most obvious of these would be a brightly colored

531. A bold geometric painting provides a point of strong emphasis in the dining room of a house designed by Charles Moore of MLTW/Moore Associates.

textile or a dramatic painting (Fig. 531). But even without these accents, a home has built-in points of emphasis. A door, especially an entrance door, may be such a focal point. For example, the Spanish, living secluded lives behind thick walls and small grilled windows, use their doors as dramatic portals to impress the visitor with the importance of crossing the threshold. Stairways, too, may have a strong ceremonial connotation. Not only does a staircase act as a sculptural element, molding the space between two vertically related areas, but it also creates a feeling of suspense—literally and figuratively—between two levels. Perhaps for this reason filmmakers often set their most dramatic scenes on stairways (Fig. 532).

Proportion and *scale* in the home take their cue from the scale of the occupants—that is, human scale. Chairs, beds, tables, and other furnishings must be on the *scale* of the people who will use them in order to be comfortable, and the interior space as a whole should be in some kind of satisfying *proportion* to human size. The room shown in

532. "The Barbecue at the Wilkes'," an early scene from *Gone With the Wind.* Scarlett O'Hara (Vivian Leigh) and Ashley Wilkes (Leslie Howard) are posed momentously on a grand staircase.

left: 533. A heavy, large-scale fireplace creates a satisfying sense of proportion for the lofty living room of a house designed by Mark Mills.

right: 534. Elegant rattan furnishings and classic side tables, plus the display of paintings and precious objects, contribute to the "formal" quality of this room. Courtesy McGuire Company, San Francisco.

Figure 533 shows how these relationships can operate. Here the built-in furniture is modest in scale and low to the ground, with comfortable proportions for sitting. The major elements in the room, however, are large and lofty. The high ceiling, heavy beams, and large windows might seem out of proportion to the furnishings, except for a strong transitional device—the fireplace. This massive structure bridges the gap between the two scales, bringing them into proportion with each other. Heavy, rocky, and rough near the top, the fireplace gradually becomes smoother near the bottom, and the fire opening is in perfect proportion to the seating units. Proportion and scale can always be considered in terms of relationships—to the architecture and to the people.

Interior Design and Individuality

Effective interior design always emerges from the particular way of life followed by the people who live in a home. Some families entertain a great deal, others hardly at all. Those who do entertain may do so with casual snacks around the television set or with formal sit-down dinners. The way one lives and the things one expects to do in the home will have more to do with its design than any other factor.

The room shown in Figure 534 has a rather "formal" quality reminiscent of the old-fashioned ceremonial parlor. No doubt its owners entertain frequently in this room and use it primarily for that

left: 535. A way of life that includes weaving and other crafts calls for looms and a work table brought right into the main living area. Kipp Stewart, owner-architect.

below: 536. An easy, casual living style sets the design quality for this very personal loft-home renovated by Polly Myhrum and Myron Adams.

purpose. This is a space for special occasions, not one for casual lounging. Another style of living led to the design of the room shown in Figure 535. Both of the people who live in this house are involved in crafts and natural materials, and one is a weaver. The loom is brought directly into the living area to mark this space as one in which things are created, not merely enjoyed. While the room could also be used for social events, it functions as a workroom, reflecting the serious interests of the owners.

Figure 536 shows a very casual living area in a home that was renovated by the owners. This space actually functions as a common room, an area in which all the activities of life take place. People gather here to talk, to work, to eat, or simply to relax. Furnishings and design take their character from the lives of the people within.

The success of the three designs shown here can be measured by the fact that, without ever having met them, we know much about the people who designed and live in these spaces.

Influences on Interior Design

The influences that bear upon interior design in the United States today are as diverse as a history of civilization and as far-reaching as a geography book. It is still possible to buy furniture similar in design to that used by Cleopatra, Henry VIII, or Josephine. Many people respond to the appeal of period furnishings, especially French and English designs from the 18th century, considering these styles to be a height of elegance never matched since. However, a room done entirely in period furniture seems out of keeping with today's way of life. When unoccupied, such rooms tend to look like stage settings, and with people in them the effect may be even ludicrous. We are not 18th-century people, and it is inevitable that a person wearing blue jeans sitting on a Louis XV chair will present a jarring image.

More successful are designs that take their style and spirit from other cultures yet remain modern in outlook. The room shown in Figure 537 might be considered Persian or Indian in influence, with its profusion of patterns, colors, low furniture, cushions, and wicker. But this is clearly a room occupied by 20th-century Western people.

A daring adaptation of forms from another culture can be seen in a modern American house (Fig. 538). The raised ceiling, soaring upward in a curved triangle, has been borrowed from the Chinese pagoda shape, yet the effect is absolutely contemporary. This particular device enables the house to have very high ceilings without their height seeming overwhelming, and the glass insets between the "pagoda" sections bring a great deal of light into the house.

There is no set formula for interior design today. Rather, designs emerge from the living styles of people who borrow from many different cultures and periods. Some of the most effective designs result when objects gathered for their special meanings to the individual are assembled according to the principles of design.

left: 537. Wicker furniture, a low mattress, colorful prints, and many plants lend an "Eastern" quality to this room in a California house. Taylor and Ng, architects.

right: 538. A raised pagoda-like roofline transforms this house into a Western version of a Chinese temple. Warren Callister, architect.

27 Architecture and Landscape

Architecture is the art of enclosing space for effective use. Since the first inhabited cave, the different styles in which space has been enclosed have been largely responsible for—and responsive to—the richness, effectiveness, and variety of human life. The skyscraper, the igloo, the cathedral, and the tent all represent spatial enclosures for particular purposes.

The Meaning of Space

Space as a limitless expanse stretching to infinity is an awesome concept that defies imagination, yet this same space exists on the earth, both inside and outside enclosures. Scientists would differentiate between the vacuum of outer space and the atmosphere of the earth or another planet. In a design sense, however, the two are identical, since they indicate the absence of form. As mentioned in Chapter 4, we do not become aware of space until it has been demarcated by forms and shapes (Fig. 539). During the 19th century, when the frontier of the United States was pushing westward, hostilities were acute between the cattle ranchers who wished to maintain the "wide open spaces" for their herds to roam, and the farmers, who circumscribed space with fences to protect their crops. Some people when confined in a small space suffer what is known as claustrophobia; others, confronted with vast reaches of plains or desert or water, become victims of an opposite fear, which psychologists label agoraphobia. Both are terrifying emotional handicaps caused by one aspect or another of the human response to space.

The understanding of space and its effective use has a great deal to do with successful design. Positive and negative spaces are the components of sculpture (Figs. 81, 82), and the space that remains within a ceramic bowl or a silver chalice determines its capacity and its use. The importance of space to architecture becomes clear if one conceives of space as being unlimited until the architect demarcates it by erecting walls. The quality of the designed space determines the success of a building, for it is only after the spaces have been established that the material, surface color, and texture of the walls will be considered. One could even say that the limitation of space is the structural design of a building, with the walls being merely the decorative design that defines and enhances it.

The dimension of time plays a greater role in architecture than in any other design field. To know a building thoroughly, one must take time to walk through it, allowing one's spirit to flow through the space, over and around the divisions or walls, and out through the doors and windows. Anyone who has learned to "feel" a building in all its possibilities can sense almost endless dimensions in its relationship to the human personality. It is this relationship that makes it possible for an individual to relate to a specific space in such a way that it becomes an integral part of existence. The space becomes "home," the most intimate of connections between space and the human spirit.

539. Paul Rudolph. Reception area of Burroughs Wellcome & Co. building, North Carolina, designed in concrete-aggregate and glass. 1974–75.

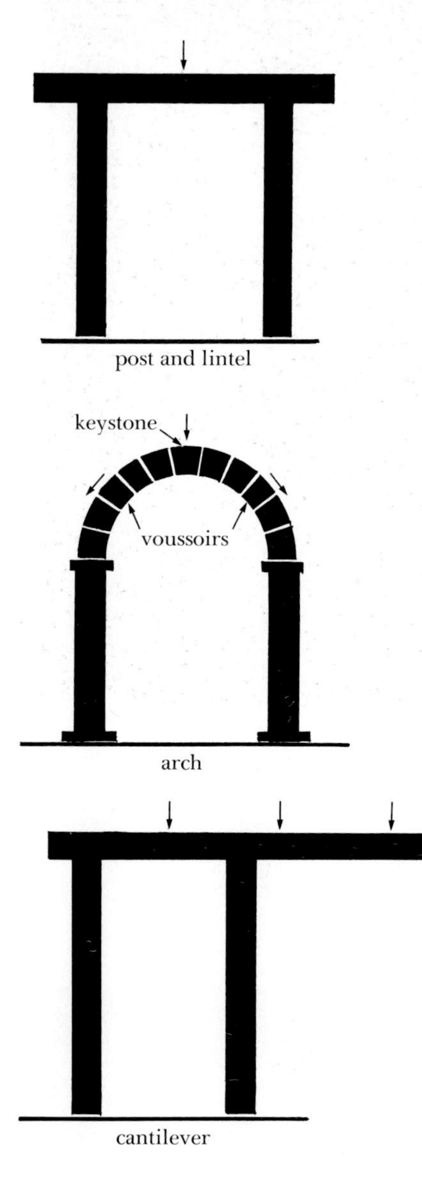

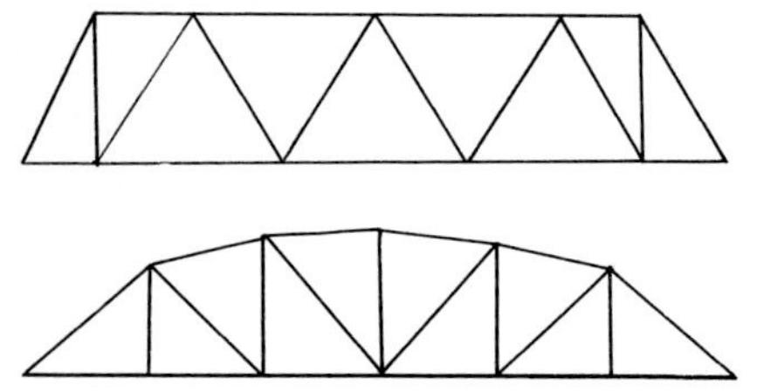

Structural Design

New methods and materials have expanded contemporary architectural processes far beyond those used in past centuries. However, any understanding of architectural design should be based on familiarity with the four traditional structural classifications: *post-and-lintel, arch, cantilever,* and *truss* (Fig. 540).

The Parthenon (Fig. 196) stands as the classic example of post-and-lintel construction. In this system two verticals are erected, and the intervening space is bridged by a beam, or lintel. This arrangement creates angular space within two walls and a flat roof (or any variation of the peaked roof) above the horizontal beams.

The development of the arch provided architects with a new concept: curved and circular space. First used by the Mesopotamians, the arch became a truly revolutionary element in the hands of the Romans. They repeated it in *arcades,* placed arches at right angles to one another to form *vaults,* and rotated the arch on its central axis to create the *dome.*

The *cantilever* system came into prominence with the development of reinforced concrete—concrete poured over steel rods or mesh to give it support and stability. With immense tensile strength, steel beams can span greater distances than either stone or wood. When this strength is combined with the strength of concrete under compression, a new and versatile material evolves. Beams imbedded in slabs of concrete and riveted or welded into place can support tremendous weights, even when they are extended into space. This extension provides a new concept of open space—an approach in which space is articulated rather than enclosed.

One of the best-known cantilever constructions was designed by Frank Lloyd Wright for the Edgar Kaufmann family in Pennsylvania—the house known as "Falling Water" (Fig. 541). Built on pylons or piers, anchored in a foundation of natural stone, the house has cantilevers of tawny-colored concrete projecting dramatically over the waterfall. The cantilevers, which also serve as terraces, have no support at one end. They form layers of solid structure counterbalanced by open space. Glass walls carry the feeling of space indoors and contrast in texture with the stone of the chimney and the rugged quality of the surrounding woods.

above: 540. The four traditional structural systems: post-and-lintel, arch, cantilever, and truss.

right: 541. Frank Lloyd Wright. Kaufmann House ("Falling Water"), Bear Run, Pa., 1936. Cantilevered concrete balconies and rough walls of local stone.

542. Bernard Judge's design for an experimental house of aluminum rods and plastic skin, Hollywood, California. Based on the geodesic dome principle developed by R. Buckminster Fuller.

Trusses are employed when it is necessary to span longer distances than can be bridged by post-and-lintel construction. The truss consists of a rigid framework of bars, beams, or other material that is so strong it cannot be pushed out of shape. Trusses have long been used for steel bridges, as well as for large pavilions and aircraft fuselages.

The materials and technology of the 20th century have added immeasurably to the vocabulary of structural design for architecture. Plastic foams, sprayed or otherwise applied to a frame of some kind, can form a rigid, self-supporting structure of any shape the architect desires, with the framework either remaining in place or being removed (Fig. 552). The same is true of *ferrocement* or ferroconcrete, which consists of layers of steel mesh sprayed with cement mortar. Because of its superior strength and elasticity, ferrocement can stand great strains without cracking, even when used in thin slabs and shells. The wooden molds ordinarily used for pouring concrete can be dispensed with; instead, the cement mortar is applied directly to mesh that has been previously shaped, often in free-form designs.

A quite different but equally innovative approach to structure is the *geodesic dome,* patented by R. Buckminster Fuller in the 1940s. Just as a flat sheet of paper can be made into a dome by crumpling its surface into a series of small planes, an architectural dome can be created by the arrangement of small triangles combined with tetrahedrons. This system of building expands the possibilities of the dome to cover much larger areas than had ever before been enclosed by a circular construction. The triangular modules can be made of lightweight metal, and the resulting structure covered with any suitable material, such as plastic, cloth, or wood. Since 1947 more than three thousand geodesic domes have been built, ranging in size from the huge one that housed the United States pavilion at Expo 67 in Montreal to the smaller ones intended for family housing (Fig. 542).

A concept that has totally revolutionized architectural design is *modular* construction, which depends upon prefabricated modules or units shipped intact to the building site and attached to one another.

right: 543. Architect Myron Goldfinger's design for a vacation house combines three basic modules—a 15-foot curve, triangular roof section, and a cantilevered deck. 1971. Westchester County, New York.

below: 544. Christopher Owen's design for a house in New York's suburbs is a contemporary version of the International Style of architecture. 1975.

The modules vary from simple boxes to more elaborate geometric shapes. The overriding advantage of this system is the cost saving, since units mass-produced at the factory are much less expensive than on-site construction. The result is not necessarily stereotyped, for different combinations of modules can offer a wonderfully free architectural approach (Fig. 543).

545. Jorn Utzon's design for multiple housing in Denmark.

546. F. Kissler and A. Bartos. The Shrine of the Book, Israel Museum, Jerusalem. The shrine houses the Thanksgiving Scroll from the 1st century C.E.

Decorative Design

In architecture, decorative design is so closely wedded to structure that the two can be separated for discussion only theoretically. The decorative design of a building may emerge from the relationships of different structural parts to each other, as well as from embellishments such as stairways, cornices, moldings, window frames, and railings (Fig. 544). The arrangement of openings for doors and windows also contributes substantially to decorative design. Buildings in the so-called International Style, for example, like the one shown in Figure 544, feature pristine geometric shapes, usually painted pure white. They have little or no superficial detailing but rely on functional elements such as metal railings for linear emphasis. The Victorian house (Fig. 173), of course, provides an extreme contrast, with its abundant decorative enhancements. However, while such details may seem purely external, they are integral with the exuberant architecture—emerging from structure rather than being merely stuck on.

An important part of decorative design is the texture and character of wall siding. Patterns of wood, masonry, or brick give a subtle enrichment to architectural planes, as do the accents at the edges of walls (Fig. 545). Projecting members and changes in elevation create patterns of light and shade on a building's surface, causing the "decorative design" of the sun to change constantly during the day.

Elements and Principles of Architectural Design

Throughout this text we often have used architectural examples to illustrate ways in which the elements and principles of design function. In architecture, these ingredients exist on a grand scale, so their harmonious integration is perhaps all the more vital.

Form

Architectural form is almost indistinguishable from mass. The overwhelming majority of buildings erected throughout history have been based on geometric form (Fig. 544), because the stability of the cube, the sphere, the pyramid, and the cone provide not only physical but also visual strength. Especially in cities and towns, cubes predominate simply for their ability to fit together neatly. With the introduction of new materials and building techniques, however, architects have been able to branch out into freer shapes, including forms so organic they seem to have grown right out of the earth (Fig. 546). The contempo-

547. William Turnbull's design for a house at Pajaro Dunes, Calif.

rary architect can "sculpt" a building just as freely as the artist creates form in malleable materials, whether that form be nonrepresentational or evocative of a familiar shape.

Line

As discussed in Chapter 3, line is one of the most important elements in architectural design. When we see a building from a distance, we are most aware of its lines—lines of roof, walls, and major projections. The house shown in Figure 547, set low on a hill covered with brush, makes splendid use of line for design impact. From the approach to the house the visitor would be struck first by the strong line of the roof against the sky, then perhaps by the counterpoint of short parallel lines in the steps leading up to the house. In drawing nearer the visitor can appreciate the subtle lines of vertical siding that offset the dominant horizontal. The house is meant to seem low to the ground, to blend with the hillside, and the strong horizontal roofline helps to create this impression. The opposite situation prevails in our large cities, where the lines of skyscrapers provide a predominant verticality. Line can act as a kind of symbolism, as in the vertical lines of cathedrals, which represent the aspirations of humankind toward heaven. Every medieval town was dominated by its church, for the spires would be the highest point—the dominant line—on the landscape.

Color

Most people, particularly those living in northern climates, do not associate architecture with color, so conditioned are we to the neutral grays and browns of buildings. The standard building materials—wood, masonry, steel, and concrete—have generally muted hues and do not lend themselves readily to color being introduced. Of course, wooden houses always have been painted, but homeowners generally limit themselves to the more subtle earth colors that blend with the surrounding terrain, or else to pure white, considered "appropriate" for a home.

In warmer climates color is more readily accepted in architecture, perhaps because the intense southern sun seems to vibrate with saturated colors. Also, the hues of the natural landscape are brighter in tropical regions—bluer sky, yellower sun, exotic birds and foliage. The Mexican architect Luis Barragán has become famous for buildings drawn in pure, planar shapes, often of masonry that has been dyed in hot colors—reds, pinks, oranges, and purples (Pl. 49, p. 356). In Barragán's hands these vivid structures become stable, authoritative megaliths—as classic in their context as the Parthenon is in its own.

The newer building materials such as ferrocement and plastic can be colored easily by adding dye to the mixture before it hardens. It may be that in the future we will see more color being introduced into architecture. The philosophy of each architect will largely decide whether a building should blend with its surroundings or function as an accent to them.

Texture

Texture is one of the most important elements in architecture. Most buildings have broad, flat planes that function as perfect surfaces for textural embellishment. Sometimes texture emerges from the surface quality of the actual building material, as with rough masonry or wood shingles (Fig. 548). In other cases textural decoration will be applied for a richer effect. The half-timbered houses so common in England (Fig. 549) originated because of a scarcity of lumber. However, the textural pattern of lights and darks that results from this method of construction makes a perfect background for added decorative design. By contrast, the International Style emphasizes absolutely smooth, clean surface textures, with the stress more on machined form (Fig. 544).

Unity and Variety

As with any other field of design, variety is among the most obvious traits in architecture. Our cities and towns and countryside abound

left: 548. Wood siding and shingles contribute to the eccentric appearance of a house in Oklahoma, by Herb Greene.

above: 549. Half-timber cottage in Stratford-on-Avon, England.

550. Architect Alex Riley's own house in Inverness, Calif. The recycled wood siding carries through from exterior to interior.

with buildings of incredibly diverse character. To a great extent, the architect's task is the establishment of unity—between a building's shell and its interior, its immediate surroundings, and the environment as a whole. There are many devices for creating unity between architecture and interior. Figure 550 shows one example—a house in which the same wood siding, old recycled beams, was used for both the exterior sheathing and the inside wall finish. The pattern and warm color of the wood carry through the whole house, making it seem like an entity, rather than a decorated shell.

Sometimes an architect will be faced with the problem of designing a building to blend with its environment or with nearby structures. Such was the case when Philip Johnson was commissioned to create a new wing for the Boston Public Library, a classic edifice designed by the famed architectural team of McKim, Mead, and White (Fig. 551). Johnson's solution was to keep the spirit of the original 1895 building but with thoroughly contemporary lines. Bound by the initial concept to maintain a height no greater than the main library, he designed the new wing with three large arcades that suggest but do not mirror the arched windows of the old building. In all, Johnson's design offers a striking new variety, while maintaining the unity of Copley Square.

551. Philip Johnson and John Burgee. New wing of the Boston Public Library, on Copley Square. Original building by McKim, Mead, & White 1888–92; new wing completed 1973.

Architectural Materials

The first habitable structures were made from the natural rock of caves and the skins of animals draped over temporary frames. Later, wood and brick were added to the list of materials for architecture, and the Romans made extensive use of concrete. Glass was employed sparingly until the early 20th century, when it joined with steel in the elevation of the new skyscrapers. As discussed above, ferrocement, developed in the 1940s, greatly expanded the possibilities for architectural form, allowing rounded shapes and extensions into space that would not be possible with conventional building materials.

The newest material for architecture is plastic, either attached in sheets or sprayed as a foam to some kind of framework. The house shown in Figure 552 was initially framed in wood, covered with fiberglass mesh, then sprayed with isocyanurate foam, next mineral cement, then fireproof cellular foam plastic. The resulting finish is an excellent insulator, repels water and cleans with a hose, can be painted or sprayed with color, and will not crack when penetrated by nails. With the increasing scarcity and expense of traditional materials, it may well be that architects will turn to new and untried substances.

Architecture and Function

The expression "form follows function" applies more concretely to architecture than to any other design field. Every building has a purpose, whether it is to provide a suitable place for worship of a deity, to contain offices and shops, or to house a family.

We become most aware of form in relation to function when it proves unsuccessful—when the air conditioning fails in a building that has immovable windows, for example. Similarly inappropriate would be the church allowing no provision for weddings and processions, the museum that makes it difficult to view the art, or the home in which one cannot be comfortable. Regardless of the pure architectural beauty the shell may embody, a building fails if it does not work.

In a home, the function seems obvious: shelter from weather and protection from intruders. However, function can also be a highly personal matter. Some people use their homes as centers for entertaining; others require a quiet retreat from the noises of the outside world. Many homes double as studios for painting or writing or making pottery. A doctor or dentist might maintain a home office,

552. "Environ A," architect Valerie Batorewicz' home in New Haven, Conn., combines conventional building techniques with synthetic materials.

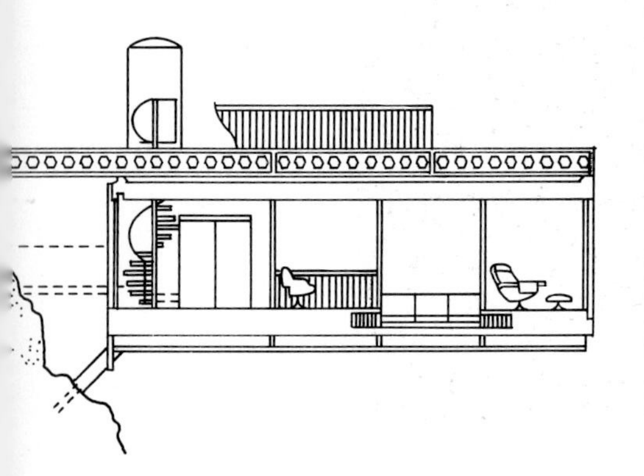

553. The great tensile strength of steel allows this house to project outward from its steep cliff site with minimum support. Harry Weese, architect.

where the public could arrive at any hour. Each of these aspects of the home suggests a different treatment from a design standpoint.

Function also takes into consideration the size and relationships of the group who will live in a particular home. In addition to the requirements for physical space, a well-designed home reflects the natural rhythms. The rhythm of the seasons dictates placement and landscaping. The daily rhythms of waking and sleeping must be considered in the arrangement of rooms and the provision for light and air. The rhythms of family growth and development should enter into the overall design. A home, if properly designed, will fulfill not only physical but psychological needs as well.

Oftentimes, function will be an expression of the site on which a home will be constructed. As a shelter, a home should minimize or absorb the natural elements according to their beneficial or adverse conditions. Though relatively few buildings consider this factor, it makes good sense to orient a house according to the climate and the effects of wind and sun. In warm climates most openings can be placed on the northern side, to present a solid front to the scorching sun from the south. Cold climates reverse the procedure.

Unusual site conditions can lead to unusual architectural solutions. The house shown in Figure 553 was almost literally "stuck into" a sharply precipitous hillside. Steel girders imbedded in the cliff give the house its only support, and most of the structure extends over thin air. The great tensile strength of steel makes this construction

554. Jorn Utzon and others. Opera House, Bennelong Point, Sydney Harbor. 1957–1973.

555. "San Simeon," the estate of William Randolph Hearst in southern California.

possible. For people capable of living in such a psychologically unstable building, the great benefit would be a dramatic view over the surrounding countryside.

Architecture as Symbol

In public architecture, symbolism may be an overriding concern. The Parthenon was intended to represent the noble ideals of the Greek civilization, a Christian church—with its cross plan and lofty spires (Fig. 221)—stood for aspirations toward heaven. Today city planners still dream in terms of concrete embodiments of a particular spirit or quality. The people of Sydney, Australia, spent more than $150 million and nearly twenty years in the construction of their magnificent Opera House (Fig. 554), whose overlapping arched roofs suggest a sailing ship in full rig—symbolic of the great harbor into which the building juts.

Nowhere in the field of design is *personal* symbolism more important than in the designing of individual shelters, for the home symbolizes a philosophy and a way of life with all its memories and goals. Ideally, the style in which the structure ultimately evolves is an expression of the preferences of the owners in materials, color, line, form, and texture. Ideas of beauty in architecture vary widely, and the design of any specific home should be a highly personal matter. In the early part of the 20th century the residential areas of most large cities revealed a great deal about their owners, for a single street might include small versions of a Norman castle, a Mediterranean villa, and a Renaissance palace. People of great wealth recreated medieval castles—sometimes stone by stone—to symbolize their identification with the elevated status of those who had occupied the originals (Fig. 555).

The present generation has a completely new set of symbols evident in the quality of their dwellings. Mobility and freedom from the bonds of material possessions are symbolized by tents and mobile homes. The distaste for grandeur and sameness has resulted in a crop of handmade houses, with materials recycled from almost anything. To a large extent, the design of a home symbolizes the particular qualities an individual feels and wishes to project to the outside world.

Architecture and Environment

In visual terms, there are two basic approaches to architectural design. One maintains that a building should stand out from its background and become an architectural statement—an imprint of human hands upon the world. The opposite point of view is held by those who feel a structure should blend into the landscape and be as unobtrusive as possible. The latter is the aesthetic behind homes painted dark brown or green, as well as those that appear to nestle into their surroundings as though they had grown there (Fig. 556).

Environmental concerns also come into play in the *functional* design of a building. The conventional house, for instance, requires considerable energy to heat, cool, and light it, and to bring in running water. The wastes generated by the house are simply carted away, with no attempt made to utilize them. With serious concern today about energy shortages, much study has been devoted to finding ways to avoid this wasteful usage.

Solar energy has attracted a great deal of attention in recent years. Houses built specifically to capture and store the energy of the sun gain much critical acclaim, but to date only prototypes have been built. Two physicists at the Massachusetts Institute of Technology took the concept of self-sufficiency even further with the design for an "autonomous" house (Fig. 557). This structure, which exists only on the drawing board, has a windmill for generating power, plus a greenhouse in which heating, cooling, and food needs would be met.

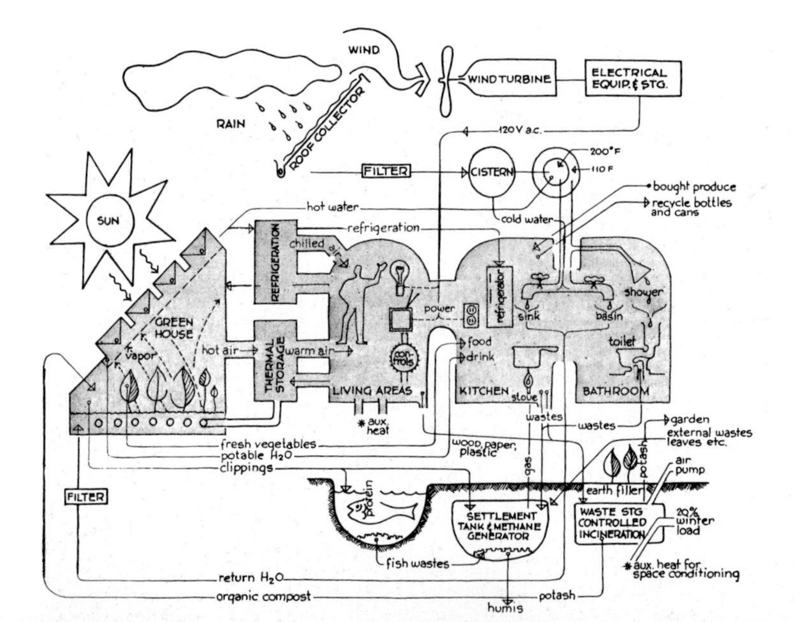

above: 556. A house design by William Turnbull of MLTW/Turnbull Associates, nestles into the Colorado landscape.

right: 557. Day Chahroudi and Sean Wellesley-Millar's design for an "autonomous house" provides for living space, a greenhouse, aquiculture, cooling and heating, waste conversion, water and electrical supply, and energy storage. Courtesy Sumtek Research Associates.

Water would be gathered naturally and wastes separated for productive reuse. There is even provision for aquiculture—the artificial cultivation of fish for protein.

Plans like the autonomous house are so far nothing but dreams. However, their vision is so drastically removed from the present reality that it seems likely a compromise can be achieved. Architectural designs that make even one step toward reconciling structure with environment serve as landmarks in the quest for function in form.

Architecture and Landscape

The landscape surrounding a building is integral with its total design. We have all seen houses erected on land flattened by the bulldozer. They seem naked and exposed, almost embarrassed. The design of an appropriate landscape creates a transition to the outside world, allowing the spaces of a house to flow beyond the walls and doors, to blend with the environment.

Landscape design, which was once something that happened to parks and large estates, today is everywhere—in parking lots with trees and planters, on rooftops with potted shrubs, in the parking strips of banks and department stores. Many towns have planters along their main streets or have hanging baskets suspended from the lampposts. All of this is an effort to bring nature into an environment built by and for human beings.

The elements and principles of design play a vital role in the planning of a landscape. Line and shape will establish the degree of order, so that the overall effect can be flowing and natural (Fig. 558), or it can mimic the geometric treatment of historic formal gardens. Vertical line is created by the use of trees, whose trunks form strong, dark accents contrasting with the colors of the garden (Fig. 559). In the winter, the stark bare branches become dramatic linear accents against the sky.

Probably the first element that comes to mind in landscape design is color, because flowers and flowering trees make up such an important part of the designed landscape. Tree trunks and branches contribute much to color as well, for even bark tone often changes from season to season. A landscape designer must consider winter color as well as summer, including evergreens and plants whose bare branches have interesting reds or yellows to replace the more spectacular colors of summer flowers. Beautiful gardens have been designed around

left: 558. A natural garden centered around a pond, in Carmel, Calif.

above: 559. Trees provide the accent of vertical lines and, when in blossom, a splash of color in a garden.

greens alone, with lawns, evergreens, and border plants that require little upkeep but offer almost unlimited variety. Fences and walls supply yet more color, and colored gravel for walks and drives, or low plants for small areas of ground cover may be effective.

After color, texture is no doubt the most obvious element in landscape design. The possibilities for textural contrast are unlimited, considering the rough textures of bark, the billowing effects of flowers or shrubs, the smooth relief of lawn or paved walk (Fig. 560).

560. A Japanese-style garden is a study in textural contrasts. Design by G. K. Scott.

The Japanese garden is a masterpiece of simplicity. Japanese philosophy envisions human beings as tiny figures in a vast natural setting; consequently, the Japanese gardener adapts the natural environment, accentuating its charm with a few plants selected carefully for the lines of their branches and the texture of their leaves. A single azalea or chrysanthemum may be given major importance, so the viewer can fully appreciate the details of its beauty. Bonsai—miniature plants and trees—are a feature of any Oriental garden (Fig. 560), as are stone lanterns in a variety of shapes, each carrying an important philosophical connotation. Trees and shrubs may be radically pruned to create dramatic or symbolic lines, contrasting with round stepping stones across a pool or stream. The Japanese see plants as possessing human traits of character and attribute specific personalities to the wild plum, the willow, the chrysanthemum, and so on. The bamboo is considered to have the ideal combination of gentlemanly virtues, judged by its behavior under diverse conditions. In spite of the difference in basic philosophy, the western world has long admired the Japanese garden and attempted to copy it.

If there is one principle of design that comes naturally to a garden, it is variety. There are more than 300,000 different kinds of plants in the world, and the variety is infinite—in color, shape, line, texture, and size.

The visual rhythm of a garden is achieved by the controlled use of space for plantings and for walkways. Sweeping lawns possess a kind of rhythm, as do flower beds with curving edges. The biomorphic shape of a pond is rhythmic, and there is rhythm in curved walks or in the shape of a patio. Repetition comes from patterns of similar shapes or from a fence or wall that reappears at intervals under the growth of vines or climbing bushes. Emphasis may be focused on a pond, a piece of sculpture, a furniture grouping, or a single beautiful plant or tree.

Balance derives from color, texture, and mass played against one another in satisfying proportions. Evergreens spaced to appear on both sides of a patio, colors of flowers or shrubs repeated in various places along a wall, trees of similar species located in more than one position in a yard—these are typical of the manner in which balance transforms a landscape into a total unity. Balance and unity are implicit in nature, and the landscape designer who learns to work with the natural processes and rhythms finds that these principles appear readily with a little conscious direction.

Architecture and landscape provide the most dramatic opportunity for the designer to make an imprint on the natural world. They are integral with one another and with the broader environment, for each building is part of a community and each community is part of the earth as a whole. The ultimate extension of the designer's art is the planning of whole communities and environments—the essence of total design.

Community and Environment

The opportunity to plan a whole environment has tempted designers since the beginning of civilization. In the 5th century B.C. Pericles, the Athenian leader, superintended the complete reconstruction of the Acropolis in Athens along lines that would symbolize the noble ideals of Greek culture. Nearly 2500 years later Adolf Hitler, with a purpose more grandiose than grand, set his architect Albert Speer to the task of redesigning Berlin as an imperial city. In between there were many other projects of total design, which were initiated for one of three reasons: some disaster had leveled a preexisting complex, thus wiping the slate clean for new building; a serious problem existed which could be eliminated only by a whole new design; or it became desirable to open up new territory—either geographically or conceptually.

All three of these potential stimuli for design still operate today. The designer faced with the overwhelming task of creating an environment has at once tremendous power and the possibility of failure on a monumental scale. A painting that does not come off as the artist intended can be stuck away in the back of the studio or simply destroyed. But an unsuccessful city cannot be hidden.

So many considerations enter into environmental design that the designer must be at once architect, engineer, psychologist, sociologist,

561. The Plaza, Place Ville Marie, Montreal.

social worker, visionary, and—all too often—publicist. In any community design one must always remember that large numbers of people will be affected, and people's reactions are not predictable to any high degree. The basic material of the community is not stone and glass and steel, but human lives.

Community Design

The motivations behind design for a self-contained community may be any one of the following: total planning for new construction; redesign of an existing area; rebuilding something that has been destroyed; preservation and restoration of historical sites; or simply beautification. Each of these gives the designer broad latitude in establishing the character of a community.

During the post-World War II era, one of the most fertile areas for the designer was in the suburbs that began to spring up around all the large cities. The major population trend before the war had been from rural areas to the cities; afterwards, it shifted from cities to "bedroom communities." As the people moved out of the cities, commerce followed them. Downtown merchants and banks had no choice but to build branches in the suburbs.

The suburban shopping center was one of the phenomenal developments of the mid-20th century. It provided shoppers with ample parking space, attractive surroundings, and large landscaped areas where they were free from the hazards of traffic while they shopped (Fig. 561). Centers became increasingly elaborate, with restaurants, small theaters, flower beds, fountains, statuary, and architectural embellishments.

The idea of a traffic-free shopping area really is not new. In 1860 the city of Milan, Italy, staged a competition inviting all citizens to submit designs for a covered *galleria,* to be built in the center of town. The winning plan was that of Giuseppe Mengoni, and in 1867 the Galleria Vittorio Emanuele was officially opened to the public (Fig. 562). It consists of two covered streets, 643 and 344 feet long respectively, intersecting in the form of a Latin cross. The glass roof soars to a height of 88 feet and culminates in a central cupola 160 feet above

the ground. Within this spectacular enclosure are nearly a hundred smart shops, plus elegant restaurants and cafés. Since its inception the Galleria has been a meeting place for artists, writers, and musicians, as well as a gathering point for the entire population of Milan. In summer the airy coolness of the Galleria attracts throngs of tourists. The structure was heavily damaged in World War II, but it was completely rebuilt within twelve years. Today it stands as a monument to intelligence and foresight in city planning.

Not all designed communities are meant for people. Under special circumstances the designer may be called upon to plan an environment for animals outside their natural habitat—in other words, a zoo. Many cities around the world vie for the honor of maintaining the "best" zoo, but in the United States few would challenge the absolute distinction of the zoo built by the city of San Diego. Although adjacent to the downtown area, the San Diego Zoo (Fig. 563) sprawls over a huge area comprising hundreds of acres. Like any zoo, it is intended as a place for people to see animals they would not normally be exposed to, but all design was considered from the point of view of the animals. Enclosures resemble as closely as possible the native terrain of each species, and the animals are provided with ample space in which to hide, if that is their inclination. The success of this designed environment is demonstrated by the large population of baby animals.

above: 562. Giuseppe Mengoni. Galleria Vittorio Emanuele, Milan. Completed 1867.

below: 563. Cascade Canyon and sitatunga, San Diego Zoo.

564. Larimer Square in Denver is graced by intersecting arcaded walkways and attractive shop fronts.

Redesign of an existing area often begins with the desire to eliminate urban blight. Larimer Street was the "skid row" of Denver until a group of inspired citizens formed the Larimer Square Association and renovated a block-long segment of the area (Fig. 564). Oldtime façades were retained, while arcades leading into courts and walkways encouraged artists and shopkeepers to establish galleries. Such oases have blossomed throughout the United States—Old Town in Chicago, Pioneer Square in Seattle, Ghirardelli Square in San Francisco, and many others. Renovation of this kind represents community design at its best, the cooperation of local vision and abilities to transform an eyesore into an attraction.

Design for rebuilding usually follows some natural or man-made disaster. It operated in San Francisco after the great earthquake and fire of 1906; in London after the catastrophic fire of 1666 leveled the city; and in most of Europe following World War II. A striking example of urban reconstruction can be seen in Rotterdam, where the core of the city had to be entirely rebuilt (Fig. 565). The Town Hall, one of only two major buildings that survived the bombing, today stands as the focal point of a new pedestrian mall and town center. A disaster area was converted into a model city that has provided inspiration to people in all parts of the world.

A major approach to the problem of preserving the city has been made in Norfolk, Virginia. Old Ghent, a rundown former residential community, has been rehabilitated by the Norfolk Rehabilitation and Housing Authority. This agency uses private funds to provide low-interest loans for conserving and rebuilding the big, comfortable houses of a former era, which subsequently have come into great demand (Fig. 566). The success of the venture has inspired the renovation of a blighted area adjacent to Old Ghent and extending into the downtown area, a development known as Ghent Square. Slum land was cleared and rezoned to accommodate more than four hundred middle- and upper-income houses, as well as specialty shops and boutiques. Textures and materials are consistent in both developments. A Colonial lighting system and extensive use of maples and magnolias in parks and malls unify Old Ghent with Ghent Square.

Attempts to beautify the cityscape have taken many forms, including large murals, mosaics, "pocket" parks, and landscaping. Gene Davis' approach to the Washington Mall is unique (Pl. 50, p. 356). The painting of huge multicolor stripes down the length of the mall was not intended as a permanent fixture. Like Christo's earthworks (Fig. 10), its point is to place art in a new context, to consider the landscape (or in this case the cityscape) from a completely different point of view. Such a work accomplishes more in opening our eyes to the possibilities for community design than it does in and of itself.

Design for Cities

The city originated as a solution to a problem. When medieval cities were built, they consisted of clusters of people gathered together for mutual protection. Strong walls encircled the houses and shops, and as the population grew, outer walls were erected, creating the faubourg or "false city" between the two walls. Central areas grew up around plazas, civic buildings, and churches (Fig. 567).

above left: 565. Town Hall of Rotterdam, seen from the Lijnbaan shopping center, the first post-war pedestrian mall and town center in Europe.

above right: 566. Renovated attached houses in Old Ghent, a residential community in Norfolk, Va.

right: 567. View of Siena, Italy.

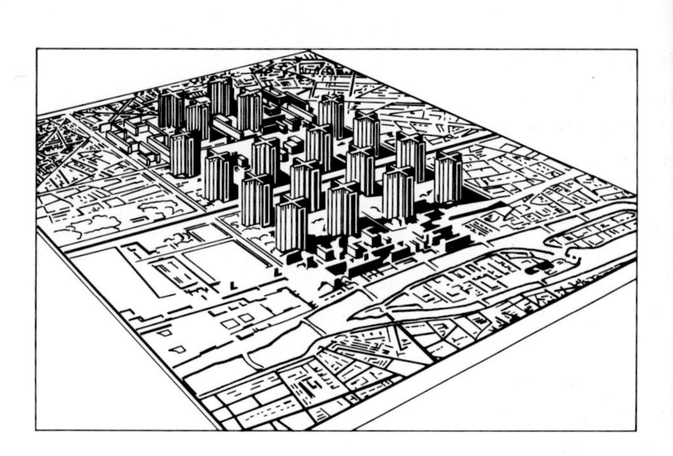

left: 568. A model of Le Corbusier's Voisin Plan (1925), which would have redesigned the center of Paris to provide skyscraper housing and much open space.

right: 569. The Paseo del Rio, or River Walk, is the focus of downtown San Antonio, Tex.

The advent of the machine in the 18th and 19th centuries brought dramatic changes to the city—new developments in transportation that revolutionized commerce and the beginnings of industry that would eventually transform the world. It also brought the metropolitan slum and the industrial factory district, which rapidly became breeding places for civic turmoil. In the two centuries since the Industrial Revolution began, the situation in the cities has become so critical that many plans have been formulated to correct it.

Among the first designers to take an interest in rebuilding 20th-century cities was Le Corbusier, who in 1925 designed a model for the reconstruction of Paris (Fig. 568). This model, known as the Voisin (neighbor) Plan, embodied his theory that most cities need sweeping renovation rather than small and often uncoordinated reforms. Corbu's theory is widely endorsed today, yet his Voisin Plan has been deemed inadequate to the psychological and sociological problems of contemporary cities. In this plan, housing was to be centralized in sixteen glass-walled skyscrapers in the heart of the city, thus stacking houses vertically instead of allowing them to spread horizontally. Such a system would lift people above the fumes and noise of the city, as well as conserving land area. The keynote of the plan was balance. Each building was to be designed in such a way that the negative space surrounding it was at least equal to the positive area of the building, providing each of four wings with air, sunlight, and a view of the city. Landscaped areas were to surround the buildings, balancing the structure with the soft textures and colors of nature. The plan did not materialize in Paris, but it served as a model for many other cities.

In a few cases, the total redesign of a city has taken advantage of some natural feature, such as a river. This was the case with San Antonio, Texas, whose river, winding through the downtown area, had become a city dump, its shores lined with trash, old tires, and rusting automobiles. Because the San Antonio River brought periodic devastation by flooding, city planners suggested covering it with concrete and using it as a sewer. Farsighted citizens had other ideas. After 23 years of study, they set up a River Walk Commission to prepare a master plan for the development of the river as a scenic attraction. Today the Paseo del Rio is a thriving business area, lined with shops and exotic restaurants, featuring beautifully landscaped vistas that serve as a center of attraction for both residents and visitors (Fig. 569). The entire downtown area focuses on the River Walk.

The opportunity to design an entire new town or city provides the ultimate in creative possibilities. In the depression years of the 1930s the U.S. Federal Government purchased land near three large cities for the purpose of creating jobs by building model communities. The new towns would house workers near industrial areas, yet give them an attractive and satisfying life away from the noise and overcrowding of the city. The three towns constructed were Greenbelt, Maryland, Greenhills, Ohio, and Greendale, Wisconsin. The planners followed the example set earlier by Radburn, New Jersey, the first community in the United States to separate traffic from residential areas in such a way that the pedestrian could move without encountering automobiles.

Typical of the design concept is Greendale (Fig. 570), in which open areas and belts of trees curve in biomorphic shapes that soften the rectangles of the residential streets. These shapes are integrated throughout the community in such a way that all living areas face parks or open country. Kitchens and utility rooms open onto quiet service roads, so that daily chores can be carried out in an unobtrusive manner, and each house is set on a plot of ground large enough to ensure real privacy. The individual home is more important than any arbitrary consistency of line along a street. Many residential streets terminate in dead ends or curve to join other streets adapted to the topography of the land. Wherever possible, sidewalks cross thoroughfares by means of underpasses. Materials for houses were chosen with variety in mind, and paint colors were selected to make each home as individual as possible. Fulfilling the original designers' hopes, these three towns have provided inspiration to other cities seeking to escape the deadly monotony of the usual suburban patterns and to find a means of establishing a full and attractive community life.

One of the most impressive steps toward the city of the future was the construction during the middle of the 20th century of a new capital city for Brazil. For centuries the capital of Brazil had been Rio de Janeiro, a thriving but increasingly crowded metropolis squeezed along the coastal region. Far inland a vast plateau offered a wealth of natural resources, an invigorating climate, and unlimited space and land. For more than a century, successive governments had pledged themselves to move the capital inland, but it was not until 1956, when Juscelino Kubitschek took office as president, that the promise was realized. The result was Brasilia, a completely new city built in a record-breaking four years (Fig. 571). In 1960 the government was formally moved into new and dramatically modern buildings, in a city that was planned in every aspect for its specific purpose.

The plan for Brasilia was chosen in a worldwide competition, and the winning design was the work of Lucio Costa. Costa's plan is particularly appropriate to a new city in the space age, for it roughly

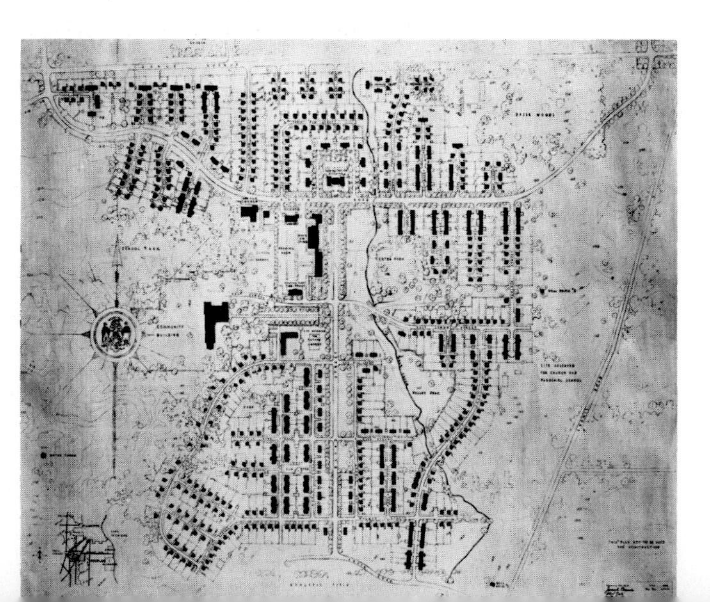

570. An architect's drawing of the city of Greendale, Wis., shows a balance between structures and open green areas.

left: 571. View of the government center, Brasilia, showing the Senate dome, the Palácio do Planalto, Congress Administrative Offices, and the Chamber of Deputies.

right: 572. R. Buckminster Fuller's model of "Triton City," a single floating neighborhood module designed to house approximately 5000 people.

approximates the shape of an airplane. Buildings and development follow the contours of a large lake that was created as part of the design. Structures are arranged according to function: the ministry and legislative group are placed where the engine of the plane would be; commerical establishments, public parks, and the stadium correspond to the fuselage; and residential structures fill the area of the wings. Architect Oscar Niemeyer designed all the public buildings, integrating them into an overall unity of stark modern lines. The president's palace, with its silhouetted forms like huge paper cutouts across the front, has become the symbol of Brasilia.

Most of the architecture is of concrete block and glass, a fitting contemporary expression that stands between the Portuguese colonial architecture of the coastal area and the art of the Indians in the Amazon Basin. The buildings are set wide apart so that their spacious surroundings preserve the spirit of the frontier. There are no street intersections, for all crossings are cloverleafs, overpasses, or underpasses. The conventional grid pattern of the typical city has been abandoned. Brasilia has no hub with avenues radiating from it; rather, it follows an organic arrangement consistent with the contours of a carefully designed location.

Brasilia is an interesting experiment because of its contribution to the art of city design and also because of its sociological implications. When the new city was opened, population came slowly, and the lawmakers had a tendency to fly back to Rio immediately after discharging their official duties. The question of whether an entire

573. Paolo Soleri's design for "Arcosanti," a community dedicated to the arts and handcrafts. The structure is being built in the Arizona desert.

population can be transplanted intact from one area to another with lasting success is still in the process of being answered. City growth is an organic phenomenon, involving many personal tastes and needs. The mere planning of an ideal situation on paper, or even the execution of the plan, does not always prove to be the answer to the requirements of a group of individuals who, even in an era of mobility, have a tendency to resist change.

Design for the Future

Since the city is recognized as one of the major problems of the 20th century, it is a favorite project for designers, and the city of the future as designed on paper takes many forms. The space age and its discoveries make even the most fantastic designs a possibility. Suggestions have been made for platform towns with traffic moving in corridors under the ground, and for multitiered cities a mile wide and 20 miles long, that eventually would join city to city. Plans have been drawn for satellite cities to be situated in "rural rings" around existing metropolises, and for cellular cities and towns in which a number of community units are placed around a central urban core. R. Buckminster Fuller, developer of the geodesic dome, has formulated designs for a floating city (Fig. 572). There are several versions of this—one intended for anchorage just offshore, another meant to float, in total self-sufficiency, in mid-ocean.

One of the most interesting designs for total living is Paolo Soleri's "Arcosanti," now under construction in the desert of Arizona (Fig. 573). The underlying principle of Arcosanti is concentration of citizens in a small area, this area to be surrounded by miles of open space. Soleri feels that people function best when bound into coherent groups, but that broad areas for farming and recreation should be immediately at hand. His city design is the direct opposite of suburban sprawl. It is as though one could take the entire population of a spreading metropolis, stack it efficiently in one huge megastructure, and leave the rest of the land free. Soleri's designs are truly visionary. The ultimate "arcology" in his system might stand three hundred stories high and cover 14 square miles of land.

Total design for cities does not stop with the earth. Space scientists are right now planning the configuration of orbiting space communities as well as fixed extraterrestrial towns (Fig. 574). The construction of cities beyond the earth gives the designer infinite space to mold—a space undreamed of in the history of human design. As in every other design field, a primary concern must be for balance—balance between imagination and practicality, between technology and nature, between the future and the past, and between science and the living individual.

574. Design for a 20th-century space colony orbiting between the earth and the moon. The cylinder is 19 miles long and 4 miles in diameter, with a potential to accommodate a population ranging between 200,000 and several million people.

Glossary

Terms italicized within the definitions are themselves defined in the Glossary.

abstract Broadly, *nonobjective, nonrepresentational;* originating with a recognizable form, but simplified or distorted in some way.

Abstract Expressionism An art style, also called the "New York School," that emerged after World War II, and which emphasized *nonobjective* form, spontaneous invention, and frequently evidence of energetic activity on the part of the artist, leading to the term "Action Painting."

achromatic Having no color, a *neutral* such as black, white, or gray.

acrylic A *plastic* which in solid form is usually rigid, clear, and transparent; also, a *binder* for *pigments* used in painting.

Action Painting See *Abstract Expressionism.*

additive primary colors In light, those *primary* colors—red, blue, and green—which in theory can be blended to add up to white light, or all light.

additive Descriptive of a sculptural method in which *form* is created by building up material, as by *modeling* or welding. Compare *subtractive.*

afterimage A physiological phenomenon in which the retina of the eye becomes fatigued after viewing any *hue* for a sustained period of time, causing the *complementary color* to be seen.

analogous Referring to colors adjacent on a *color wheel.*

appliqué A fabric-decorating technique in which various shapes, colors, and types of material are stitched onto a background to create a design.

aquatint In *printmaking,* a variation of the *intaglio* process in which a porous *ground* of resin is applied to a plate, after which the plate is dipped by stages into an acid bath to create a range of tonal *values.*

arcade A series of *arches* supported by piers or columns to form an open passageway.

arch A structural device, generally any opening spanned by a curved top supported by two uprights. The true arch consists of wedge-shaped blocks placed in a semicircle and in counterthrust, so that they converge on a keystone at the center of the opening.

Art Nouveau A decorative design style of the 1890s, based primarily on flowing, curvilinear plant and animal forms.

assemblage The act of creating a work of art by joining together objects or fragments of objects that often initially served some other purposes; also, the work so created.

atmospheric perspective The effect of an intervening body of air between an object and a viewer, causing a softening of outlines, blurring and cooling of colors, and loss of detail at the horizon; the simulation of depth in two-dimensional art by the portrayal of this effect.

bas relief or **low relief** Sculpture in which the figures are attached to a background, projecting only slightly from it.

batik A form of resist dyeing for fabric in which nonprinting portions of a design are "stopped out" with wax to prevent color penetration.

Bauhaus A school of design founded in Germany in 1919, known for its adaptation of design principles to mass production; also descriptive of the works, especially furniture, designed by the staff.

bilateral symmetry A type of design balance in which the two halves of a composition formed by a bisector are mirror images of one another.

binder A substance in paints that causes the *pigment* particles to hold together and to a *support.*

biomorphic Taken from nature; from the Greek meaning structure based on life.

calligraphy The art of beautiful writing.

cantilever A structural member, as in architecture, projecting from an upright and unsupported at the opposite end.

cartoon A drawing, made to scale on paper, used in transferring designs as a basis for painting, mosaic, or tapestry.

casein A painting *medium* in which the *pigment* is bound with milk curd.

casting The process of forming a liquid or *plastic* substance into a specific shape by pouring it into a mold and allowing it to harden.

chasing A decorative technique for metal in which the exterior surface is repeatedly struck by a rounded tool propelled by a hammer.

chiaroscuro The use of dark and light *value* areas in a painting to imitate effects of light and shadow found in nature.

china A commercial white ceramic ware similar to *porcelain,* firing in the higher temperature ranges.

chroma See *intensity.*

cire-perdue or **lost wax** A method of *casting* metal in which a model is coated with wax and a mold built around it. When heated, the wax melts and flows out, leaving a cavity into which molten metal can be poured and allowed to solidify.

cloisonné An *enameling* technique in which color or design areas are separated by thin metal wires fused to the metal base.

coiling A forming method for clay in which rolls of *plastic* material are joined together.

collage A predominantly two-dimensional work of art to which pieces of paper, cloth, or other materials are pasted. Loosely, any assembly of materials to create a design.

collagraph A *print* made from a surface that has been built up in the manner of a *collage.*

color wheel A circular arrangement of colors that expresses their relationships according to a particular color theory.

complementary colors Colors opposite one another on a *color wheel,* which, when mixed together in equal parts, form a *neutral,* or, in the case of light, form white light.

composition An ordered relationship among parts or elements of a design.

conceptual art A work of art or an event that depends primarily upon an intellectual concept conceived by the artist.

conceptual imagery *Imagery* derived from imagination, emotion, dreams, or other internal sources; compare *perceptual imagery.*

content The subject matter of a work of art, including its emotional, intellectual, symbolic, thematic, and narrative connotations

contour In two-dimensional art, a line that represents the edge of a form or group of forms.

cross hatching A series of intersecting sets of parallel lines used to indicate shading or volume in a drawing.

Cubism An art style developed by Pablo Picasso and Georges Braque, beginning in 1907, characterized by faceted forms, flattened *pictorial space,* and *figure-ground* ambiguity.

decorative design Embellishment or surface enrichment of an object. Decorative design may be inherent in structure or may be applied once the structure is completed.

dome A hemisphere or inverted cup, theoretically the result of rotating an *arch* on its axis.

drypoint A method of *intaglio printmaking* in which a metal plate is needled with a sharp point that raises a burr, or curl of metal. The burr gives drypoint its characteristically soft, velvety quality.

ductility The capacity of metal for being drawn out or hammered thin without breaking.

earthenware A coarse, porous, usually reddish ceramic ware fired in the low temperature ranges.

earthworks Large-scale sculptural works that actually transform the landscape.

embroidery The technique of decorating fabric by use of colored threads worked in a variety of stitches.

enameling The art of creating designs in colored glassy materials, which are fused to metal.

encaustic A type of paint in which the *binder* is wax.

engraving An *intaglio printmaking* technique in which an image is created by scratching into a metal plate with a sharp tool. Ink is introduced into the depressions, and then paper is forced in to make an impression.

etching An *intaglio printmaking* process in which acid acts as the cutting agent. A metal plate is coated with acid resist, the resist is scratched away in image (or printing) areas, and then the plate is dipped in acid.

Expressionism An early-20th-century art movement that emphasized the artist's emotional response to experience, especially through the use of color and symbolic *imagery.*

façade The exterior, usually the front, of a building.

Fauvism A movement in painting originating in France in 1905, characterized by the unconventional, apparently arbitrary use of bright, contrasting colors for structural and expressive effects.

felting A method of making cloth by interlocking loose *fibers* together through a combination of heat, moisture, and pressure.

fiber A material, either natural or synthetic, capable of being made into yarn or thread.

figure-ground A relationship, usually in two-dimensional art, between a *form* and its background or surroundings. Figure-ground ambiguity refers to the inability to distinguish between the two.

foreshortening A device used in two-dimensional art to portray organic or anatomical *forms* in such a way that they appear to project from or recede behind the *picture plane;* a means of creating spatial depth in figures.

form 1. The underlying structure or *composition* in a work of art. 2. The shape or outline of something. 3. The essence of a work of art—its medium or mode of expression. 4. The substance of something, as "solid or liquid form."

fresco A painting *medium* often used for murals in which the paint is applied to a *ground* of wet plaster.

geodesic dome A *dome* first devised by R. Buckminster Fuller, composed of small *modules* based on the triangle.

gesso A mixture of white *pigment,* glue, and plaster or gypsum that serves as a *ground* for *tempera.*

glaze 1. A glassy, vitreous coating fired onto ceramic ware for decoration and/or waterproofing. 2. A thin layer of paint applied to canvas or other base in one or more layers, in an effort to achieve transparency or *luminosity* in a painting.

gouache Opaque *watercolor* paint in which the *binder* is gum arabic and a paste of zinc oxide.

graphic Descriptive of the arts involving drawing or writing. "Graphic design" usually means design for a printed format, such as advertising, books, magazines, and packaging.

gray scale A series of *value* gradations between white and black.

grisaille An *enameling* technique utilizing only black, white, and shades of gray. Thin layers of white are applied to a dark background for shaded effects.

ground 1. A preliminary material applied to a *support* in preparation for the drawing or painting *medium.* 2. The background or general area of a *picture plane* as distinguished from *forms* or figures. See *figure-ground.*

hard-edge A style of art developed in the mid-20th century, in which *forms* are depicted and separated by meticulous, regular, geometric lines.

hatching A series of closely spaced parallel lines used to indicate shading or volume in a drawing.

haut relief or **high relief** Sculpture in which *forms* project from a background to considerable depth.

hue The pure state of any color; the name by which a color is called.

iconography 1. The visual *imagery* used to convey the meaning of a work of art, and the conventions governing such imagery. 2. The study of various forms of meaning to be found in pictorial representations. 3. Loosely, the "story" behind a work of art, especially religious or mythological symbolism.

imagery The art of making images, or pictures, as in drawing or painting, to represent or evoke a particular thing. See also *perceptual imagery, conceptual imagery.*

impasto The thick application of paint to a *support;* also, the three-dimensional surface that results from such application.

Impressionism An art style originating in France in the 1870s, in which artists sought to represent in paint transitory effects of light, shade, and color that occur in nature.

inlay A method of decorating wood (and sometimes metal, ivory, shell, or other material) by inserting small and often contrasting pieces of material into a backing to form a design.

intaglio 1. A *printmaking* method in which the image area is recessed below the surface of the plate. Compare *relief.* 2. Any depressed image created by carving, cutting, or incising.

intensity The relative purity or grayness of a color. Colors that are not grayed are said to have "high intensity," and the converse.

iridescence The rainbow effect by which a material or surface seems to reflect all the *hues* of the spectrum, as a result of light playing on it.

linear perspective A system for depicting three-dimensional depth on a two-dimensional surface, dependent upon the illusion that parallel lines receding into space converge at a point, known as the "*vanishing point.*"

lithography A *planographic* or flat-surface *printmaking* technique, in which the image areas are neither depressed nor raised. (Compare *relief* and *intaglio.*) Printing depends upon the mutual antipathy of grease and water.

local color The color of things seen under standard light without shadows; the "real" color of objects in the natural world.

lost-wax casting See *cire-perdue.*

luminal art Art, especially sculpture, of which light is an element.

luminosity The actual or illusory effect of giving off light.

luster The glow of reflected light.

macramé A *fiber*-construction technique in which *form* is achieved by knotting strands into varied patterns.

medium 1. The material used for a work of art. 2. The basis for a paint, such as oil. 3. The form of expression in a work of art, such as painting or *printmaking.*

mezzotint An *intaglio printmaking* process in which the plate is initially roughened with a tool called a rocker, then gradually smoothed for intermediate *values,* working from dark to light.

Minimal Art A style of painting and sculpture in the mid-20th century in which *form* is achieved by the barest means—contour shape, flat surface, and sometimes pure, unmodulated color. Minimal works tend to be geometric and machined in their precision.

modeling 1. Shaping objects from *plastic* material, such as clay. 2. In drawing or painting, effects of light and shadow that create the illusion of three-dimensional volume.

modular Characterized by repetitive and/or interconnecting units that can be assembled in different ways, especially in furniture or architecture.

monochromatic Having only one *hue,* possibly with gradations of *value* or *intensity.*

monoprint A one-of-a-kind *print* made by transferring to paper an image drawn on a plate, usually of glass.

mosaic An art form in which pieces of glass, ceramic tile, or other materials are fitted together to form a design and then glued or cemented to a background.

neutral A color not associated with any particular *hue,* such as gray or tan.

niello A technique of decorating metal with black *pigment* forced into incised lines.

nonobjective Having no resemblance to natural forms or objects.

nonrepresentational See *nonobjective.*

normal value The *value* of any color when it is in its pure, unmixed state.

Op Art An art style of the mid-20th century concerned with optical stimulation and manipulation, including the creation of optical illusions, a sense of vibration, and *afterimages.*

palette 1. The range of colors used for a painting. 2. The range of colors characteristically used by a single artist or group of artists. 3. The surface on which an artist mixes paint.

patina A surface coating on metal that results from natural oxidation or from the application of certain chemicals.

perceptual imagery *Imagery* derived from experience or perception of the natural world.

Photorealism An art style of the mid-20th century, in which objects or people are depicted with photographic accuracy.

pictorial space The apparent or illusionary space in a painting, as it appears to recede backward from the *picture plane.*

picture plane An imaginary flat surface assumed to be at the front surface of a painting.

pigment A colorant ground into a fine powder and used to color paints or dyes.

pile weave A weave characterized by protruding tufts or loops of fiber.
pinching A method of shaping clay with the fingers.
plain weave A basic *weave* characterized by a regular alternating sequence of one-up, one-down interlacings of *warp* and *weft* yarns.
plane A flat surface. See *picture plane.*
planography A *printmaking* method in which the printing surface is flat, neither raised nor recessed. See *lithography.*
plastic 1. Capable of being molded or shaped. 2. Solid, sculptural, three-dimensional. 3. Any of numerous synthetic substances composed principally of carbon compounds in long molecular chains.
plasticity The ability of a material to be molded or shaped; also, solidity, three-dimensionality.
plique-à-jour An *enameling* technique similar to *cloisonné,* but with the metal base removed after firing for a translucent effect.
pointillism A technique of applying tiny dots of color to canvas. The term is used especially in connection with the work of Georges Seurat.
Pop Art An art style dating from the mid-1950s that takes as its subject matter popular, mass-produced symbols.
porcelain A pure, white, hard ceramic ware that fires at a very high temperature; used especially for fine dinnerware and figurines.
post-and-lintel A structural system in architecture in which beams or lintels are placed horizontally across upright posts.
post-Impressionism A loose term to designate the various painting styles following *Impressionism,* during the period 1885 to 1900. The term is applied primarily to the works of Van Gogh, Cézanne, Gauguin, Seurat, and their followers.
primary color One of the basic colors on any *color wheel,* which it is assumed cannot be mixed from other colors, but which serves as a basis for mixing all combinations on the wheel.
print An impression made (usually) on paper from a master plate, stone, or block created by an artist, most often repeated many times for multiple images that are identical or similar. Also, a similar process applied to cloth.
printmaking The art of making *prints.*
proportion Size or weight relationships among structures or among elements in a single structure. Compare *scale.*
quilting The process of sewing together small pieces of cloth (in a pattern or at random) to form a design, and then stitching to create a puffed surface.
radial symmetry Balance achieved by the arrangement of elements in a circular pattern around a central core.
refraction The bending of a ray of light as it passes through a prism or a lens.
relief 1. A printmaking process in which portions of the image to be printed are raised above the surface of the plate or block. Compare *intaglio.* 2. Any raised image, as in sculpture.
relief sculpture Sculpture attached to a background from which it projects. See *bas relief, haut relief.*
repoussé A forming technique for metal in which punches driven by hammers push the metal out from its reverse side to create a low *relief* design on the front.
saturation See *intensity.*
scale Size or weight relationships in a structure or between structures, especially as measured by some standard, such as the human body.
secco A method of painting in which color is applied to dry plaster walls.
secondary color A color created by mixing two primary colors on any *color wheel.*
serialism A visual expression, especially in painting, sculpture, or photography, in which individual works are not considered to be entities but are part of a continuum.
serigraphy A *printmaking* process based on stencils or screens. See *silk screen.*
shade A variation of any color that is darker than its *normal value.*
silk screen A *printmaking* method in which the image is transferred to paper or cloth by forcing ink through fine mesh screens, usually of silk, in which nonprinting areas are "stopped out" to prevent color penetration.
simultaneous contrast The tendency of *complementary* colors to intensify each other when placed side by side.
slab construction A method of forming clay by rolling it into flat sheets and then joining the sheets to each other or to other *forms.*
slip Liquid clay the consistency of cream, used mainly for casting.
split complement A combination of colors involving one *hue* and the hues on either side of its *complement* on a *color wheel.*
stained glass Glass that has been colored and arranged in pieces to create a design or pattern. Often the pieces are joined by strips of lead.
stitchery Any fabric decorating technique in which the thread stitches predominate on the surface and carry the major design.
stoneware A relatively hard, vitreous ceramic ware, usually gray or tan, and firing in the middle range of temperatures.
structural design Design concerned with the creation of basic *form* in an object, as distinguished from its surface enrichment.
stylization The simplification of a form to emphasize design qualities.
subtractive Descriptive of a sculptural method in which *form* is created by carving or cutting away material. Compare *additive.*
subtractive primary colors Those colors—cyan (turquoise), magenta, and yellow—which subtract from white light the wavelengths for all colors except the one seen.
successive contrast The phenomenon by which the *afterimage* of a visual impression appears to the closed eyes in the complementary colors of its original.

support In two-dimensional art, the material to which the drawing or painting *medium* is applied, as a canvas.
Surrealism An art movement originating in the early 20th century, which emphasized intuitive and non-rational ways of working as a means of recreating the chance relationships and the symbols that often occur in dreams.
synthesia A sympathetic stimulation of senses, for example, the sensing of color in relation to musical sounds.
tapestry A type of *weaving* in which the *weft* yarn carries the design and appears on the surface of the fabric only in specific design areas.
tempera A painting *medium* in which the *pigment* is bound together with egg yolk or with animal or vegetable glue.
tensile strength A characteristic of metal or other material that makes it possible for it to be stretched or extended without breaking.
tesserae Small pieces of glass, tile, stone, or other material used in a *mosaic.*
tetrad Any four colors equidistant from one another on a *color wheel.*
thermoplastic Descriptive of *plastics* that can be reheated and reshaped without undergoing chemical change.
thermosetting Descriptive of *plastics* that undergo a chemical change during curing and become permanently shaped.
tint A variation of any color that is lighter than its *normal value.*
tone A softened color achieved by mixing a pure *hue* with gray or with its *complement.*
triad Any group of three colors equidistant from each other on a *color wheel.*
trompe-l'oeil French for "fool-the-eye"; a two-dimensional visual representation so carefully contrived that the viewer has the illusion of seeing a three-dimensional object or space.
truss A structural form consisting of rigid bars or beams arranged in a system of triangles joined at their apexes; found in architecture and especially bridge design.
value The lightness or darkness of a color.
vanishing point In *linear perspective,* the point at which lines or edges parallel in nature converge at the horizon line.
vault An *arched* roof, usually of stone or concrete, created by intersecting two *arches.*
vehicle See *binder.*
visual texture Surface variety that can be seen but not felt with the fingers.
warp In *weaving,* the lengthwise yarns held stationary on the loom and parallel to the finished edge of the fabric.
watercolor A painting *medium* in which the *binder* is gum arabic.
weaving The process of interlacing two sets of parallel threads, held usually at right angles to one another, to form a fabric.
weft In *weaving,* the crosswise yarns that intersect the *warp* to make a fabric.
woodcut See *relief.*

Bibliography

Chapters 1–11 Elements and Principles of Design

Albers, Anni. *On Designing.* Middletown, Conn.: Wesleyan University Press, 1971.

Anderson, Donald M. *Elements of Design.* New York: Holt, Rinehart and Winston, 1961.

Arnheim, Rudolph. *Art and Visual Perception.* Berkeley: University of California Press, 1965.

Ballinger, Louise, and Thomas Vroman. *Design: Sources and Resources.* New York: Reinhold, 1965.

Berenson, Bernard. *Seeing and Knowing.* Greenwich, Conn.: New York Graphic, 1968.

Birren, Faber. *Light, Color, Environment.* New York: Van Nostrand Reinhold, 1969.

Brodatz, Phil. *Textures: A Photographic Album for Artists and Designers.* New York: Dover, 1966.

Collier, Graham. *Form, Space, and Vision.* 3rd ed. Englewood Cliffs, N.J.: Prentice-Hall, 1972.

Ehrenzweig, Anton. *The Hidden Order of Art.* Berkeley: University of California Press, 1967.

Ellinger, R. *Color, Structure, and Design.* Scranton, Pa.: International Textbook, 1963.

Elsen, Albert E. *Purposes of Art.* 3rd ed. New York: Holt, Rinehart and Winston, 1972.

Evans, Helen Marie. *Man the Designer.* New York: Macmillan, 1973.

Faulkner, Ray, and Edwin Zeigfeld. *Art Today.* 5th ed. New York: Holt, Rinehart and Winston, 1969.

Fleming, William. *Arts and Ideas.* 3rd ed. New York: Holt, Rinehart and Winston, 1974.

Grillo, Paul. *Form, Function, and Design.* New York: Dover, 1975.

Hambridge, Jay. *Practical Applications of Dynamic Symmetry.* New York: Devin, 1965.

Itten, Johannes. *Design and Form.* 2nd rev. ed. New York: Van Nostrand Reinhold, 1975.

———. *The Art of Color.* New York: Van Nostrand Reinhold, 1974.

Kandinsky, Wassily. *Point and Line to Plane.* New York: Guggenheim Museum, 1947.

Kepes, Gyorgy. *Language of Vision.* Chicago: Paul Theobald, 1969.

———, ed. *Vision/Value.* 6 vols. New York: Braziller, 1966–67.

Knobler, Nathan. *The Visual Dialogue.* 2nd ed. New York: Holt, Rinehart and Winston, 1971.

Lowry, Bates. *The Visual Experience.* Englewood Cliffs, N.J.: Prentice-Hall, 1965.

McHarg, Ian. *Design with Nature.* Garden City, N.Y.: Natural History Press, 1969.

Ocvirk, Otto G., Robert O. Bone, Robert E. Stinson, and Philip R. Wigg. *Art Fundamentals: Theory and Practice.* 3rd ed. Dubuque, Iowa: Wm. Brown, 1975.

Pye, David. *The Nature of Design.* New York: Reinhold, 1964.

Renner, Paul. *Color, Order and Harmony.* New York: Reinhold, 1965.

Russell, Stella Pandell. *Art in the World.* New York: Holt, Rinehart and Winston, 1975.

Sausmarez, Maurice de. *Basic Design.* New York: Reinhold, 1964.

Sommer, Robert. *Design Awareness.* New York: Holt, Rinehart and Winston, 1972.

Stix, Hugh, et al. *The Shell: Five Hundred Million Years of Inspired Design.* New York: Ballantine, 1972.

Strache, Wolf. *Forms and Patterns in Nature.* New York: Pantheon, 1973.

Chapter 12 Wood

Brodatz, Philip. *Wood and Wood Grains: A Photographic Album for Artists and Designers.* New York: Dover, 1972.

Constantine, Albert. *Know Your Woods.* New York: Scribner, 1972.

English, Kevin. *Creative Approach to Basic Woodwork.* San Francisco: Cowman, 1969.

Glenister, S. H. *Contemporary Design in Woodwork.* Levittown, N.Y.: Transatlantic Arts, 1968.

Hayward, Charles H. *Complete Book of Woodwork.* New York: Drake, 1972.

Joyce, Ernest. *The Encyclopedia of Furniture Making.* New York: Drake, 1971.

Meilach, Dona Z. *Contemporary Art with Wood.* New York: Crown, 1968.

Piepenburg, Robert. *Designs in Wood.* New York: Bruce, 1969.

Rottger, Ernst. *Creative Wood Design.* New York: Reinhold, 1961.

Shea, John. *The American Shakers and Their Furniture.* New York: Van Nostrand Reinhold, 1967.

Willcox, Donald. *Wood Design.* New York: Watson-Guptill, 1968.

———. *New Design in Wood.* New York: Van Nostrand Reinhold, 1970.

Chapter 13 Metal

Almeida, Oscar. *Metalworking.* New York: Drake, 1971.

Blackmore, Howard L. *Arms and Armour.* New York: Dutton, 1965.

Carron, Shirley. *Modern Pewter: Design and Technique.* New York: Van Nostrand Reinhold, 1973.

Granstrom, K. E. *Creating with Metal.* New York: Reinhold, 1968.

Feirer, John. *General Metals.* New York: McGraw-Hill, 1967.

Hale, Nathan Cabot. *Welded Sculpture.* New York: Watson-Guptill, 1968.

Hughes, Graham. *Modern Silver Throughout the World: 1880–1967.* New York: Viking, 1967.

Lister, Raymond. *The Craftsman in Metal.* Cranbury, N.J.: A. S. Barnes, 1968.

Meilach, Dona, and Donald Seiden. *Direct Metal Sculpture.* New York: Crown, 1966.

Morris, Joe L. *Metal Casting.* Englewood Cliffs, N.J.: Prentice-Hall, 1957.

Morton, Philip. *Contemporary Jewelry.* 2nd ed. New York: Holt, Rinehart and Winston, 1976.

Thomas, Richard. *Metalsmithing for the Artist-Craftsman.* Philadelphia: Chilton, 1960.
Untracht, Oppi. *Metal Techniques for Craftsmen.* Garden City, N.Y.: Doubleday, 1968.

Chapter 14 Clay

Arias, Paolo Enrico. *A History of 1000 Years of Greek Vase Painting.* New York: Abrams, 1962.
Berendsen, Anne, et al. *Tiles: A General History.* New York: Viking, 1967.
Berenson, Paulus. *Finding One's Way with Clay.* New York: Simon & Schuster, 1972.
Charleston, Robert J. *World Ceramics.* New York: McGraw-Hill, 1968.
DeJonge, C. H. *Delft Ceramics.* New York: Praeger, 1970.
Hambridge, Jay. *Dynamic Symmetry: The Greek Vase.* New York: Dover, 1967. Reprint of the 1920 edition.
Hughes, Bernard. *English Pottery and Porcelain Figures.* New York: Praeger, 1968.
Leach, Bernard. *A Potter's Book.* Levittown, N.Y.: Transatlantic Arts, 1965.
Nelson, Glenn. *Ceramics.* 3rd ed. New York: Holt, Rinehart and Winston, 1971.
Prodan, Mario. *The Art of the T'ang Potter.* New York: Viking, 1961.
Rhodes, Daniel. *Clay and Glazes for the Potter.* Rev. ed. Philadelphia: Chilton, 1973.
Riegger, Hal. *Raku: Art and Technique.* New York: Van Nostrand Reinhold, 1970.
Sanders, Herbert. *The World of Japanese Ceramics.* New York: Kodansha International, 1967.
Yoshida, Mitsukuni. *In Search of Persian Pottery.* New York: Weatherhill, 1972.

Chapter 15 Glass

Bernstein, Jack. *Stained Glass Craft.* New York: Macmillan, 1973.
Bovini, Giuseppe. *Ravenna Mosaics.* Greenwich, Conn.: New York Graphic, 1968.
Burton, John. *Glass: Handblown, Sculptured, Colored: Philosophy and Method.* Philadelphia: Chilton, 1968.
Chagall, Marc. *The Jerusalem Windows.* New York: Braziller, 1967.
Gardner, Paul V., and James S. Plant. *Steuben: Seventy Years of American Glassblowing.* New York: Praeger, 1975.
Johnson, James Rosser. *The Radiance of Chartres.* New York: Random House, 1965.
Koch, Robert. *Louis C. Tiffany, Rebel in Glass.* New York: Crown, 1966.
Labino, Dominick. *Visual Art in Glass.* Dubuque, Iowa: Wm. Brown, 1968.
Metcalf, Robert, and Gertrude Metcalf. *Making Stained Glass.* New York: McGraw-Hill, 1972.
Peter, John. *Design with Glass.* New York: Reinhold, 1964.
Rossi, Fernando. *Mosaics: Painting in Stone: History and Technique.* New York: Praeger, 1970.
Savage, George. *Glass.* New York: Putnam, 1965.
Unger, Hans. *Practical Mosaics.* New York: Viking, 1965.

Chapter 16 Fiber

Albers, Anni. *On Weaving.* Middletown, Conn.: Wesleyan University Press, 1965.
Blumenau, Lili. *Creative Design in Wall Hangings.* New York: Crown, 1967.
Constantine, Mildred, and Jack Lenor Larsen. *Beyond Craft: The Art Fabric.* New York: Van Nostrand Reinhold, 1972.
6th International Biennial of Tapestry. Lausanne: Musée Cantonal Des Beaux Arts, 1973.
7th International Biennial of Tapestry. 1975.
Hartung, Rolf. *Creative Textile Design: Thread and Fabric.* New York: Reinhold, 1964.
———. *More Creative Textile Design: Color and Texture.* New York: Reinhold, 1965.
Harvey, Virginia I. *Macramé: The Art of Creative Knotting.* New York: Reinhold, 1968.
Held, Shirley E. *Weaving: A Handbook for Fiber Craftsmen.* New York: Holt, Rinehart and Winston, 1973.
Kahlenberg, Mary Hunt, and Anthony Berlant. *The Navaho Blanket.* New York: Praeger, 1972.
Johnston, Medea Parker, and Glen Kaufman. *Design on Fabrics.* New York: Reinhold, 1968.
Kaufmann, Ruth. *The New American Tapestry.* New York: Reinhold, 1968.
Krevitsky, Nik. *Batik: Art and Craft.* New York: Reinhold, 1973.
———. *Stitchery: Art and Craft.* New York: Van Nostrand Reinhold, 1973.
Kybalova, Ludmila. *Coptic Textiles.* London: Hamlyn, 1967.
Plath, Iona. *Handweaving.* New York: Scribner, 1964.
Proud, Nora. *Introducing Textile Printing.* New York: Watson-Guptill, 1968.
Stitching. New York: Museum of Contemporary Crafts, 1967.
Thorpe, Azalea Stuart, and Jack Lenor Larsen. *Elements of Weaving.* Garden City, N.Y.: Doubleday, 1967.
Tovey, John. *The Technique of Weaving.* New York: Reinhold, 1966.

Chapter 17 Plastics

Hollander, Harry. *Plastics for Jewelry.* New York: Watson-Guptill, 1974.
Kobayashi, Akira. *Machining of Plastics.* New York: McGraw-Hill, 1967.
Lawrence, John R. *Polyester Resin.* New York: Reinhold, 1960.
Newman, Jay, and Lee Newman. *Plastics for the Craftsman.* New York: Crown, 1973.
Newman, Thelma. *Plastics as an Art Form.* Rev. ed. Philadelphia: Chilton, 1969.
———. *Plastics as Design Form.* Philadelphia: Chilton, 1972.
Plastic as Plastic. New York: Museum of Contemporary Crafts, 1969.
Quarmby, Arthur. *Plastics and Architecture.* New York: Praeger, 1974.
Rees, David. *Creative Plastics.* New York: Viking, 1973.
Roukes, Nicholas. *Sculpture in Plastics.* New York: Watson-Guptill, 1968.
Yarsley, V. E., and E. G. Couzens. *Plastics in the Modern World.* New York: Penguin, 1969.

Chapter 18 Painting

Arnason, H. H. *History of Modern Art.* New York: Abrams, 1968.
Berenson, Bernard. *The Italian Painters of the Renaissance.* New York: Phaidon, 1968.
Gardner's *Art Through the Ages.* 5th ed. Rev. by Horst de la Croix and Richard G. Tansey. New York: Harcourt, Brace & World, 1970.
Geldzahler, Henry. *New York Painting and Sculpture: 1940–1970.* New York: Dutton, 1969.
Hartmann, Werner. *Painting in the Twentieth Century.* 2 vols. New York: Praeger, 1965.
Hamilton, George Heard. *Painting and Sculpture in Europe: 1880–1940.* Baltimore: Penguin, 1967.
Janson, H. W. *History of Art.* Rev. ed. New York: Abrams, 1969.
Lippard, Lucy R. *Pop Art.* New York: Praeger, 1966.
Mendelowitz, Daniel M. *A History of American Art.* 2nd ed. New York: Holt, Rinehart and Winston, 1973.
Muller, Joseph-Emile. *Fauvism.* Trans. by S. E. Jones. New York: Praeger, 1967.
Parola, René. *Optical Art: Theory and Practice.* New York: Reinhold, 1969.
Read, Sir Herbert. *A Concise History of Modern Painting.* New York: Praeger, 1968.
Rewald, John. *The History of Impressionism.* New York: Museum of Modern Art, 1962.
Rosenblum, Robert. *Cubism and Twentieth-Century Art.* New York: Abrams, 1966.

Rubin, William S. *Dada and Surrealist Art.* New York: Abrams, 1969.

Chapter 19 Sculpture

Baldwin, John. *Contemporary Sculpture Techniques: Welded Metal and Fiberglass.* New York: Van Nostrand Reinhold, 1967.
Brett, Guy. *Kinetic Art: The Language of Movement.* New York: Reinhold, 1968.
Burnham, Jack. *Beyond Modern Sculpture.* New York: Braziller, 1968.
Coleman, Ronald L. *Sculpture.* Dubuque, Iowa: Wm. Brown, 1968.
Elsen, Albert E. *Rodin.* New York: Museum of Modern Art, 1967.
Goldwater, Robert. *What is Modern Sculpture?* New York: Museum of Modern Art, 1969.
Gordon, John. *Isamu Noguchi.* New York: Praeger, 1968.
Gray, Cleve, ed. *David Smith by David Smith.* New York: Holt, Rinehart and Winston, 1968.
Irving, Donald J. *Sculpture: Material and Process.* New York: Van Nostrand Reinhold, 1970.
James, Philip. *Henry Moore on Sculpture.* New York: Viking, 1967.
Kaprow, Allen. *Assemblage, Environments and Happenings.* New York: Abrams, 1966.
Kelly, J. J. *The Sculptural Idea.* Minneapolis: Burgess, 1970.
Kultermann, Udo. *The New Sculpture: Environments and Assemblages.* New York: Praeger, 1968.
Mills, John W. *Sculpture in Concrete.* New York: Praeger, 1968.
———. *The Technique of Sculpture.* New York: Reinhold, 1965.
Pope-Hennessy, Sir John. *Essays on Italian Sculpture.* New York: Phaidon, 1968.
Read, Sir Herbert. *A Concise History of Modern Sculpture.* New York: Praeger, 1964.
Roukes, Nicholas. *Sculpture in Plastics.* New York: Watson-Guptill, 1968.
Tuchman, Maurice. *American Sculpture of the Sixties.* Los Angeles: Los Angeles County Museum of Art, 1967.
Verhelst, Wilbert. *Sculpture: Tools, Materials, and Techniques.* Englewood Cliffs, N.J.: Prentice-Hall, 1973.

Chapter 20 Photography

Adams, Ansel. *Ansel Adams: Images 1923–1974.* Greenwich, Conn.: New York Graphic, 1974.
Caponigro, Paul. *Paul Caponigro.* Millerton, N.Y.: Aperture, 1972.
Cartier-Bresson, Henri. *The World of Henri Cartier-Bresson.* New York: Viking, 1968.
Dixon, Dwight R., and Paul B. Dixon. *Photography: Experiments and Projects.* New York: Macmillan, 1976.
Eisenstadt, Alfred. *Witness to Nature.* New York: Viking, 1971.
———. *Witness to Our Time.* New York: Viking, 1966.
Feininger, Andreas. *The Complete Photographer.* Englewood Cliffs, N.J.: Prentice-Hall, 1965.
Gernsheim, Helmut, and Alison Gernsheim. *Concise History of Photography.* New York: Grosset & Dunlap, 1965.
Life Library of Photography. New York: Time-Life Books, 1970–71.
Lyons, Nathan. *Photography in the Twentieth Century.* New York: Horizon Press, 1967.
Newhall, Beaumont. *History of Photography from 1839 to the Present Day.* New York: Museum of Modern Art, 1964.
Swedlund, Charles. *Photography.* New York: Holt, Rinehart and Winston, 1974.
Szarkowski, John. *The Photographer's Eye.* New York: Museum of Modern Art, 1966.
Weston, Edward. *My Camera on Point Lobos.* New York: Da Capo, 1968.

Chapter 21 Prints

Artist's Proof: The Annual of Prints and Printmaking. New York: Pratt Graphics Center and Barre Publishers. Annually.
Chieffo, Clifford. *Silkscreen as a Fine Art.* New York: Reinhold, 1967.
The Complete Woodcuts of Albrecht Dürer. New York: Dover, 1963.
Eichenberg, Fritz. *The Art of the Print.* New York: Abrams, 1976.
Escher, M. C. *The Graphic Work of M. C. Escher.* New York: Meredith, 1967.
Hayter, S. W. *About Prints.* London: Oxford University Press, 1962.
Heller, Jules. *Printmaking Today.* 2nd ed. New York: Holt, Rinehart and Winston, 1972.
Mayor, A. Hyatt. *Prints and People.* New York: The Metropolitan Museum of Art (dist. New York Graphic), 1971.
Peterdi, Gabor. *Printmaking.* New York: Macmillan, 1971.
Robertson, Ronald G. *Contemporary Printmaking in Japan.* New York: Crown, 1965.
Ross, John, and Clare Romano. *The Complete Printmaker.* New York: The Free Press, 1972. Also available in four paperback volumes.
Weaver, Peter. *Printmaking: A Medium for Basic Design.* New York: Reinhold, 1968.

Chapter 22 Graphic Design

Anderson, Donald M. *The Art of Written Forms: The Theory and Practice of Calligraphy.* New York: Holt, Rinehart and Winston, 1969.
Bowman, William J. *Graphic Communication.* New York: Wiley, 1968.
Brunner, Felix. *A Handbook of Graphic Reproduction Processes.* New York: Hastings, 1962.
Cleaver, James. *A History of Graphic Art.* New York: Philosophical Library, 1963.
Croy, Peter. *Graphic Design and Reproduction Techniques.* New York: Hastings, 1968.
Fletcher, Alan, with Colin Forbes and Bob Gill. *Graphic Design: Visual Comparisons.* New York: Reinhold, 1963.
Hutchinson, Harold F. *The Poster: An Illustrated History from 1860.* New York: Viking, 1960.
Jacobsen, E., ed. *Trademark Design.* Chicago: Paul Theobald, 1952.
Leach, Mortimer. *Letter Design in the Graphic Arts.* New York: Reinhold, 1960.
Nelson, Roy P. *Design of Advertising.* Dubuque, Iowa: Wm. Brown, 1967.
Shahn, Ben. *Love and Joy About Letters.* New York: Grossman, 1963.
Wingler, Hans M. *Graphic Work from the Bauhaus.* Greenwich, Conn.: New York Graphic, 1969.

Chapter 23 Industrial Design

Ambasz, Emilio, ed. *Italy: The New Domestic Landscape.* New York: Museum of Modern Art, 1972.
California Design 76. Pasadena, Calif.: California Design, 1976.
Drexler, Arthur. *Design Collection: Selected Objects.* New York: Museum of Modern Art, 1970.
Giedion, Siegfried. *Mechanization Takes Command.* New York: Norton, 1969.
Hulten, K. G. Pontus. *The Machine as Seen at the End of the Mechanical Age.* Greenwich, Conn.: New York Graphic, 1969.
Portable World. New York: Museum of Contemporary Crafts, 1973.
Read, Herbert. *Art and Industry.* Bloomington, Ind.: Indiana University Press, 1961.

Chapter 24 Apparel

Body Covering. New York: Museum of Contemporary Crafts, 1968.
Fairservis, Walter A. *Costumes of the East.* Riverside, Conn.: Chatham Press with American Museum of Natural History, 1971.

Hill, Margot Hamilton, and Peter A. Bucknell. *The Evolution of Fashion, Pattern and Cut.* Garden City, N.Y.: Doubleday, 1965.
Laury, Jean Ray, and Joyce Aiken. *Creative Body Coverings.* New York: Van Nostrand Reinhold, 1974.
Levin, Phyllis Lee. *The Wheels of Fashion.* Garden City, N.Y.: Doubleday, 1965.
Rudofsky, Bernard. *Are Clothes Modern?* Chicago: Paul Theobald, 1947.
———. *The Unfashionable Human Body.* Garden City, N.Y.: Doubleday, 1974.
Sronkova, Olga. *Fashions Through the Centuries: Renaissance, Baroque, and Rococo.* New York: Tudor, 1962.
Volland, Virginia. *Designing Woman.* Garden City, N.Y.: Doubleday, 1966.

Chapter 25 The Performing Arts

Bay, Howard. *Stage Design.* New York: Drama Book Specialists, 1974.
Burris-Meyer, Harold, and Edward C. Cole. *Scenery for the Theatre.* 3rd ed. Boston: Little, Brown, 1972.
Fernald, Mary, and Eileen Shenton. *Costume Design and Making.* New York: Theatre Art Books, 1967.
Mielziner, Jo. *Designing for the Theatre.* New York: Atheneum, 1965.
Parker, W. Oren, and Harvey K. Smith. *Scene Design and Stage Lighting.* 3rd ed. New York: Holt, Rinehart and Winston, 1974.
Pecktal, Lynn. *Designing and Painting for the Theatre.* New York: Holt, Rinehart and Winston, 1975.
Russell, Douglas. *Stage Costume Design: Theory, Technique, and Style.* New York: Appleton-Century-Crofts, 1973.
Schubert, Hannelore. *The Modern Theatre: Architecture, Stage Design, Lighting.* New York: Praeger, 1971.

Chapter 26 Interiors

Aronson, Joseph. *The New Encyclopedia of Furniture.* New York: Crown, 1967.
Ball, Victoria Kloss. *The Art of Interior Design.* New York: Macmillan, 1960.
Faulkner, Ray, and Sarah Faulkner. *Inside Today's Home.* 4th ed. New York: Holt, Rinehart and Winston, 1975.
Halse, A. O. *Use of Color in Interiors.* New York: McGraw-Hill, 1968.
Harling, Robert, ed. *Dictionary of Design and Decoration.* New York: Viking, 1973.
Hatje, Gerd, and Peter Kaspar. *1601 Decorating Ideas for Modern Living.* New York: Abrams, 1974.
Hayward, Helena, ed. *World Furniture: A Pictorial History.* New York: McGraw-Hill, 1965.
Peluzzi, Giulio, ed. *The Modern Room.* New York: Universe Books, 1967.
Praz, Mario. *An Illustrated History of Furnishing.* New York: Braziller, 1964.
Savage, George. *A Concise History of Interior Decoration.* New York: Grosset & Dunlap, 1966.
Stepet-DeVan, Dorothy. *Introduction to Home Furnishings.* New York: Macmillan, 1971.
Whiton, Sherrill. *Elements of Interior Design and Decoration.* 4th ed. Philadelphia, Pa.: Lippincott, 1974.

Chapter 27 Architecture and Landscape

Berrall, Julia S. *The Garden: An Illustrated History.* New York: Viking, 1966.
Chermayeff, Serge, and Christopher Alexander. *Community and Privacy: Toward a New Architecture of Humanism.* Garden City, N.Y.: Doubleday, 1963.
Clifford, Derek. *A History of Garden Design.* New York: Praeger, 1966.
Eckbo, Garrett. *The Art of Home Landscaping.* New York: McGraw-Hill, 1956.
Fitch, James Marston. *American Building: The Historical Forces That Shaped It.* New York: Schocken, 1973.
Giedion, Siegfried. *Space, Time and Architecture.* 5th ed. Cambridge, Mass.: MIT Press, 1968.
Gropius, Walter. *The New Architecture and the Bauhaus.* Cambridge, Mass.: MIT Press, 1968.
Hitchcock, Henry-Russell, and Philip Johnson. *The International Style.* New York: Norton, 1966.
Hoffman, Hubert. *Row Houses and Cluster Houses: An International Survey.* New York: Praeger, 1967.
Ito, Teiji. *The Japanese Garden: An Approach to Nature.* New Haven, Conn.: Yale University Press, 1972.
Kassler, Elizabeth B. *Modern Gardens and the Landscape.* New York: Museum of Modern Art, 1964.
Moore, Charles, and Gerald Allen. *The Place of Houses.* New York: Holt, Rinehart and Winston, 1974.
Nervi, Pier Luigi. *Aesthetics and Technology in Building.* Cambridge, Mass.: Harvard University Press, 1967.
Pevsner, Nikolaus. *An Outline of European Architecture.* Baltimore: Penguin, 1968.
Scully, Vincent. *Frank Lloyd Wright.* New York: Braziller, 1960.
Stern, Robert A. *New Directions in American Architecture.* New York: Braziller, 1969.

Chapter 28 Community and Environment

Bacon, Edmund N. *Design of Cities.* New York: Viking, 1967.
Eckbo, Garrett. *Urban Landscape Design.* New York: McGraw-Hill, 1964.
Faltermayer, Edmund K. *Redoing America: A Nationwide Report on How to Make Our Cities and Suburbs Livable.* New York: Harper & Row, 1968.
Gibberd, Frederick. *Town Design.* New York: Praeger, 1967.
Gruen, Victor. *The Heart of Our Cities.* New York: Simon and Schuster, 1964.
Howard, Ebenezer. *Garden Cities of Tomorrow.* Cambridge, Mass.: MIT Press, 1968.
Jacobs, Jane. *The Death and Life of Great American Cities.* New York: Random House, 1961.
Kepes, Gyorgy, ed. *Arts of the Environment.* New York: Braziller, 1972.
Kurtz, Stephen A. *Wasteland: Building the American Dream.* New York: Praeger, 1973.
Le Corbusier. *Towards a New Architecture.* New York: Praeger, 1970.
Lynch, Kevin. *The Image of a City.* Cambridge, Mass.: MIT Press, 1968.
Moholy-Nagy, Sibyl. *Matrix of Man.* New York: Praeger, 1968.
Mumford, Lewis. *The Highway and the City.* New York: Harcourt, Brace and World, 1963.
Rudofsky, Bernard. *Streets for People.* Garden City, N.Y.: Doubleday, 1969.
von Eckardt, Wolf. *A Place to Live: The Crisis of the Cities.* New York: Dell, 1967.
Venturi, Robert, et al. *Learning From Las Vegas.* Cambridge, Mass.: Harvard University Press, 1972.
Wall, David. *Visionary Cities: The Arcology of Paolo Soleri.* New York: Praeger, 1970.

Index

Photographic Sources

Joseph Abeles Studio, New York (518); Harry N. Abrams, Inc., New York (223, Pl. 3); John Adden Furniture, Boston (526); Jay Ahrend, Los Angeles (499); Alinari-Art Reference Bureau, Ancram, N.Y. (3, 15, 91, 203, 224, 405, 492, 567); American Honda Motor Co., Gardena, Calif. (49); American Museum of Natural History, New York (2, 8, 48, 86, 102, 137, 159, 178, 204, 264, 294, 310, 336, 485); American Telephone and Telegraph Co., New York (236, 479); Anderson-Art Reference Bureau, Ancram, N.Y. (93, 170); Neil Anderson (268); Wayne Andrews, Grosse Pointe, Mich. (263, 280); Archives of American Art, Washington, D.C., David Smith Papers (269); Archives Photographiques, Paris (38, 88); Archivo Amigos de Gaudí, Barcelona (402); Arts Council of Great Britain, London, and John Hedgecoe Ltd., Burgates, Eng. (156); Asian Art Photographic Distribution, Ann Arbor, Mich. (58, 152); Australian Information Service, New York (554); Morley Baer, Monterey, Calif. (87, 146, 527–529, 531, 533, 535, 537, 547, 556, 558–560); Bettmann Archive, New York (207); Bibliothèque Nationale, Paris (214); Black Star, New York (53); Ferdinand Boesch, New York (353); British Tourist Authority, New York (101, 549); Brogi-Art Reference Bureau, Ancram, N.Y. (562); C.J. Bruce, Calgary (301); Doris Bry, New York (Pl. 1); J. E. Bulloz, Paris (13); Rudolph Burckhardt, New York (389); René Burri, Magnum Photos, Inc., New York (Pl. 49); O. R. Cabanban, Chicago (553); Jarrold Cabluck (282); California Computer Products, Inc., Anaheim (55); Canadian Government Office of Tourism, New York (230); Canadian Government Travel Bureau, Ottawa (18); Leo Castelli Gallery, New York, and Jacob Burckhardt (369); Leo Castelli Gallery, New York, and Rudolph Burckhardt, New York (393); Channel 13, New York (136, 509); Chase Manhattan Bank, New York, and Arthur Lavine (83); Ciceri, Milan (271); William Claxton, Beverly Hills, Calif. (491); Geoffrey Clements, Staten Island, N.Y. (68, 81, 180, 232, 409); John Clemmer (342); Columbia Artists Management, Inc., New York (506); Consulate General of the Netherlands, New York, and Bart Hofmeester, Rotterdam (565); Paula Cooper Gallery, New York (351); Cosmopress, Geneva (378, Pl. 15); *Craft Horizons,* New York, and Marc Slivka, New York (313); *Craft* Magazine, Crafts Advisory Committee, London (292); Bob Cramp (366); Dallas Market Center, and Jess Alford (4); Danish Information Office, New York (545); Bevan Davies, New York (388); Russell Dian, New York (139); Editions du Cercle d'Art, Paris (171); Eliot Elisofon, *Time-Life* Picture Agency, © Time Inc., New York (219); Fred Fehl, New York (52, 176, 515); John T. Ferrari, Brooklyn, N.Y. (89, 262, 274); Festspiele Bayreuth, W. Ger., and Wilhelm Rauh (511); Fondation Vasarely, Gordes, Fr. (99); Fotocielo, Rome (6); Fotostudio Otto, Vienna (Pl. 14); Alison Frantz, Princeton, N.J. (196); Buckminster Fuller Archives, Philadelphia (572); Roger Gass (343); Michael Geiger, New York (530); German National Tourist Office, New York (357); Edmund V. Gillon, Jr., New York (276); Giraudon, Paris (368); Gianfranco Gorgoni, New York (65); Greek National Tourist Office, New York (507); Hella Hammid, Rapho/Photo Researchers, Inc., New York (505); Bob Hanson, New York (Pl. 20); O. K. Harris Gallery, New York (355, 410); Hedrich-Blessing, Chicago (36, 541); Helmsley Spear, Inc., New York (115); Holle Bildarchiv, Baden-Baden, W. Ger., and K. Schwarz, Munich (9); Harry Holtzman, Lyme, Conn. (11, 12); Mel Howard Presents, New York (516); Mel Howard Presents, New York, and Alain Béjart (179); Mel Howard Presents, New York, and R. Kayaert, Brussels (125, 522); Robert Hunt Library, London, and Stuart Lisson (296); Hurok Concerts, New York (177); *Industrial Design* Magazine, New York (472); Bruce C. Jones, Centerport, N.Y. (390); Phokian Karas, Cambridge, Mass. (174); Matthew Klein (302); Knoll Associates, New York (470); Edo Koenig, Black Star, New York (208); Koninklijk Museum voor Schone Kunsten, Antwerp (Pl. 19); Koppes (184); Balthazar Korab, Troy, Mich. (283); Gerald Kornblau Gallery, New York (278); Russell Dixon Lamb, Photo Researchers, Inc., New York (124); Elliott Landy, Magnum Photos, Inc., New York (520, Pl. 10); Robert Lautman, Washington, D.C. (194); The Lee Company, Shawnee Mission, Kan. (493); Library of Congress, Washington, D.C. (424); Nathaniel Lieberman, New York (551); London Weekend Television (513); Mats Wibe Lund, Jr., Icelandic Photo and Press Service, Reykjavik (Pl. 5); Magnum Photos, Inc., New York (486); Verena and Erling Mandelmann, Lausanne (50); Marburg-Art Reference Bureau, Ancram, N.Y. (84); Marlborough Gallery, New York (Pl. 16); Marlborough Gallery, New York, and Robert E. Mates, New York (386); MAS, Barcelona (37, 287); Maserati Automobiles, Englewood, N.J. (42); McAllister of Denver (564); Laurie McDonald, Providence, R.I. (117); Norman McGrath, New York (145, 543, 544); McGuire Furniture, San Francisco, and Ezra Stoller © ESTO, Mamaroneck, N.Y. (534); D. L. McKinley, Mississagua, Ont. (298); Mercedes-Benz of North America, Montvale, N.J. (39); Metropolitan Transit Authority, New York, and Vance Henry, Photo Researchers, Inc., New York (466); Joseph W. Molitor, Ossining, N.Y. (539); Philip Molten, Tiburon, Calif. (173, 201, 523–525, 550); John Morgan (324); Museum of Contemporary Crafts of the American Crafts Council, New York (16, 330); Museum of Modern Art, New York (27); Museum of Modern Art, New York, Film Stills Archive (517, 521, 532); Hans Namuth, New York (381); National Aeronautics and Space Administration, Washington, D.C. (490, 574); O. E. Nelson, New York (382, 399); Norfolk Rehabilitation and Housing Authority, Va. (566); Anne Odom, West Point, N.Y. (258); Oleaga (519); Pan American World Airways, New York (571); Betty Parsons Gallery, New York (199); Ruth Pasquine (293); Hans Petersen, Hornbaek, Den. (449); Max Petrelius, Helsinki (494, 500, 503); Richard L. Plaut, Jr. (211, 212); Eric Pollitzer, Hempstead, N.Y. (189, 348, 451, 457, Pls. 11, 29, 30); Josephine Powell, Rome (327); Blake Praytor (305); Orion Press, Tokyo, © Idemitsu Art Gallery (100); Nathan Rabin, New York (97, 253); Redevelopment Authority of Philadelphia (205); Stan Ries, New York (394); Riproduzioni d'Opera d'Arte, Milan (251); Roberts, Boulder, Colo. (360); Sam Sawdon Studios, London (181); Scala, New York/Florence (182); Sculpture Now, Inc., New York, and Lippincott, Inc., New Haven, Conn. (206); Walter Seng (126, 359); Mark W. Sexton, Salem, Mass. (275); Julius Shulman, Los Angeles (85, 542, 548); Shunk-Keneder, Copyright Valley Curtain Corp. (10); Kenneth Snelson, New York (71); Kristin Staubitz, Cincinnati (345); Stone and Steccati, San Francisco (538); Evon Streetman, Penland, North Carolina (308); Soichi Sunami, New York (14, 69); Suntek Research Associates, Corte Madeira, Calif. (557); Eric Sutherland, Walker Art Center, Minneapolis (314); John Tennant (Pl. 32); Frank J. Thomas, Los Angeles (358); J. Walter Thompson Co., Chicago (Pl. 44); *Time-Life* Picture Agency, © Time Inc., New York (54, 421); Tiofoto, Stockholm, © Hans Hammarskiold (363); Trizec Corp., New York (561); Charles Uht, New York (185, 277); United Press International, New York (423); O. Vaering, Oslo (Pl. 18); Malcolm Varon, New York (Pl. 31); David Vine, New York (536, Pl. 25); The Wallnuts, Philadelphia (323); Washington Cathedral, D.C. (403); David Watkins (266); Achille B. Weider, Zurich (217); Wide World Photos, Inc., New York (497, 498); Rosalie Winesuff, Placentia, Calif. (255); Zabriskie Gallery, New York (361); Zoological Society of San Diego (563).